LOVE MANGA?
LET US KNOW WHAT YOU THINK!

OUR MANGA SURVEY IS NOW
AVAILABLE ONLINE. PLEASE VISIT:
VIZ.COM/MANGASURVEY

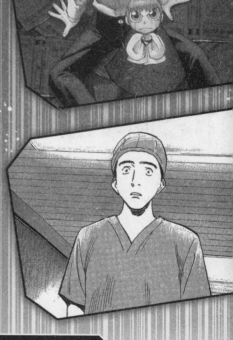

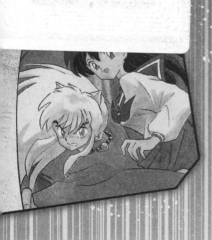

HELP US MAKE THE MANGA
YOU LOVE BETTER!

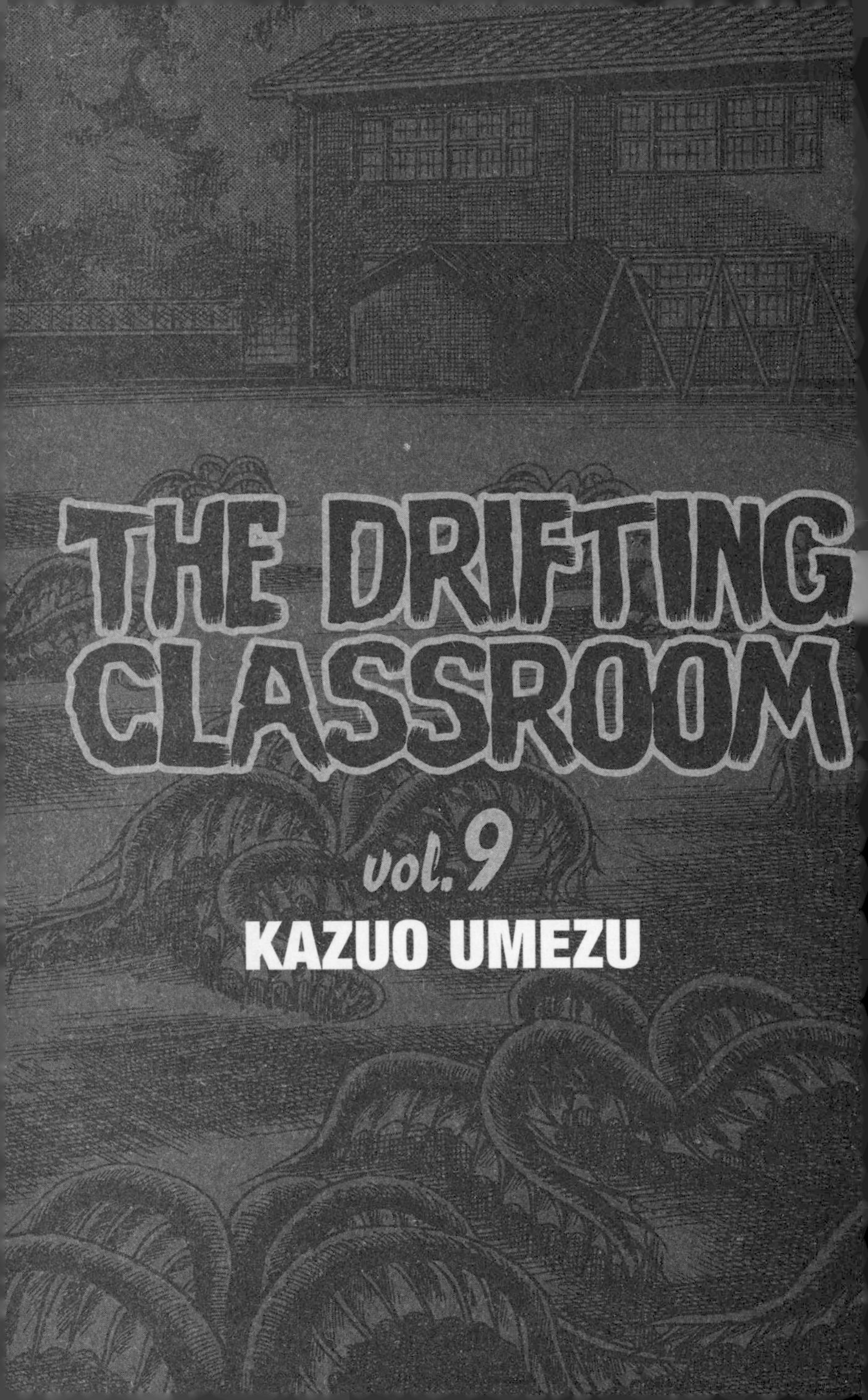
THE DRIFTING CLASSROOM
vol. 9
KAZUO UMEZU

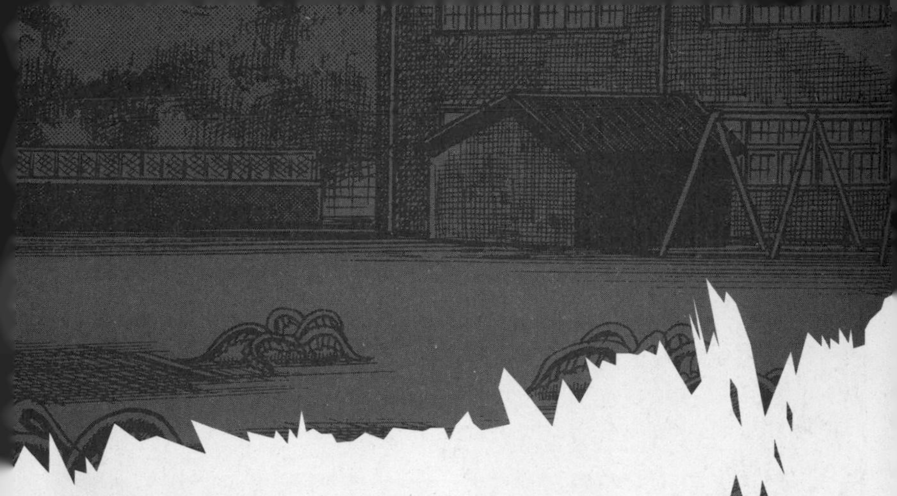

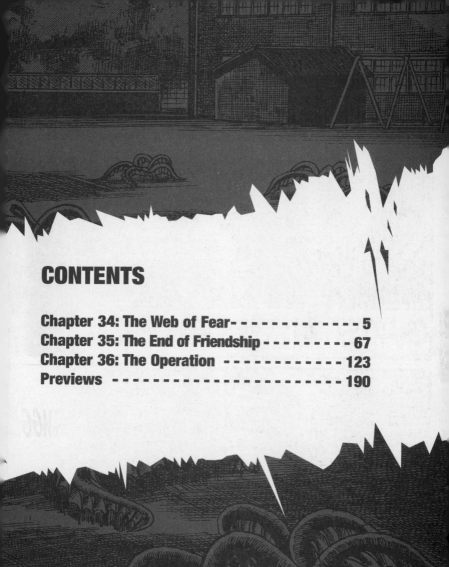

CONTENTS

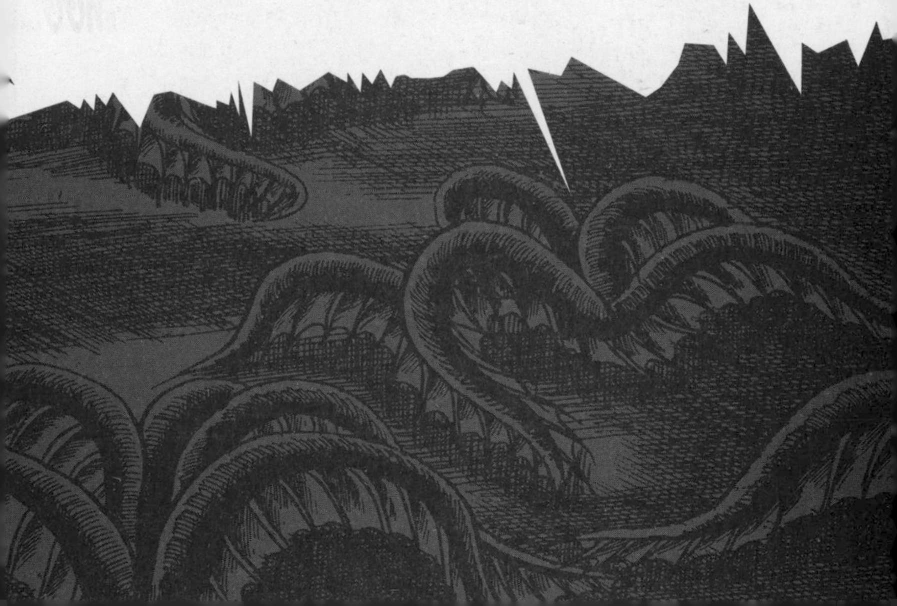

CHAPTER 34: THE WEB OF FEAR

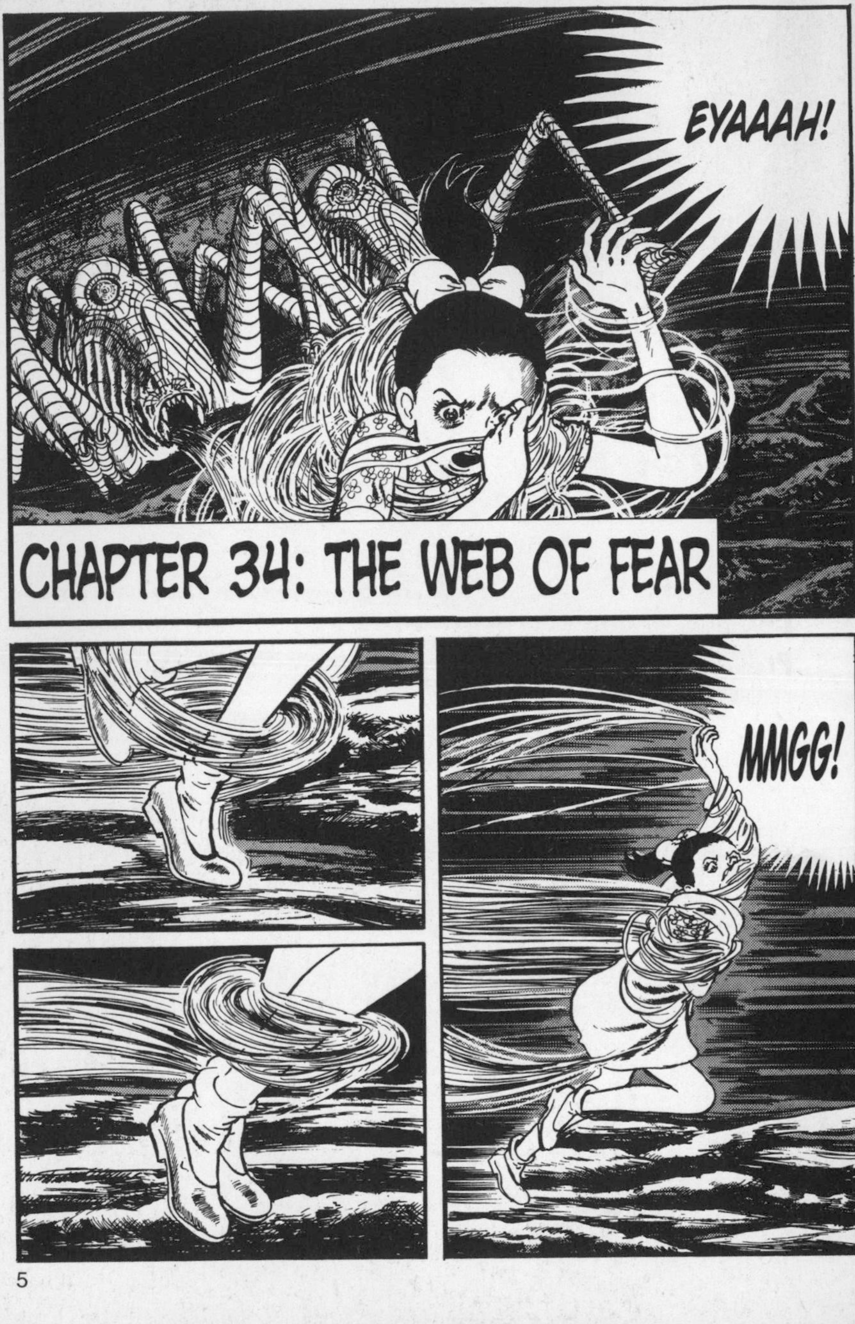
EYAAAH!
MMGG!

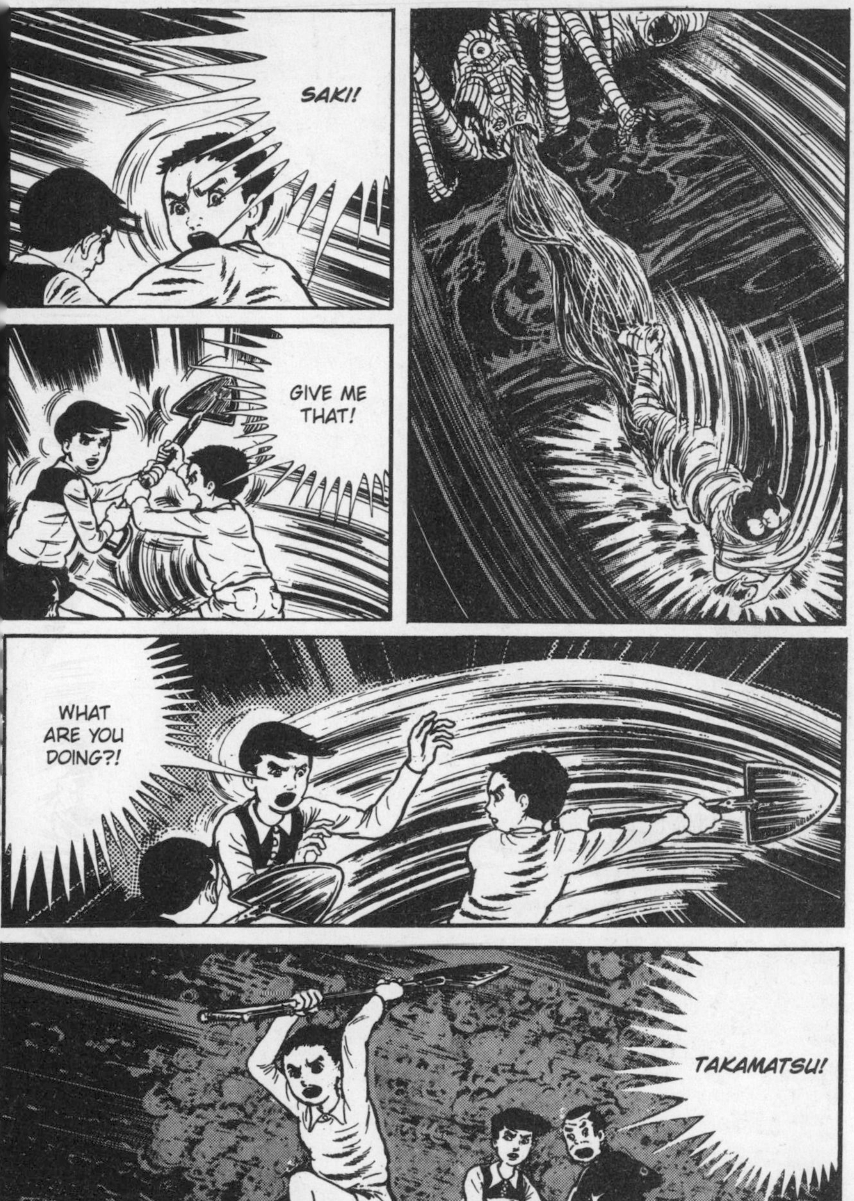
SAKI!
GIVE ME THAT!
WHAT ARE YOU DOING?!
TAKAMATSU!

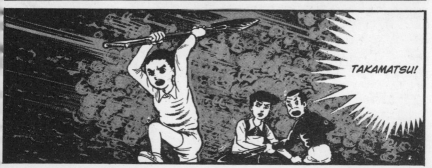

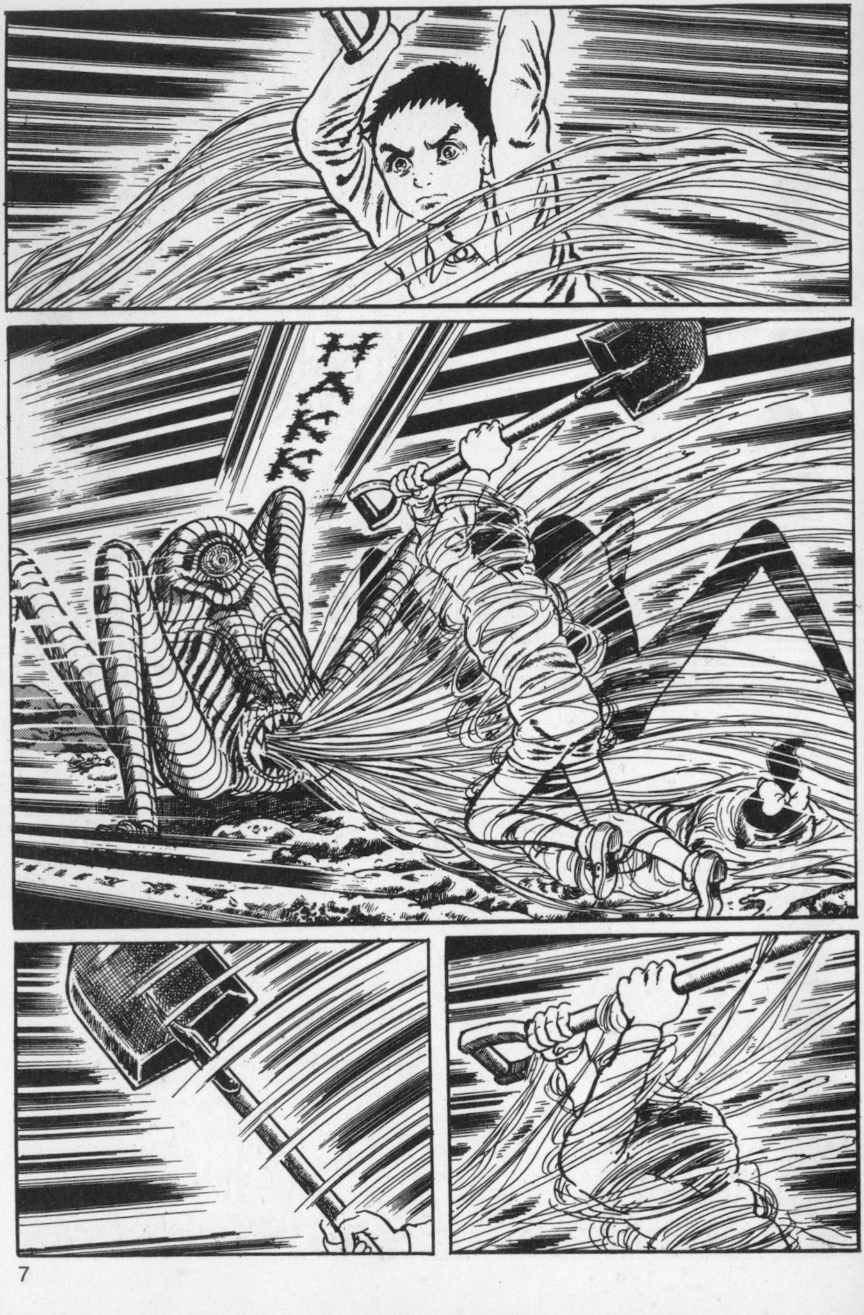
HAKKK

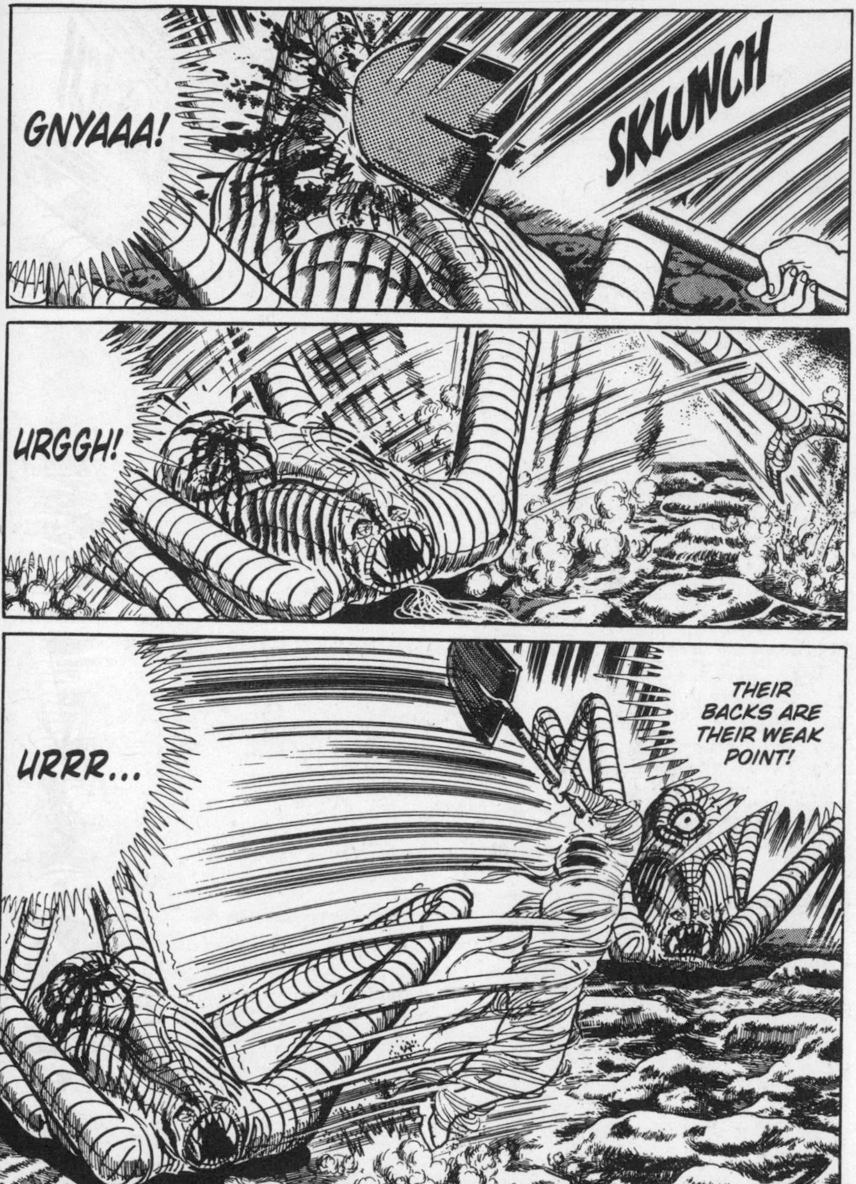
SKLUNCH
GNYAAA!
URGGH!
THEIR BACKS ARE THEIR WEAK POINT!
URRR...

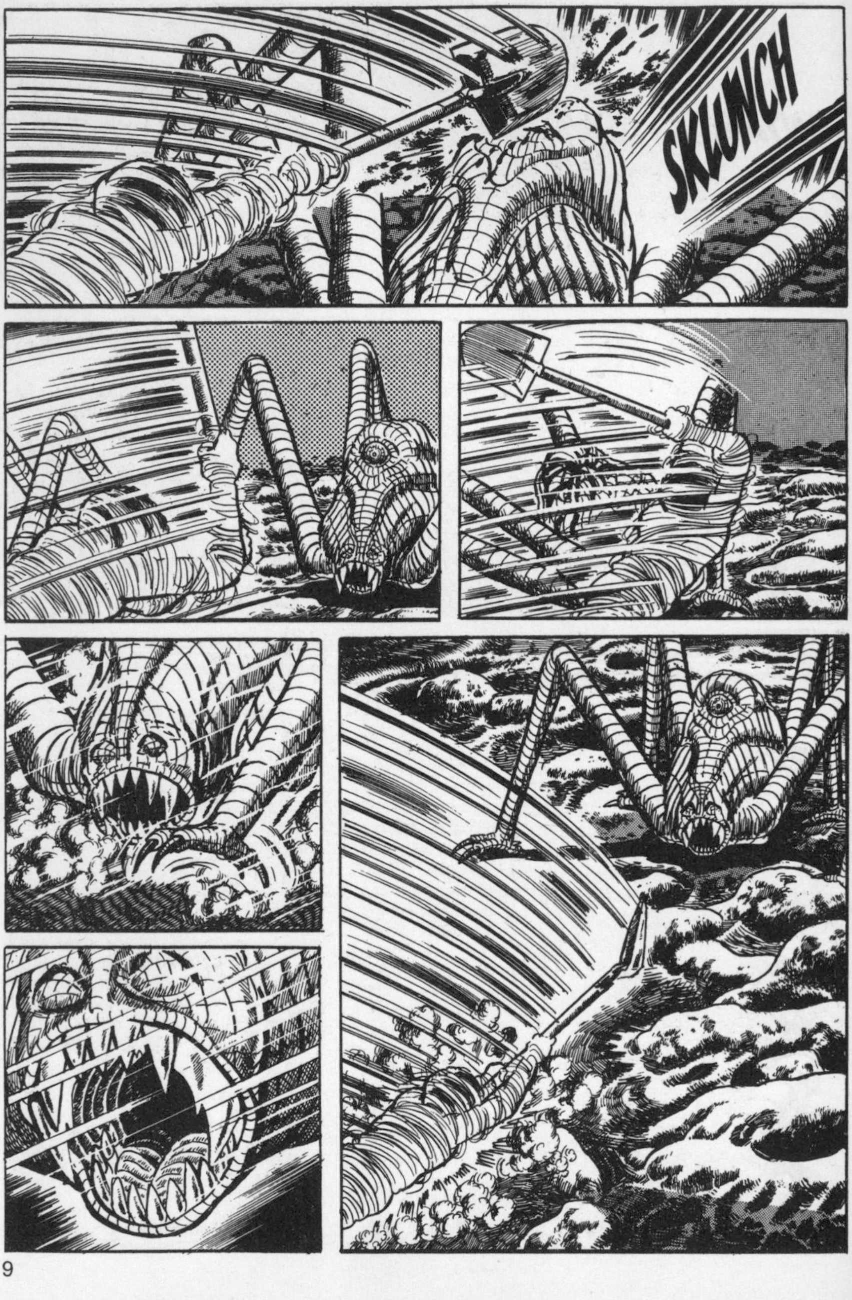
SKLUNCH

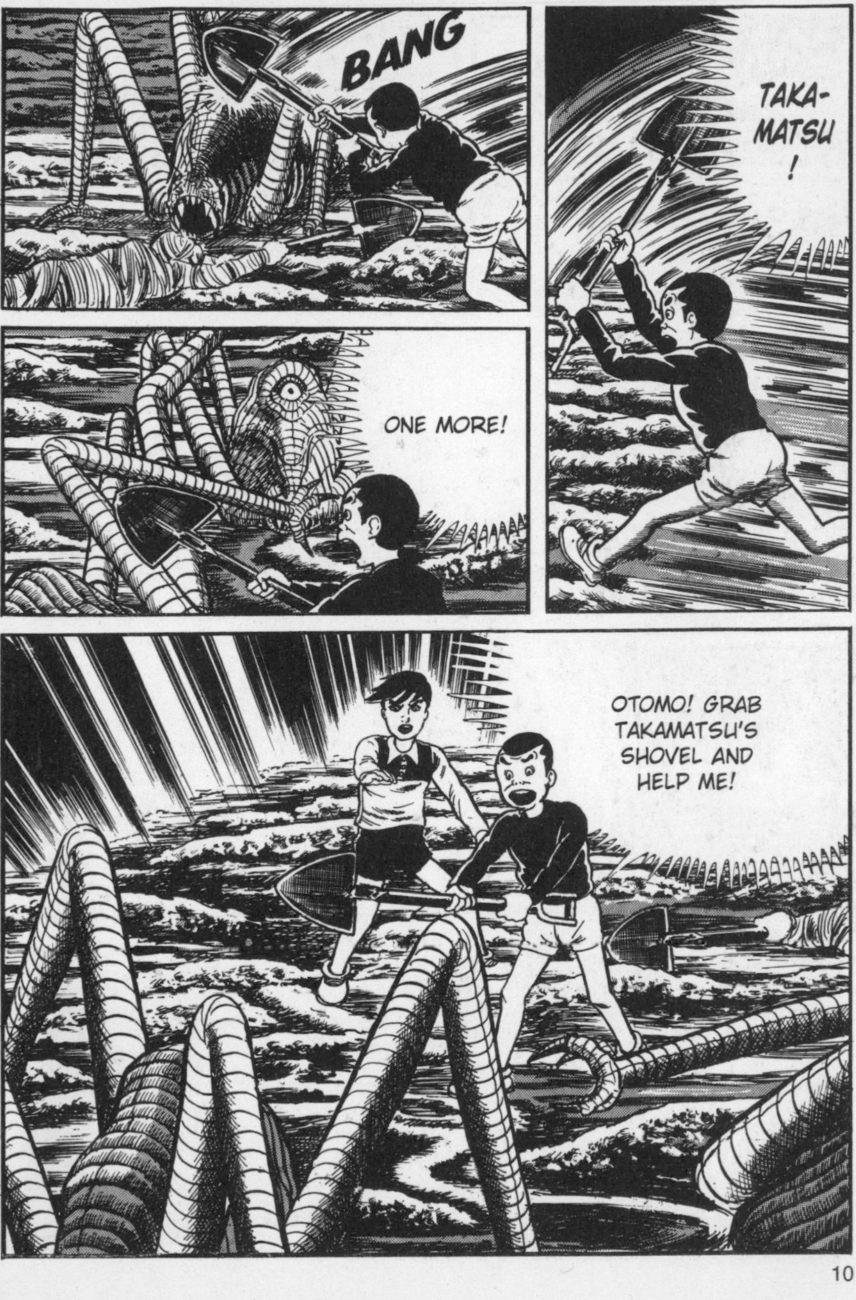
TAKA-
MATSU
!
BANG
ONE MORE!
OTOMO! GRAB TAKAMATSU'S SHOVEL AND HELP ME!

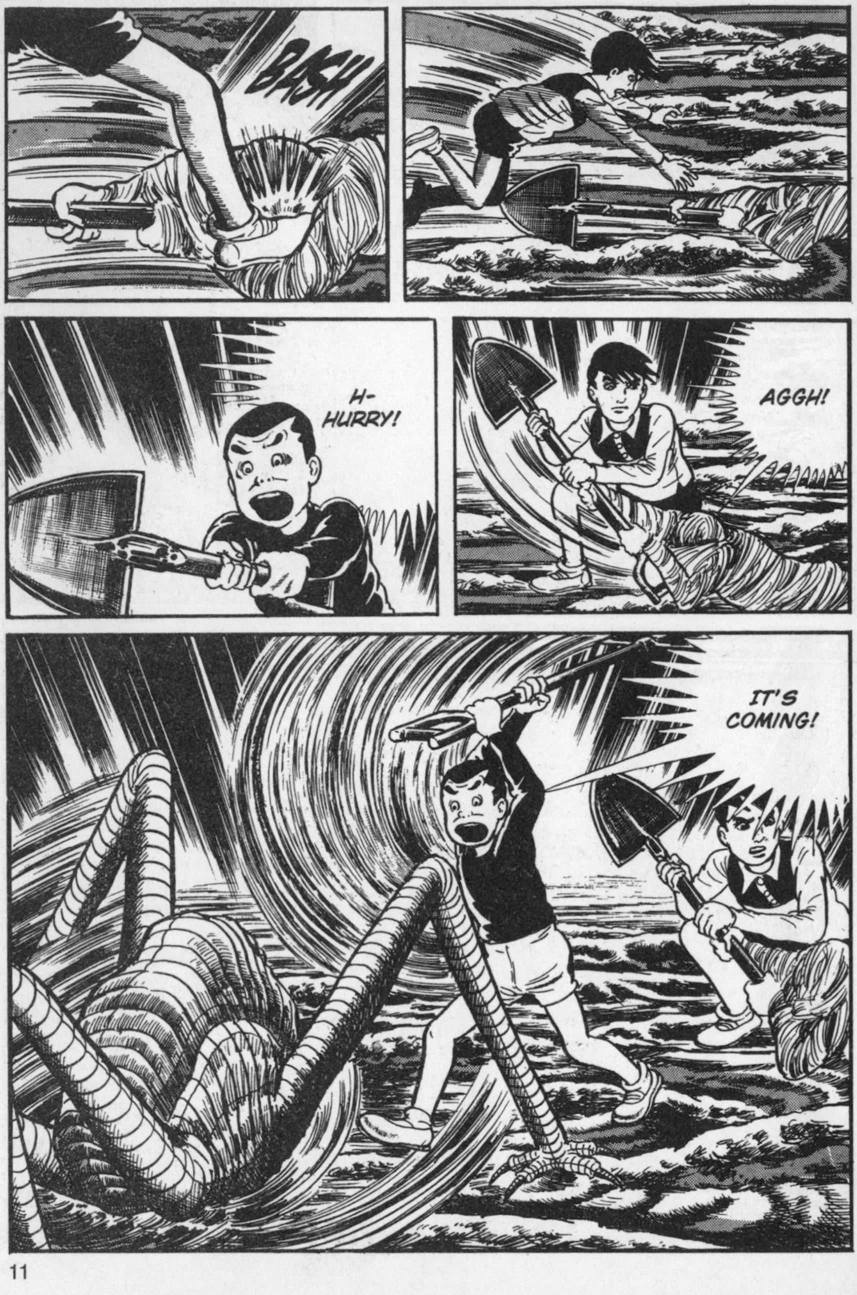
BASH
AGGH!
H-
HURRY!
IT'S
COMING!

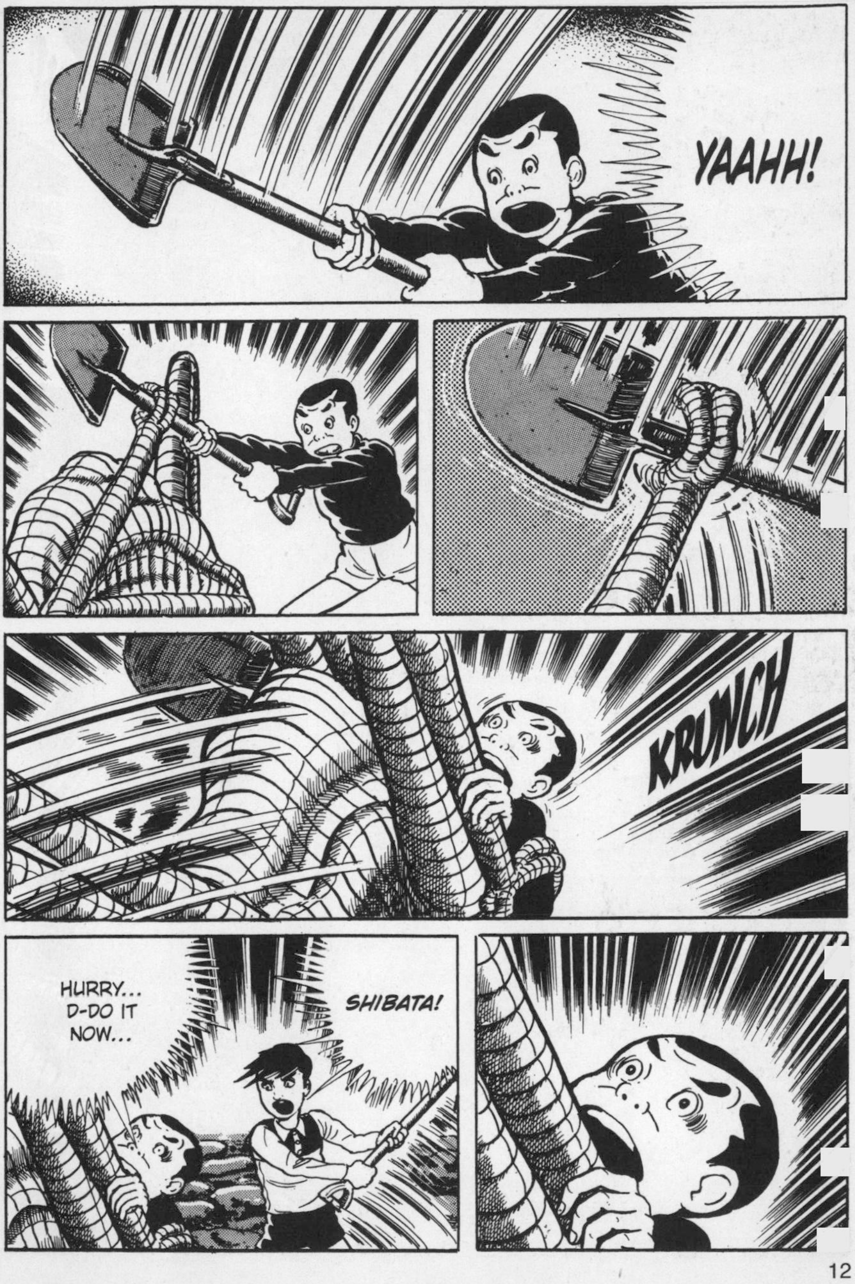
YAAHH!
KRUNCH
SHIBATA!
HURRY... D-DO IT NOW...

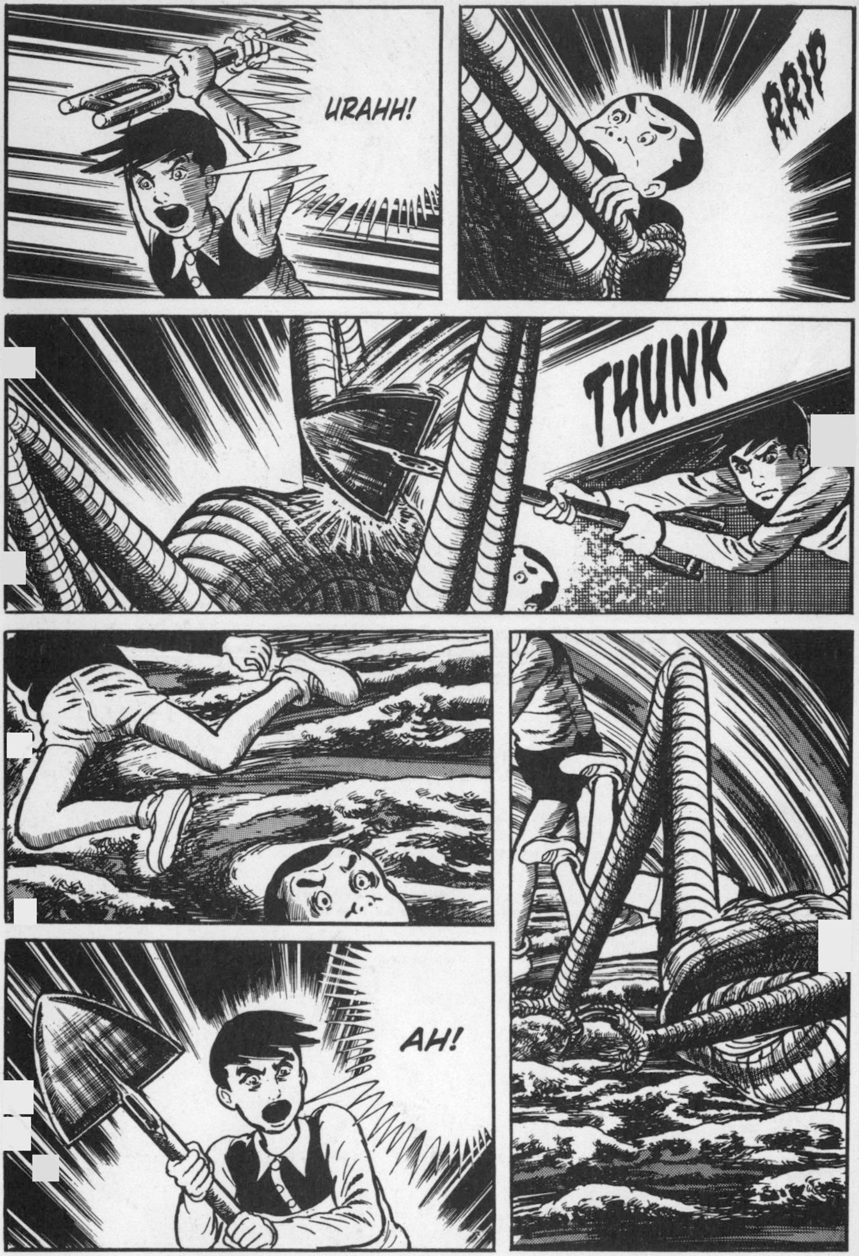
RRIP
URAHH!
THUNK
AH!

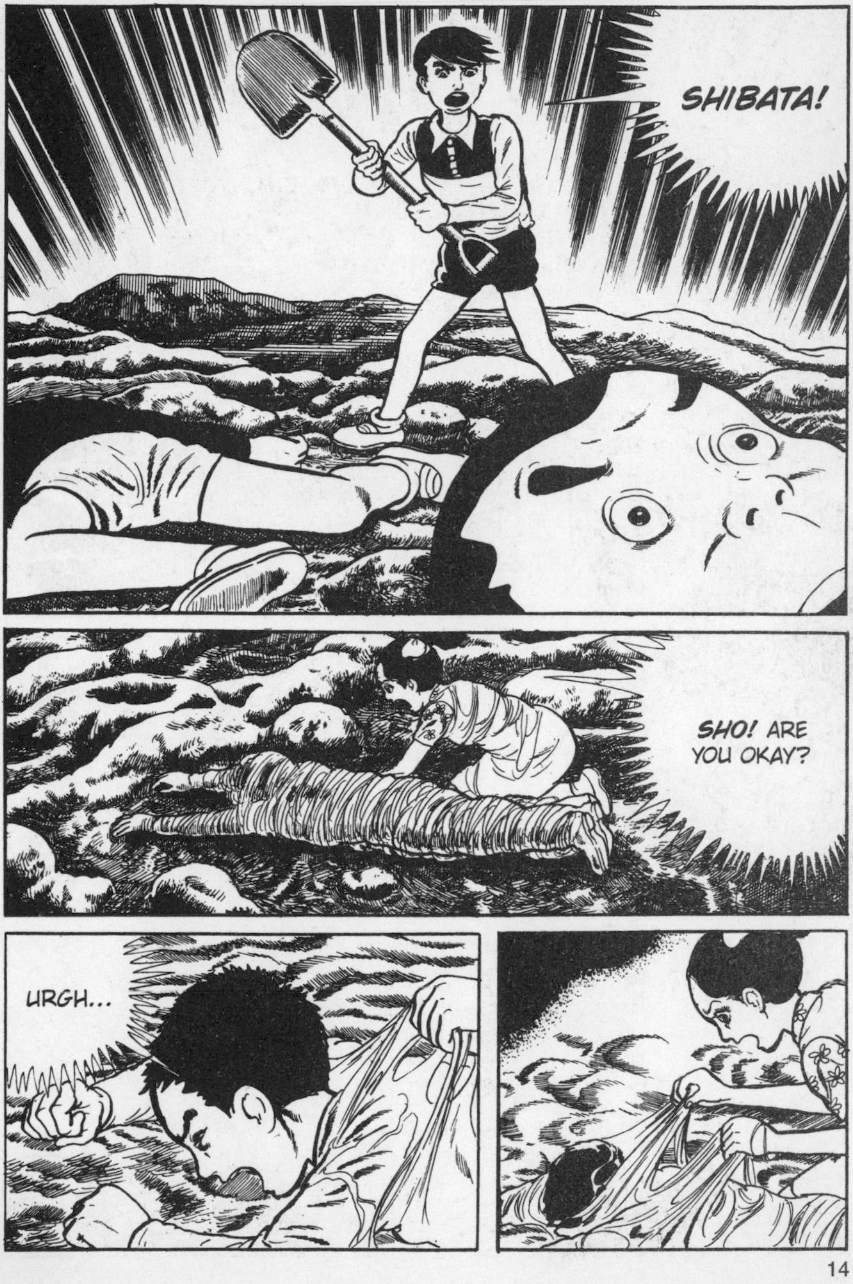
SHIBATA!
SHO! ARE YOU OKAY?
URGH...

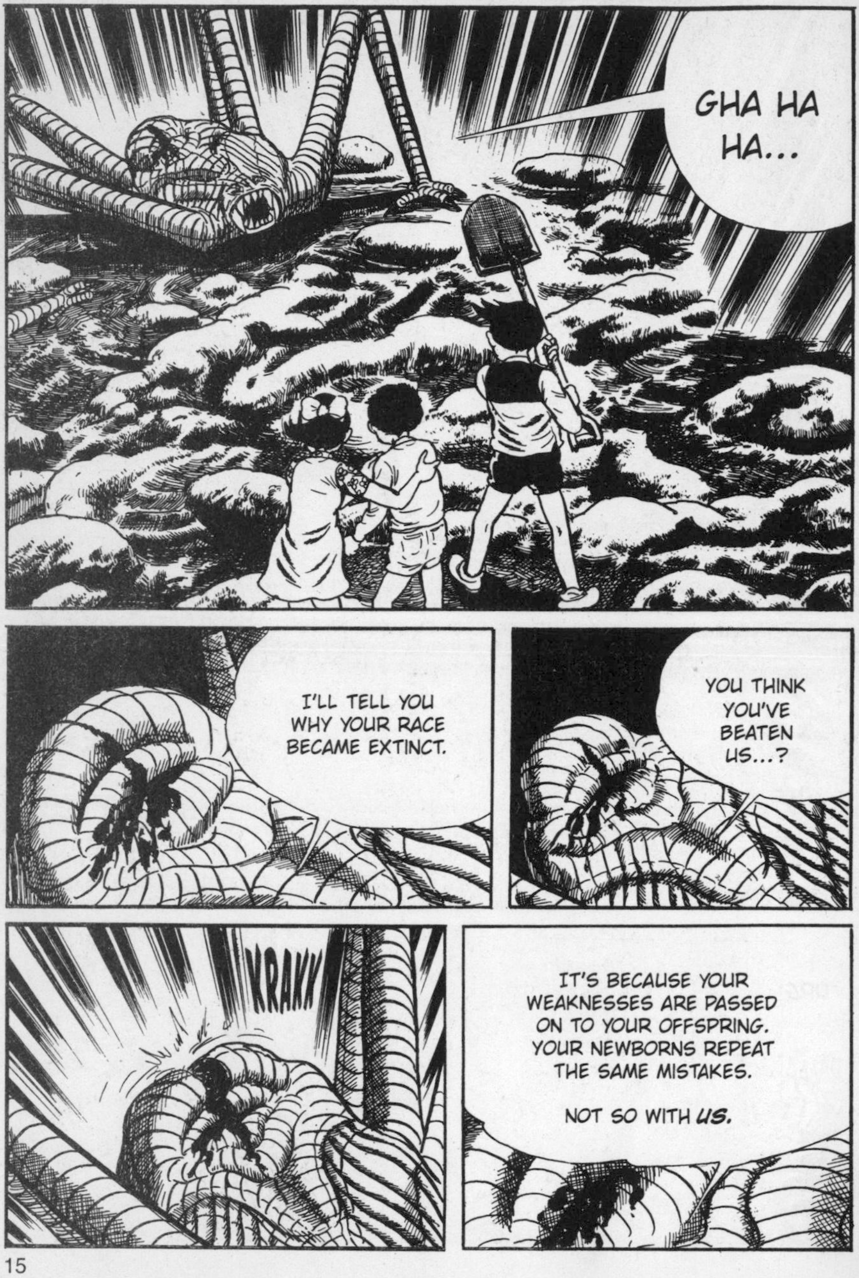
GHA HA HA...
YOU THINK YOU'VE BEATEN US...?
I'LL TELL YOU WHY YOUR RACE BECAME EXTINCT.
IT'S BECAUSE YOUR WEAKNESSES ARE PASSED ON TO YOUR OFFSPRING. YOUR NEWBORNS REPEAT THE SAME MISTAKES.
NOT SO WITH *US.*
KRAKK

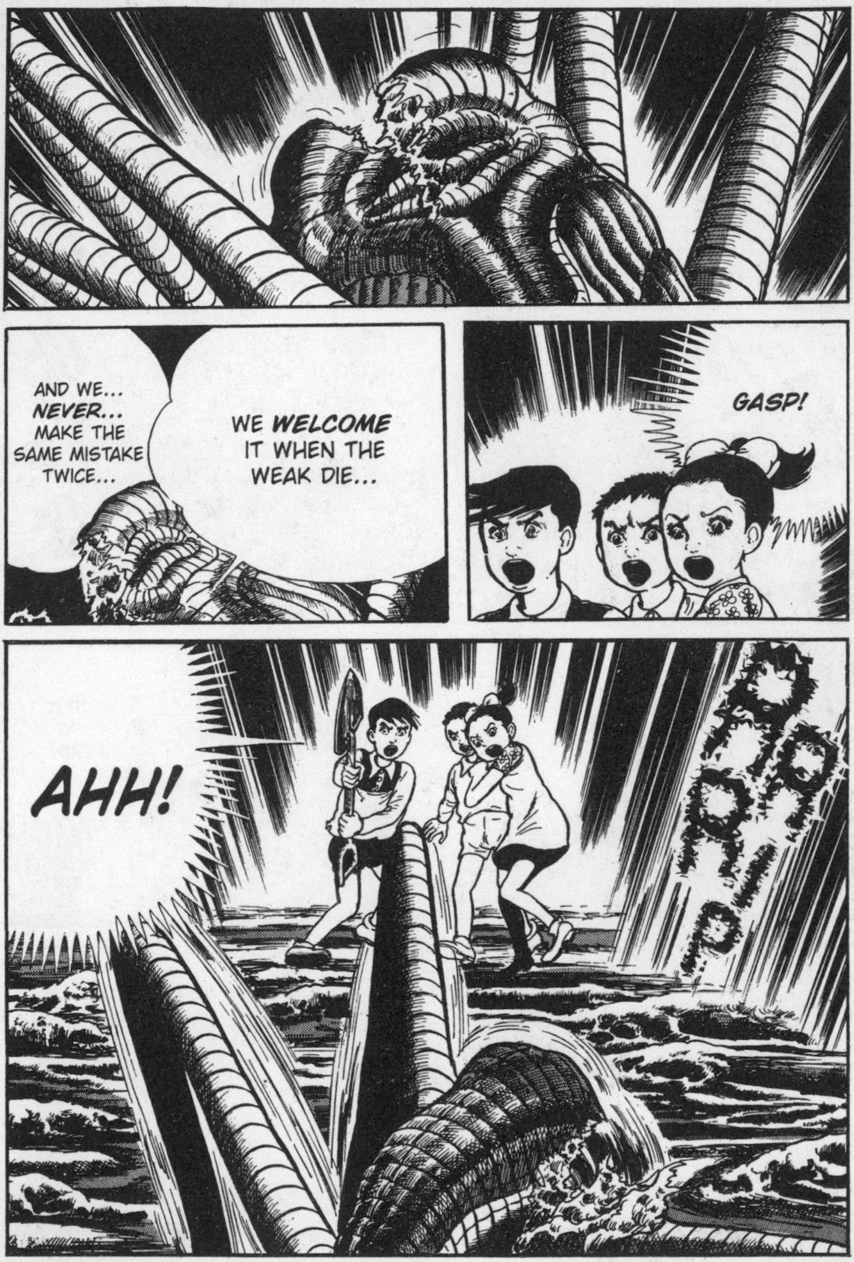
GASP!
WE WELCOME IT WHEN THE WEAK DIE...
AND WE... NEVER... MAKE THE SAME MISTAKE TWICE...
AHH!

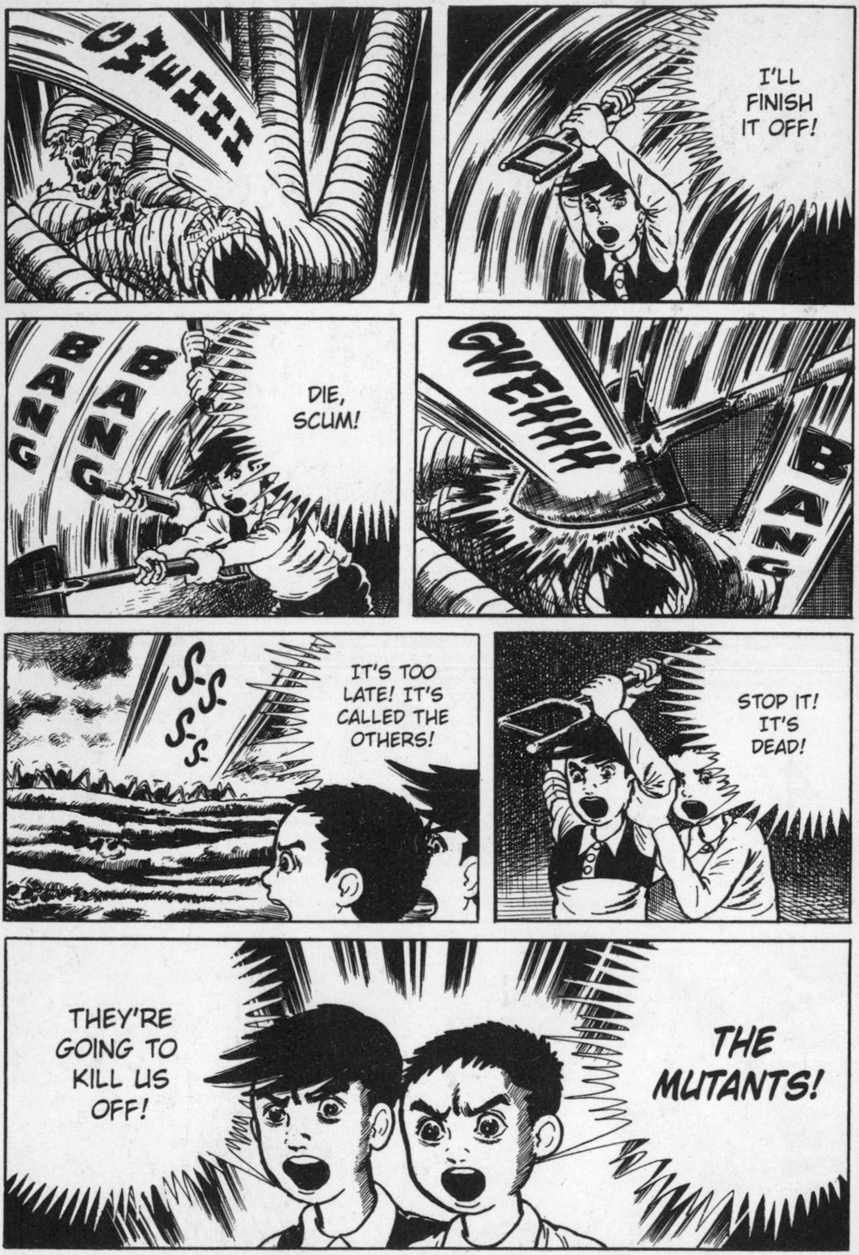
I'LL FINISH IT OFF!
GWEIII
GWEHHH
BANG
DIE, SCUM!
BANG
BANG
STOP IT! IT'S DEAD!
IT'S TOO LATE! IT'S CALLED THE OTHERS!
S-S-S-S-
THE MUTANTS!
THEY'RE GOING TO KILL US OFF!

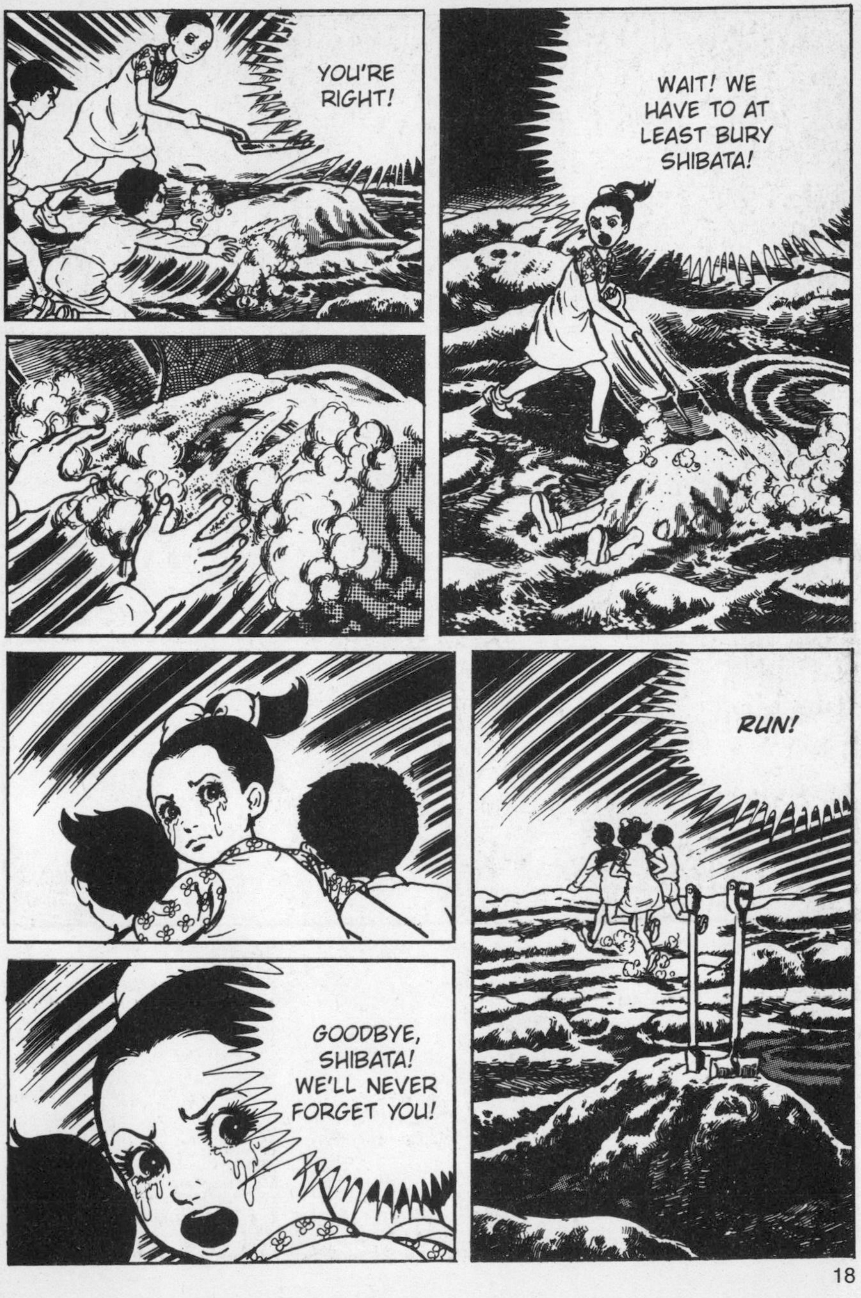
WAIT! WE HAVE TO AT LEAST BURY SHIBATA!
YOU'RE RIGHT!
RUN!
GOODBYE, SHIBATA! WE'LL NEVER FORGET YOU!

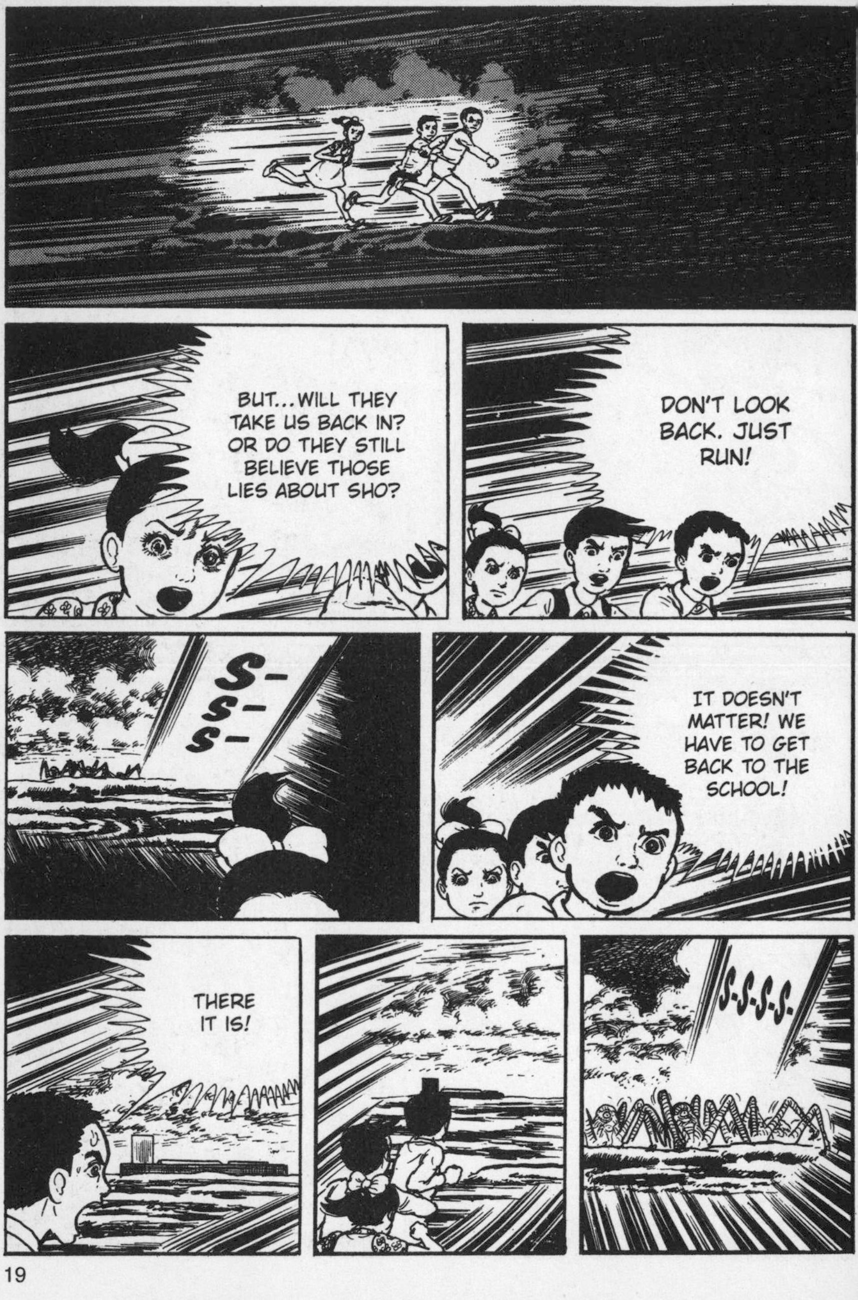
DON'T LOOK BACK. JUST RUN!
BUT...WILL THEY TAKE US BACK IN? OR DO THEY STILL BELIEVE THOSE LIES ABOUT SHO?
IT DOESN'T MATTER! WE HAVE TO GET BACK TO THE SCHOOL!
S-S-S-
S-S-S-S-
THERE IT IS!

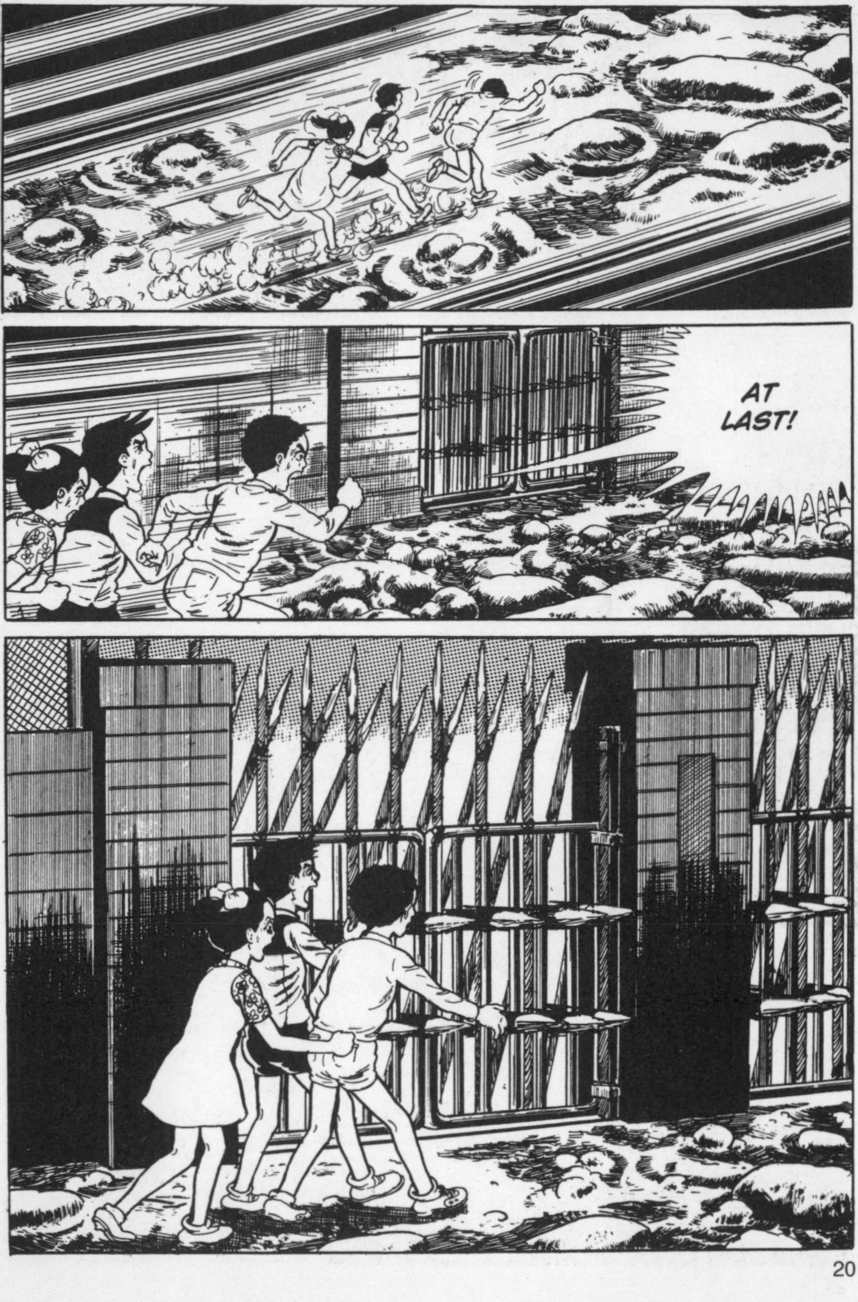
AT LAST!

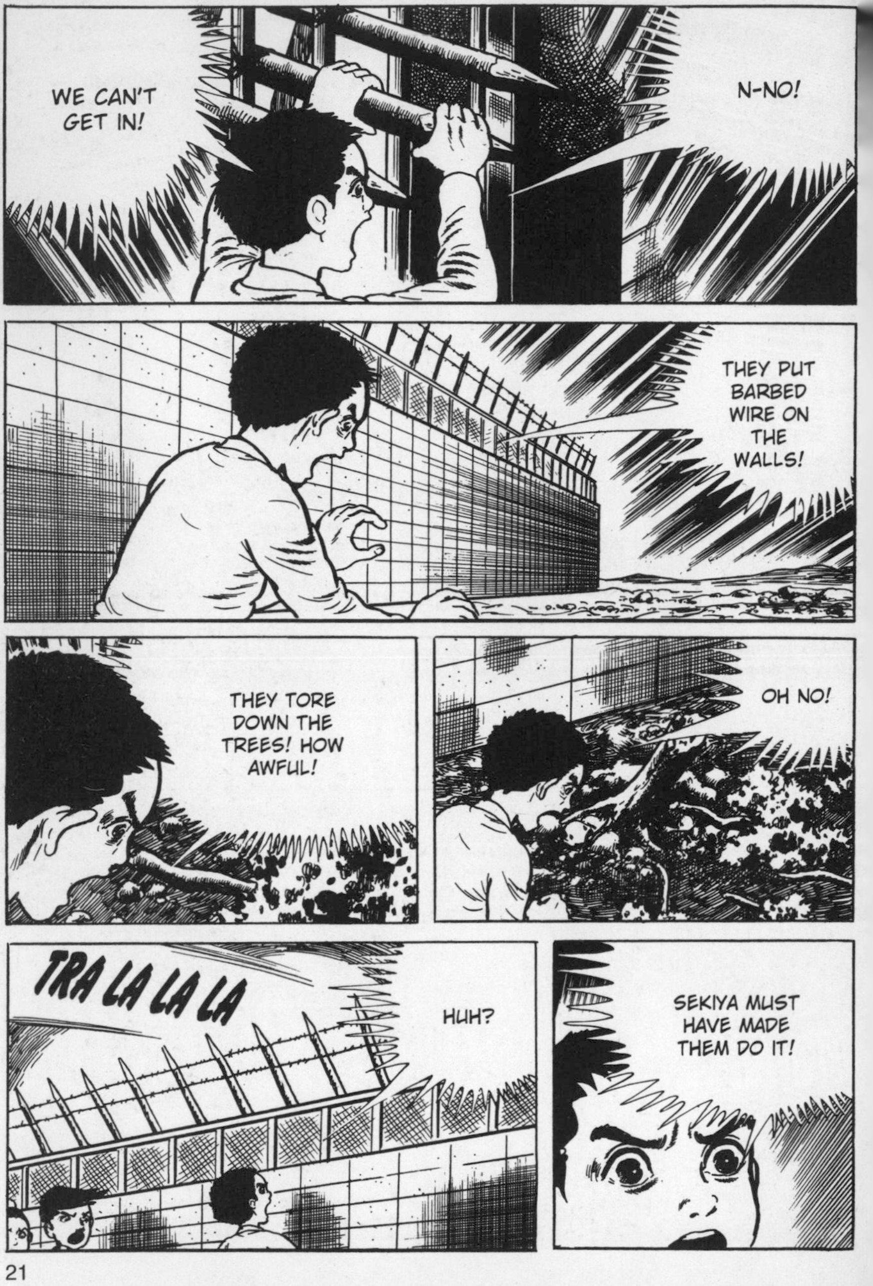
N-NO!
WE CAN'T GET IN!
THEY PUT BARBED WIRE ON THE WALLS!
OH NO!
THEY TORE DOWN THE TREES! HOW AWFUL!
SEKIYA MUST HAVE MADE THEM DO IT!
TRA LA LA LA
HUH?

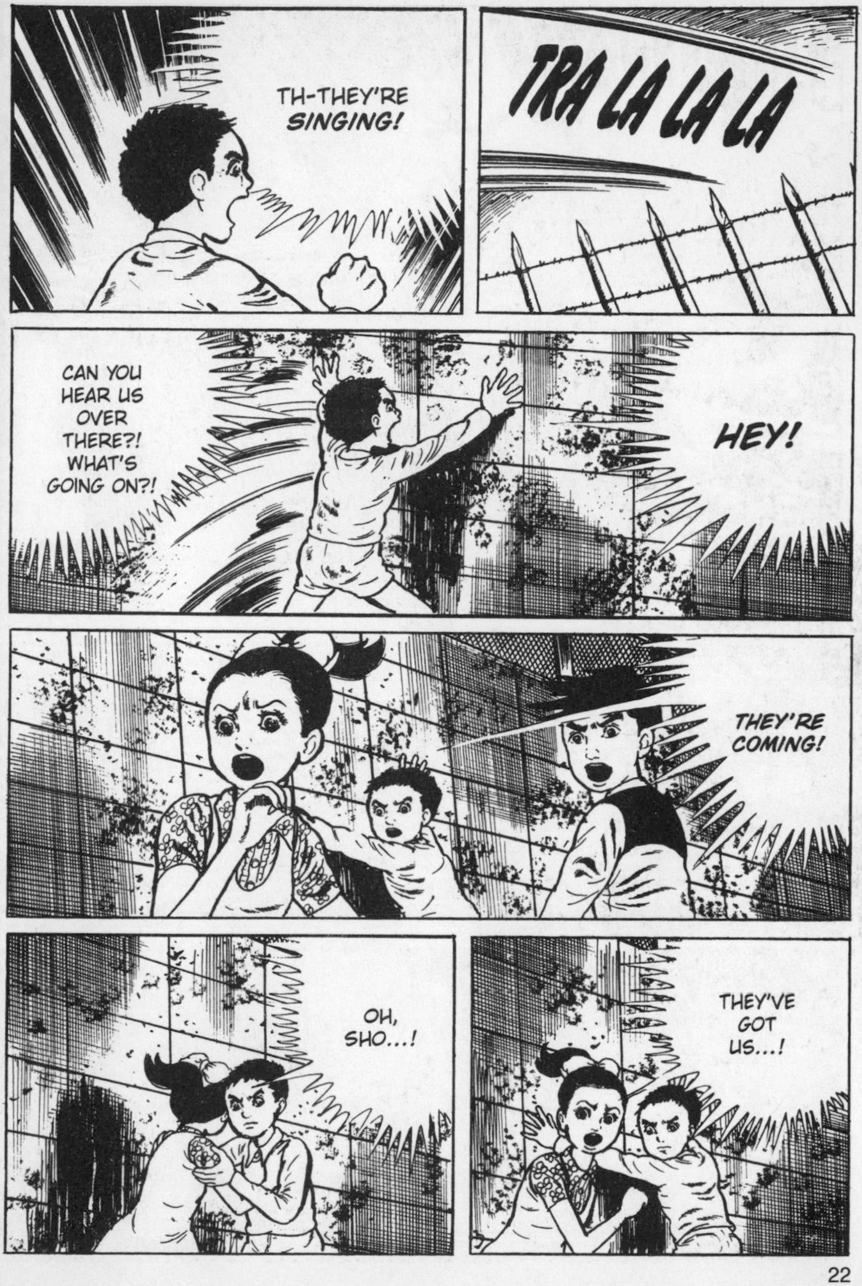
TRA LA LA LA
TH-THEY'RE SINGING!
HEY!
CAN YOU HEAR US OVER THERE?! WHAT'S GOING ON?!
THEY'RE COMING!
THEY'VE GOT US...!
OH, SHO...!

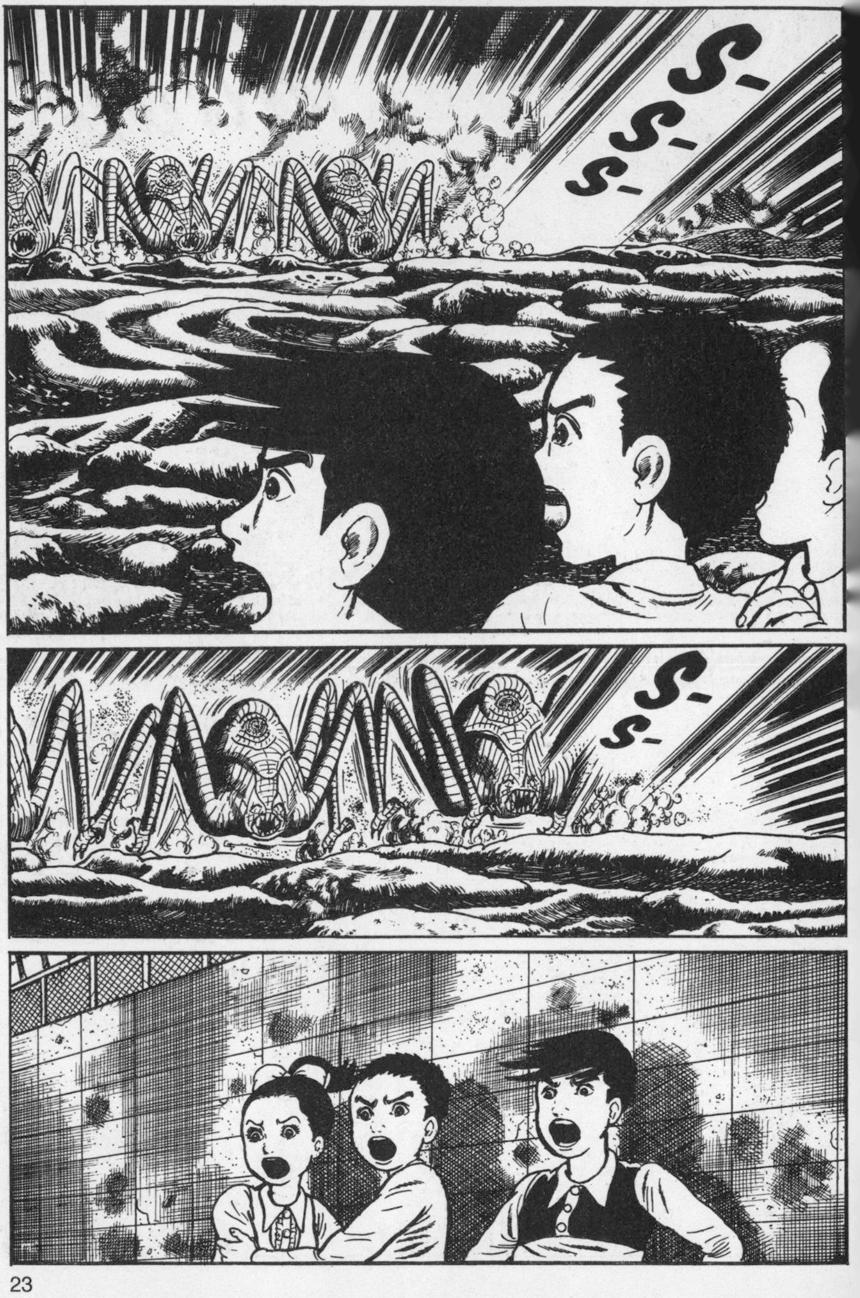
S- S- S-
S- S-

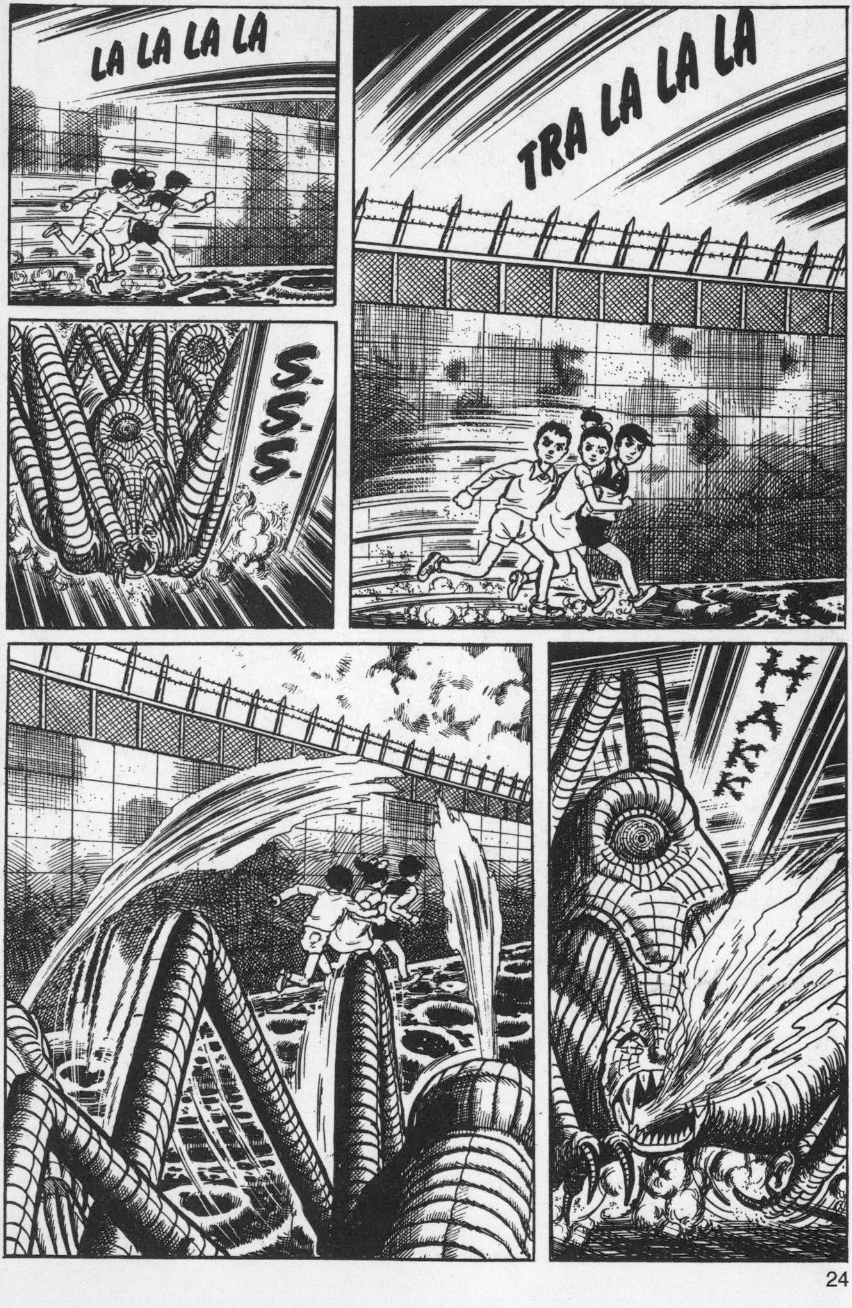
TRA LA LA LA
LA LA LA LA
S-S-S-
HAKK

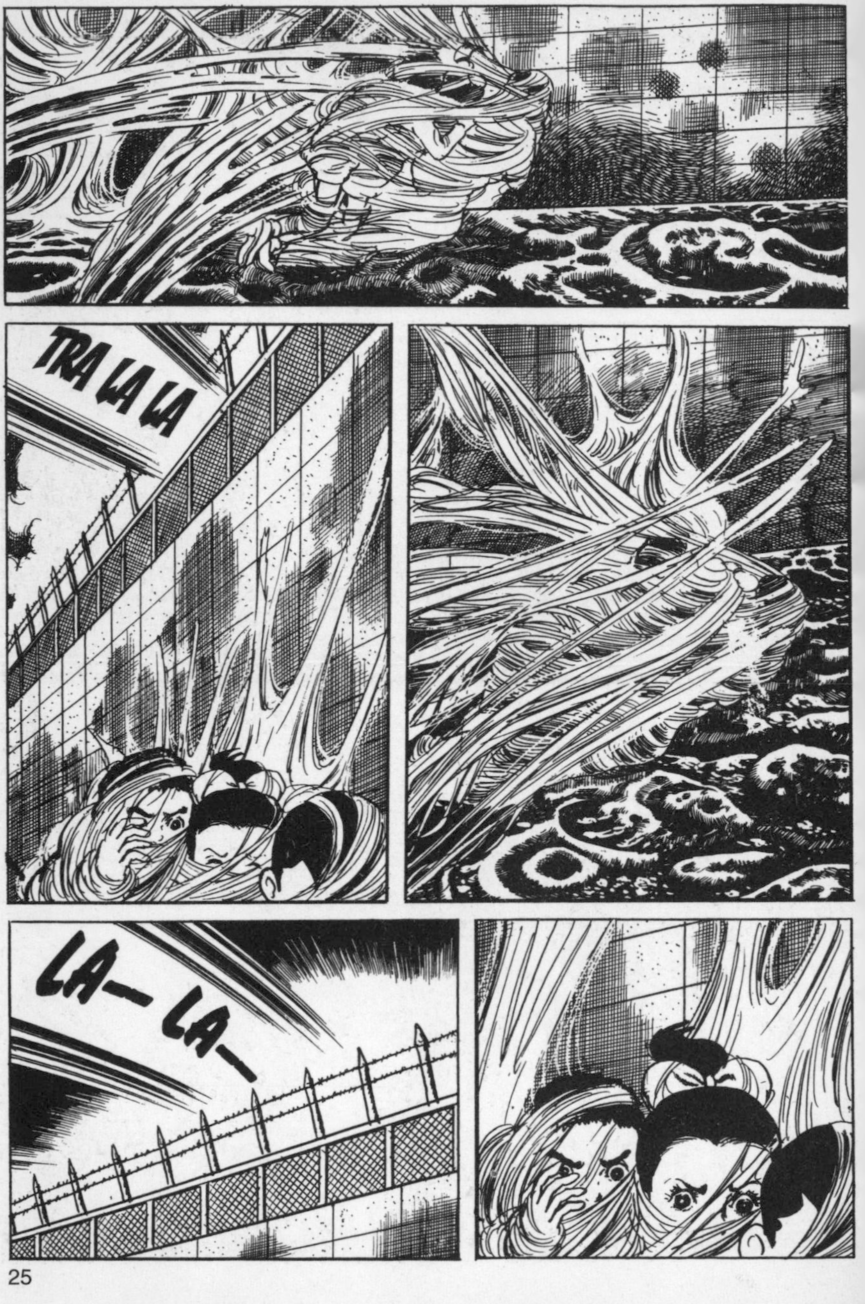
TRA LA LA
LA— LA—

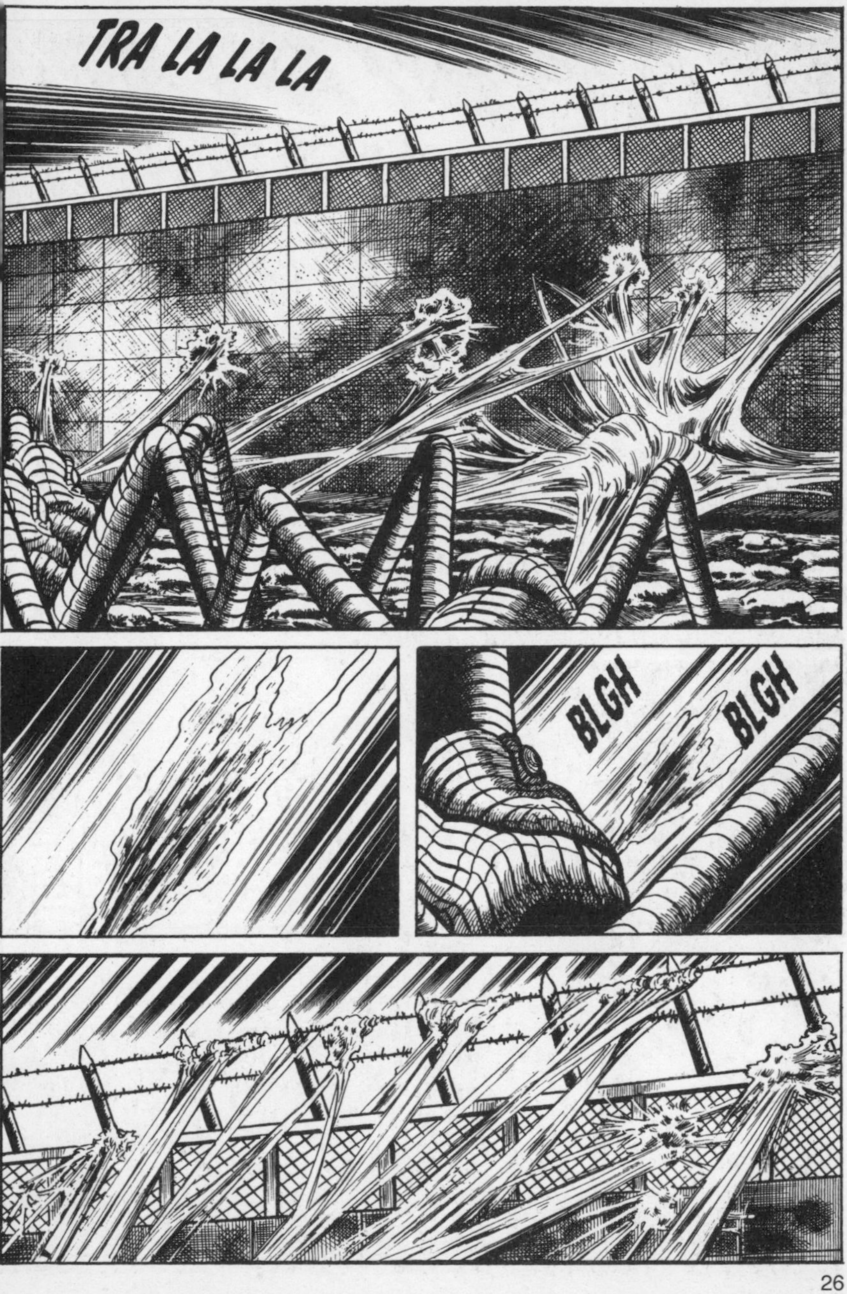
TRA LA LA LA
BLGH
BLGH

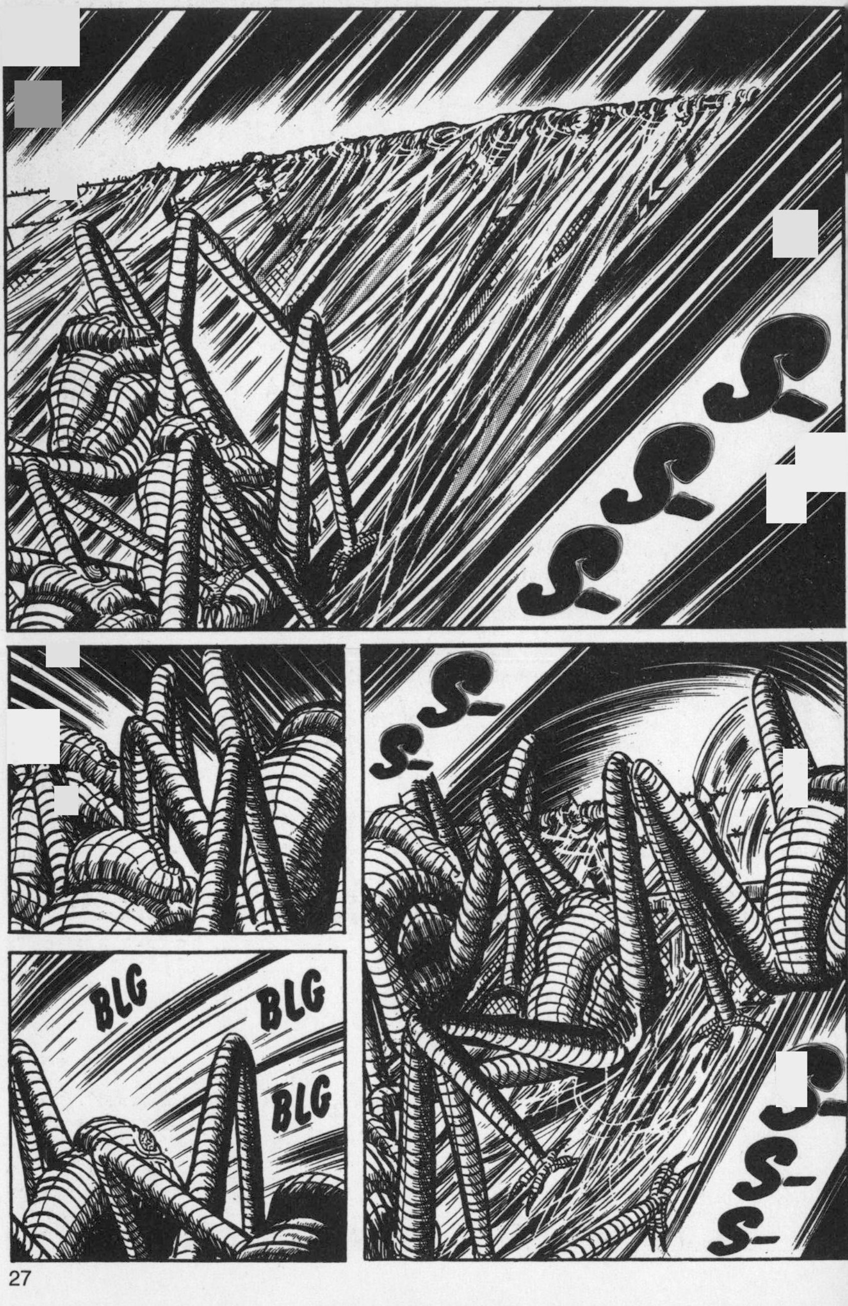
S-
S-
S-
S-
S-
S-
S-
S-
BLG
BLG
BLG

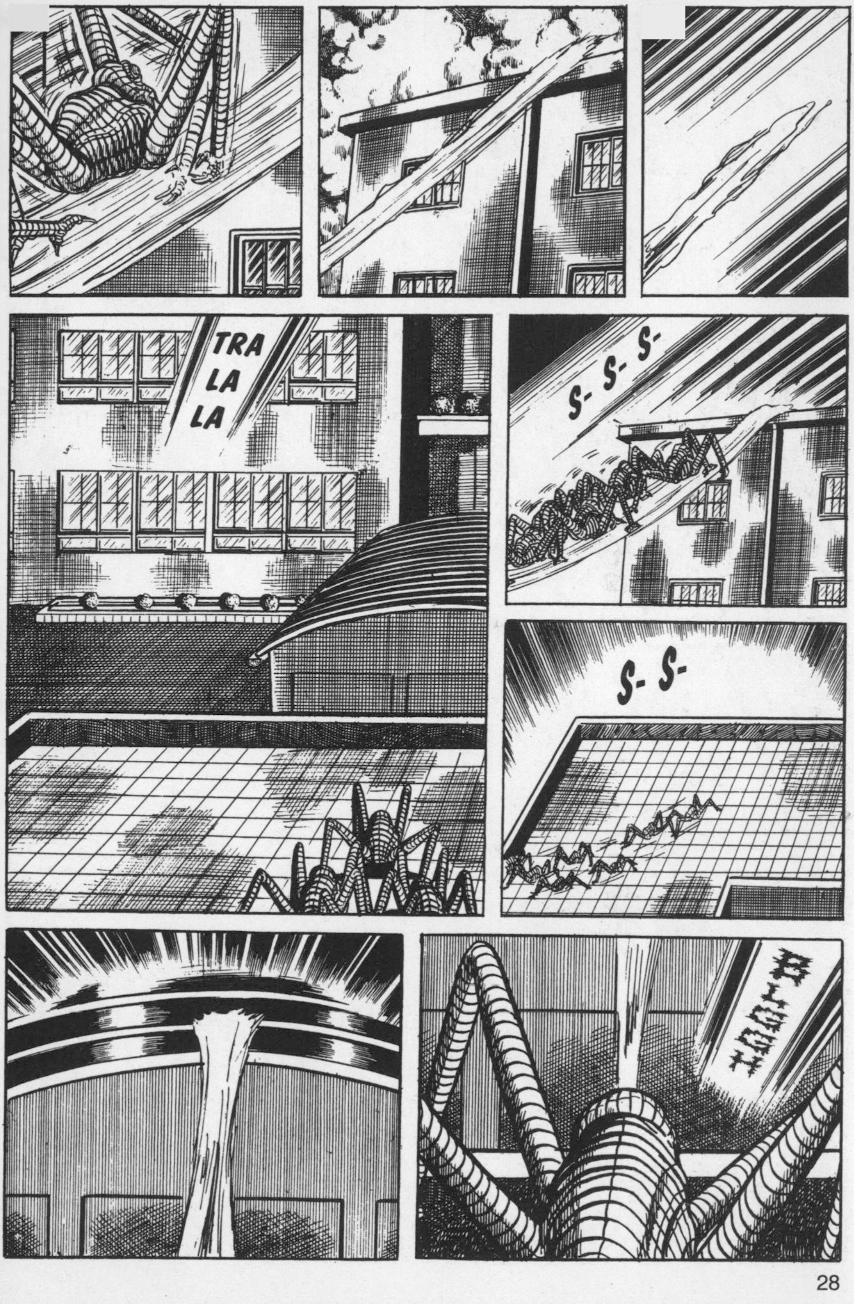
S- S- S-
S- S-
TRA LA LA
BLOGH

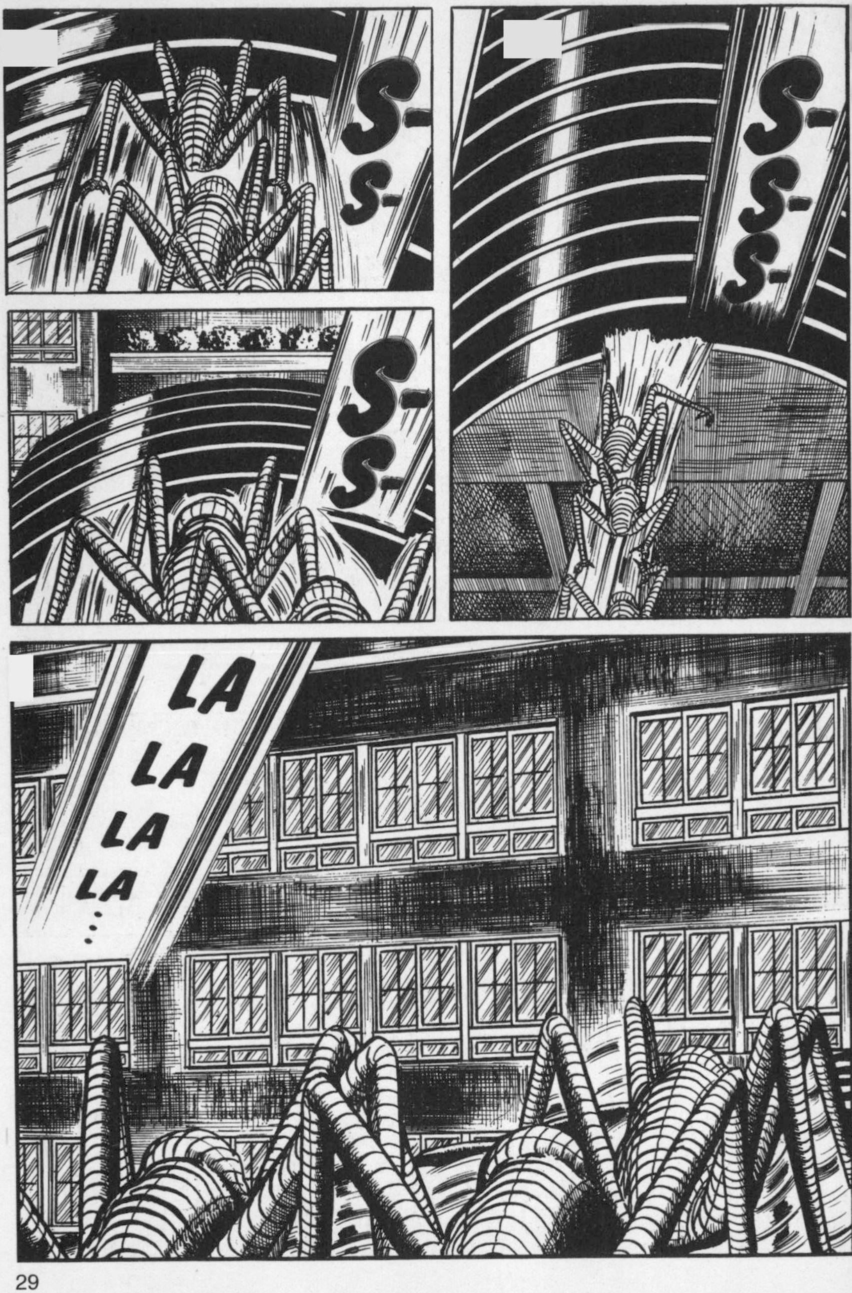
S-S-S-
S-S-
S-S-
LA LA LA LA...

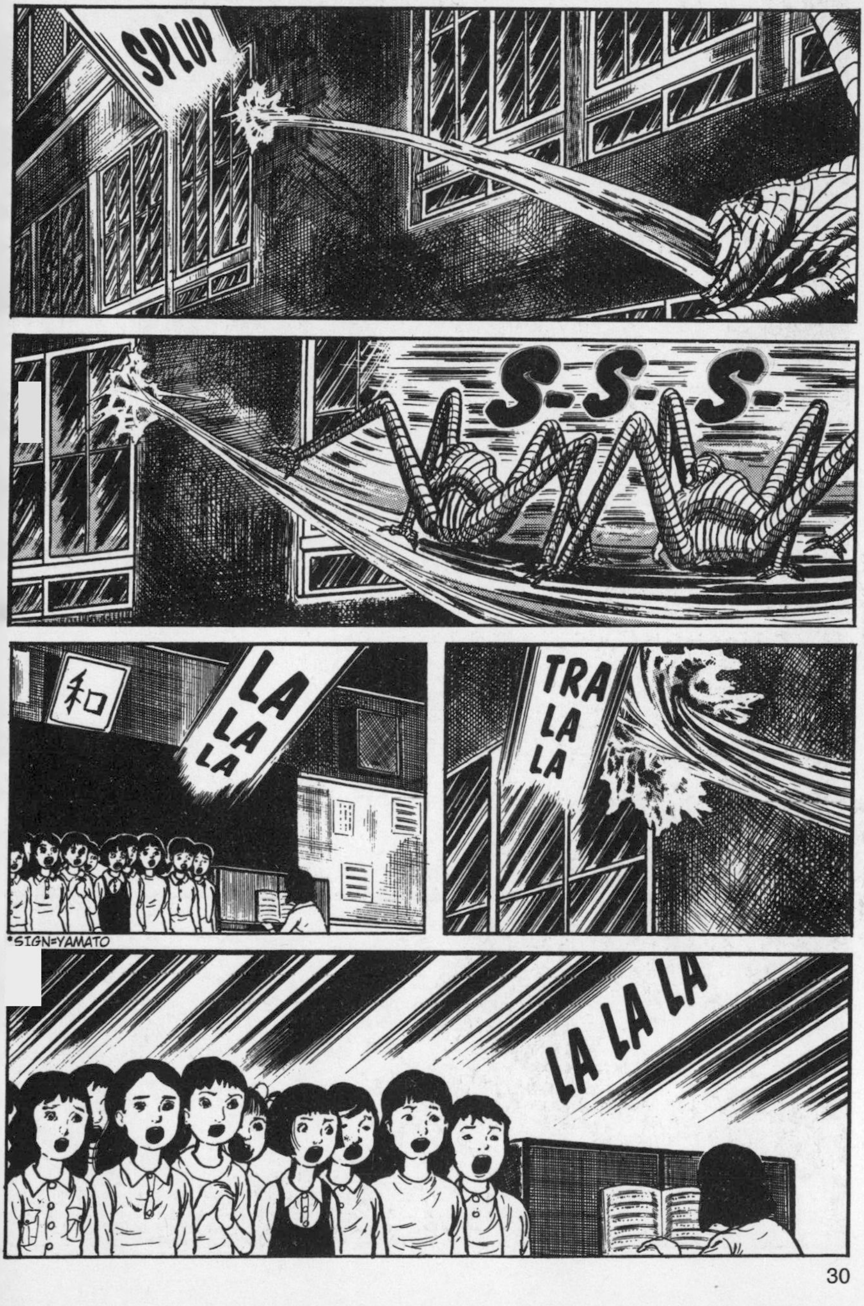
SPLUP
S-S-S-
TRA LA LA
和
LA LA LA
*SIGN=YAMATO
LA LA LA

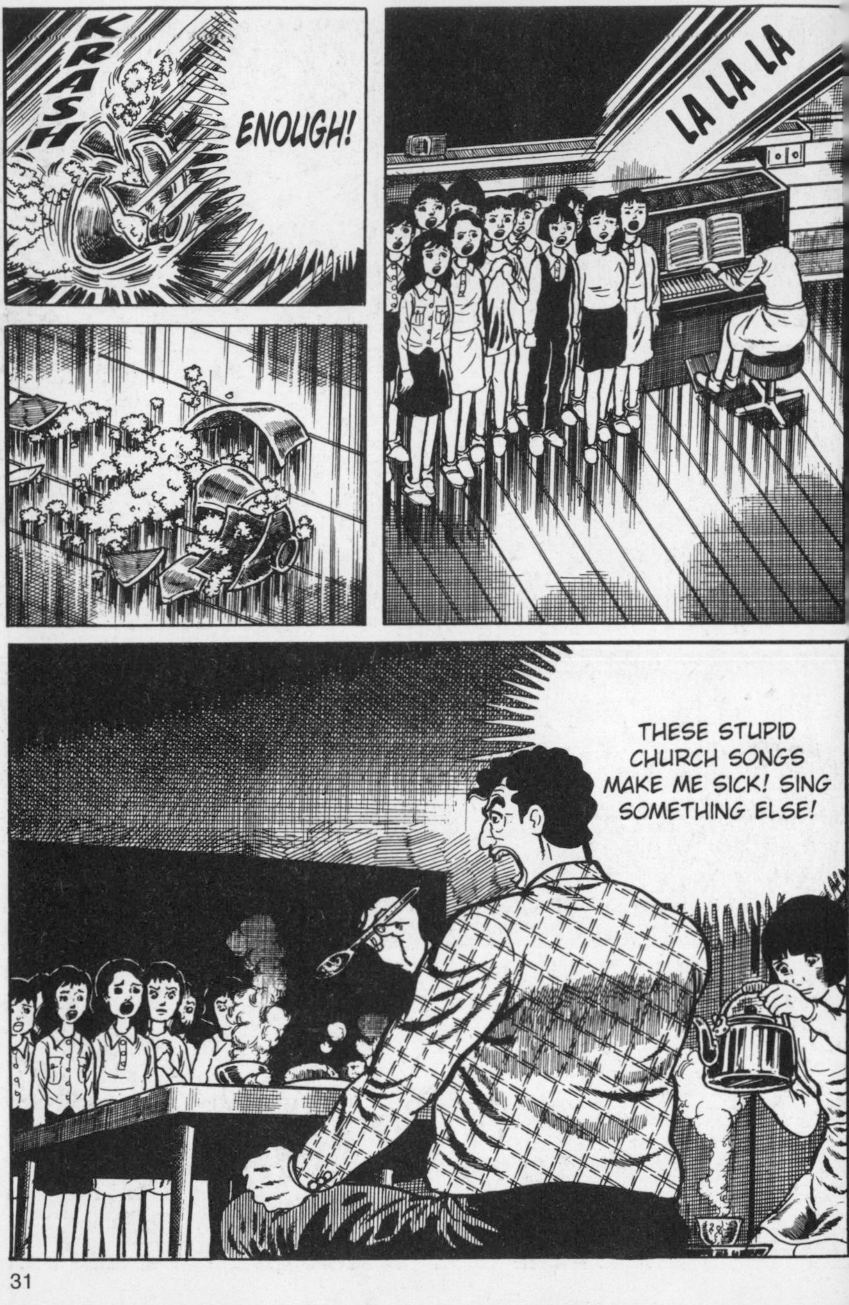
LA LA LA
KRASH
ENOUGH!
THESE STUPID CHURCH SONGS MAKE ME SICK! SING SOMETHING ELSE!

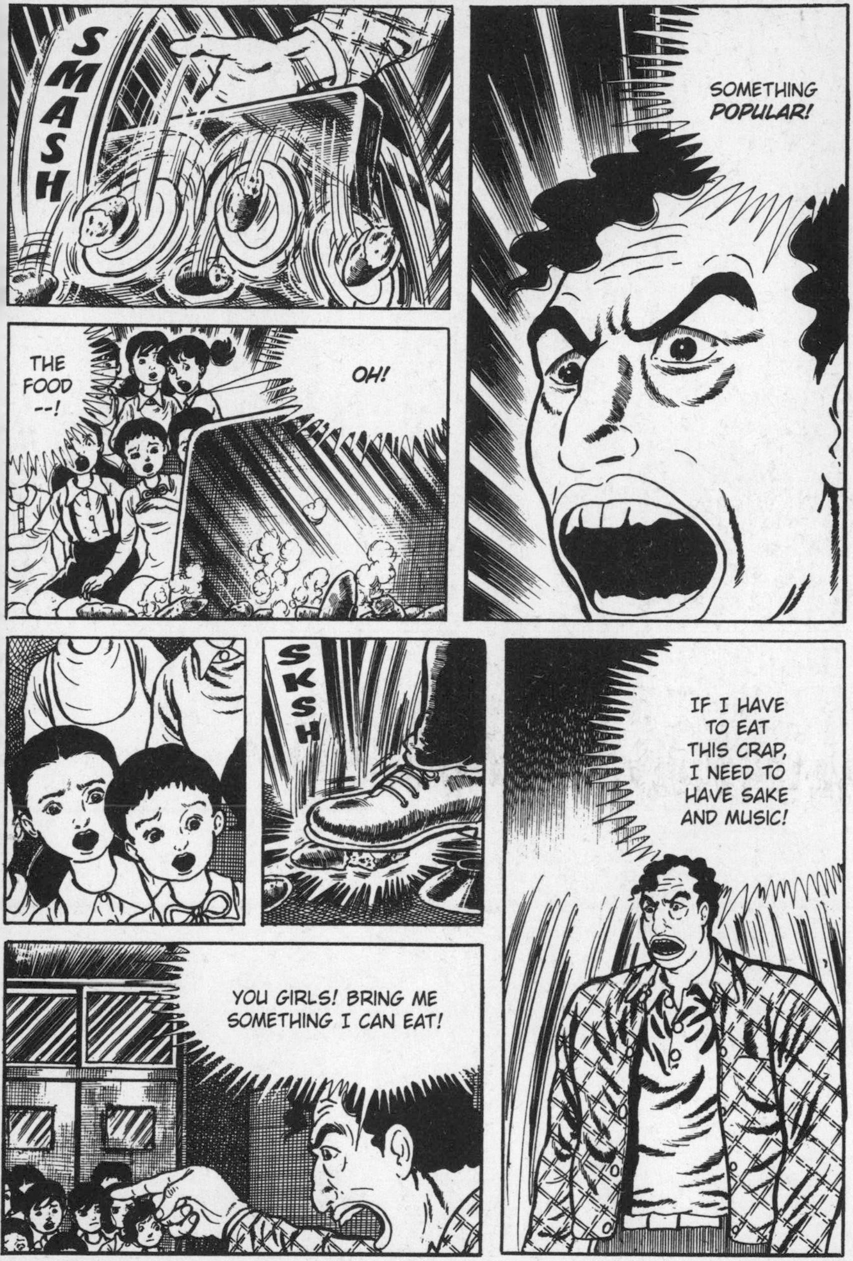
SOMETHING POPULAR!
SMASH
OH!
THE FOOD --!
IF I HAVE TO EAT THIS CRAP, I NEED TO HAVE SAKE AND MUSIC!
SKSH
YOU GIRLS! BRING ME SOMETHING I CAN EAT!

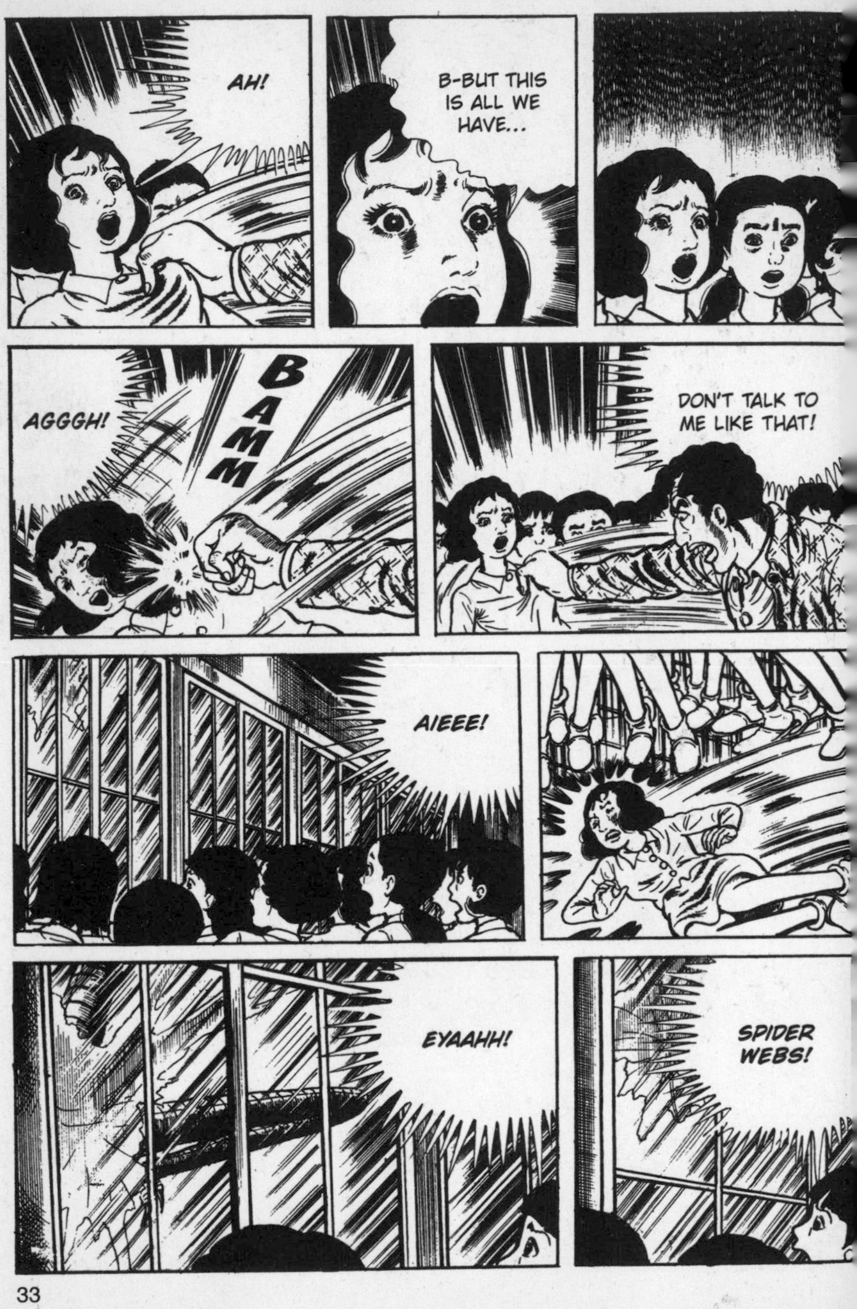
B-BUT THIS IS ALL WE HAVE...
AH!
DON'T TALK TO ME LIKE THAT!
BAMM
AGGGH!
AIEEE!
SPIDER WEBS!
EYAAHH!

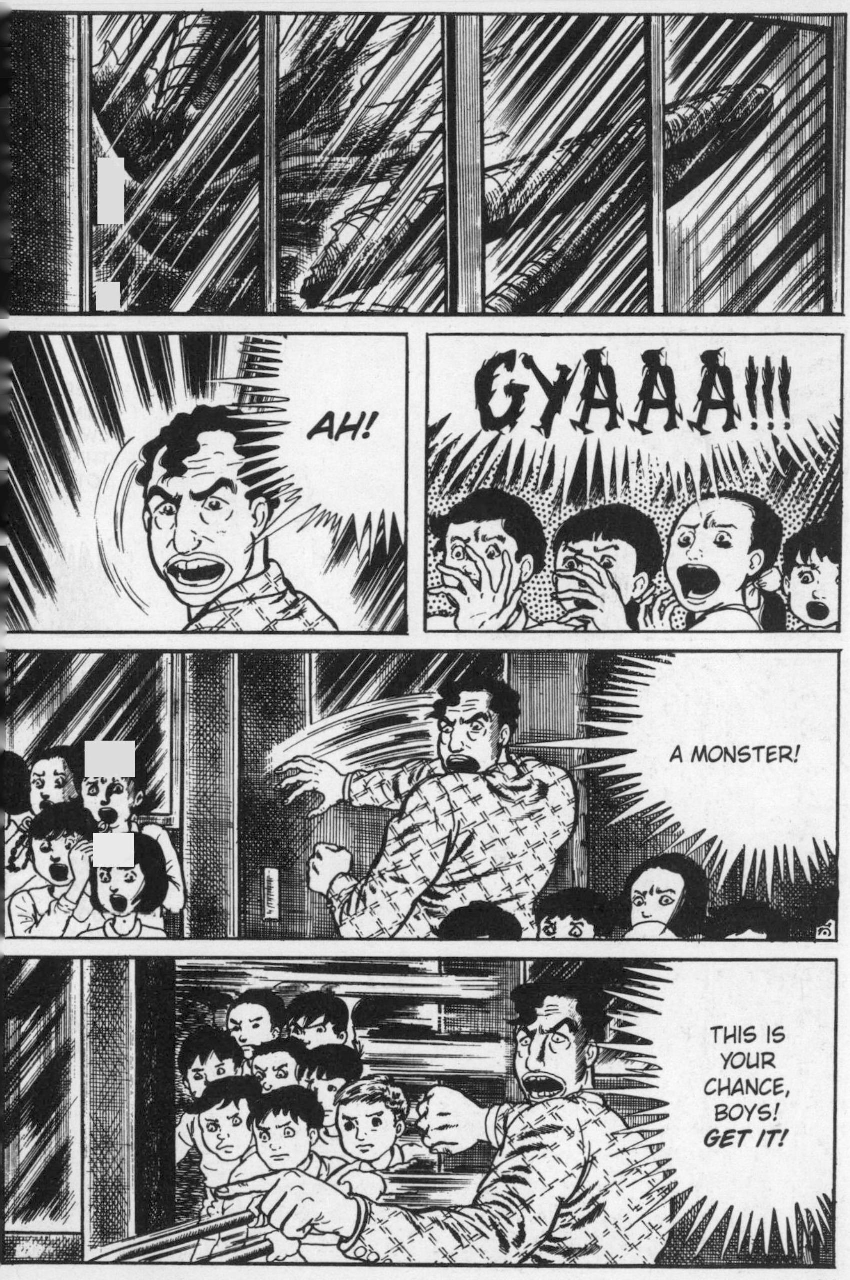
GYAAA!!!
AH!
A MONSTER!
THIS IS YOUR CHANCE, BOYS!
GET IT!

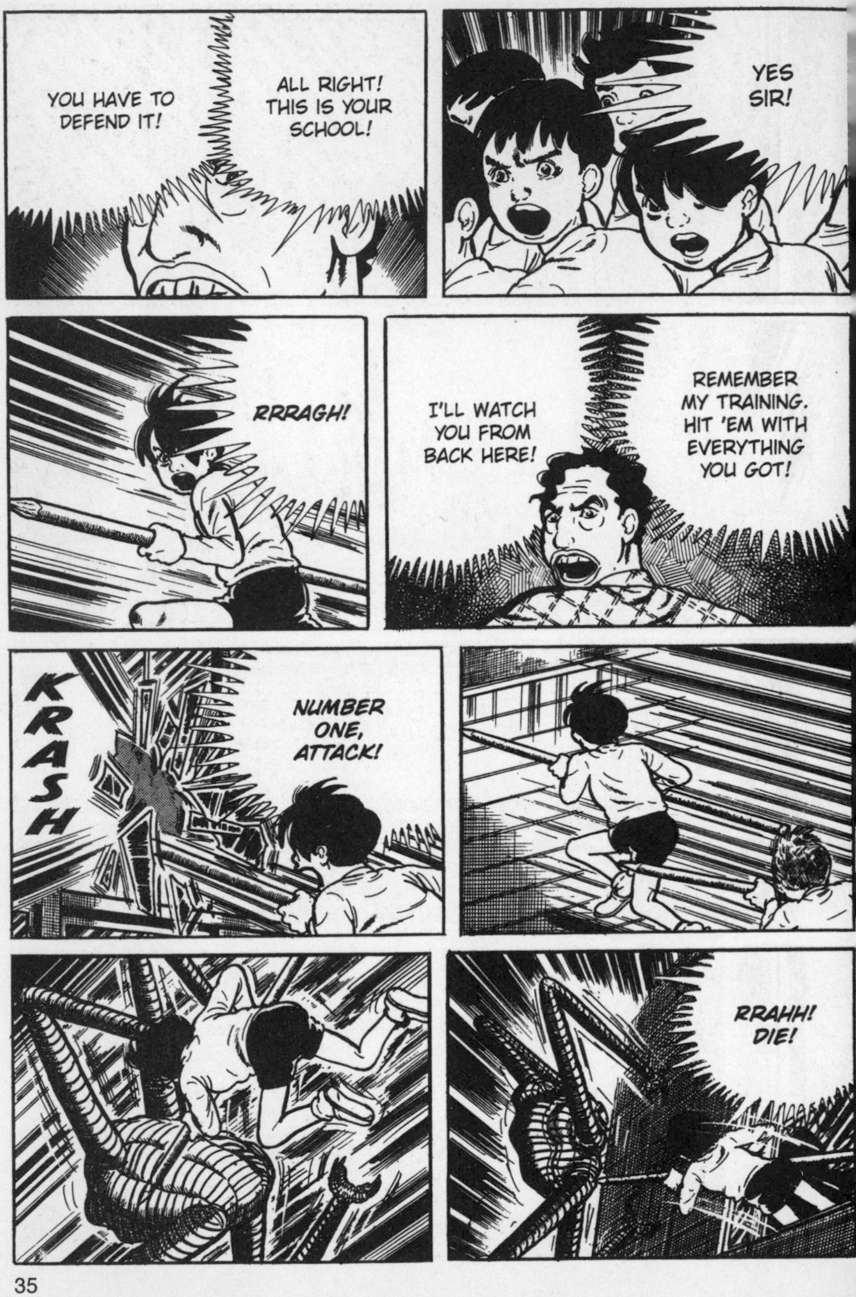
YES SIR!
ALL RIGHT! THIS IS YOUR SCHOOL!
YOU HAVE TO DEFEND IT!
REMEMBER MY TRAINING. HIT 'EM WITH EVERYTHING YOU GOT!
I'LL WATCH YOU FROM BACK HERE!
RRRAGH!
NUMBER ONE, ATTACK!
KRASH
RRAHH! DIE!

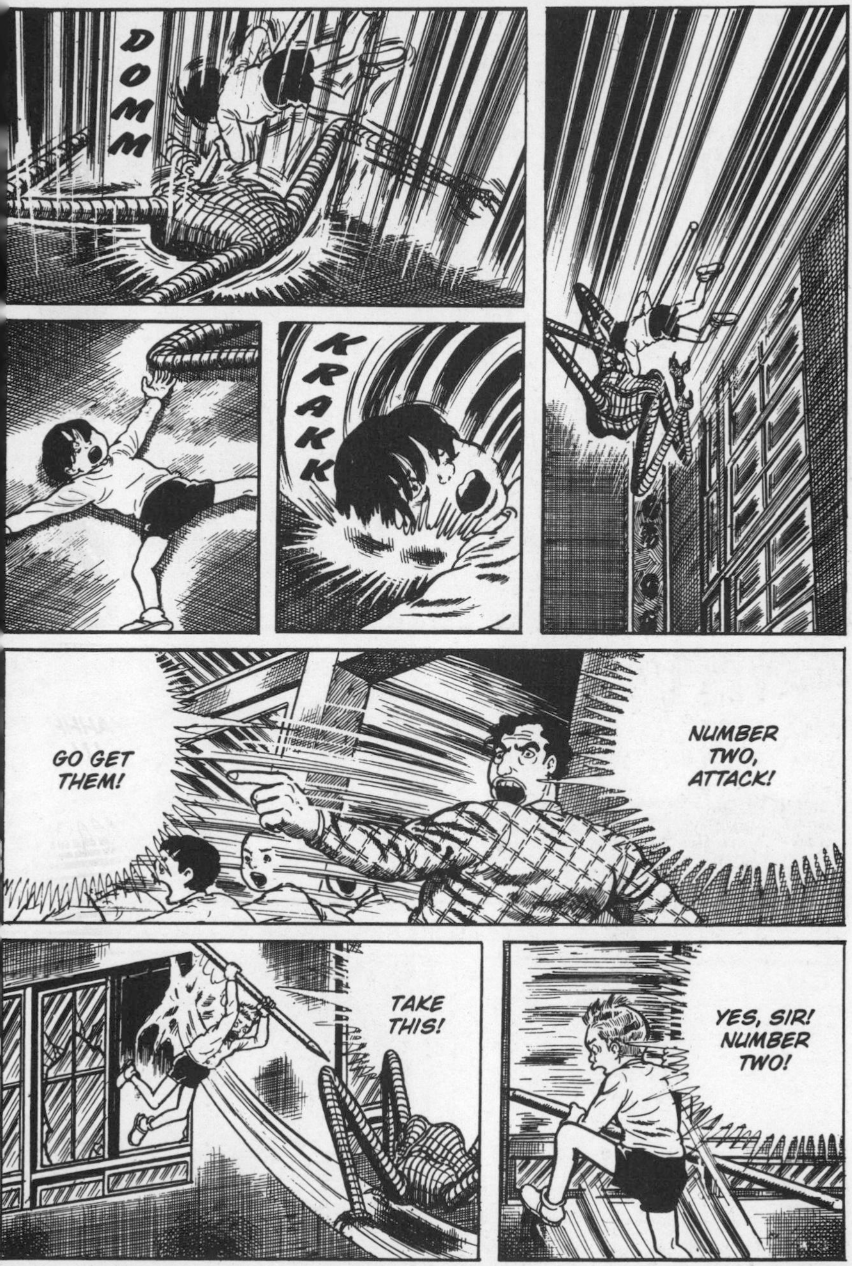
DOMM
KRAKK
NUMBER TWO, ATTACK!
GO GET THEM!
YES, SIR! NUMBER TWO!
TAKE THIS!

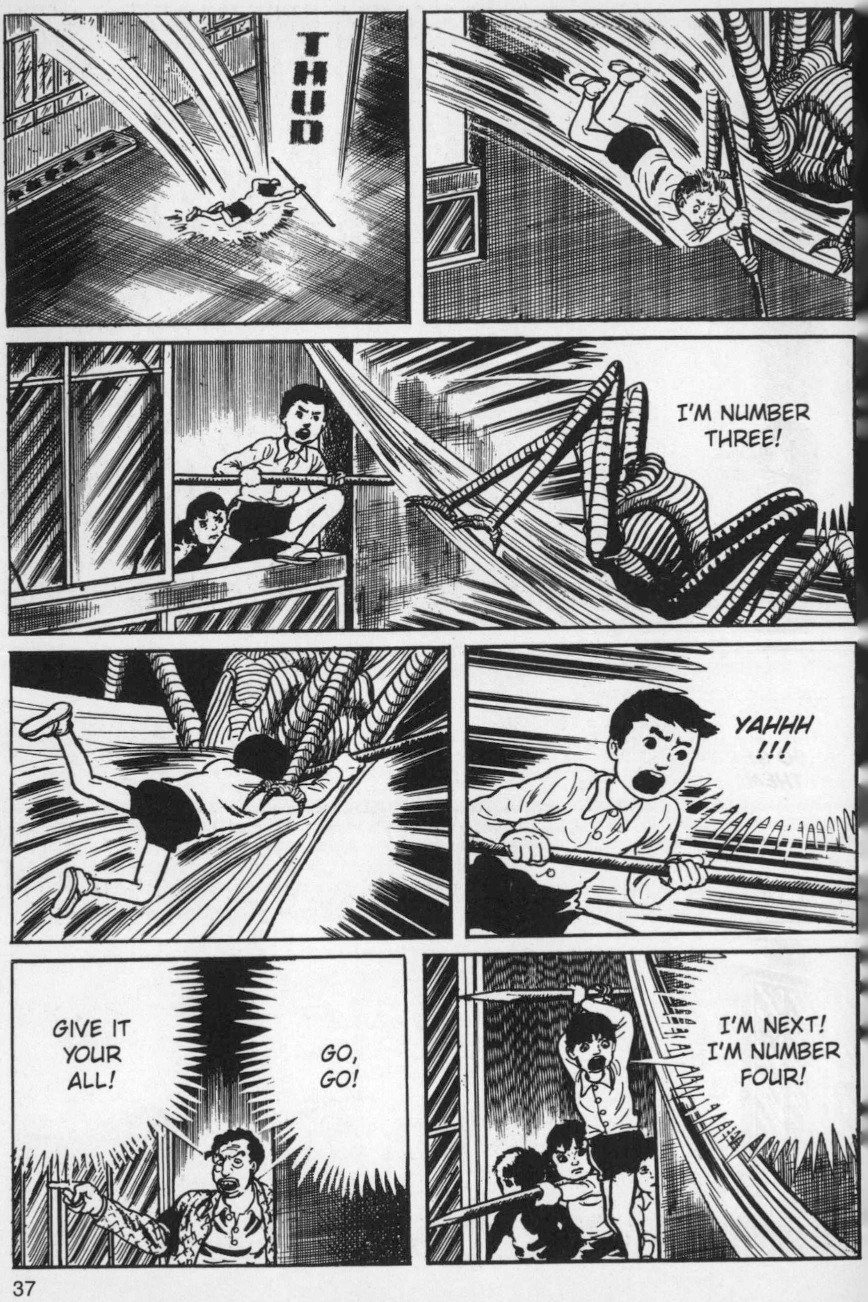
THUD
I'M NUMBER THREE!
YAHHH !!!
I'M NEXT! I'M NUMBER FOUR!
GO, GO!
GIVE IT YOUR ALL!

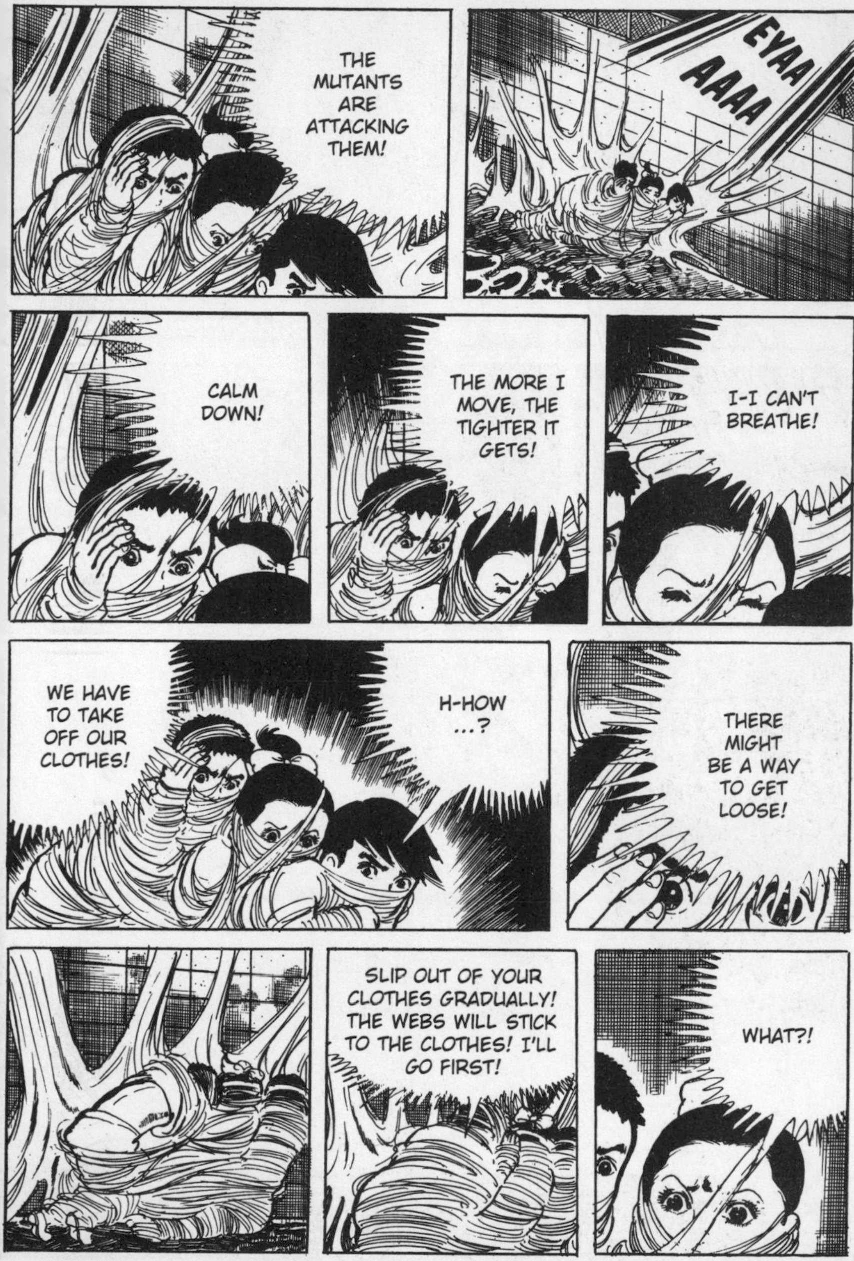
EYAA AAAA
THE MUTANTS ARE ATTACKING THEM!
I-I CAN'T BREATHE!
THE MORE I MOVE, THE TIGHTER IT GETS!
CALM DOWN!
THERE MIGHT BE A WAY TO GET LOOSE!
H-HOW ...?
WE HAVE TO TAKE OFF OUR CLOTHES!
WHAT?!
SLIP OUT OF YOUR CLOTHES GRADUALLY! THE WEBS WILL STICK TO THE CLOTHES! I'LL GO FIRST!

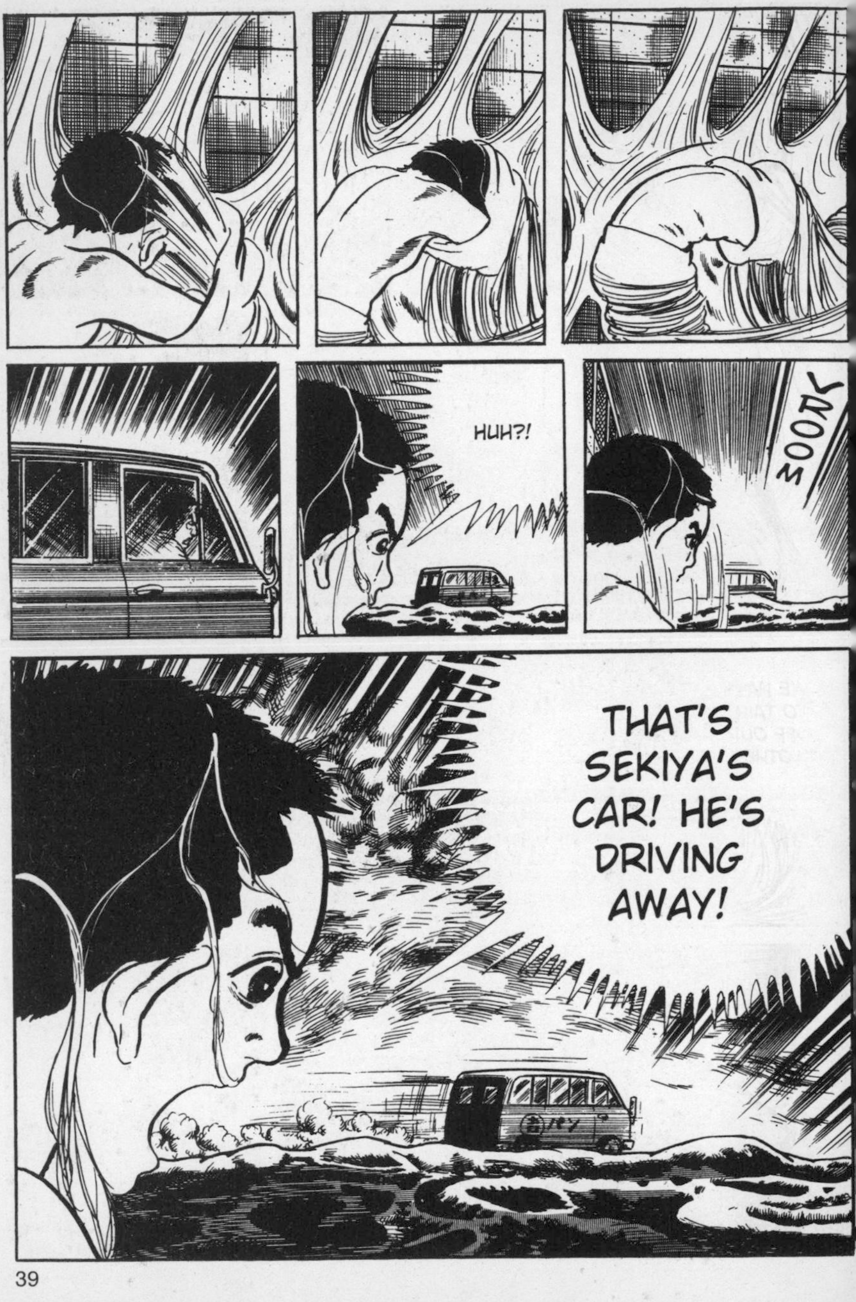
VROOM
HUH?!
THAT'S SEKIYA'S CAR! HE'S DRIVING AWAY!

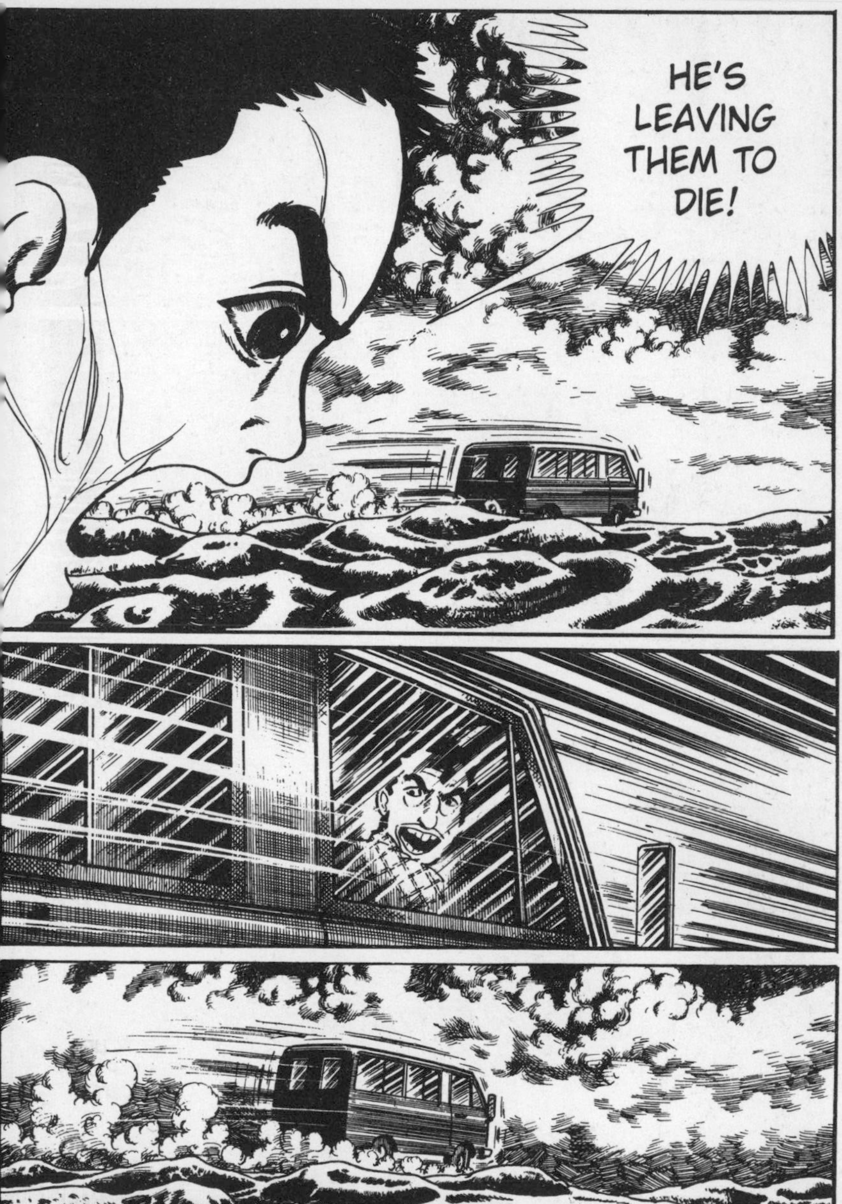
HE'S LEAVING THEM TO DIE!

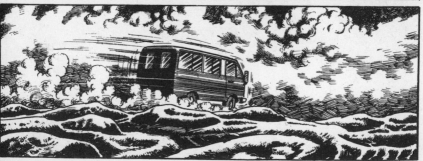

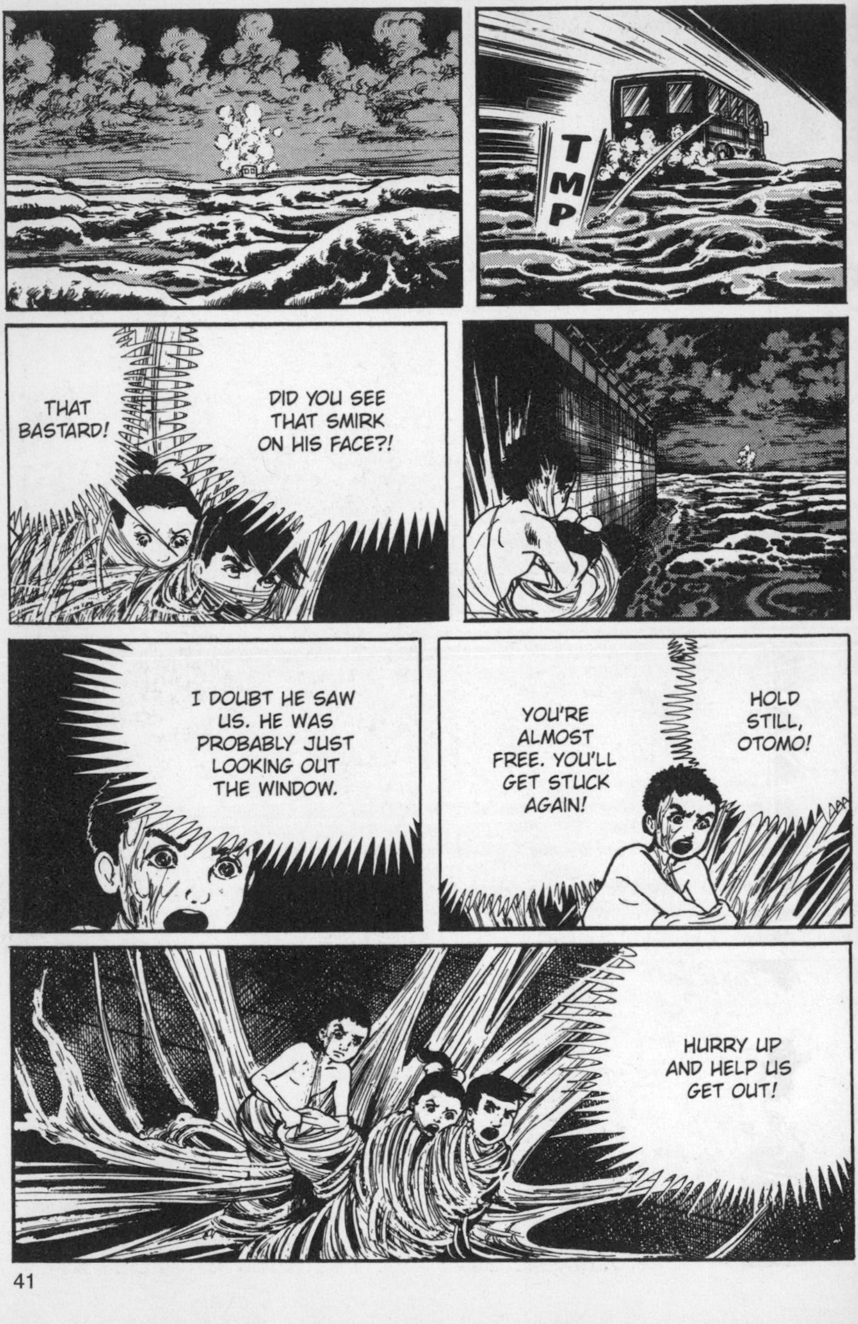
TMP
DID YOU SEE THAT SMIRK ON HIS FACE?!
THAT BASTARD!
HOLD STILL, OTOMO!
YOU'RE ALMOST FREE. YOU'LL GET STUCK AGAIN!
I DOUBT HE SAW US. HE WAS PROBABLY JUST LOOKING OUT THE WINDOW.
HURRY UP AND HELP US GET OUT!

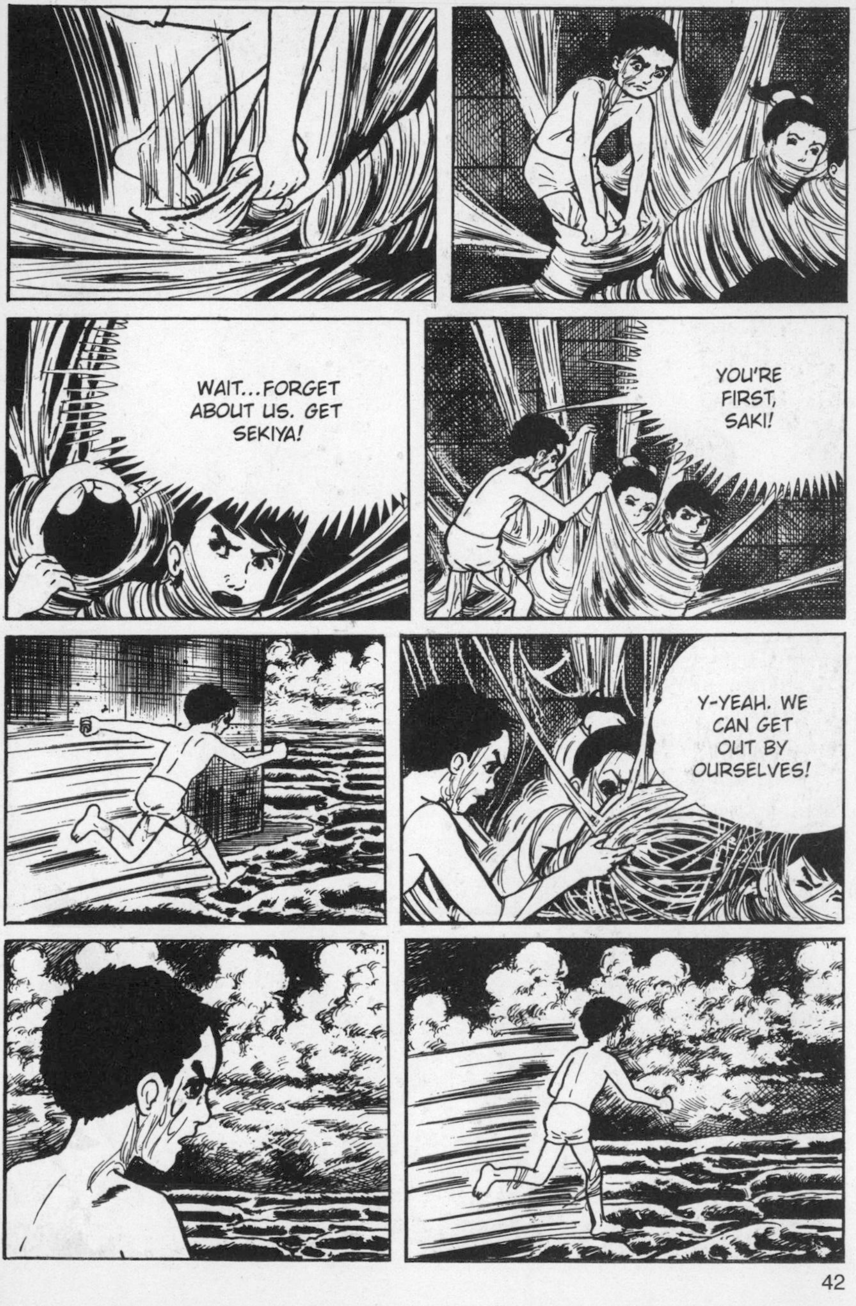
YOU'RE FIRST, SAKI!
WAIT...FORGET ABOUT US. GET SEKIYA!
Y-YEAH. WE CAN GET OUT BY OURSELVES!

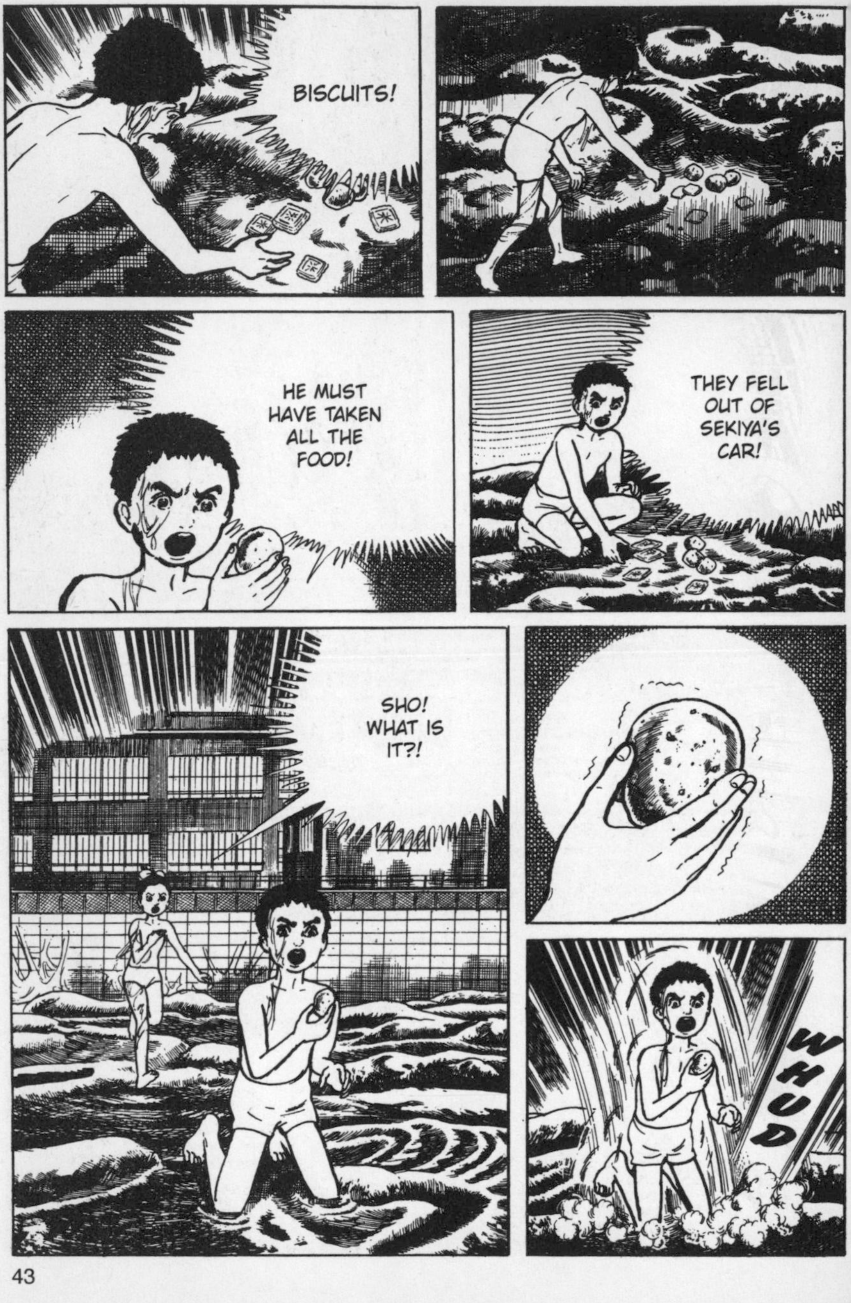
BISCUITS!
THEY FELL OUT OF SEKIYA'S CAR!
HE MUST HAVE TAKEN ALL THE FOOD!
WHUD
SHO! WHAT IS IT?!

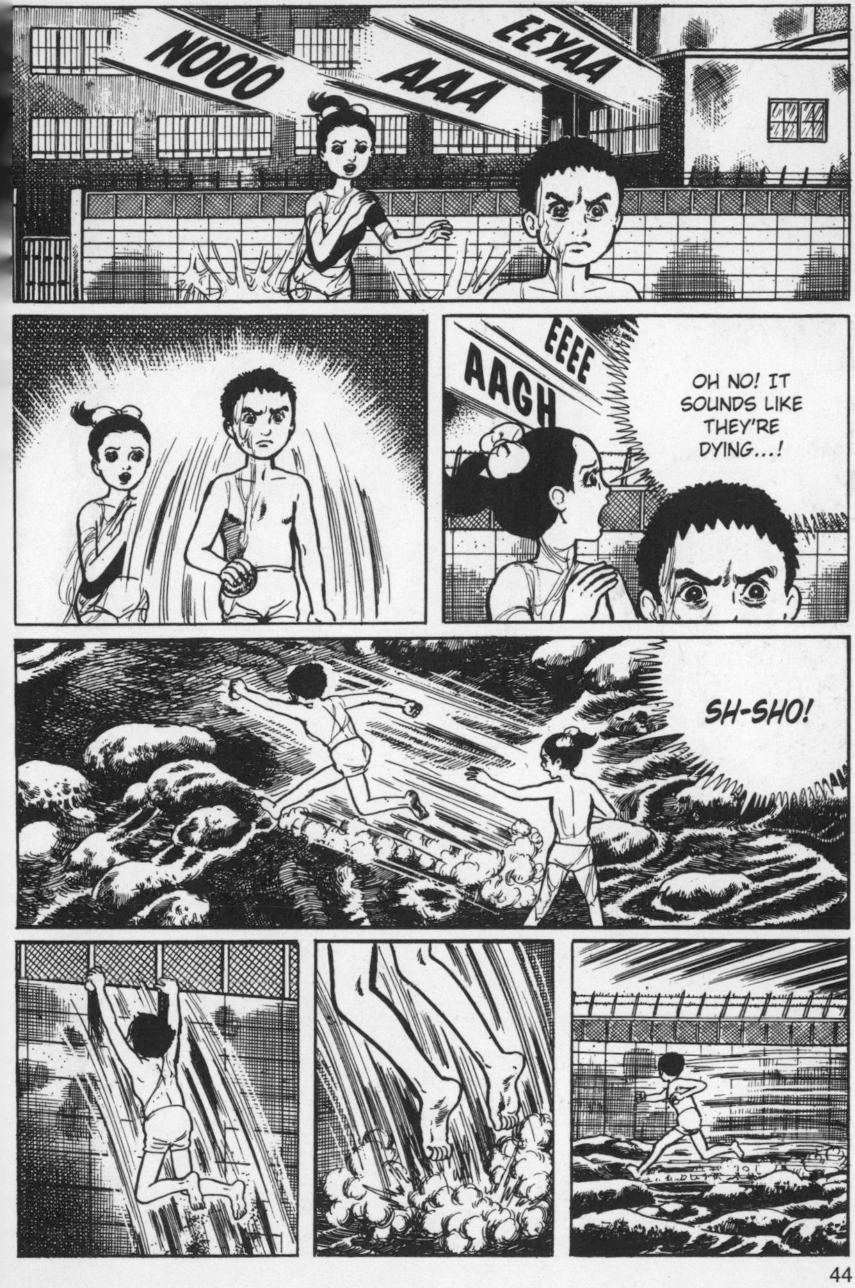
EEYAA
AAA
NOOO
OH NO! IT SOUNDS LIKE THEY'RE DYING...!
EEEE
AAGH
SH-SHO!

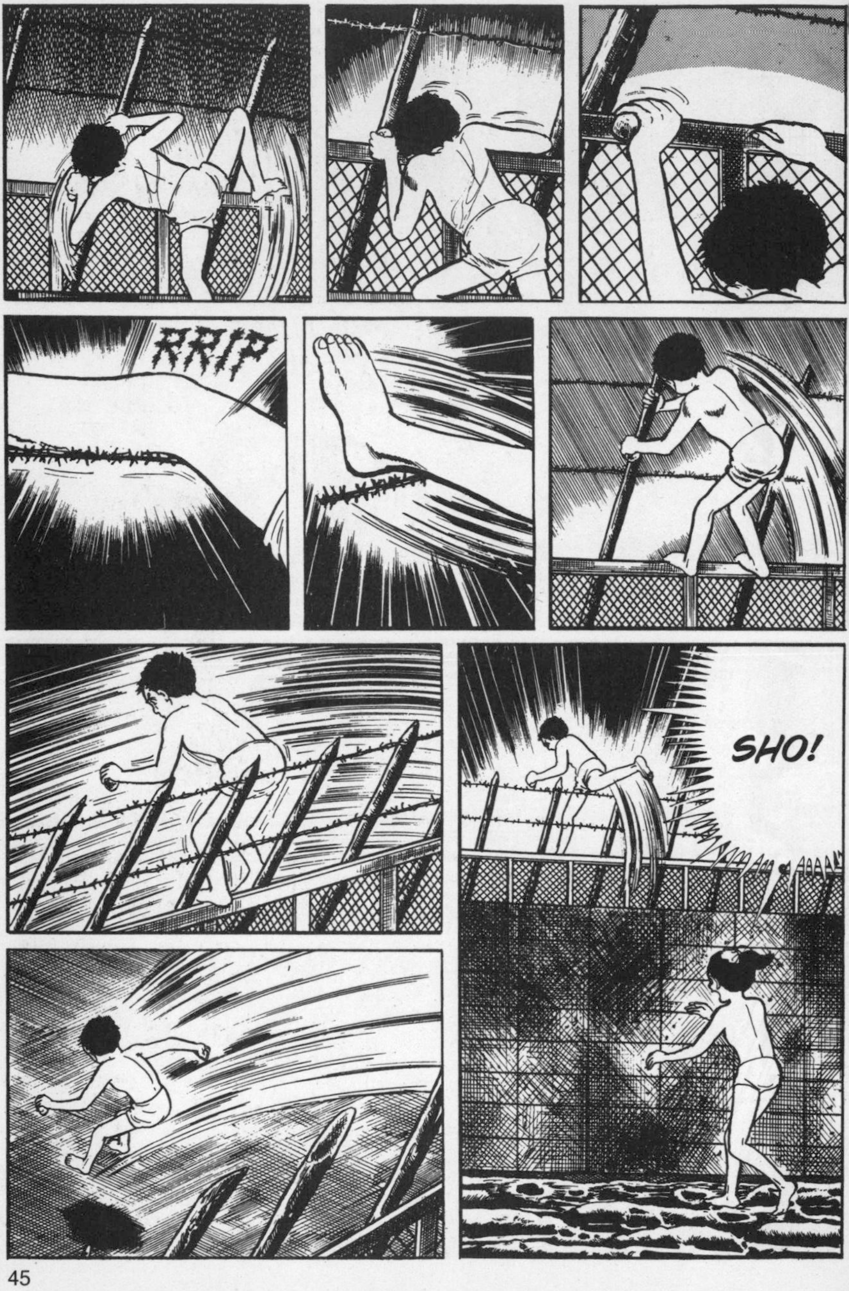
RRIP
SHO!

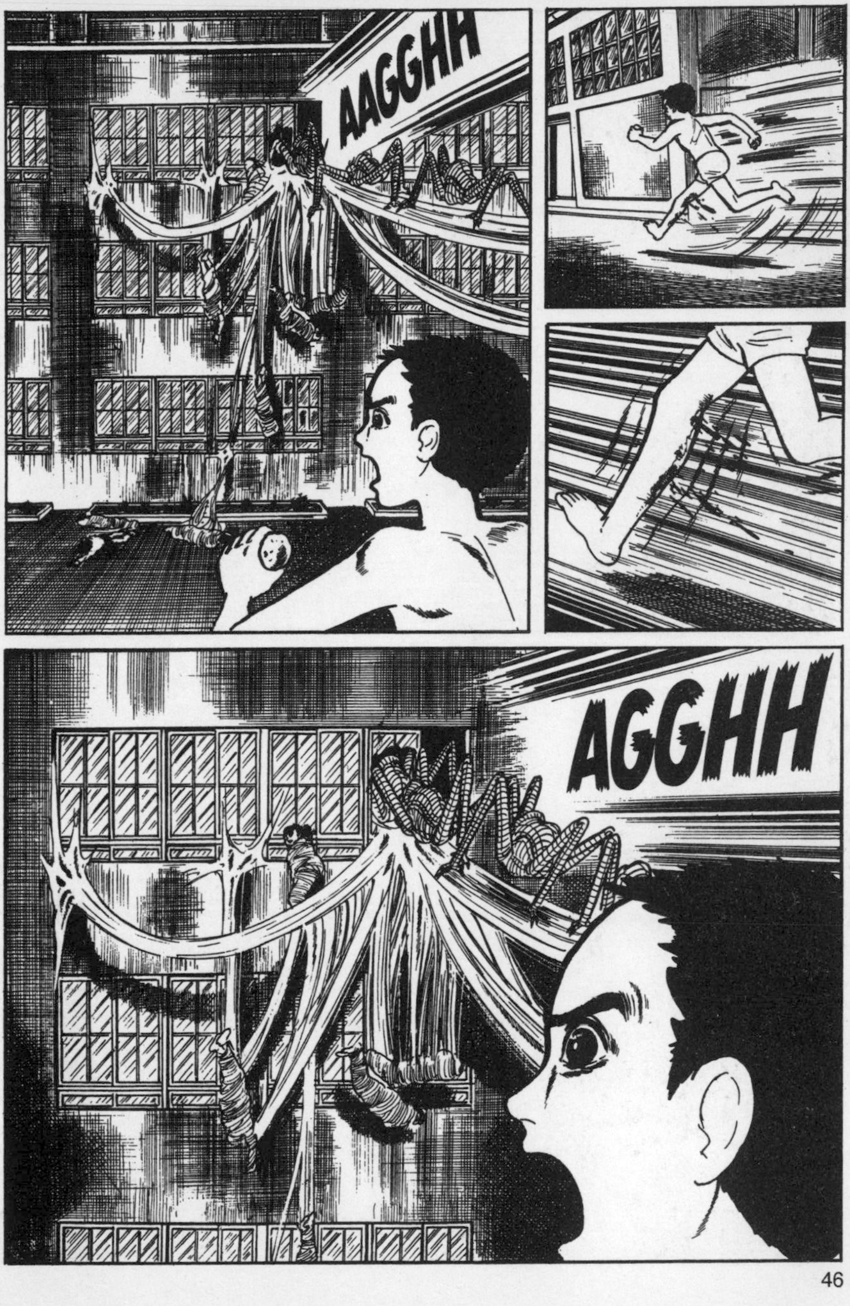
AAGGHH
AGGHH

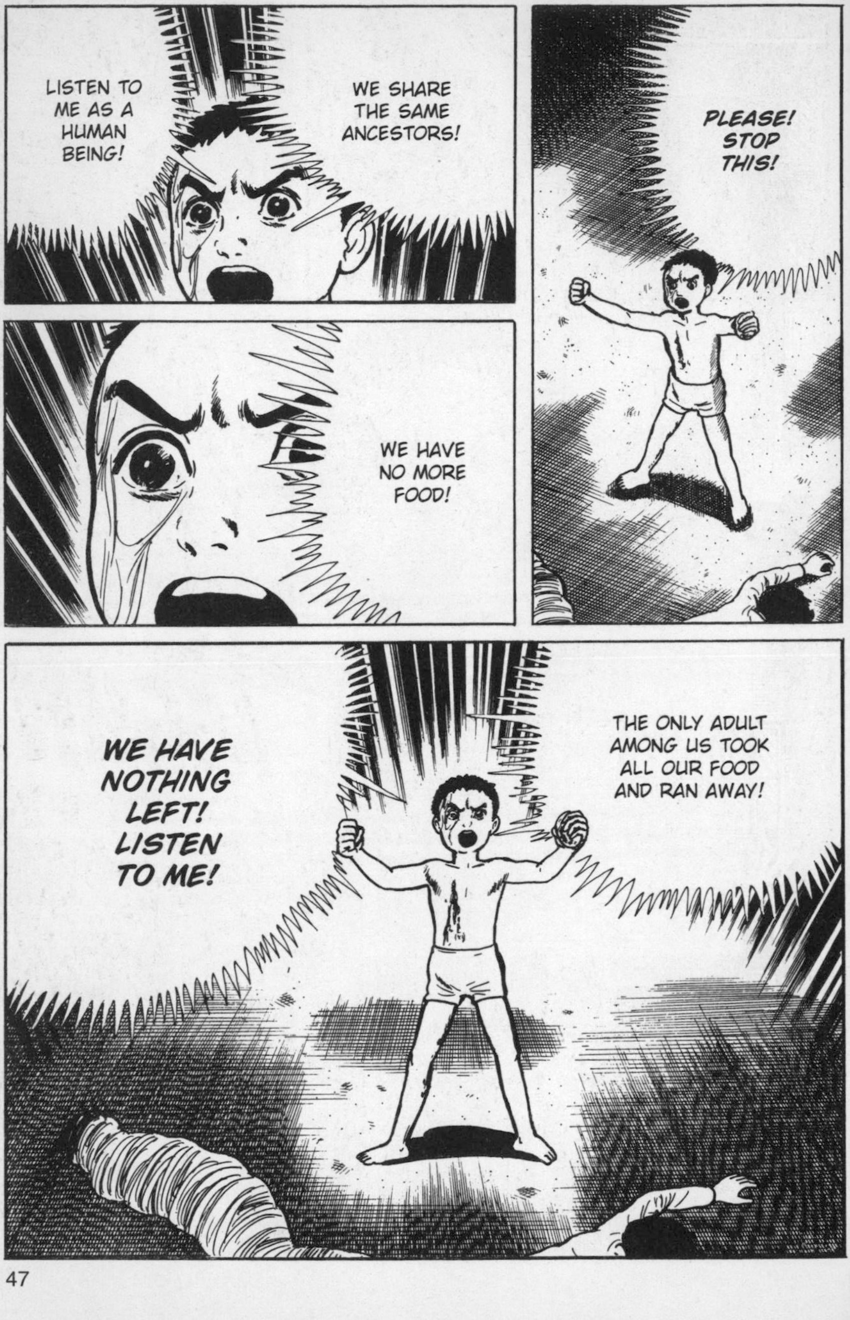
PLEASE! STOP THIS!
WE SHARE THE SAME ANCESTORS!
LISTEN TO ME AS A HUMAN BEING!
WE HAVE NO MORE FOOD!
THE ONLY ADULT AMONG US TOOK ALL OUR FOOD AND RAN AWAY!
WE HAVE NOTHING LEFT! LISTEN TO ME!

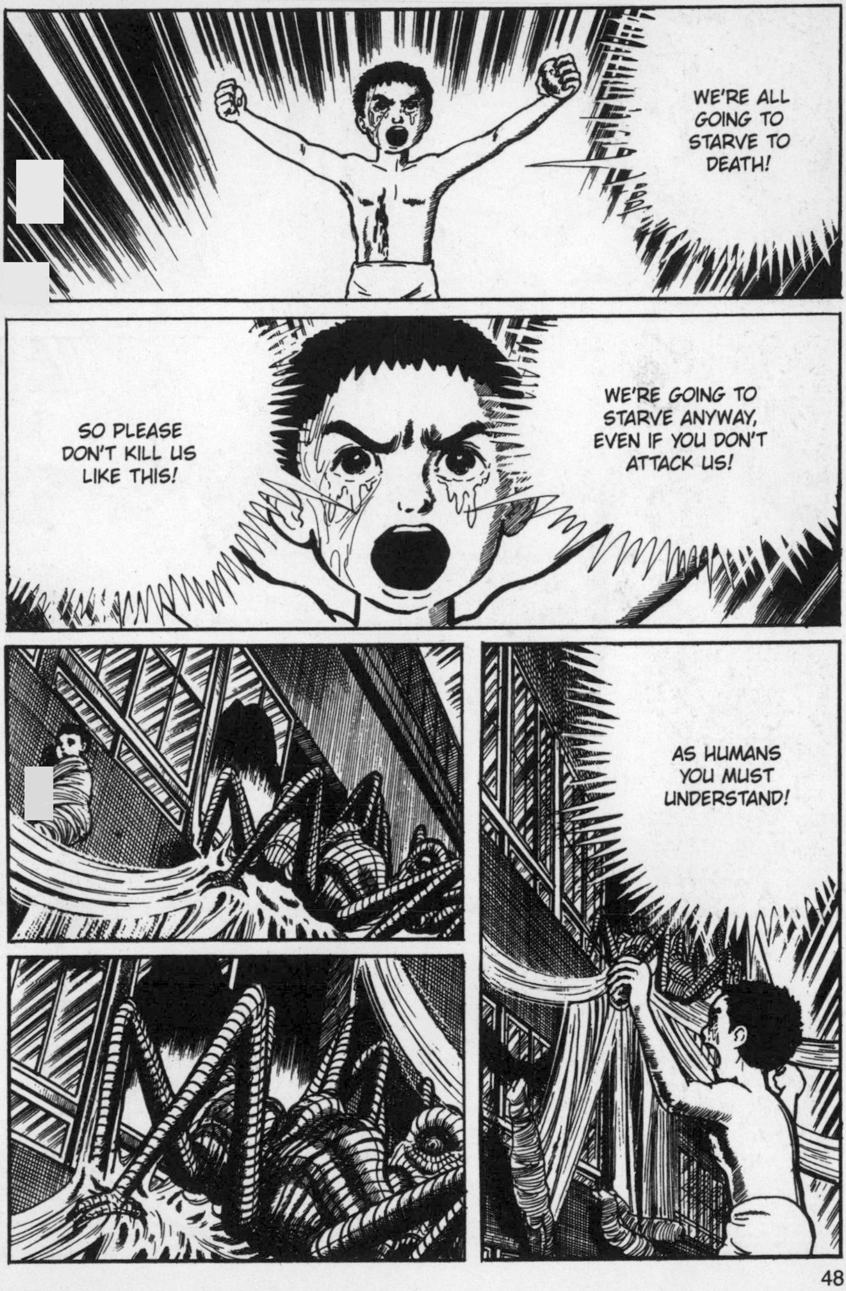
WE'RE ALL GOING TO STARVE TO DEATH!
WE'RE GOING TO STARVE ANYWAY, EVEN IF YOU DON'T ATTACK US!
SO PLEASE DON'T KILL US LIKE THIS!
AS HUMANS YOU MUST UNDERSTAND!

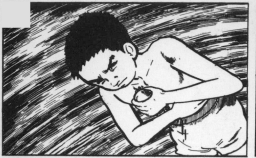

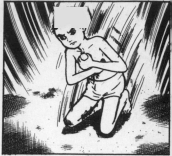

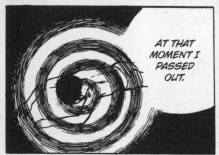

AT THAT MOMENT I PASSED OUT.

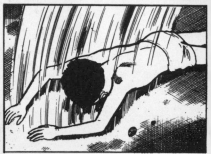

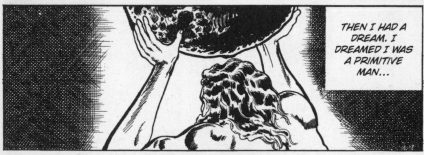

THEN I HAD A DREAM. I DREAMED I WAS A PRIMITIVE MAN...

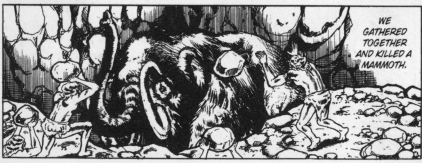

WE GATHERED TOGETHER AND KILLED A MAMMOTH.

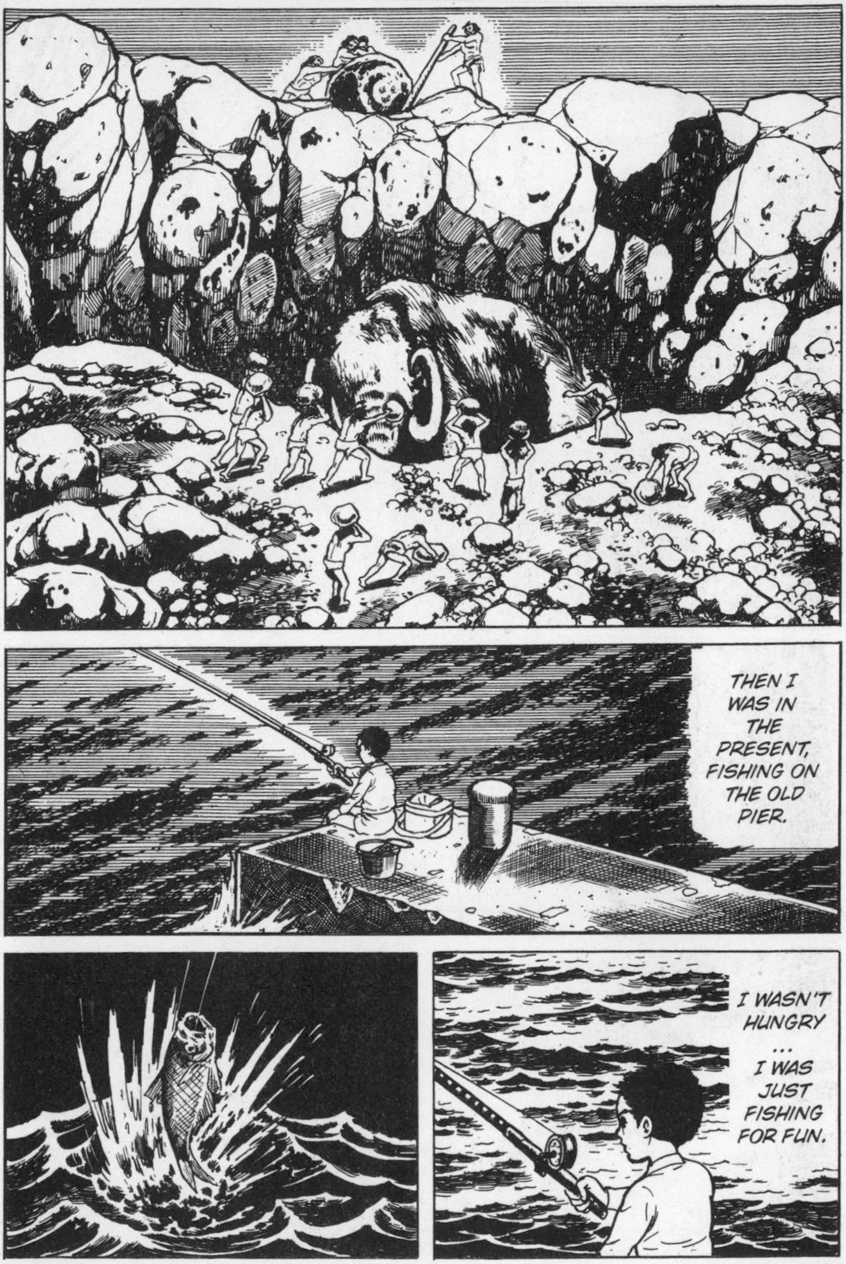
THEN I WAS IN THE PRESENT, FISHING ON THE OLD PIER.
I WASN'T HUNGRY ... I WAS JUST FISHING FOR FUN.

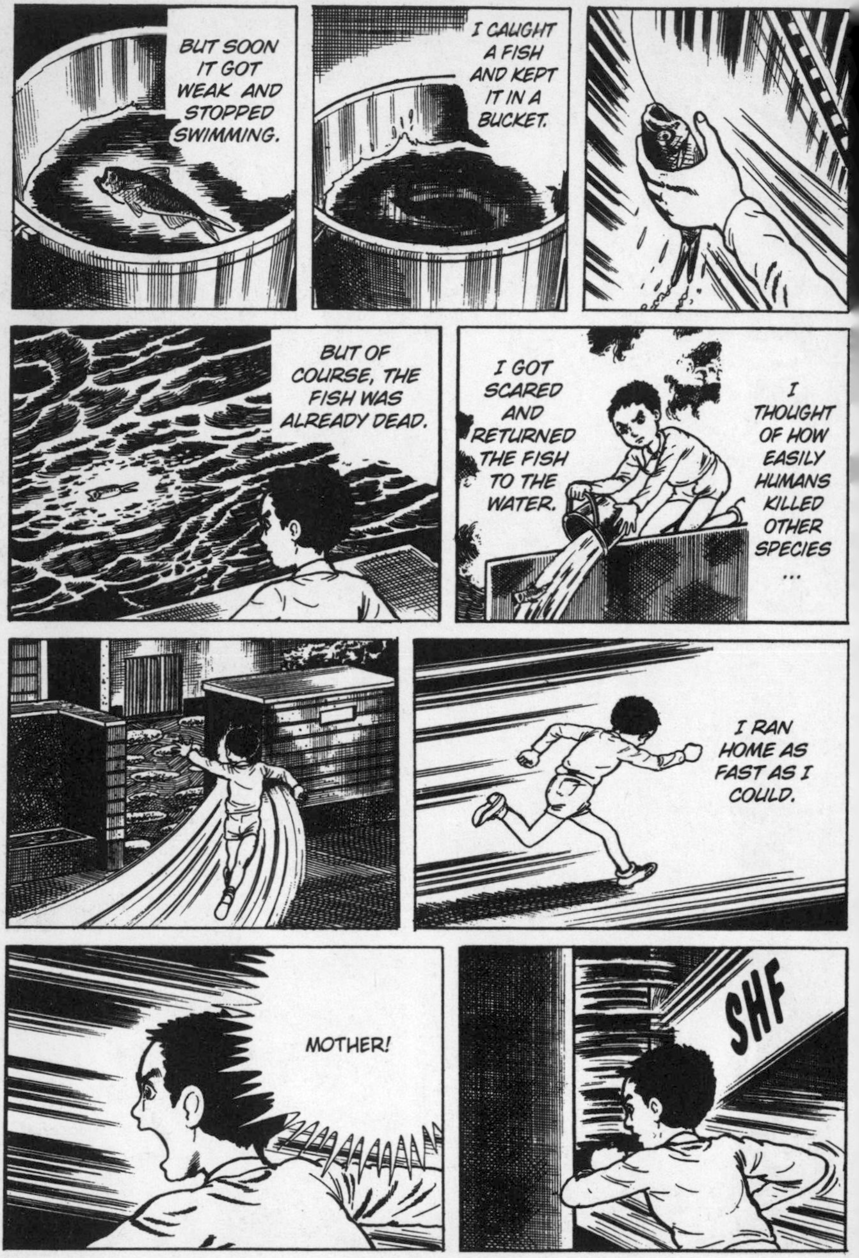
I CAUGHT A FISH AND KEPT IT IN A BUCKET.
BUT SOON IT GOT WEAK AND STOPPED SWIMMING.
I THOUGHT OF HOW EASILY HUMANS KILLED OTHER SPECIES ...
I GOT SCARED AND RETURNED THE FISH TO THE WATER.
BUT OF COURSE, THE FISH WAS ALREADY DEAD.
I RAN HOME AS FAST AS I COULD.
SHF
MOTHER!

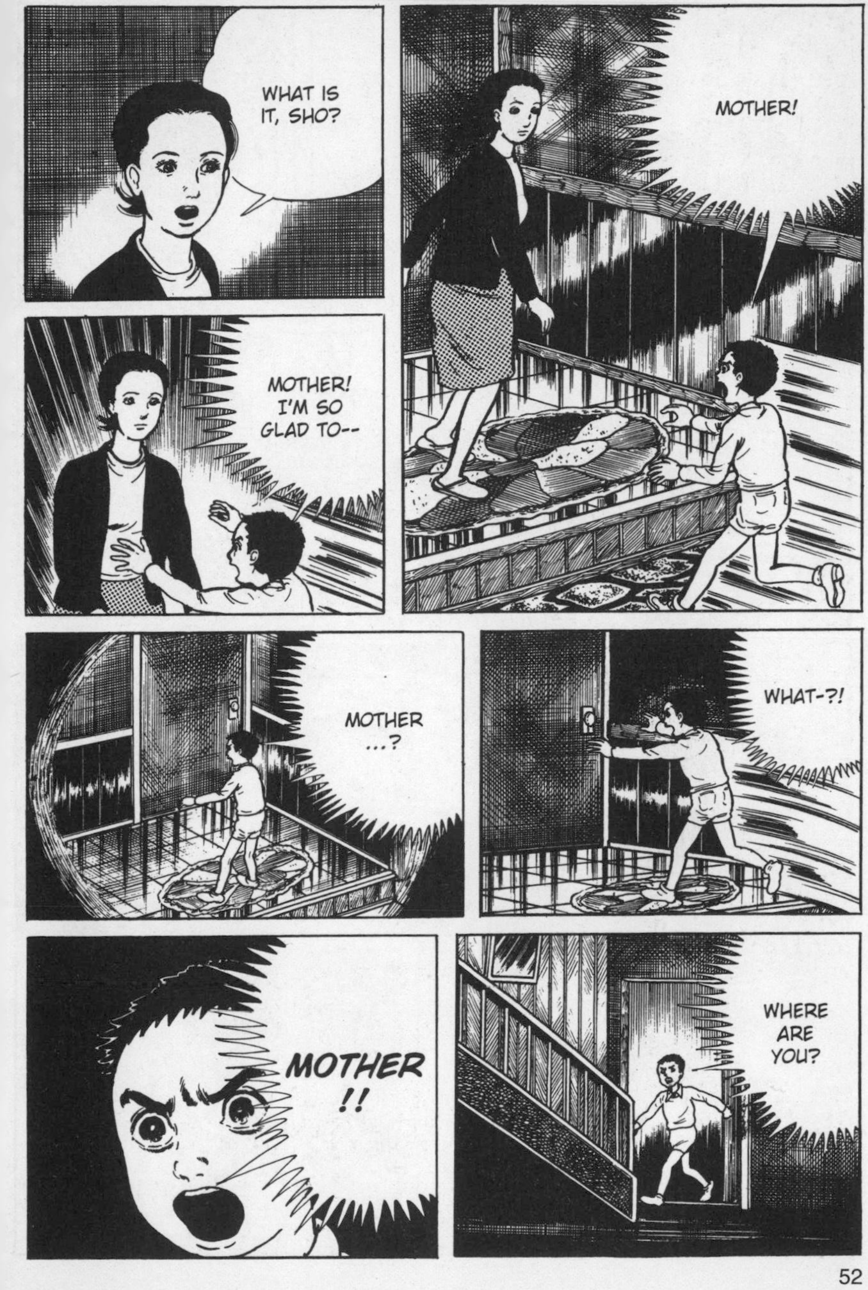
MOTHER!
WHAT IS IT, SHO?
MOTHER! I'M SO GLAD TO--
WHAT-?!
MOTHER ...?
WHERE ARE YOU?
MOTHER !!

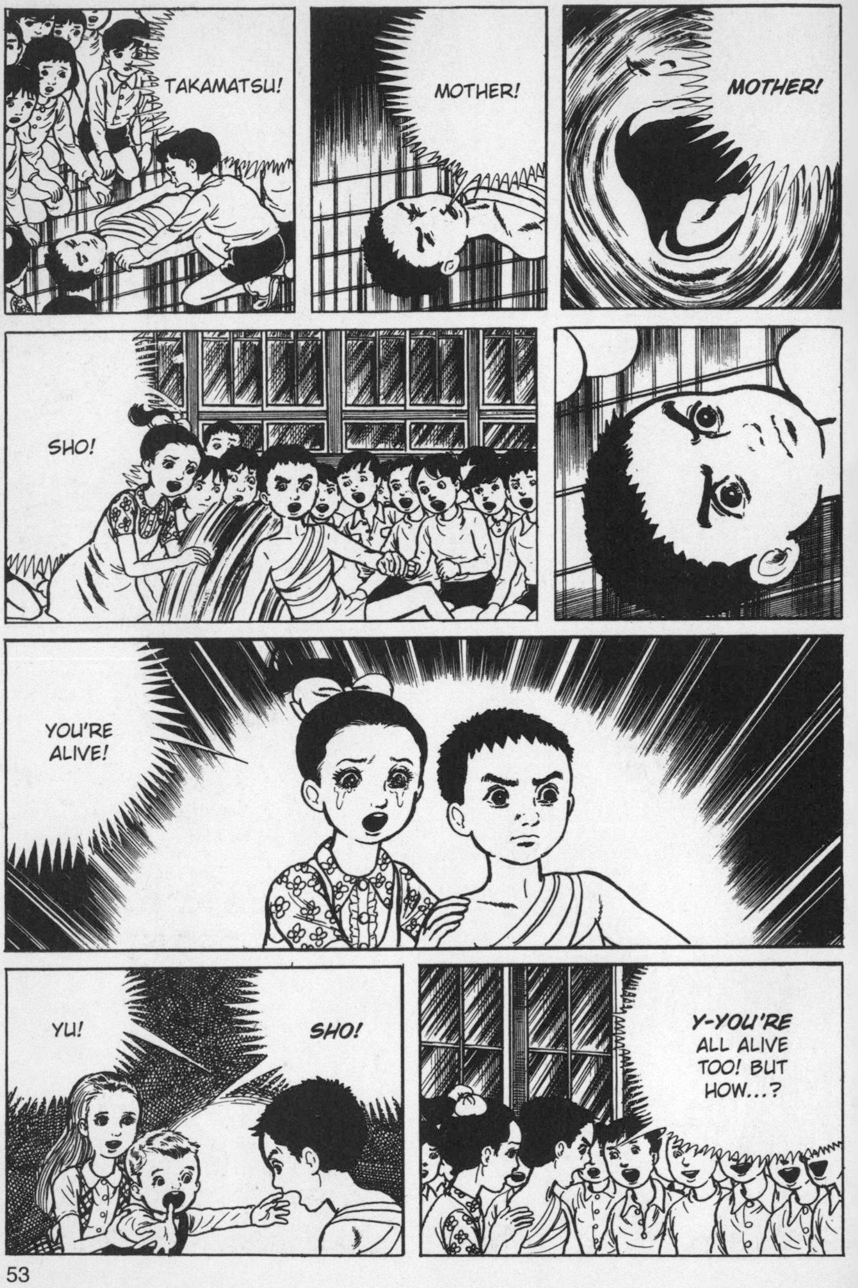
MOTHER!
MOTHER!
TAKAMATSU!
SHO!
YOU'RE ALIVE!
Y-YOU'RE ALL ALIVE TOO! BUT HOW...?
SHO!
YU!

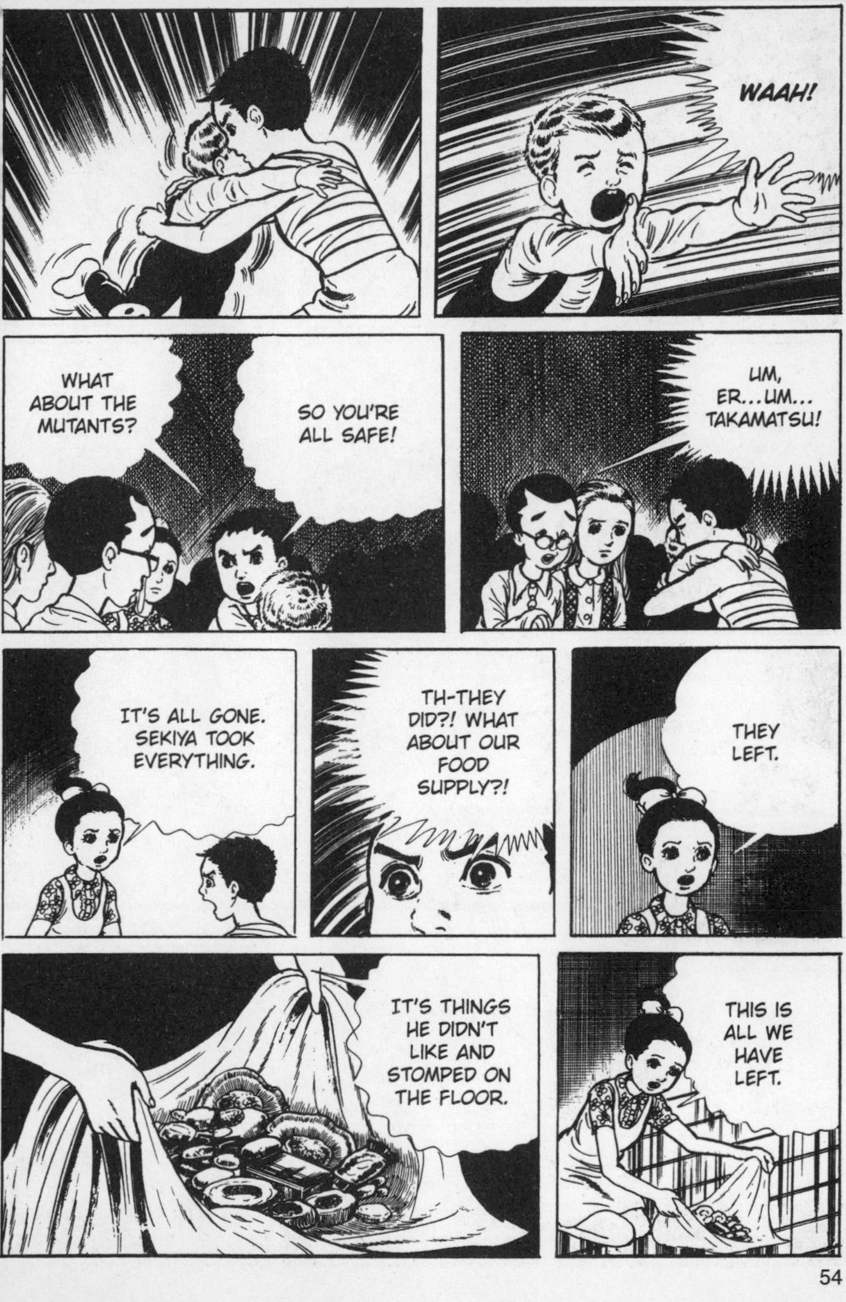
WAAH!
UM, ER...UM... TAKAMATSU!
SO YOU'RE ALL SAFE!
WHAT ABOUT THE MUTANTS?
THEY LEFT.
TH-THEY DID?! WHAT ABOUT OUR FOOD SUPPLY?!
IT'S ALL GONE. SEKIYA TOOK EVERYTHING.
THIS IS ALL WE HAVE LEFT.
IT'S THINGS HE DIDN'T LIKE AND STOMPED ON THE FLOOR.

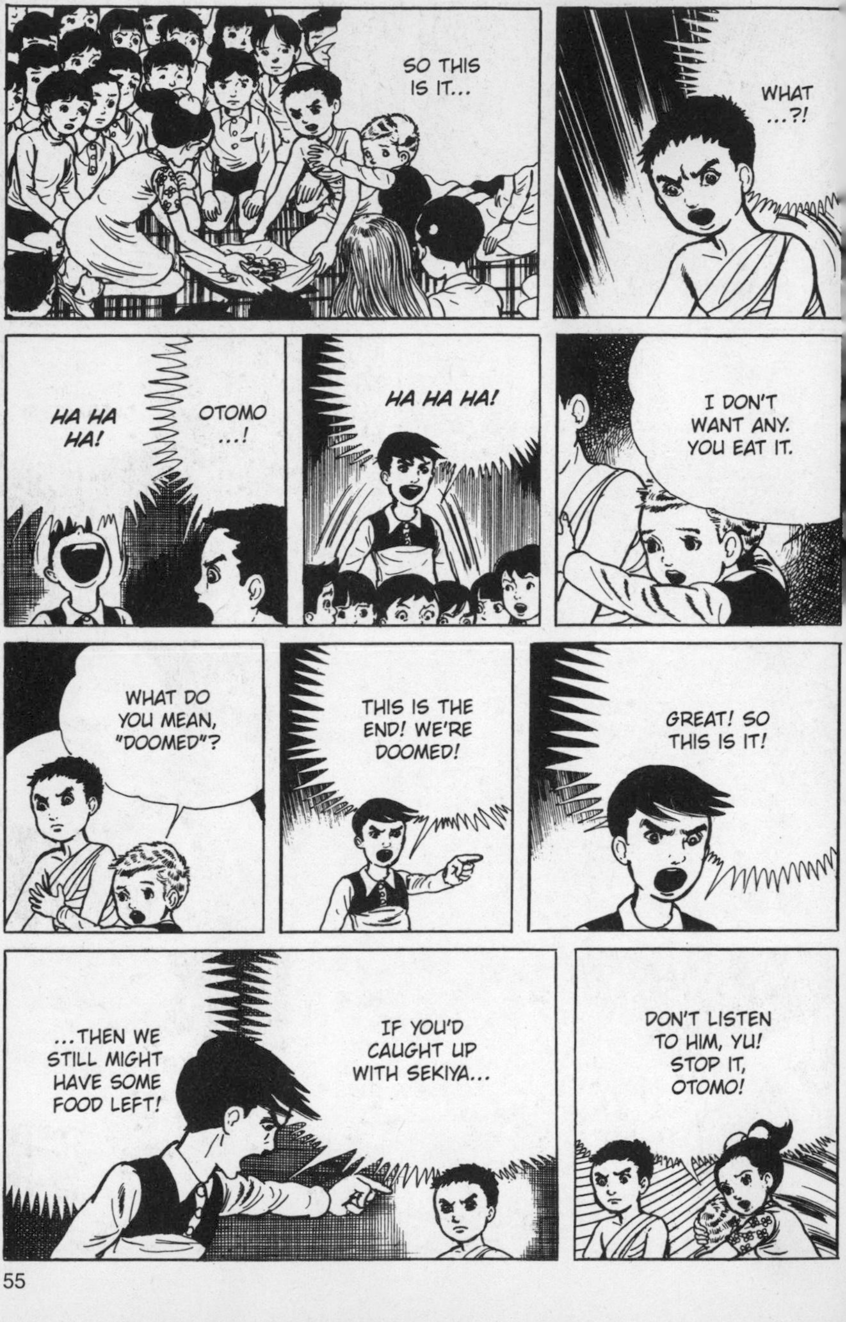
WHAT ...?!
SO THIS IS IT...
I DON'T WANT ANY. YOU EAT IT.
HA HA HA!
OTOMO ...!
HA HA HA!
GREAT! SO THIS IS IT!
THIS IS THE END! WE'RE DOOMED!
WHAT DO YOU MEAN, "DOOMED"?
DON'T LISTEN TO HIM, YU! STOP IT, OTOMO!
IF YOU'D CAUGHT UP WITH SEKIYA...
...THEN WE STILL MIGHT HAVE SOME FOOD LEFT!

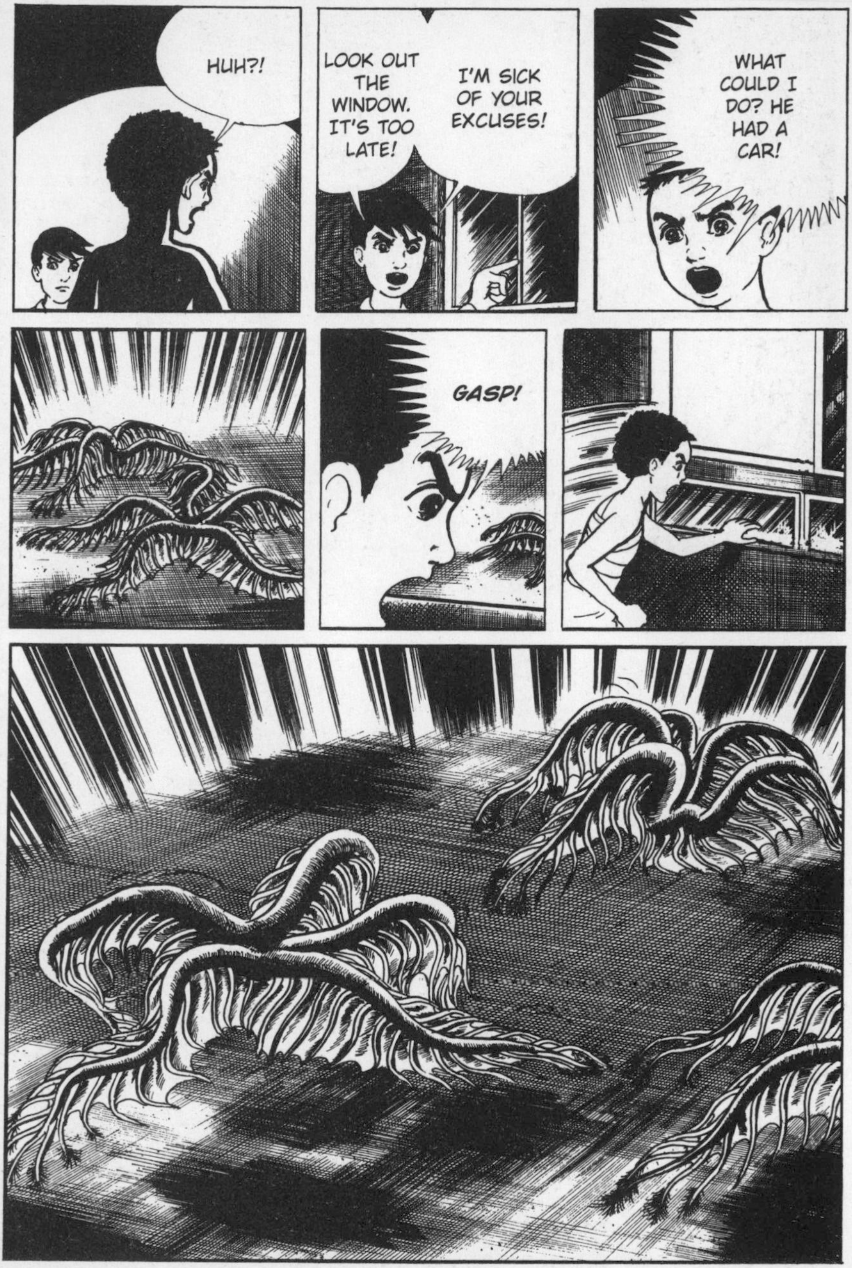
WHAT COULD I DO? HE HAD A CAR!
I'M SICK OF YOUR EXCUSES!
LOOK OUT THE WINDOW. IT'S TOO LATE!
HUH?!
GASP!

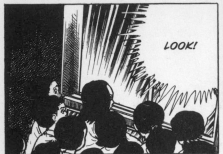

LOOK!

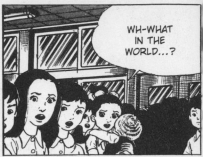

WH-WHAT
IN THE
WORLD...?

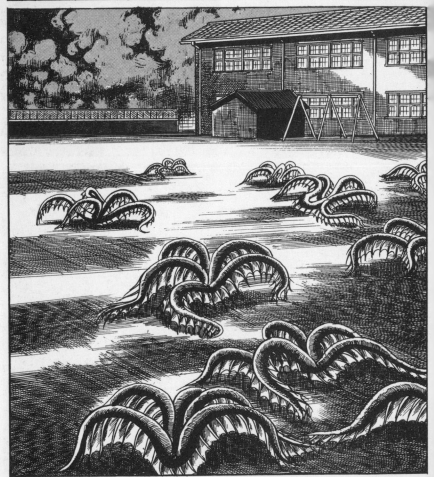

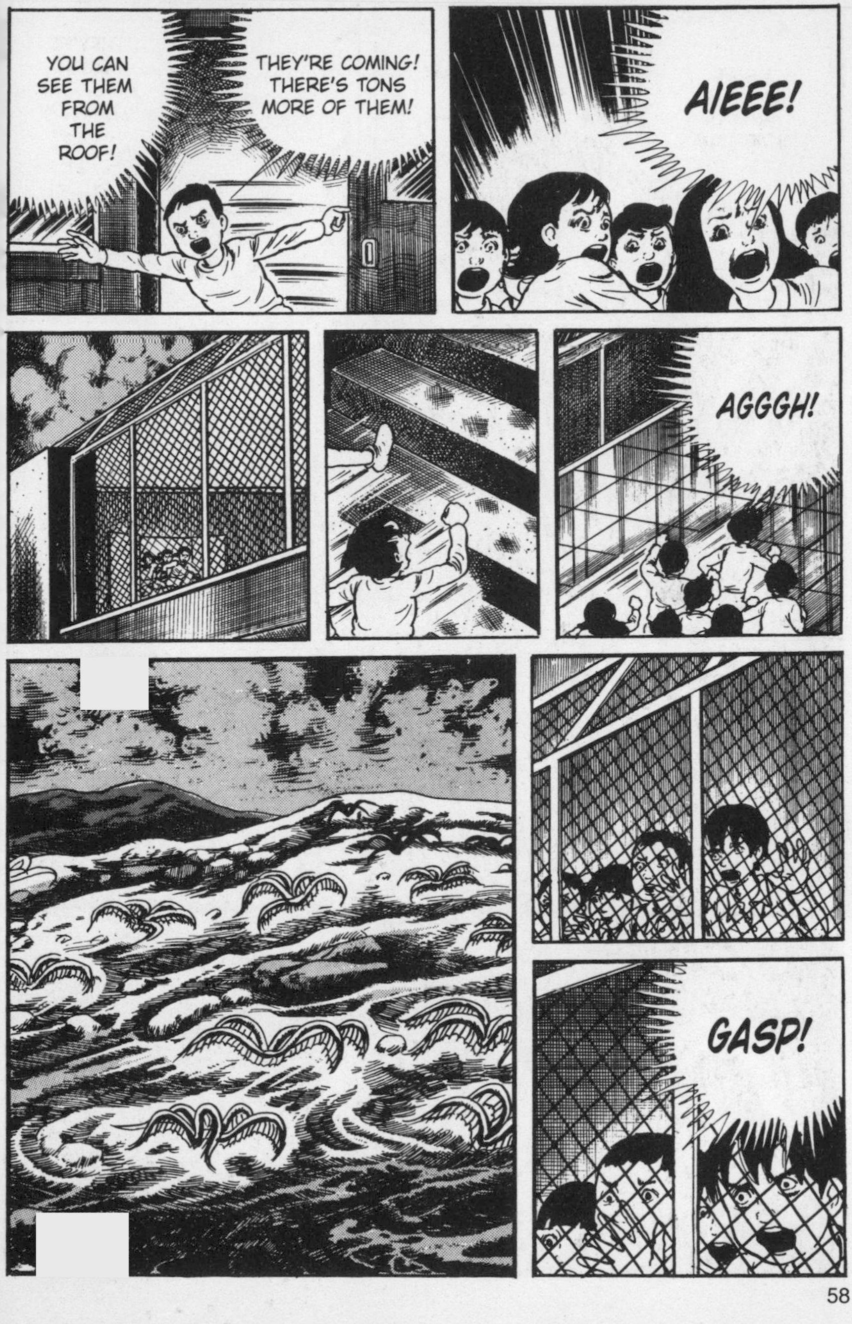
AIEEE!
THEY'RE COMING! THERE'S TONS MORE OF THEM!
YOU CAN SEE THEM FROM THE ROOF!
AGGGH!
GASP!

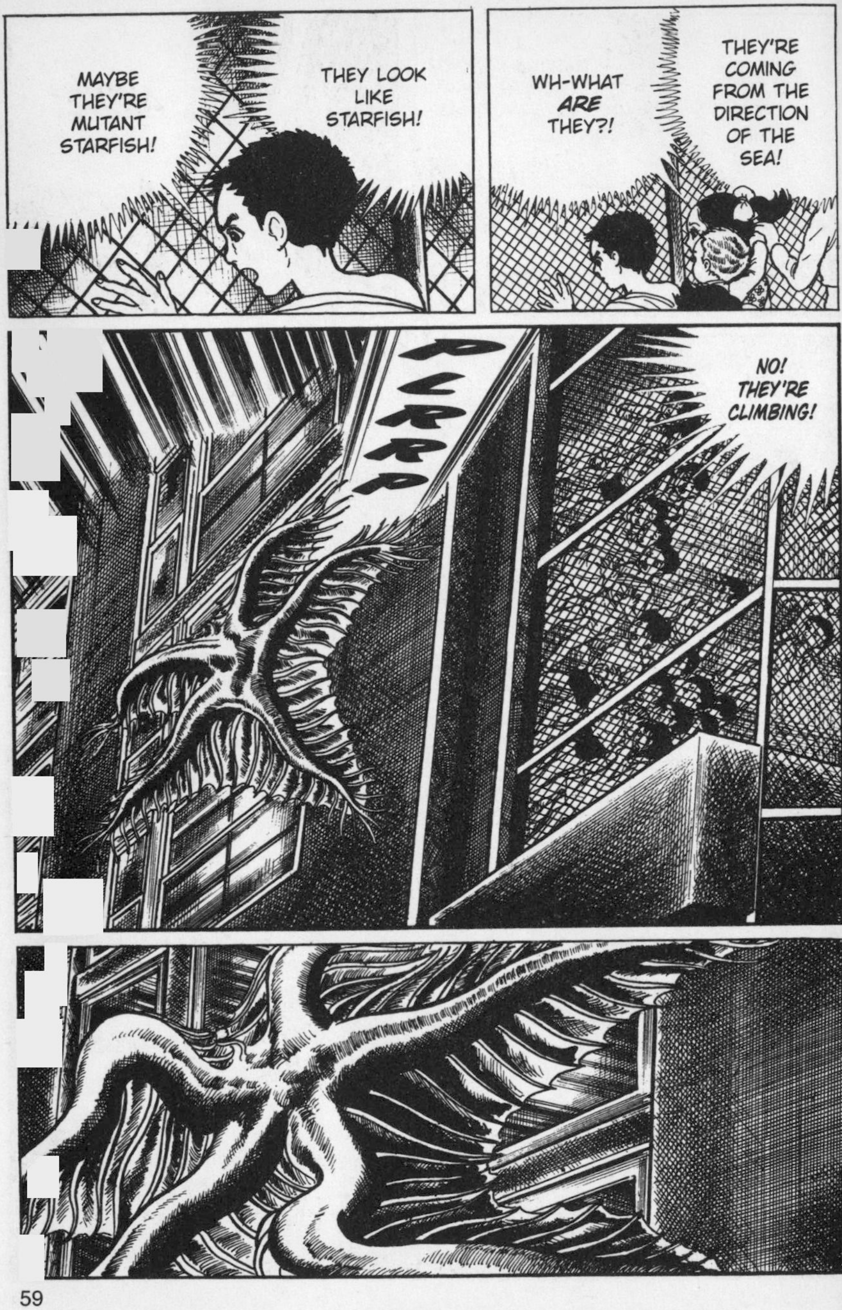
THEY'RE COMING FROM THE DIRECTION OF THE SEA!
WH-WHAT *ARE* THEY?!
THEY LOOK LIKE STARFISH!
MAYBE THEY'RE MUTANT STARFISH!
NO! THEY'RE CLIMBING!
PLRRP

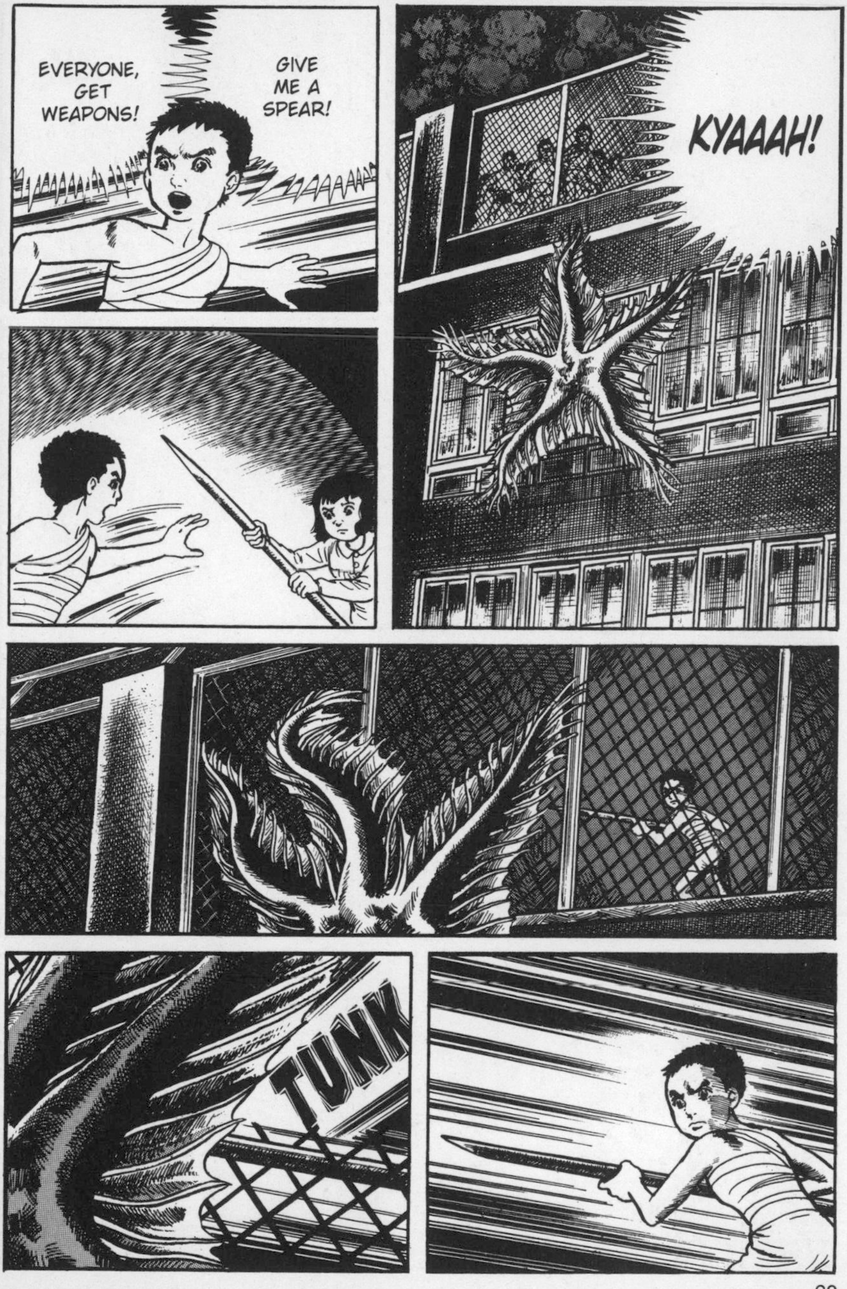
KYAAAH!
GIVE ME A SPEAR!
EVERYONE, GET WEAPONS!
TUNK

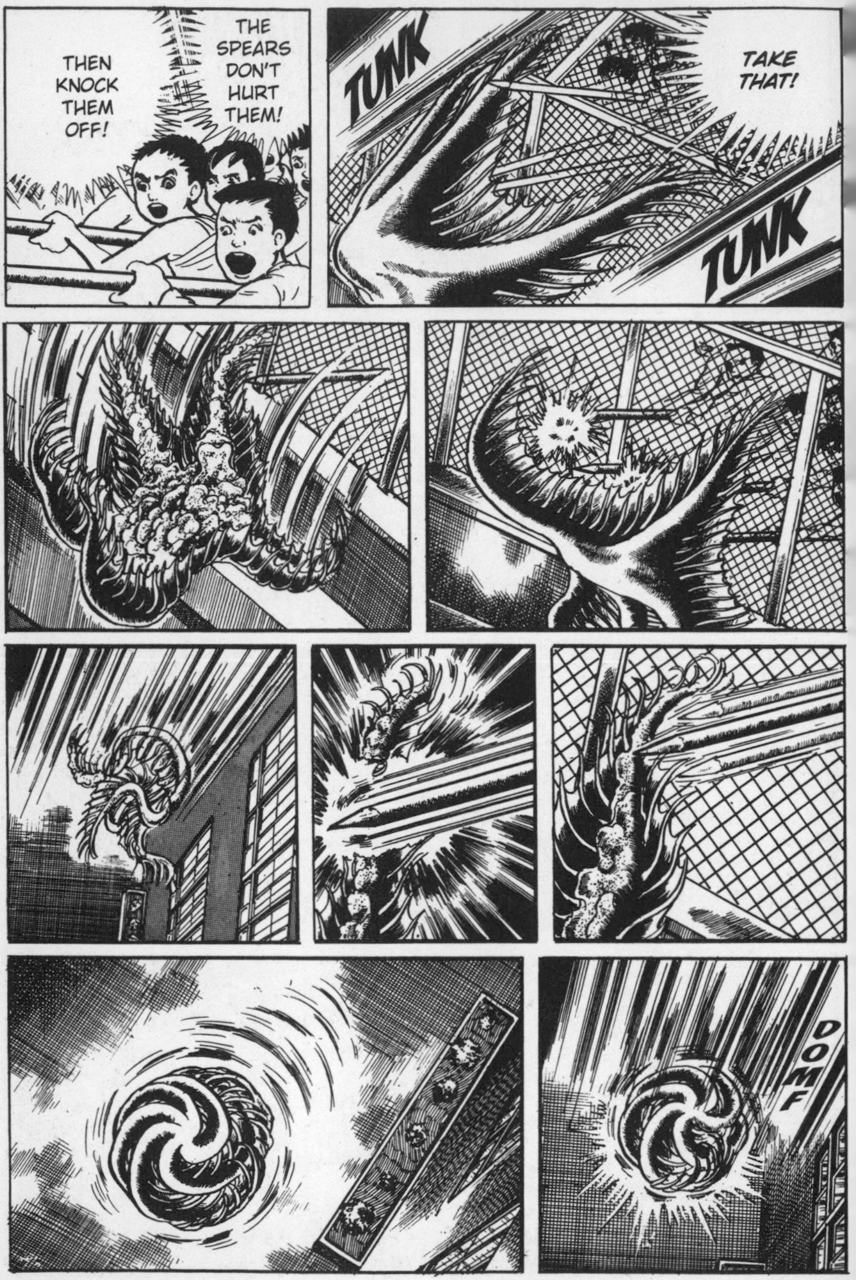
TAKE THAT!
TUNK
TUNK
THE SPEARS DON'T HURT THEM!
THEN KNOCK THEM OFF!
DOOMF

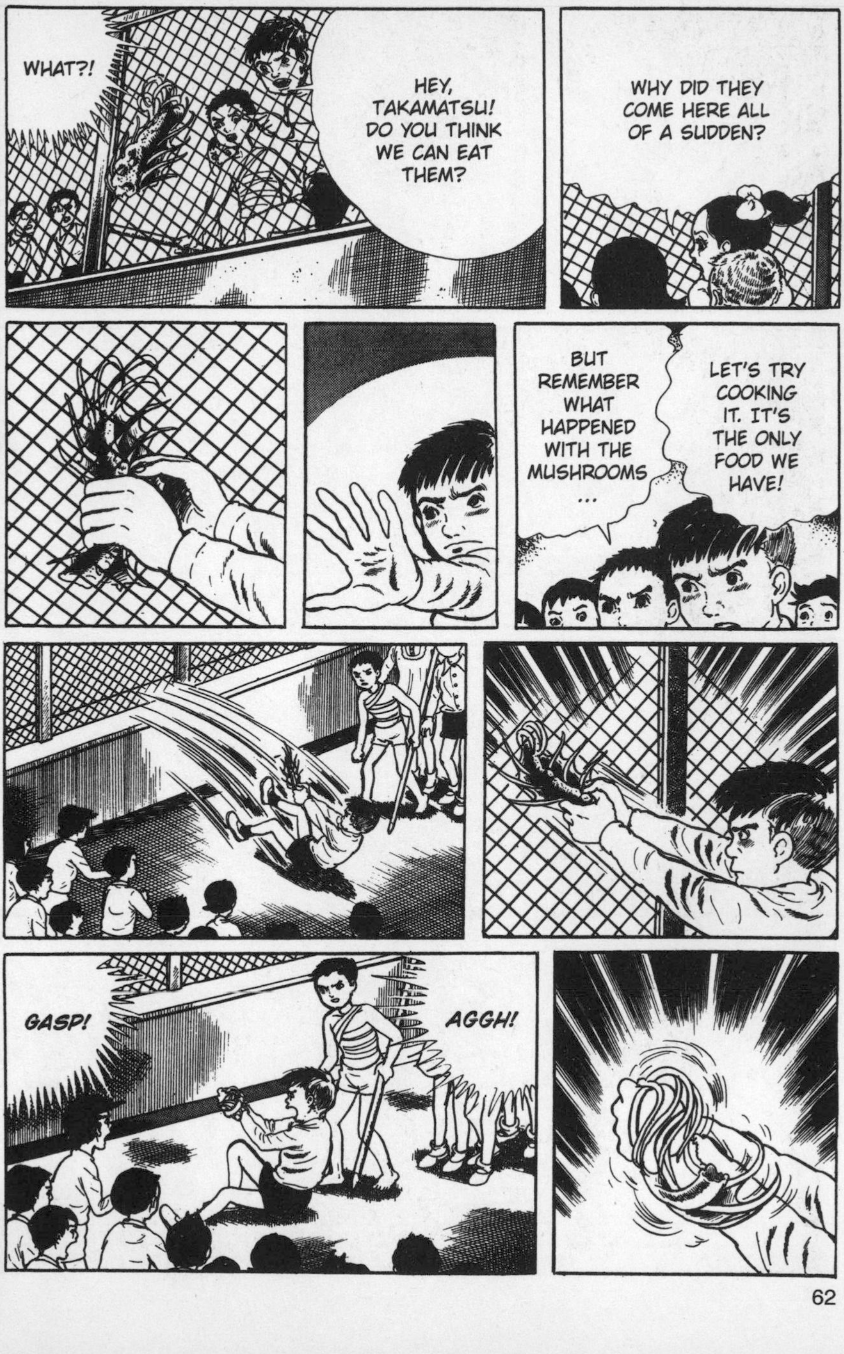
WHY DID THEY COME HERE ALL OF A SUDDEN?
HEY, TAKAMATSU! DO YOU THINK WE CAN EAT THEM?
WHAT?!
LET'S TRY COOKING IT. IT'S THE ONLY FOOD WE HAVE!
BUT REMEMBER WHAT HAPPENED WITH THE MUSHROOMS ...
AGGH!
GASP!

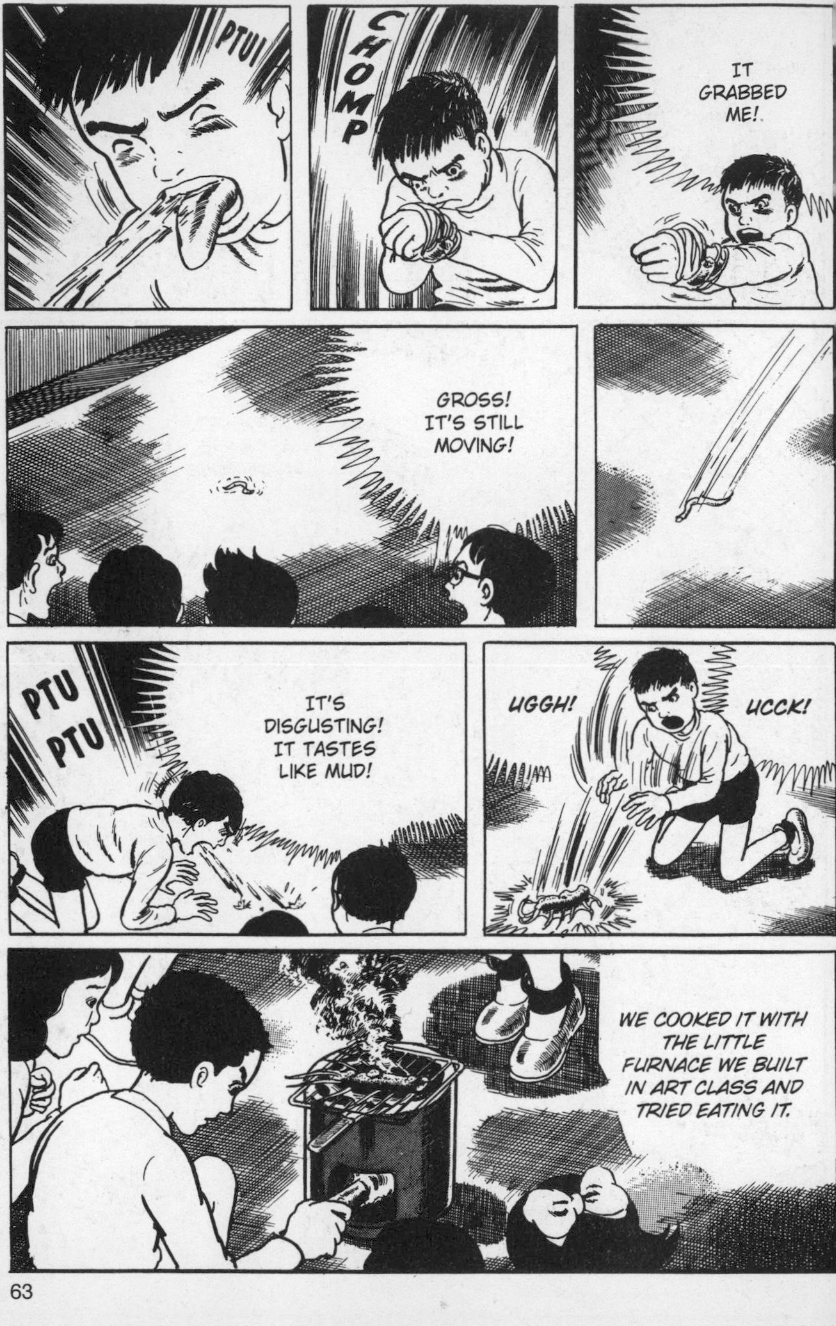
IT GRABBED ME!
CHOMP
PTUI
GROSS! IT'S STILL MOVING!
UCCK!
UGGH!
IT'S DISGUSTING! IT TASTES LIKE MUD!
PTU PTU
WE COOKED IT WITH THE LITTLE FURNACE WE BUILT IN ART CLASS AND TRIED EATING IT.

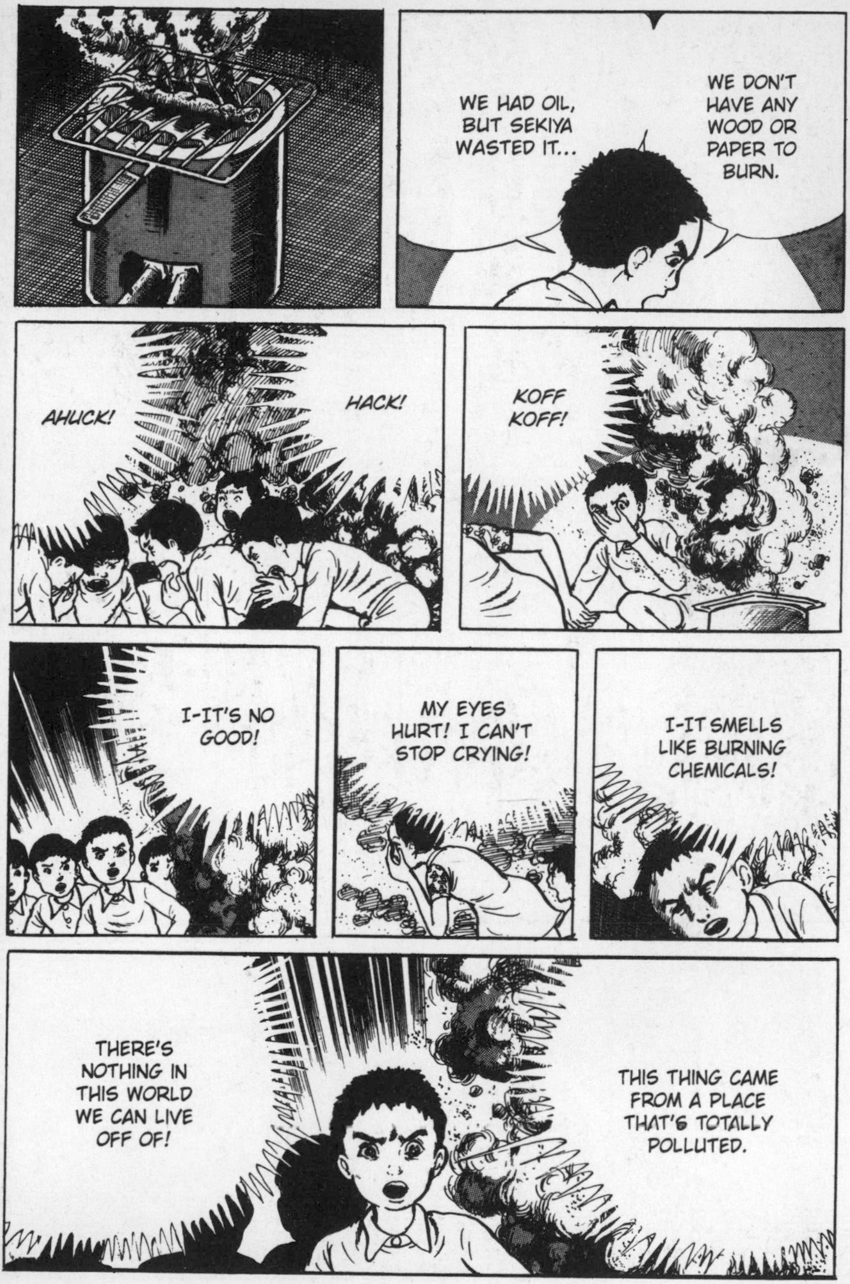
WE DON'T HAVE ANY WOOD OR PAPER TO BURN.
WE HAD OIL, BUT SEKIYA WASTED IT...
KOFF KOFF!
HACK!
AHUCK!
I-IT SMELLS LIKE BURNING CHEMICALS!
MY EYES HURT! I CAN'T STOP CRYING!
I-IT'S NO GOOD!
THIS THING CAME FROM A PLACE THAT'S TOTALLY POLLUTED.
THERE'S NOTHING IN THIS WORLD WE CAN LIVE OFF OF!

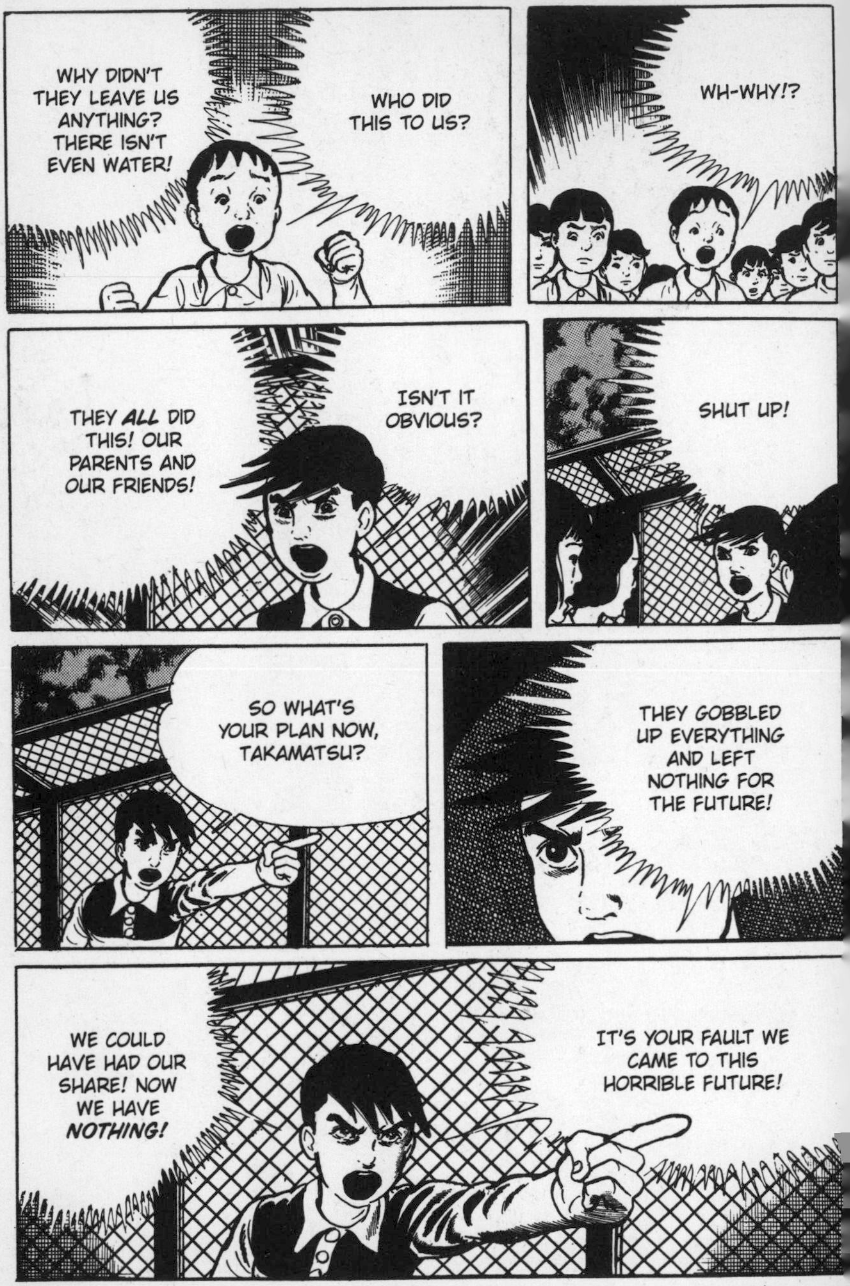
WH-WHY!?
WHO DID THIS TO US?
WHY DIDN'T THEY LEAVE US ANYTHING? THERE ISN'T EVEN WATER!
SHUT UP!
ISN'T IT OBVIOUS?
THEY *ALL* DID THIS! OUR PARENTS AND OUR FRIENDS!
THEY GOBBLED UP EVERYTHING AND LEFT NOTHING FOR THE FUTURE!
SO WHAT'S YOUR PLAN NOW, TAKAMATSU?
IT'S YOUR FAULT WE CAME TO THIS HORRIBLE FUTURE!
WE COULD HAVE HAD OUR SHARE! NOW WE HAVE *NOTHING!*

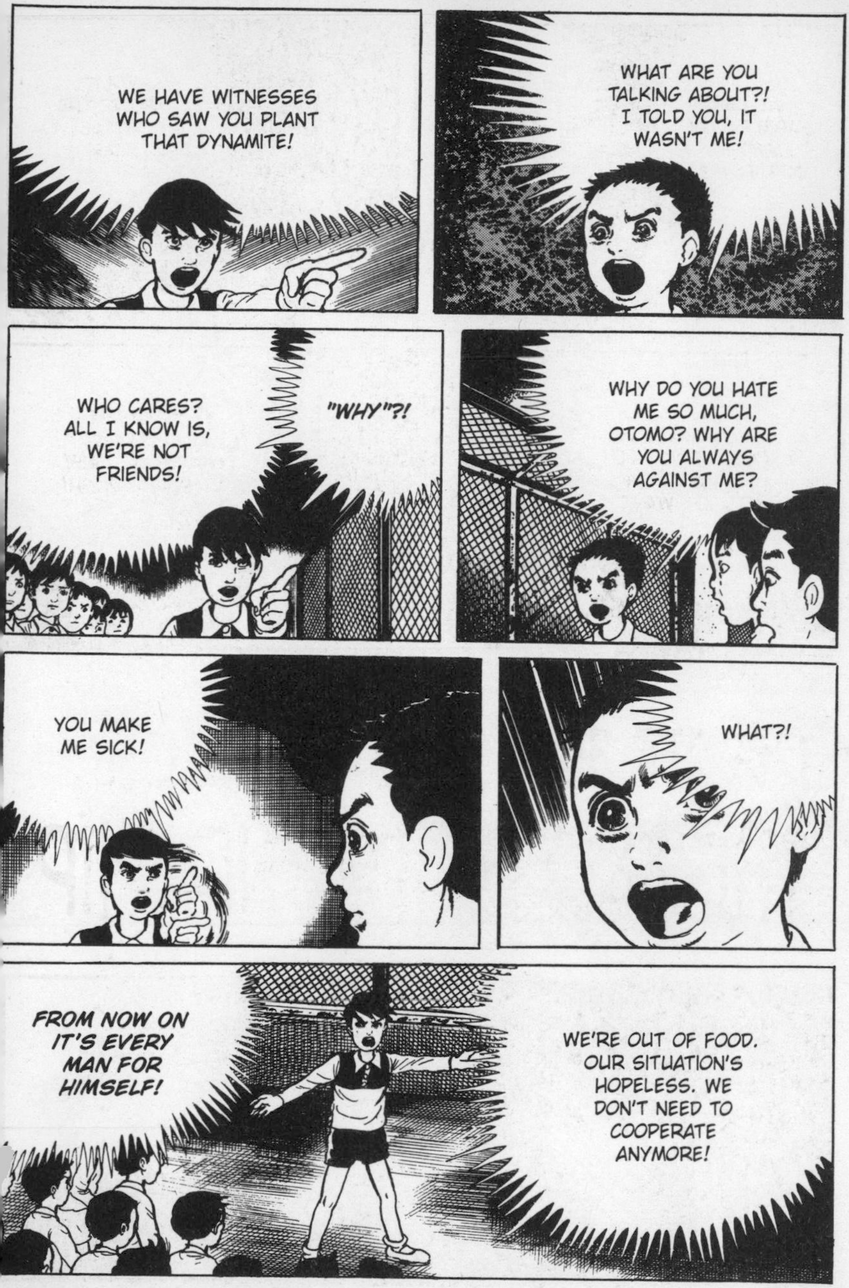
WHAT ARE YOU TALKING ABOUT?! I TOLD YOU, IT WASN'T ME!
WE HAVE WITNESSES WHO SAW YOU PLANT THAT DYNAMITE!
WHY DO YOU HATE ME SO MUCH, OTOMO? WHY ARE YOU ALWAYS AGAINST ME?
"WHY"?!
WHO CARES? ALL I KNOW IS, WE'RE NOT FRIENDS!
WHAT?!
YOU MAKE ME SICK!
WE'RE OUT OF FOOD. OUR SITUATION'S HOPELESS. WE DON'T NEED TO COOPERATE ANYMORE!
FROM NOW ON IT'S EVERY MAN FOR HIMSELF!

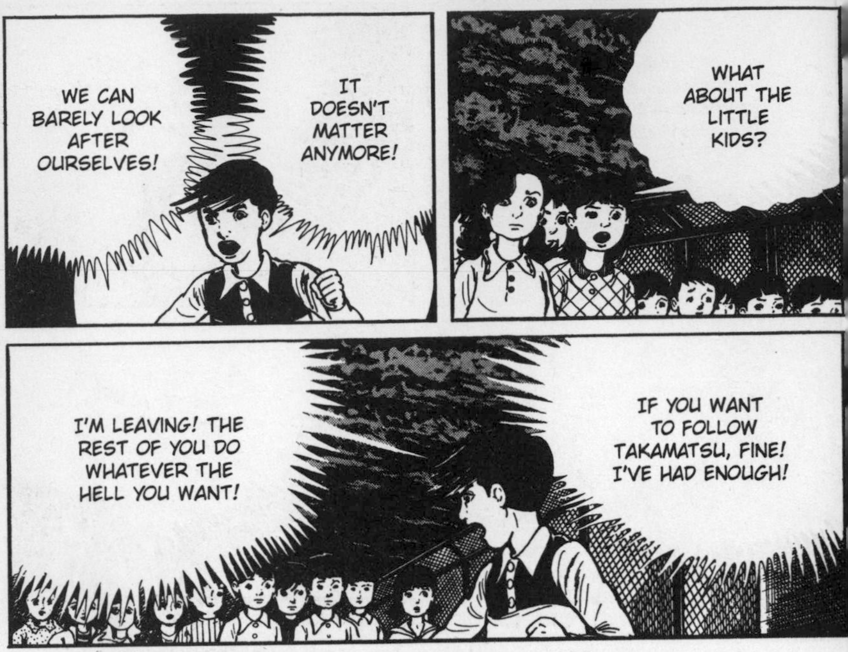
WHAT ABOUT THE LITTLE KIDS?
IT DOESN'T MATTER ANYMORE!
WE CAN BARELY LOOK AFTER OURSELVES!
IF YOU WANT TO FOLLOW TAKAMATSU, FINE! I'VE HAD ENOUGH!
I'M LEAVING! THE REST OF YOU DO WHATEVER THE HELL YOU WANT!

CHAPTER 35:

THE END OF FRIENDSHIP

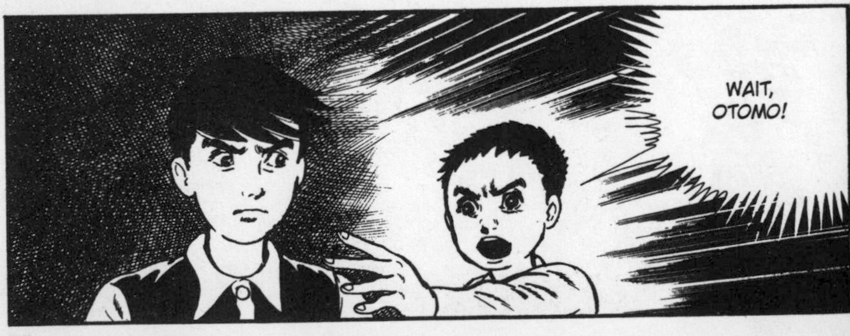
WAIT, OTOMO!

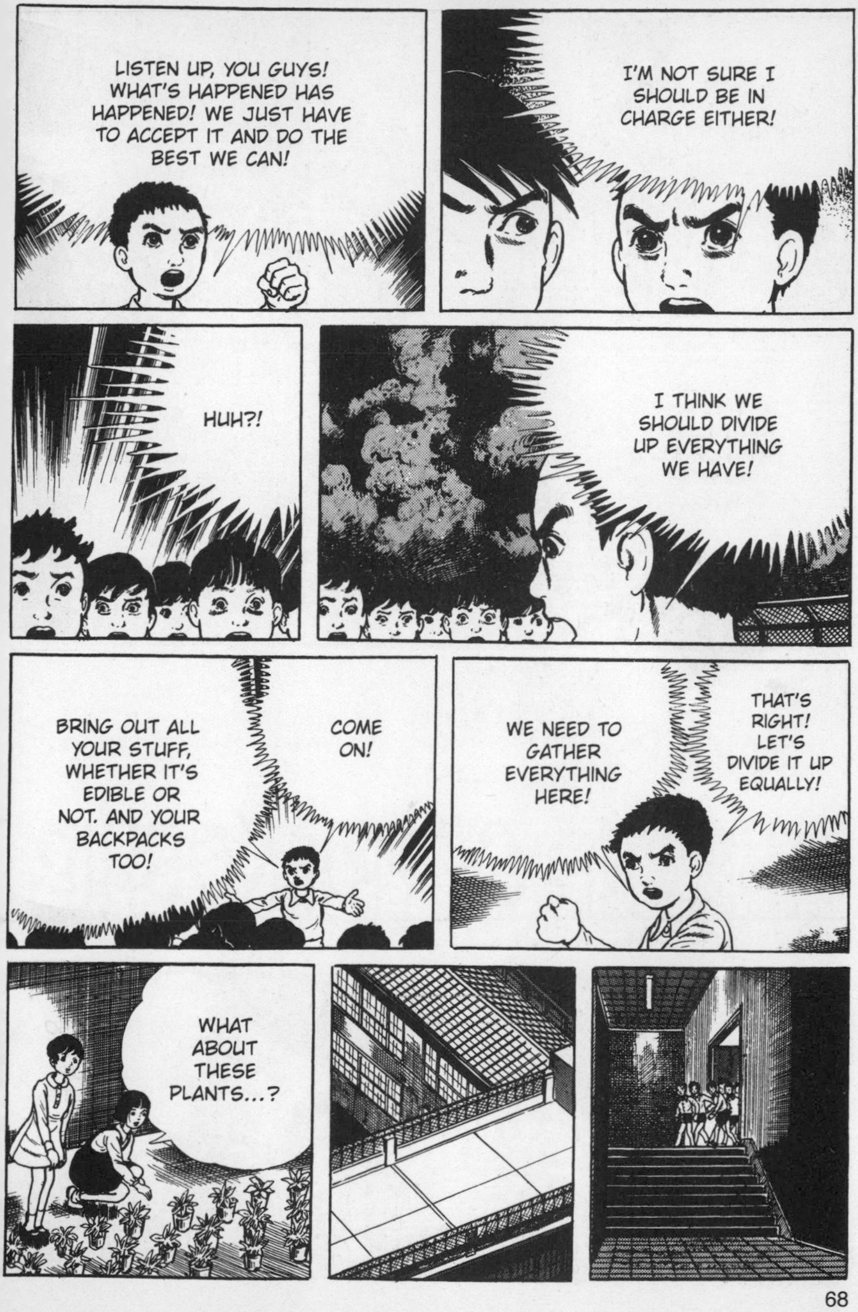
I'M NOT SURE I SHOULD BE IN CHARGE EITHER!
LISTEN UP, YOU GUYS! WHAT'S HAPPENED HAS HAPPENED! WE JUST HAVE TO ACCEPT IT AND DO THE BEST WE CAN!
I THINK WE SHOULD DIVIDE UP EVERYTHING WE HAVE!
HUH?!
THAT'S RIGHT! LET'S DIVIDE IT UP EQUALLY!
WE NEED TO GATHER EVERYTHING HERE!
COME ON!
BRING OUT ALL YOUR STUFF, WHETHER IT'S EDIBLE OR NOT. AND YOUR BACKPACKS TOO!
WHAT ABOUT THESE PLANTS...?

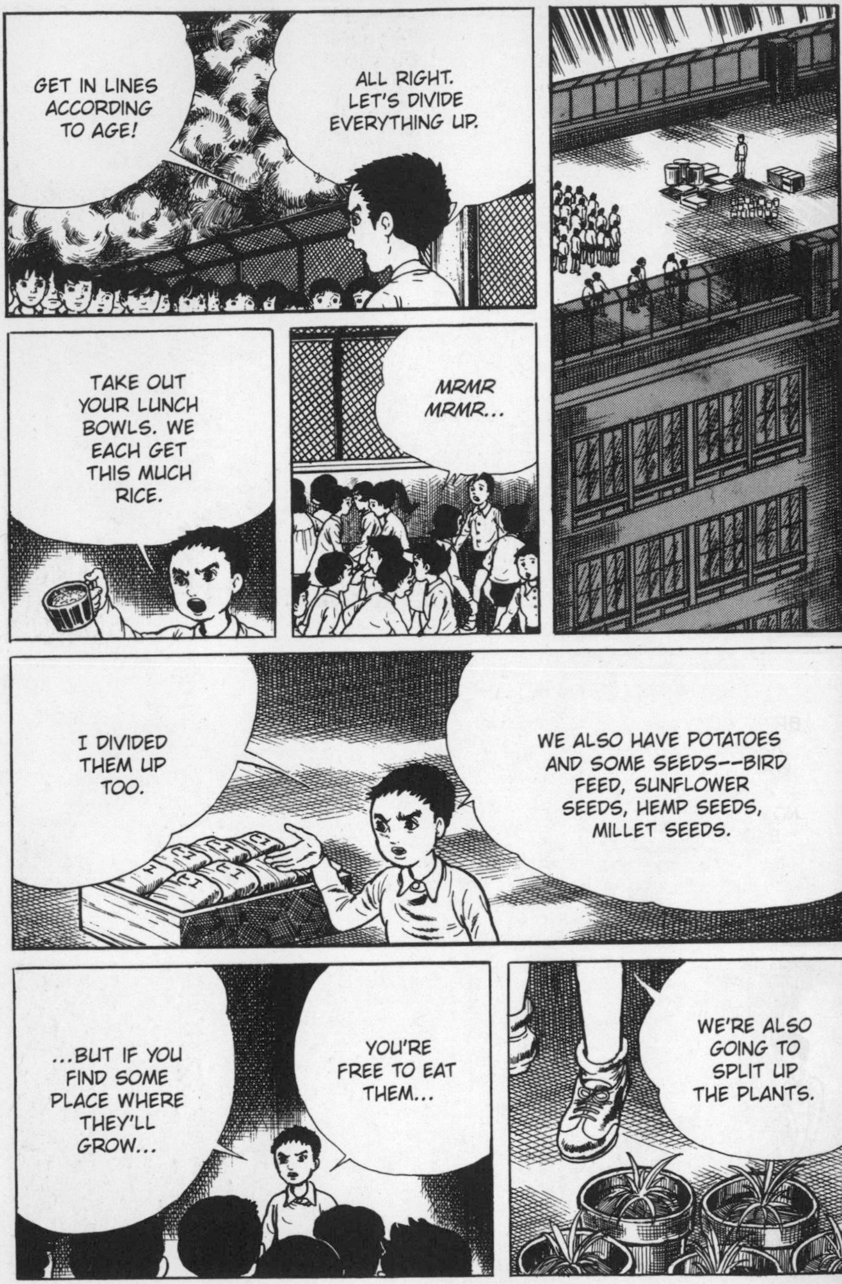
ALL RIGHT. LET'S DIVIDE EVERYTHING UP.
GET IN LINES ACCORDING TO AGE!
MRMR MRMR...
TAKE OUT YOUR LUNCH BOWLS. WE EACH GET THIS MUCH RICE.
WE ALSO HAVE POTATOES AND SOME SEEDS--BIRD FEED, SUNFLOWER SEEDS, HEMP SEEDS, MILLET SEEDS.
I DIVIDED THEM UP TOO.
WE'RE ALSO GOING TO SPLIT UP THE PLANTS.
YOU'RE FREE TO EAT THEM...
...BUT IF YOU FIND SOME PLACE WHERE THEY'LL GROW...

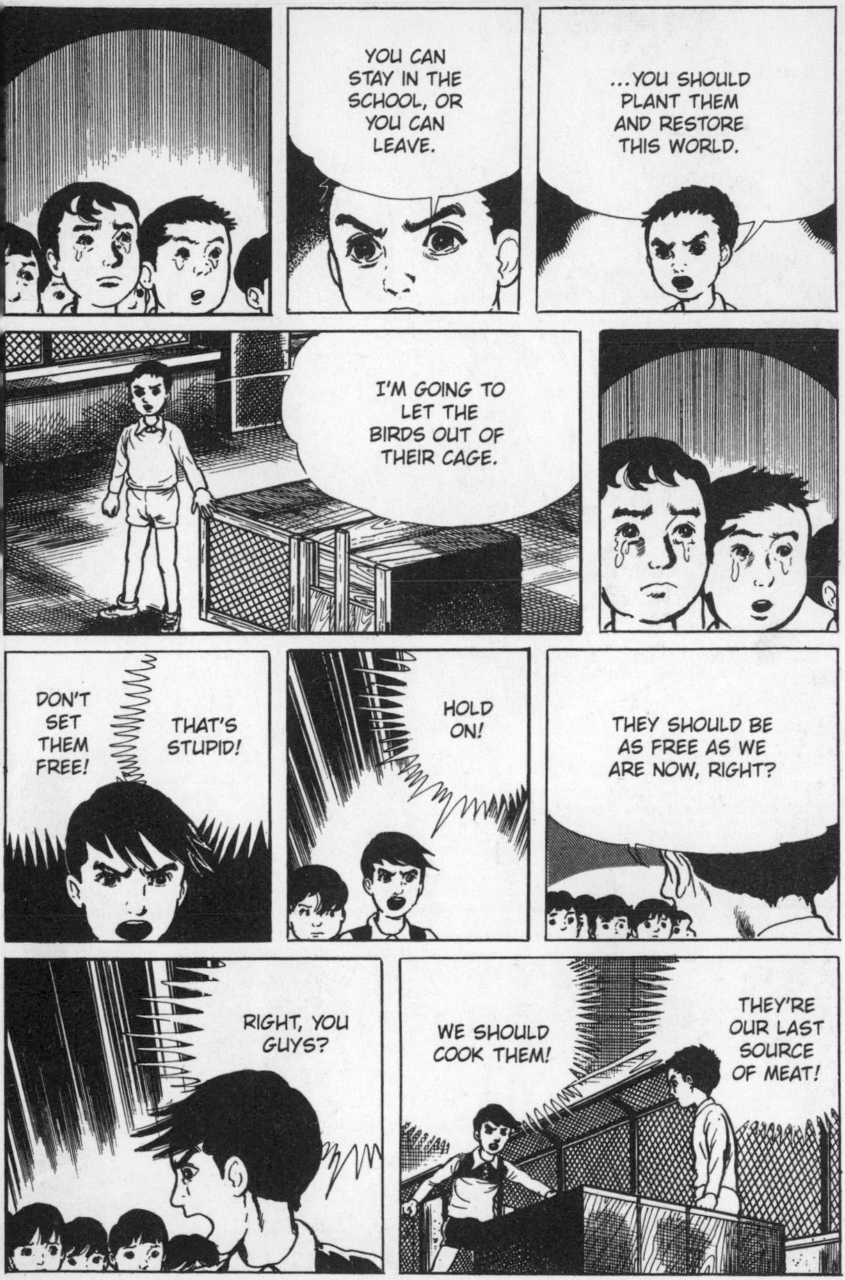
...YOU SHOULD PLANT THEM AND RESTORE THIS WORLD.
YOU CAN STAY IN THE SCHOOL, OR YOU CAN LEAVE.
I'M GOING TO LET THE BIRDS OUT OF THEIR CAGE.
THEY SHOULD BE AS FREE AS WE ARE NOW, RIGHT?
HOLD ON!
THAT'S STUPID!
DON'T SET THEM FREE!
THEY'RE OUR LAST SOURCE OF MEAT!
WE SHOULD COOK THEM!
RIGHT, YOU GUYS?

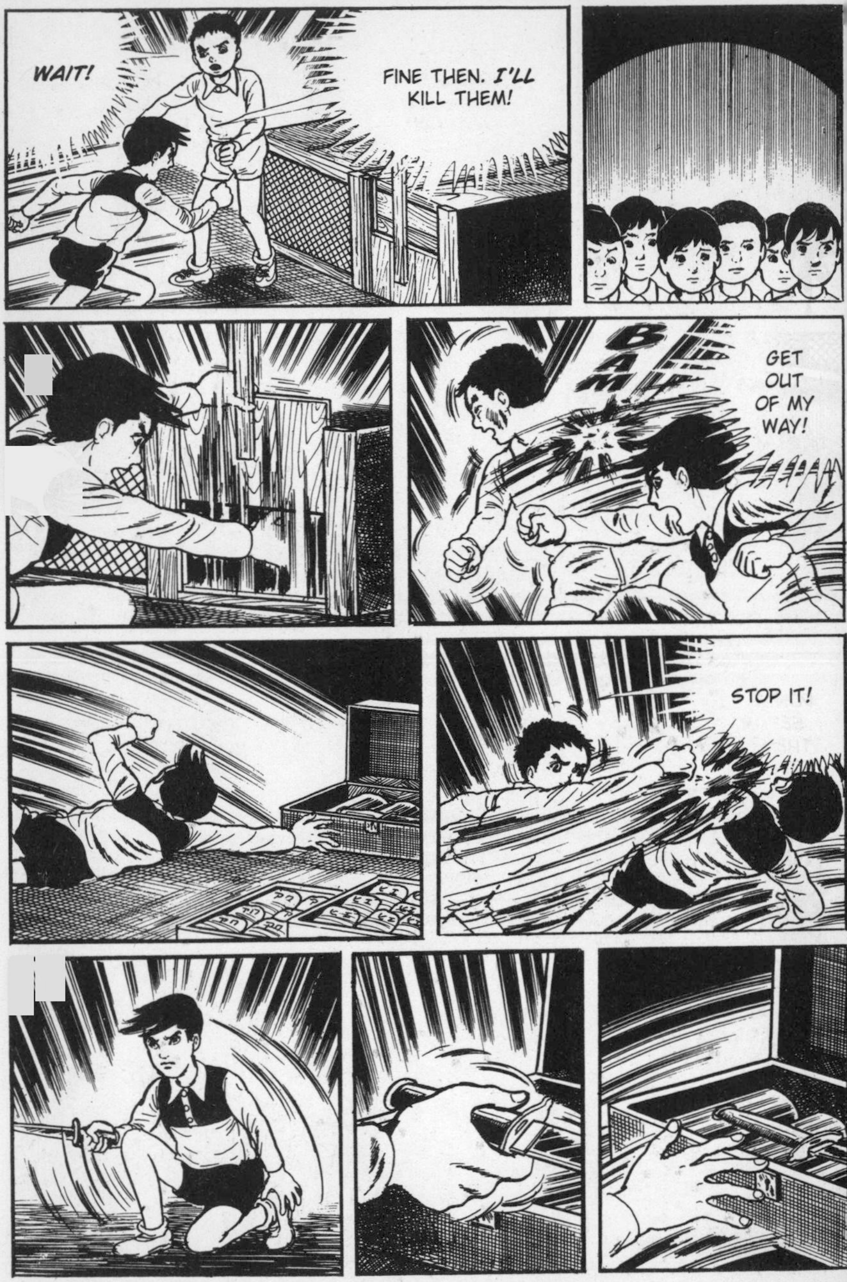
FINE THEN. *I'LL* KILL THEM!
WAIT!
GET OUT OF MY WAY!
BAM
STOP IT!

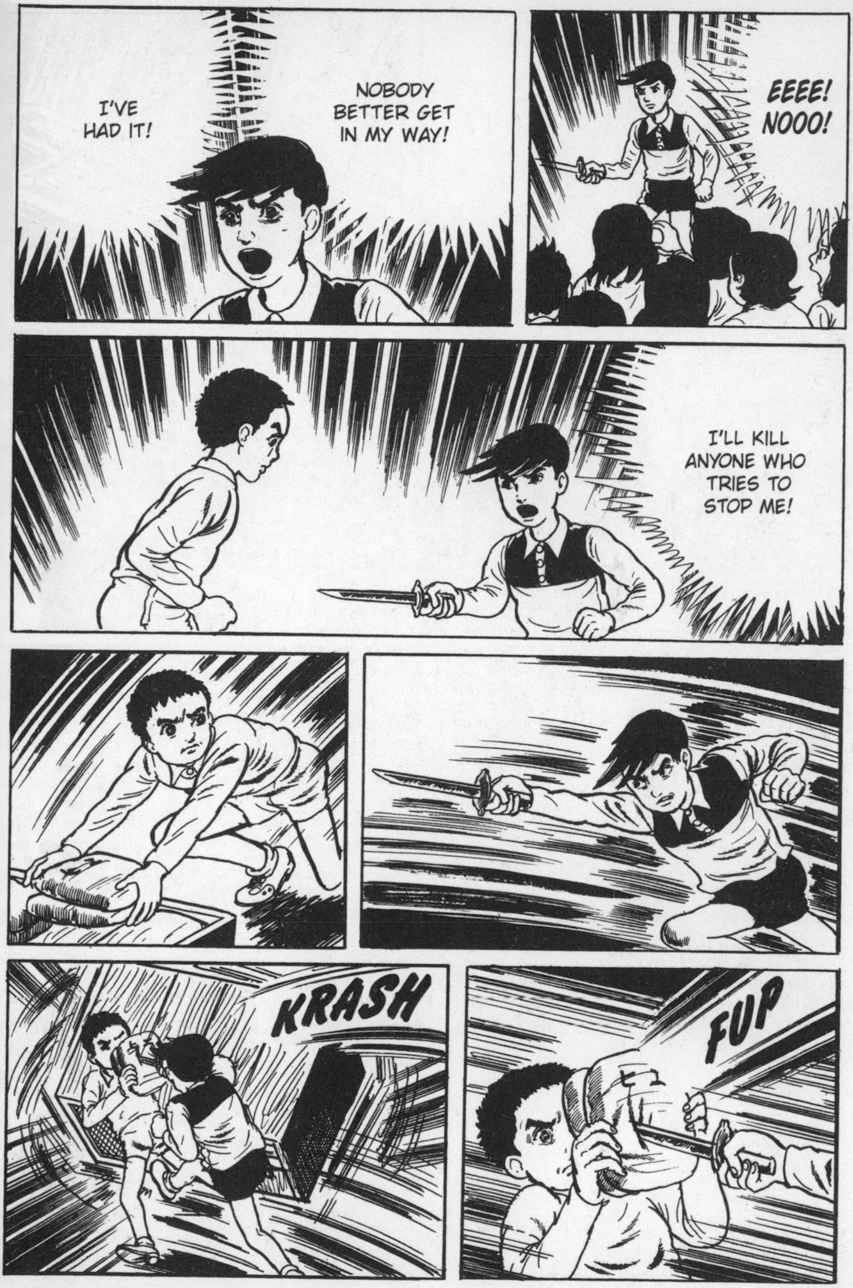
EEEE! NOOO!
NOBODY BETTER GET IN MY WAY!
I'VE HAD IT!
I'LL KILL ANYONE WHO TRIES TO STOP ME!
FUP
KRASH

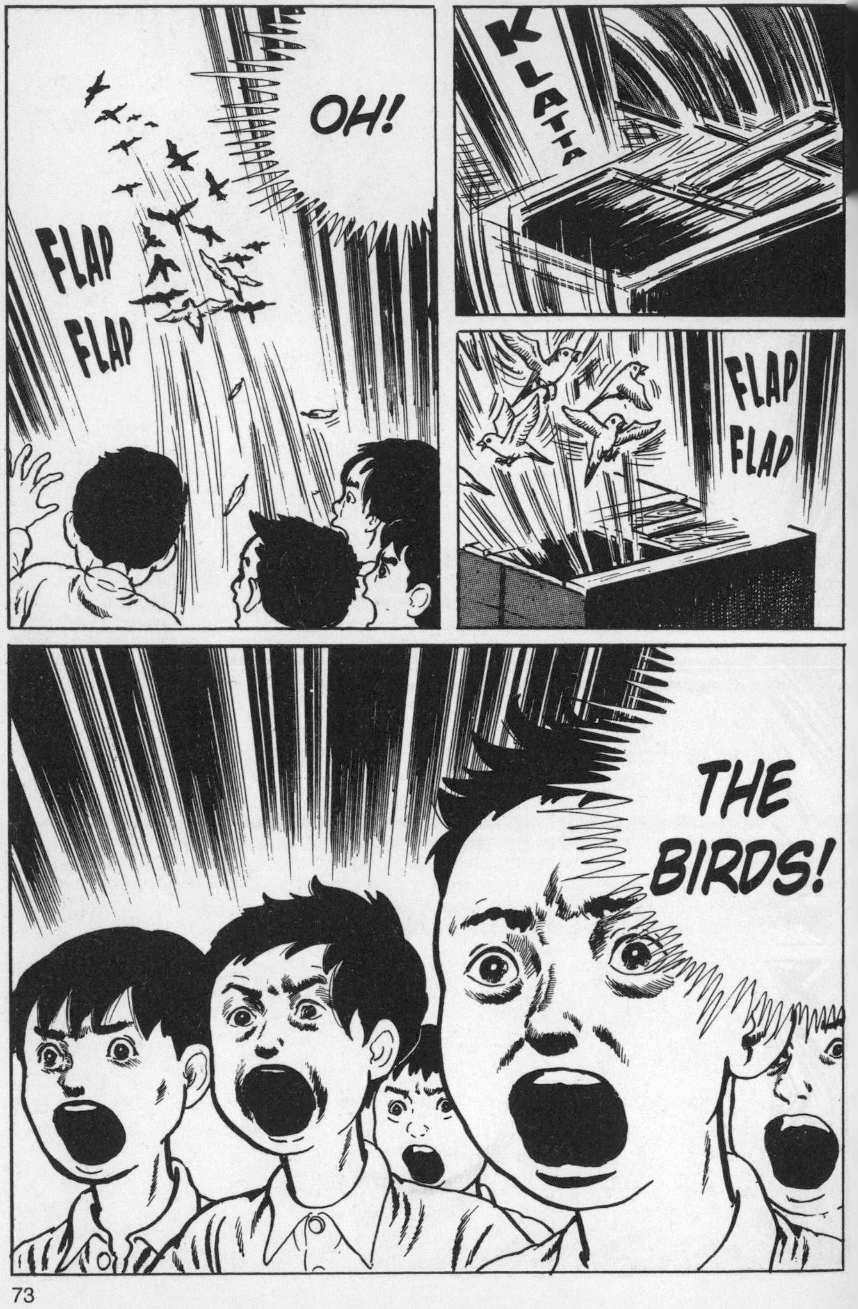
KLATTA
FLAP
FLAP
OH!
FLAP
FLAP
THE BIRDS!

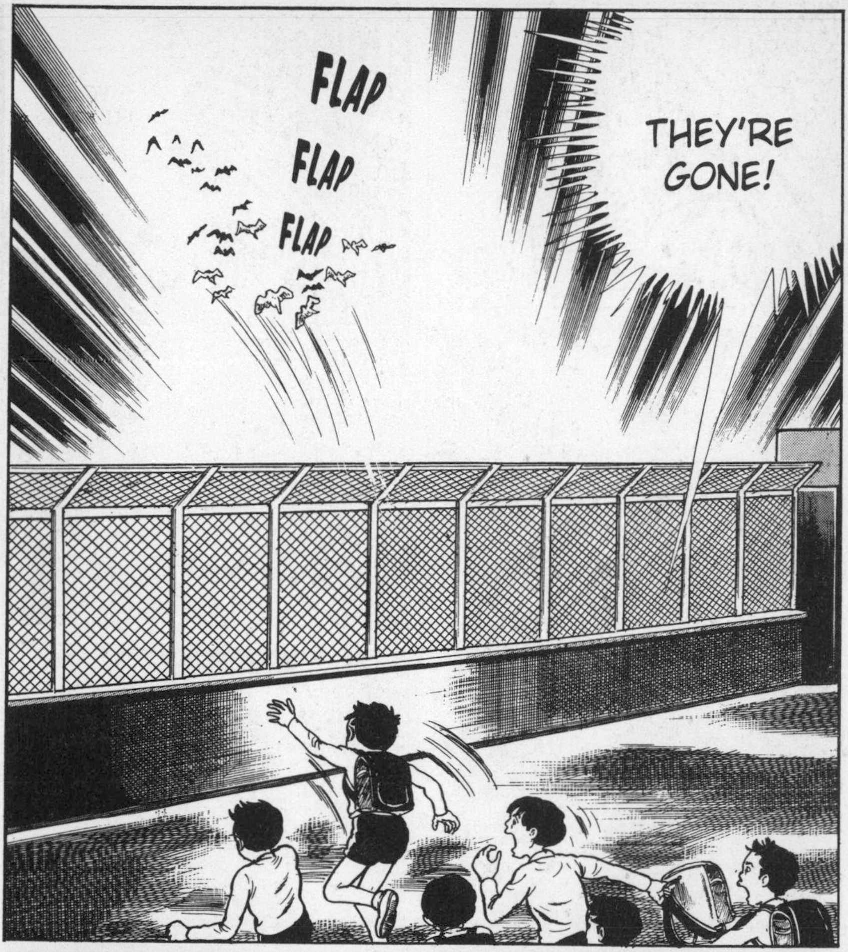
THEY'RE GONE!
FLAP
FLAP
FLAP
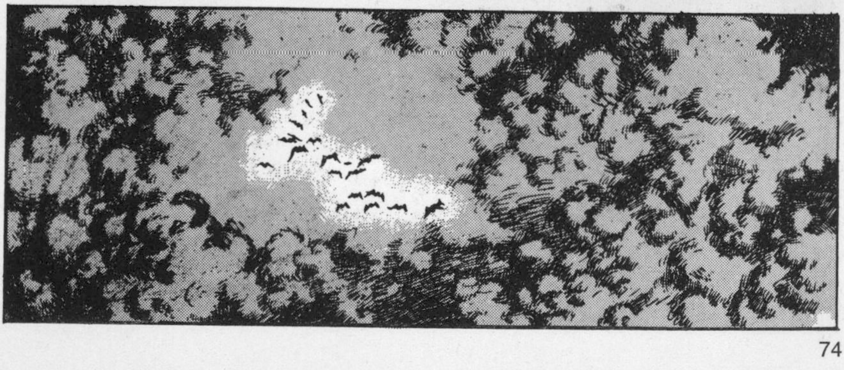

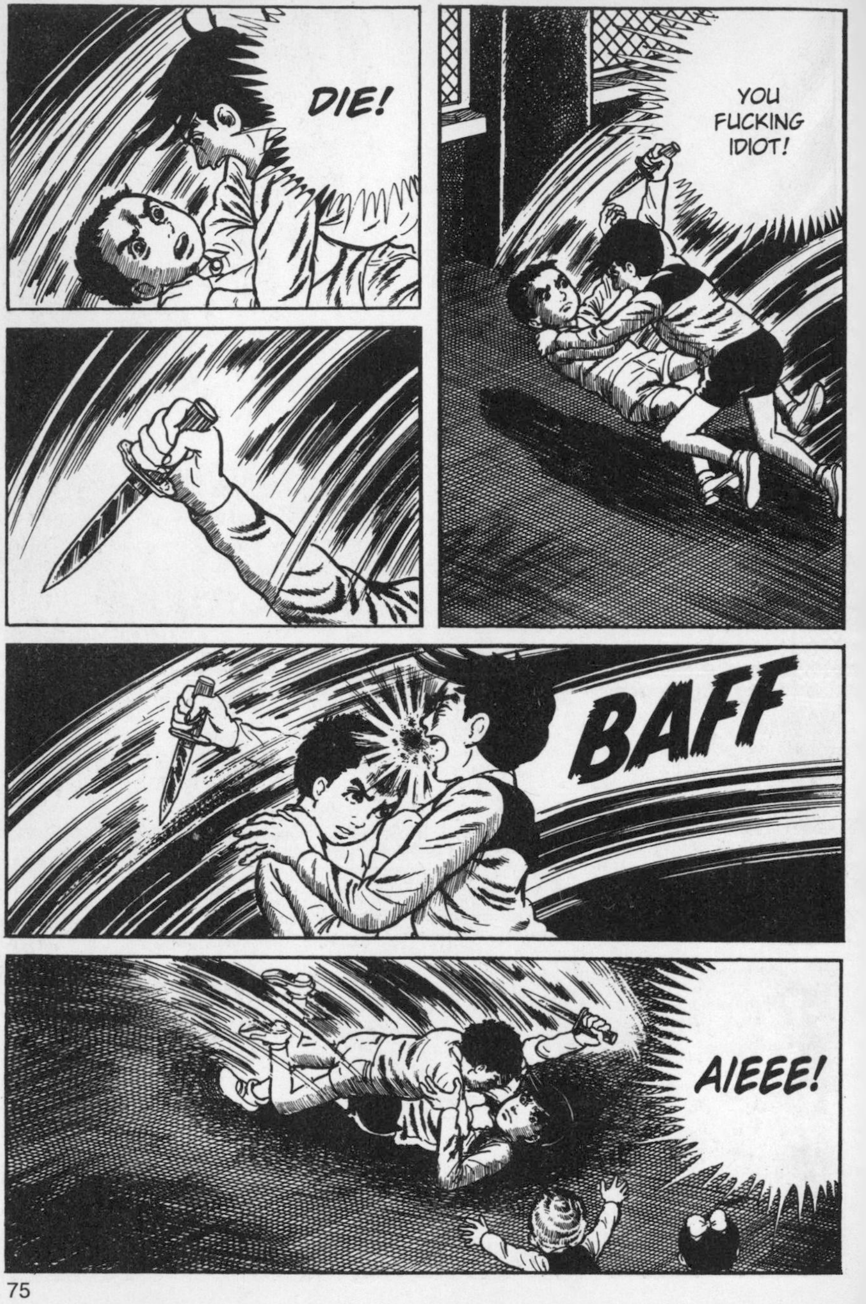
YOU FUCKING IDIOT!
DIE!
BAFF
AIEEE!

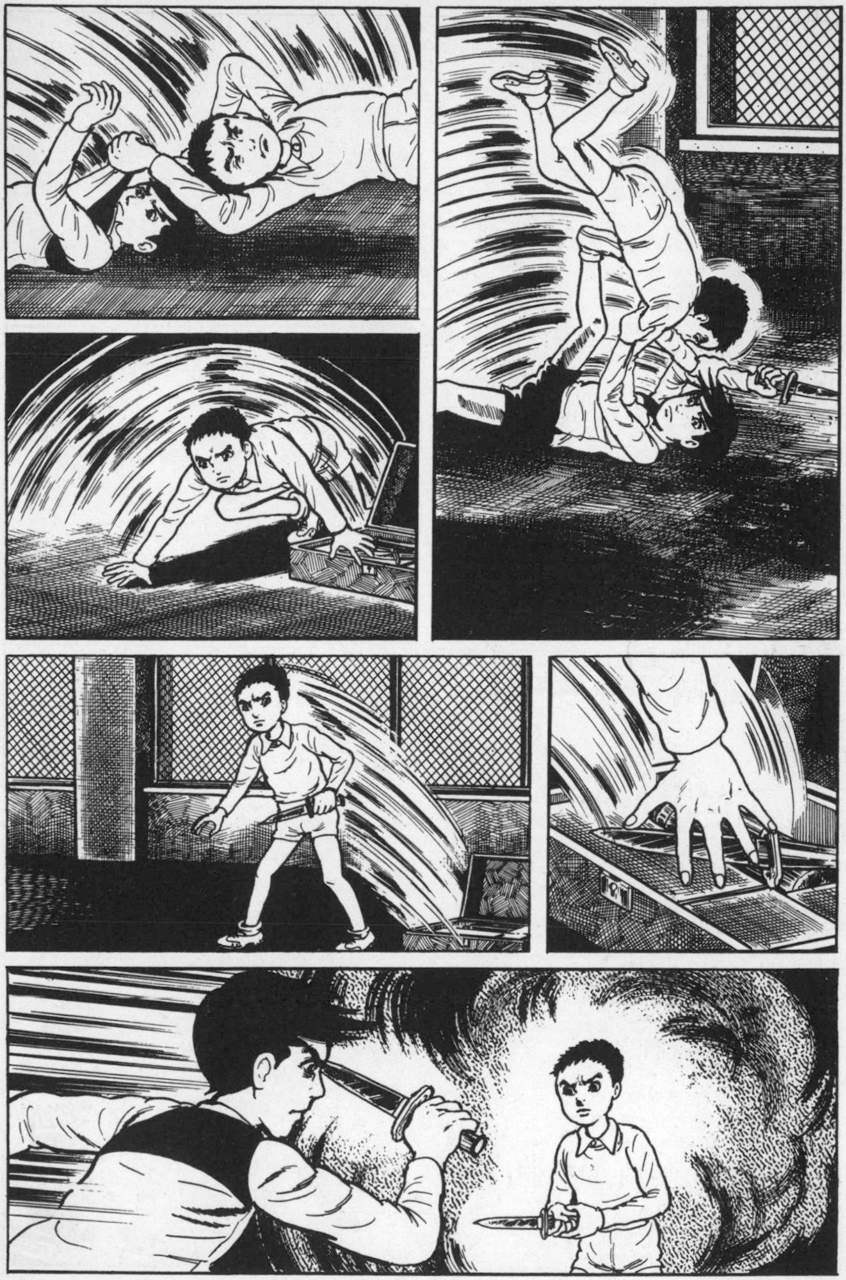

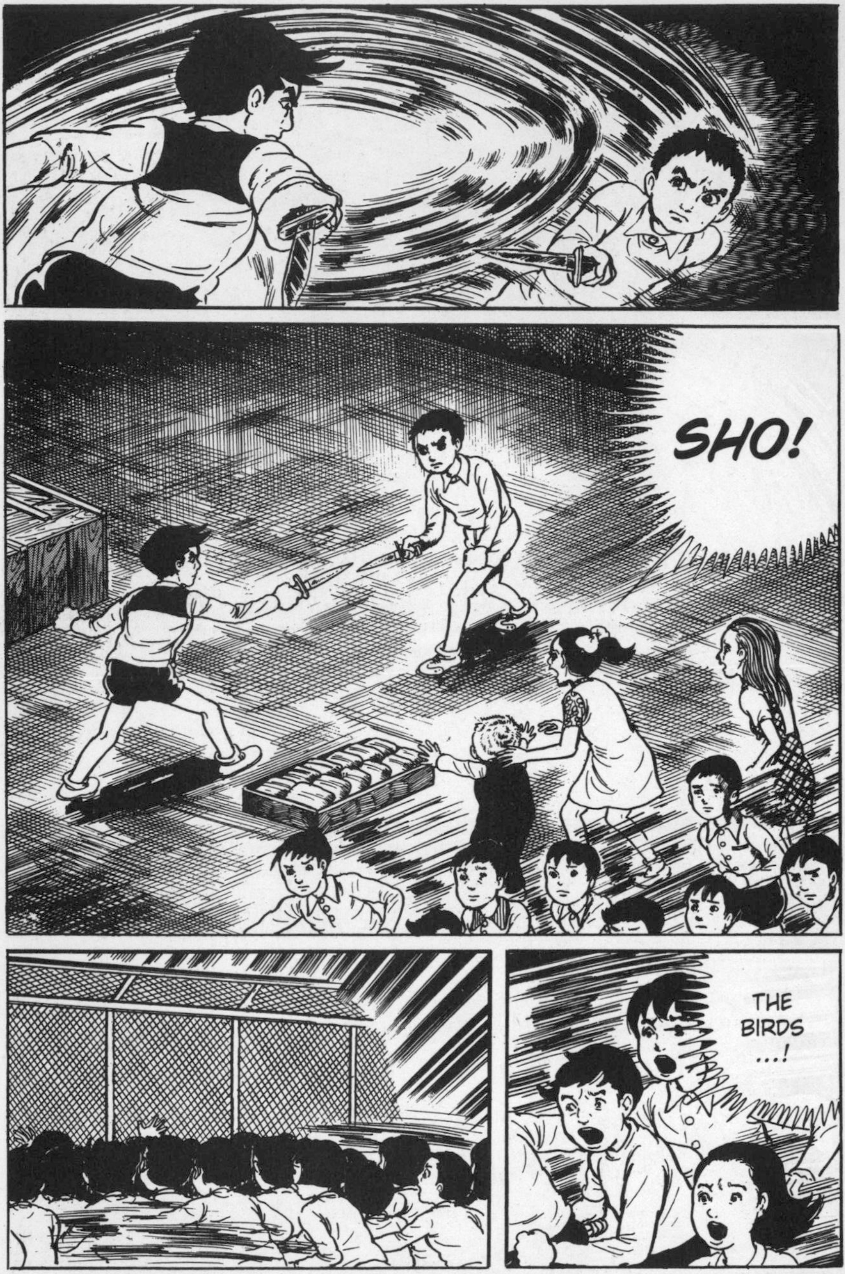
SHO!
THE BIRDS ...!

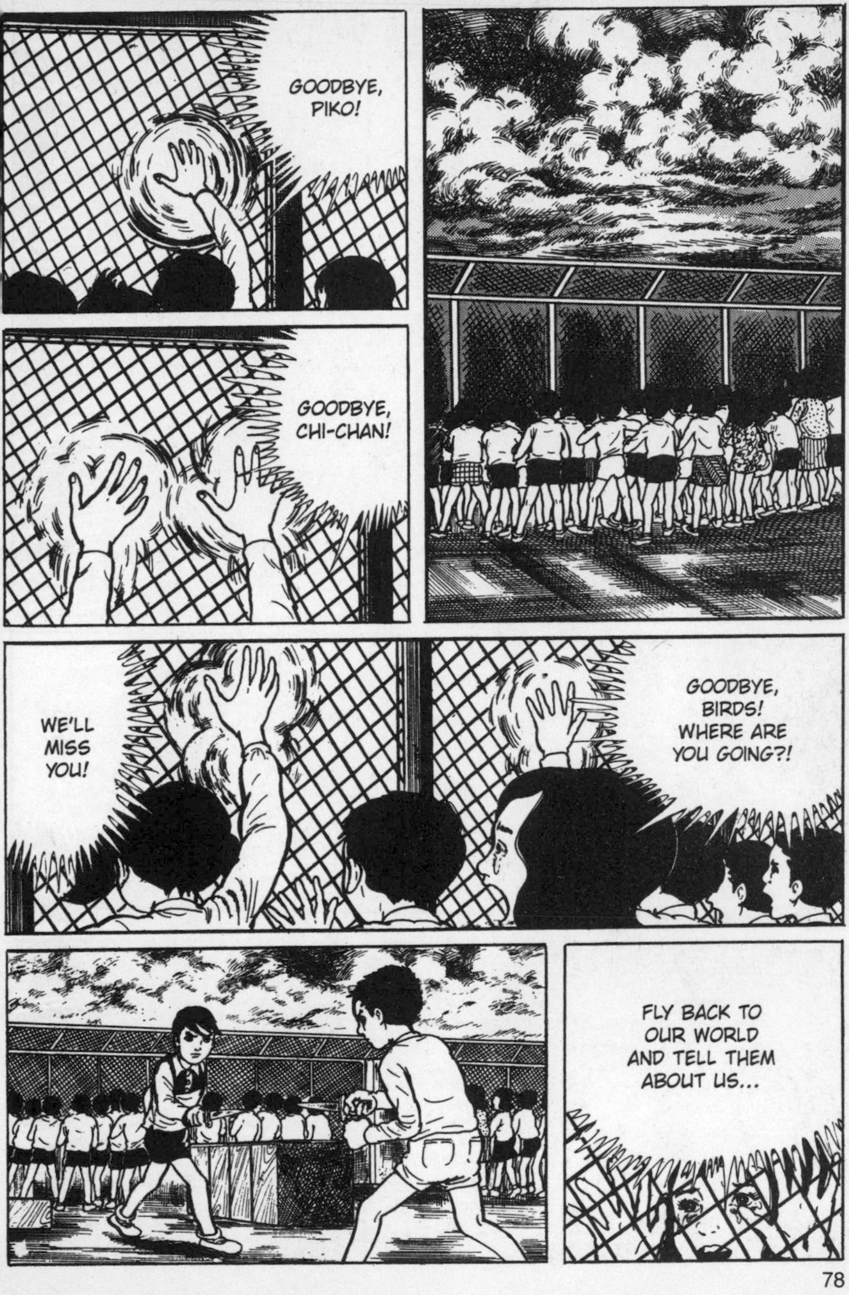
GOODBYE, PIKO!
GOODBYE, CHI-CHAN!
GOODBYE, BIRDS! WHERE ARE YOU GOING?!
WE'LL MISS YOU!
FLY BACK TO OUR WORLD AND TELL THEM ABOUT US...

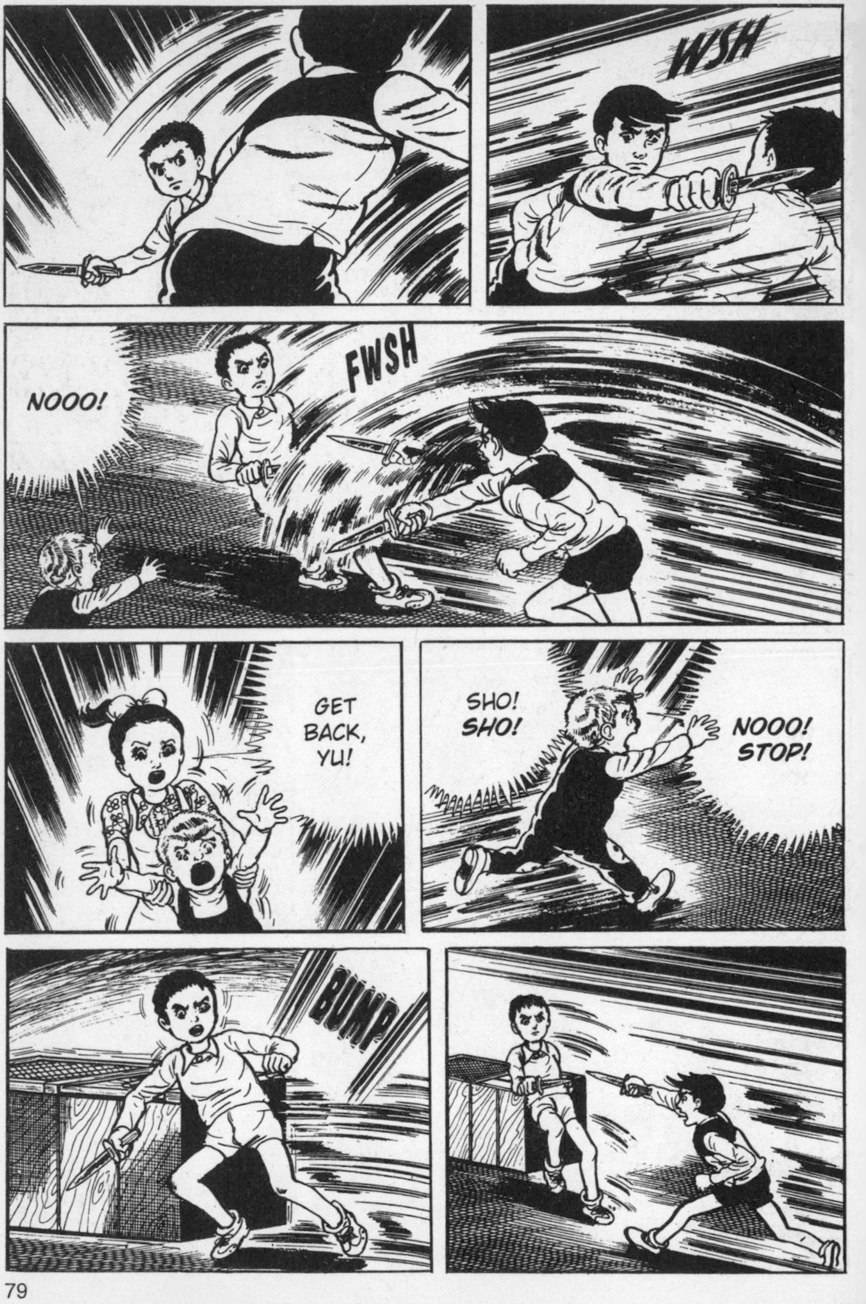
WSH
FWSH
NOOO!
NOOO! STOP!
SHO! SHO!
GET BACK, YU!
BUMP

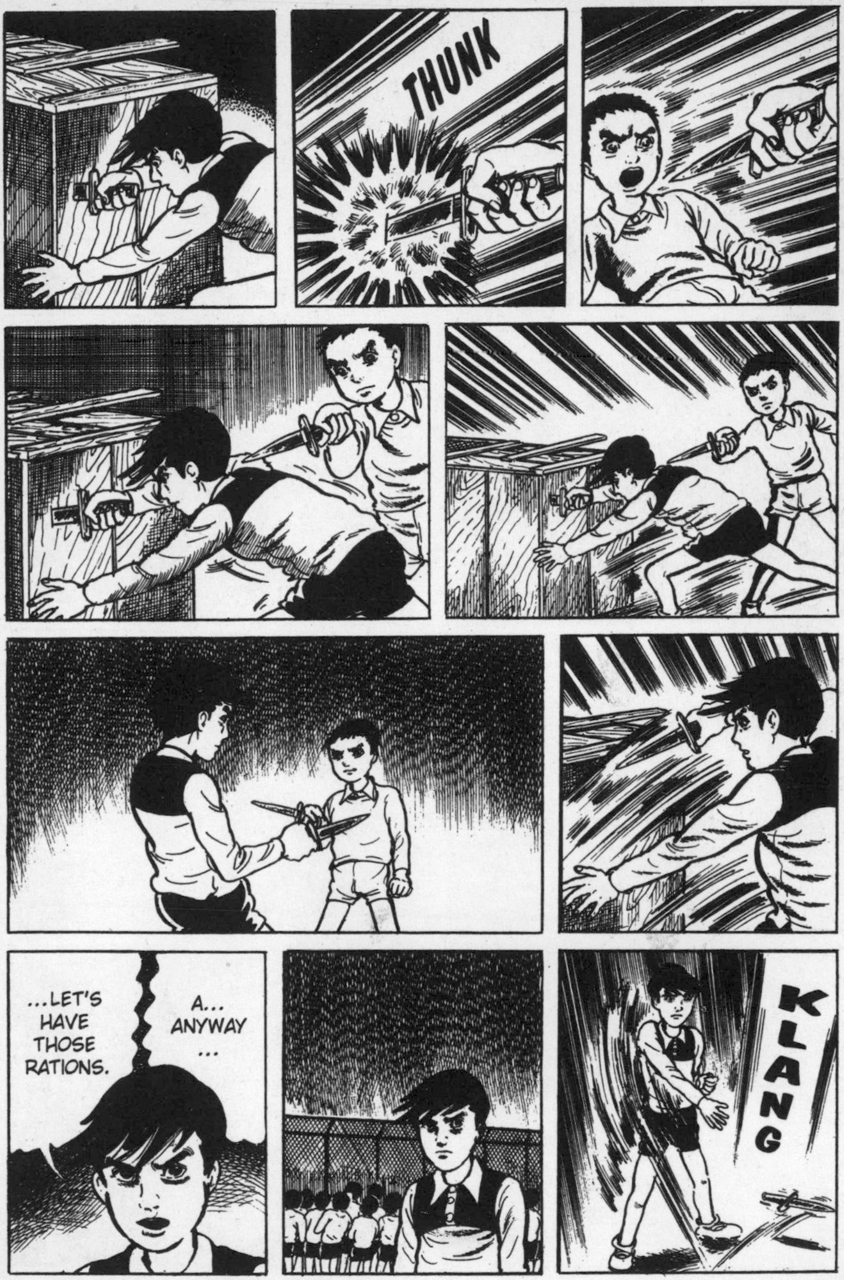
THUNK
KLANG
A... ANYWAY ...
...LET'S HAVE THOSE RATIONS.

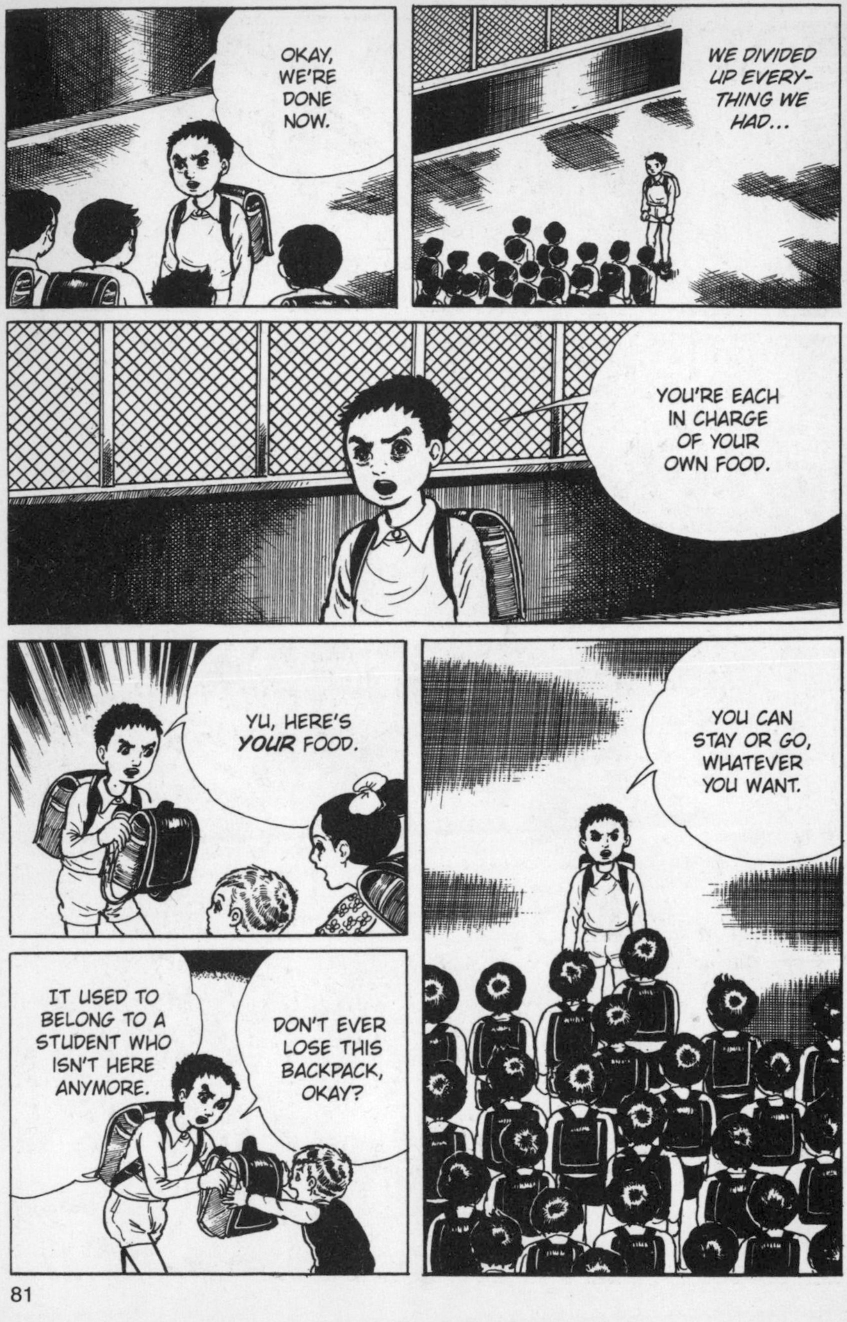
WE DIVIDED UP EVERYTHING WE HAD...
OKAY, WE'RE DONE NOW.
YOU'RE EACH IN CHARGE OF YOUR OWN FOOD.
YOU CAN STAY OR GO, WHATEVER YOU WANT.
YU, HERE'S YOUR FOOD.
DON'T EVER LOSE THIS BACKPACK, OKAY?
IT USED TO BELONG TO A STUDENT WHO ISN'T HERE ANYMORE.

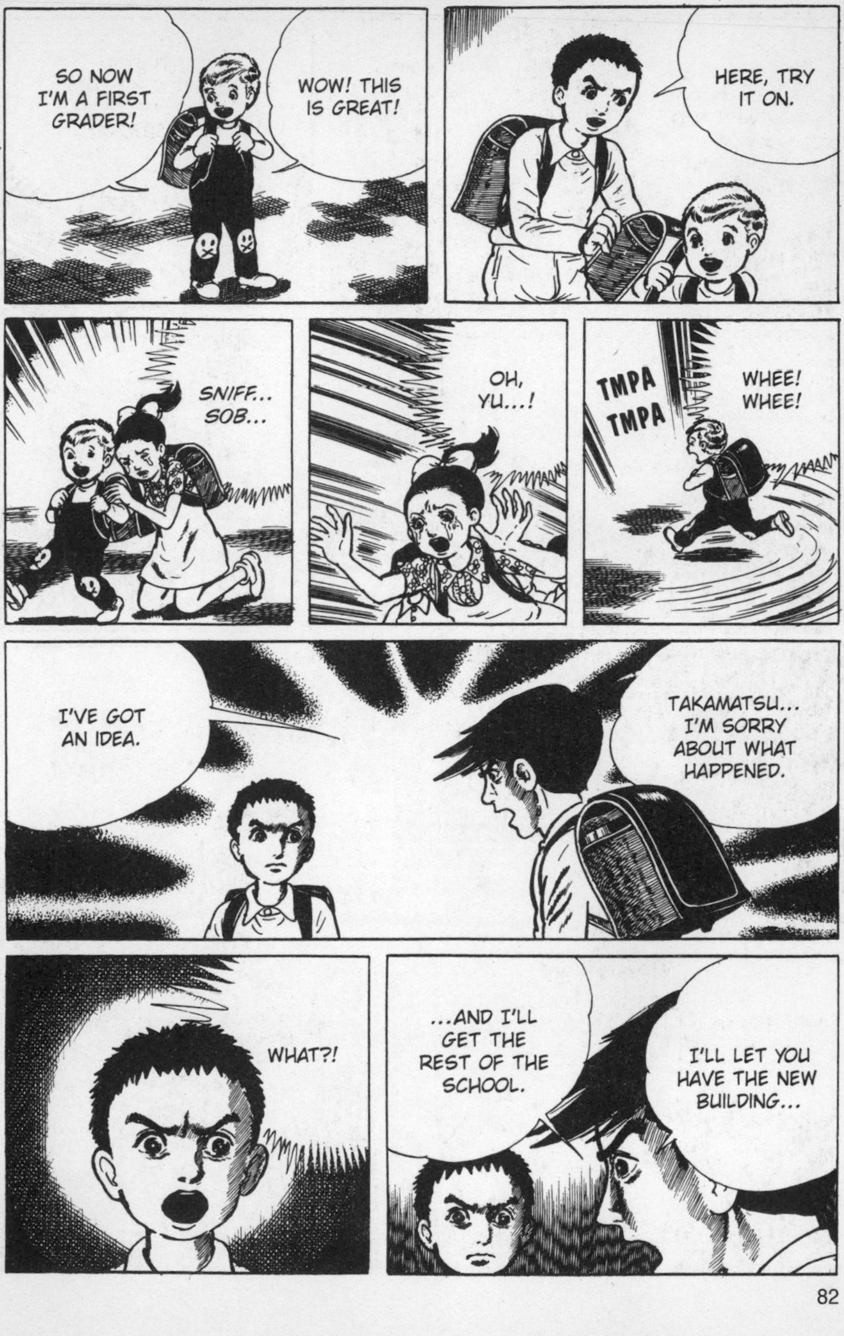
HERE, TRY IT ON.
WOW! THIS IS GREAT!
SO NOW I'M A FIRST GRADER!
WHEE! WHEE!
TMPA TMPA
OH, YU...!
SNIFF... SOB...
TAKAMATSU... I'M SORRY ABOUT WHAT HAPPENED.
I'VE GOT AN IDEA.
I'LL LET YOU HAVE THE NEW BUILDING...
...AND I'LL GET THE REST OF THE SCHOOL.
WHAT?!

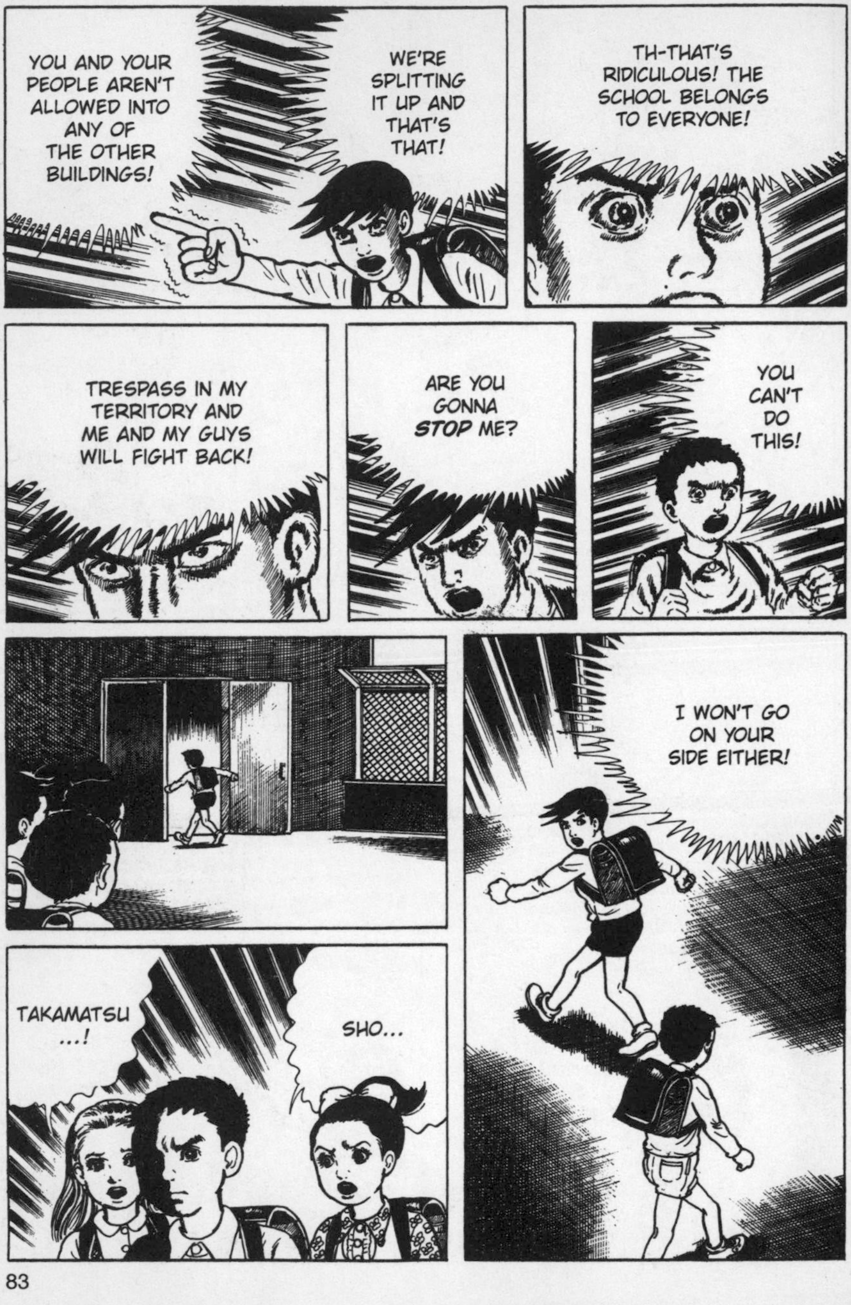
TH-THAT'S RIDICULOUS! THE SCHOOL BELONGS TO EVERYONE!
WE'RE SPLITTING IT UP AND THAT'S THAT!
YOU AND YOUR PEOPLE AREN'T ALLOWED INTO ANY OF THE OTHER BUILDINGS!
YOU CAN'T DO THIS!
ARE YOU GONNA *STOP* ME?
TRESPASS IN MY TERRITORY AND ME AND MY GUYS WILL FIGHT BACK!
I WON'T GO ON YOUR SIDE EITHER!
SHO...
TAKAMATSU ...!

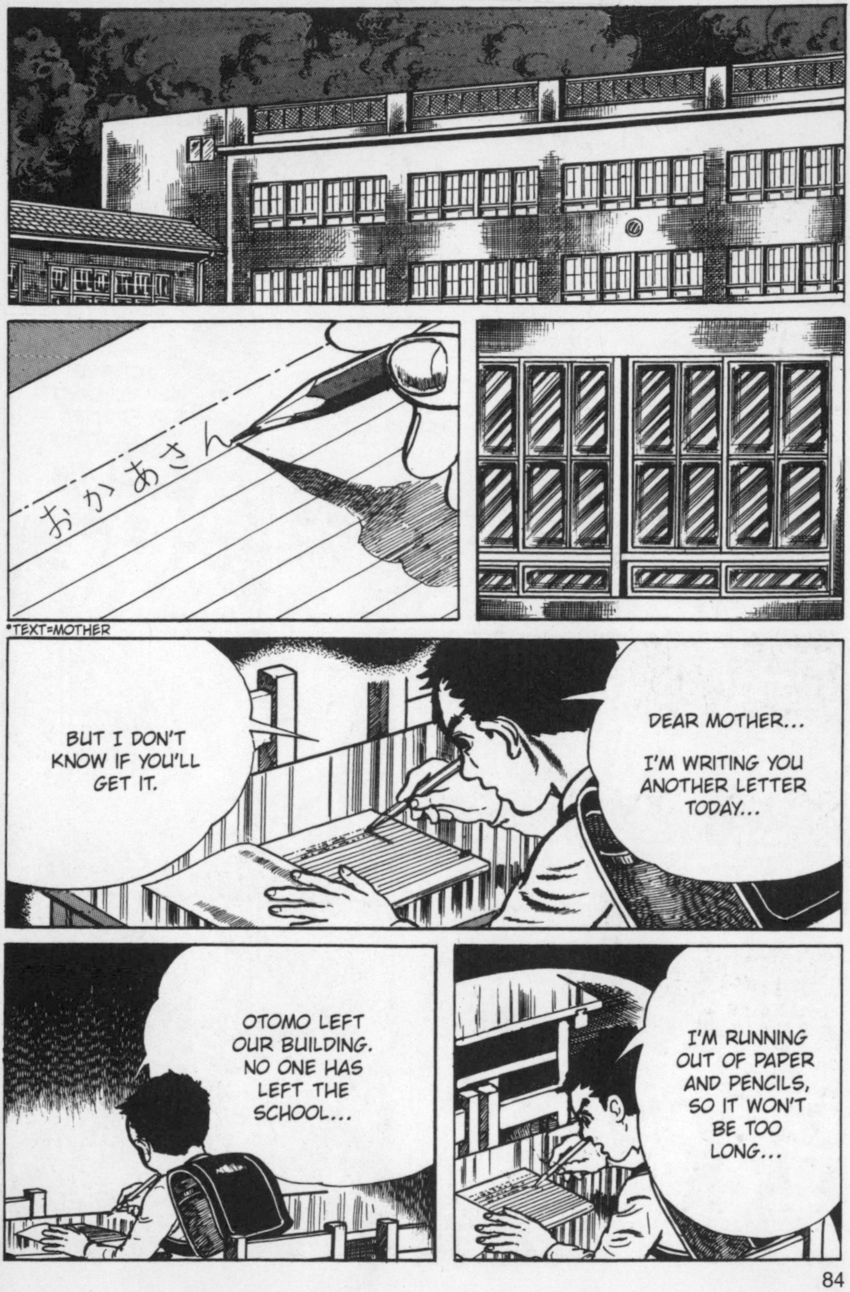
おかあさん
*TEXT=MOTHER
DEAR MOTHER...
I'M WRITING YOU ANOTHER LETTER TODAY...
BUT I DON'T KNOW IF YOU'LL GET IT.
I'M RUNNING OUT OF PAPER AND PENCILS, SO IT WON'T BE TOO LONG...
OTOMO LEFT OUR BUILDING. NO ONE HAS LEFT THE SCHOOL...

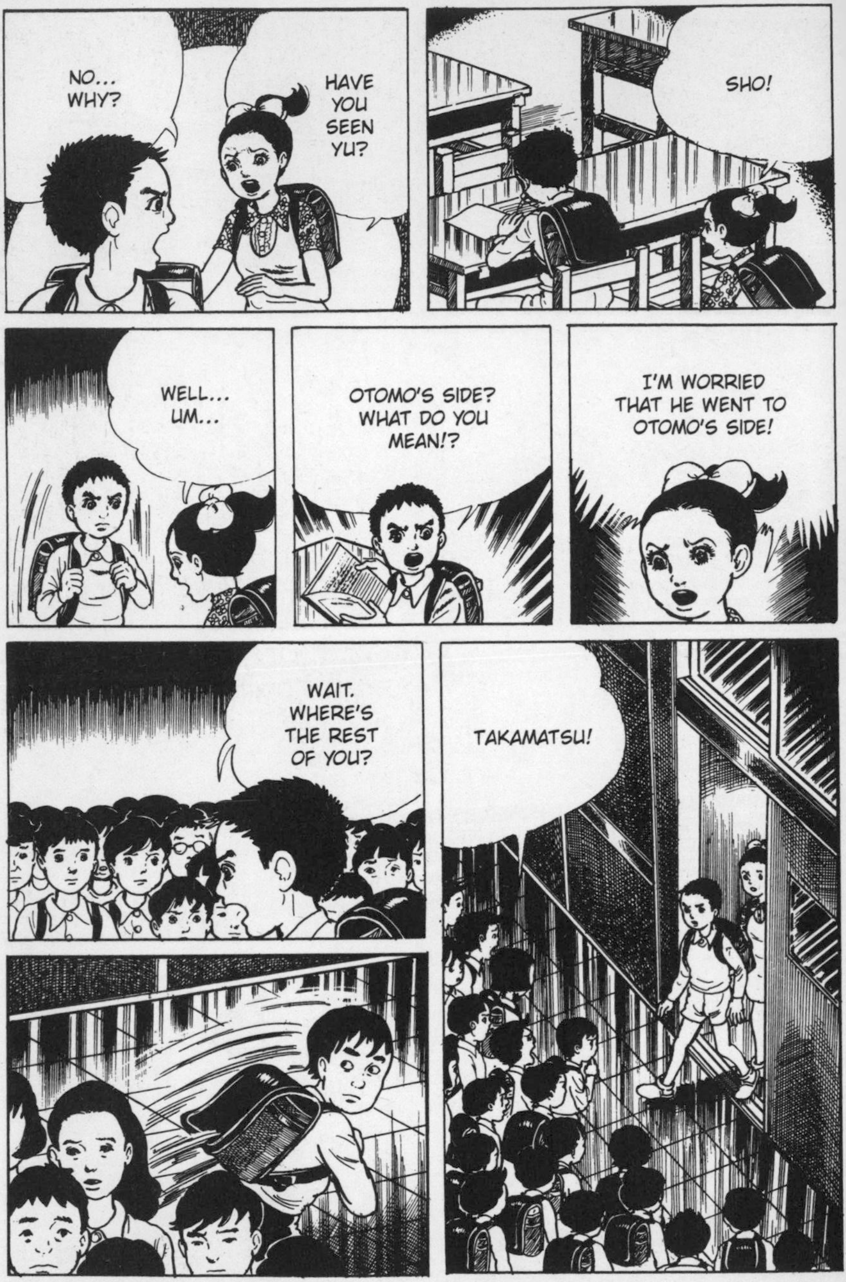
SHO!
HAVE YOU SEEN YU?
NO... WHY?
I'M WORRIED THAT HE WENT TO OTOMO'S SIDE!
OTOMO'S SIDE? WHAT DO YOU MEAN!?
WELL... UM...
TAKAMATSU!
WAIT. WHERE'S THE REST OF YOU?

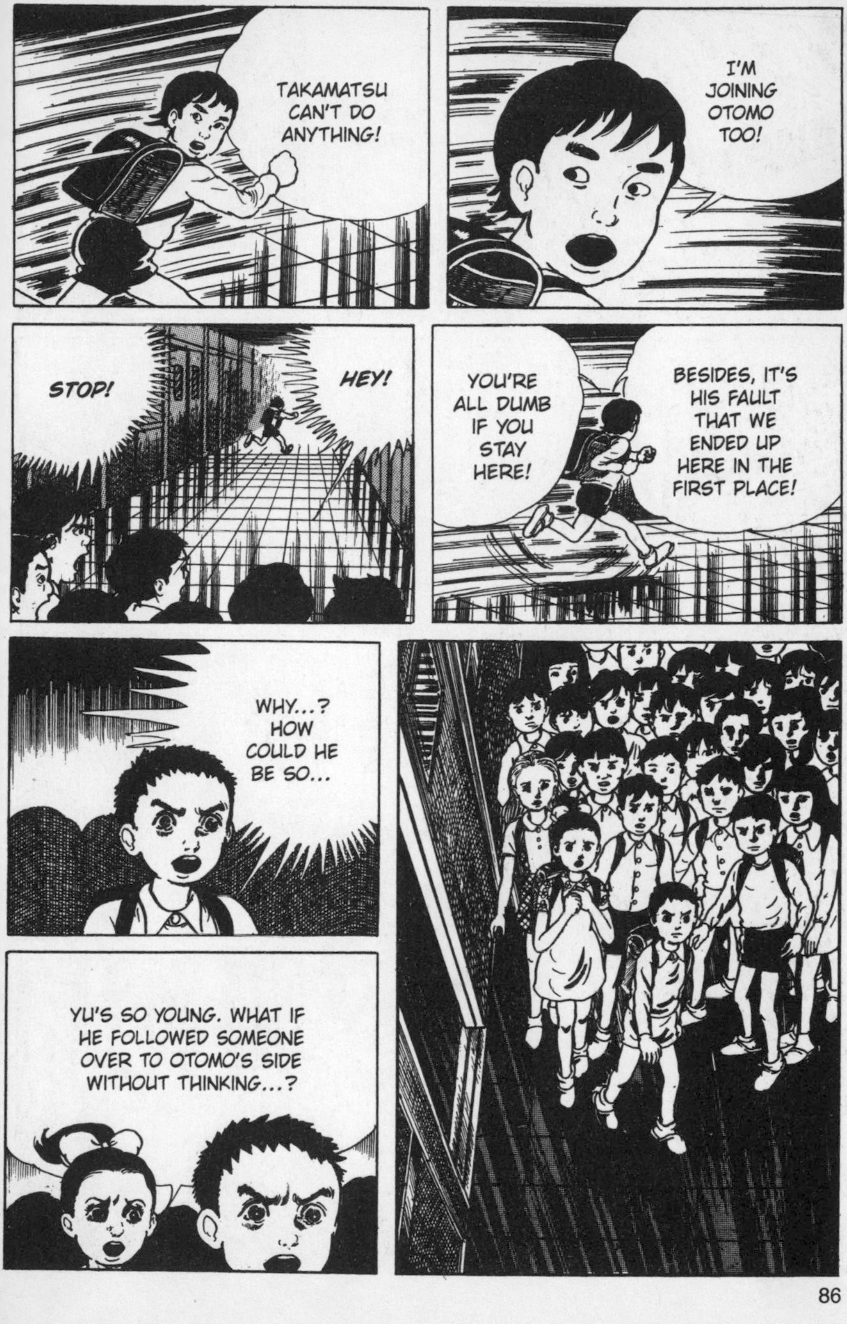
I'M JOINING OTOMO TOO!
TAKAMATSU CAN'T DO ANYTHING!
YOU'RE ALL DUMB IF YOU STAY HERE!
BESIDES, IT'S HIS FAULT THAT WE ENDED UP HERE IN THE FIRST PLACE!
HEY!
STOP!
WHY...? HOW COULD HE BE SO...
YU'S SO YOUNG. WHAT IF HE FOLLOWED SOMEONE OVER TO OTOMO'S SIDE WITHOUT THINKING...?

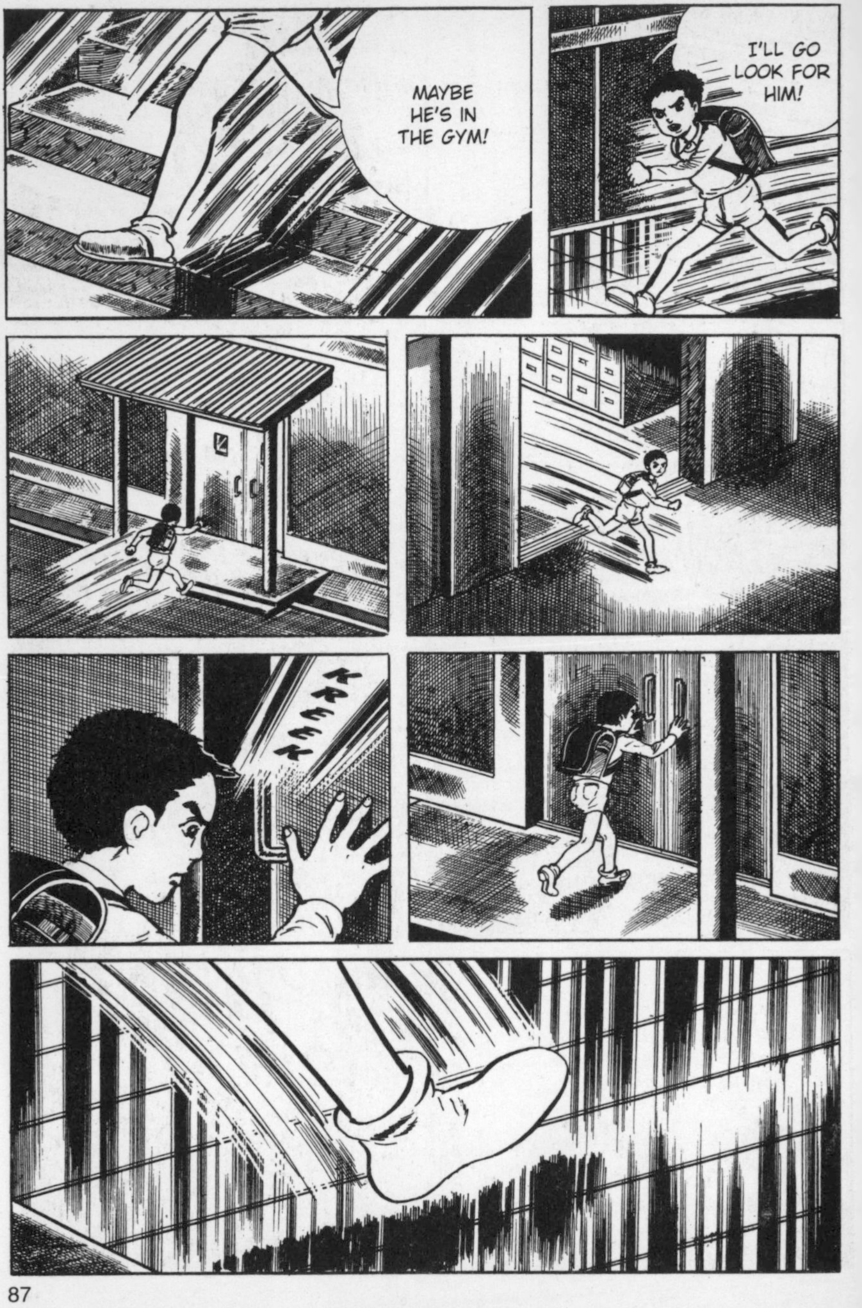
I'LL GO LOOK FOR HIM!
MAYBE HE'S IN THE GYM!
KREEK

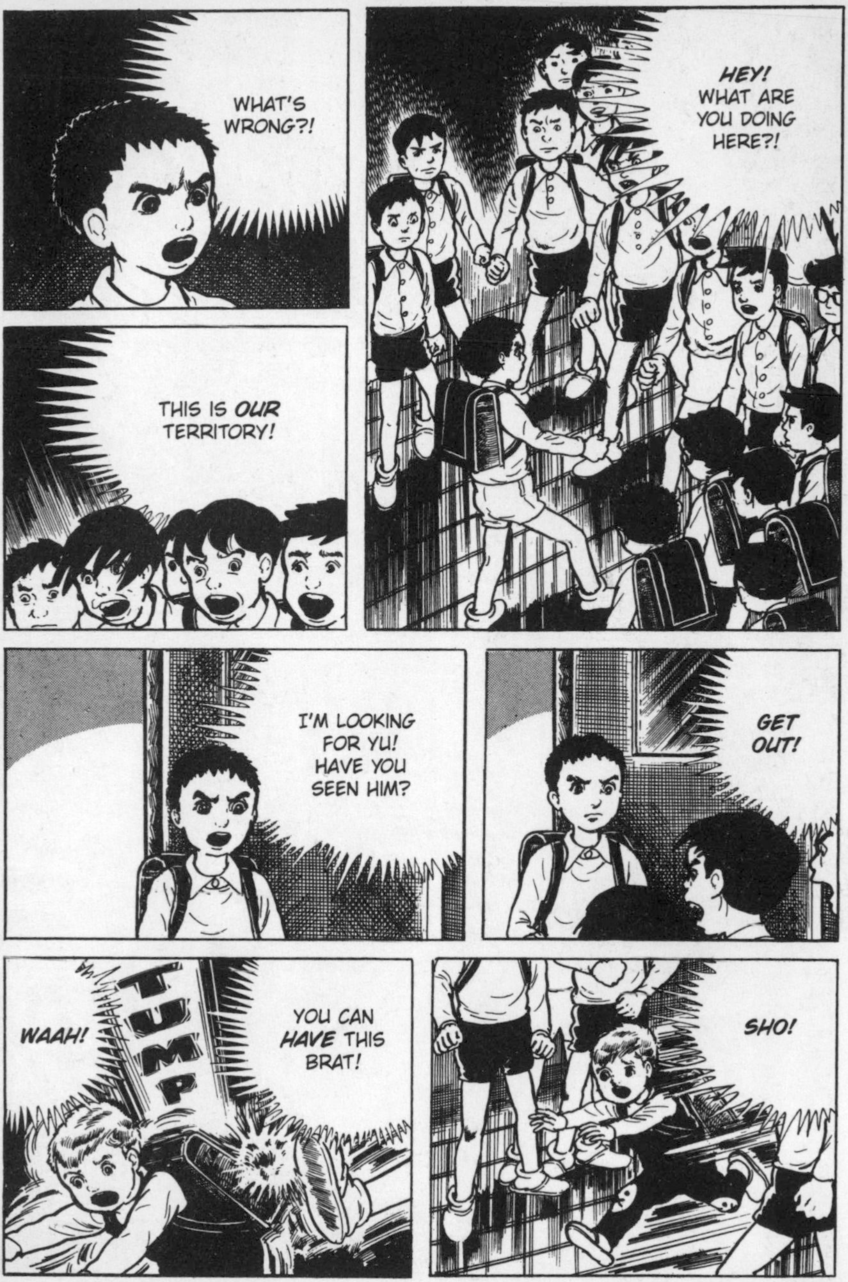
WHAT'S WRONG?!
THIS IS OUR TERRITORY!
HEY! WHAT ARE YOU DOING HERE?!
I'M LOOKING FOR YU! HAVE YOU SEEN HIM?
GET OUT!
WAAH!
TUMP
YOU CAN HAVE THIS BRAT!
SHO!

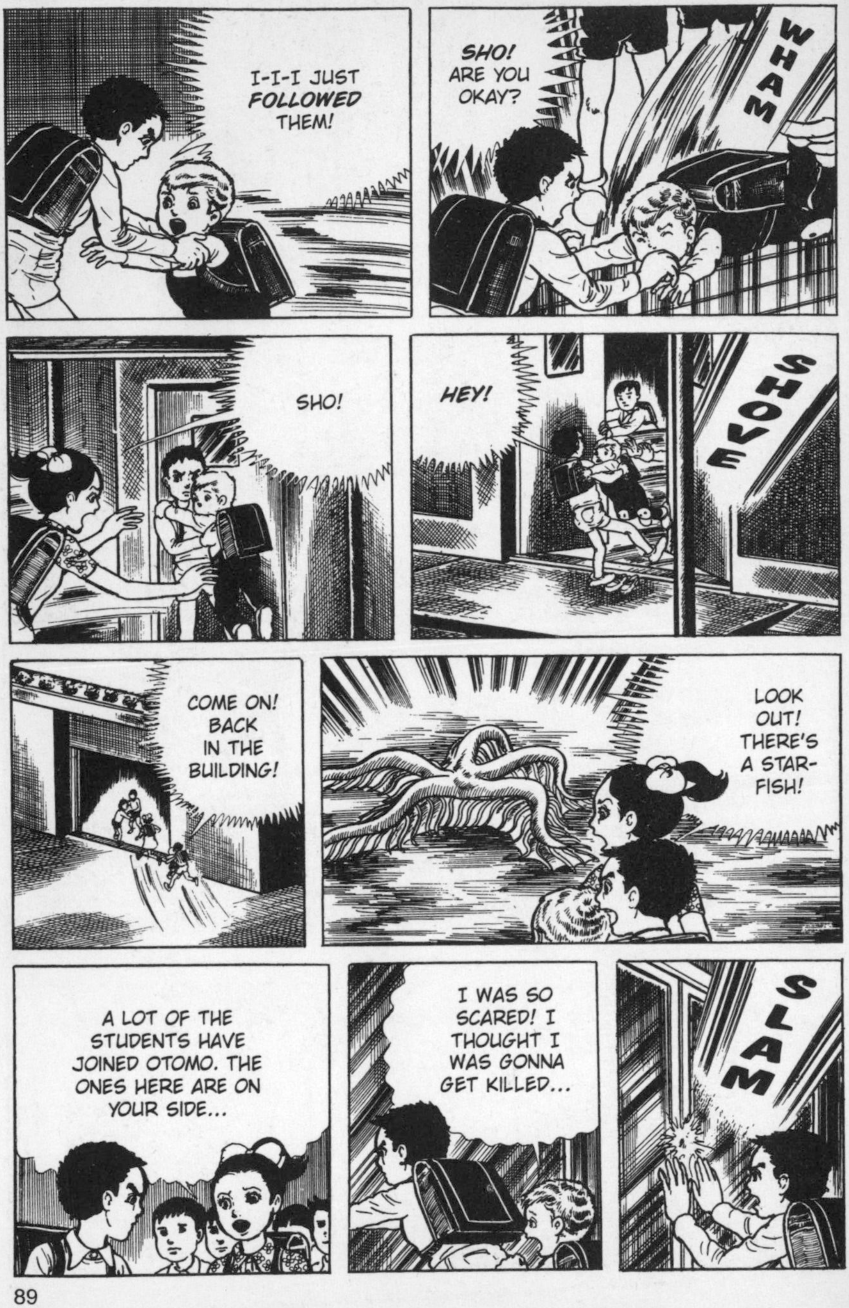
SHO! ARE YOU OKAY?
WHAM
I-I-I JUST FOLLOWED THEM!
HEY!
SHOVE
SHO!
LOOK OUT! THERE'S A STAR-FISH!
COME ON! BACK IN THE BUILDING!
SLAM
I WAS SO SCARED! I THOUGHT I WAS GONNA GET KILLED...
A LOT OF THE STUDENTS HAVE JOINED OTOMO. THE ONES HERE ARE ON YOUR SIDE...

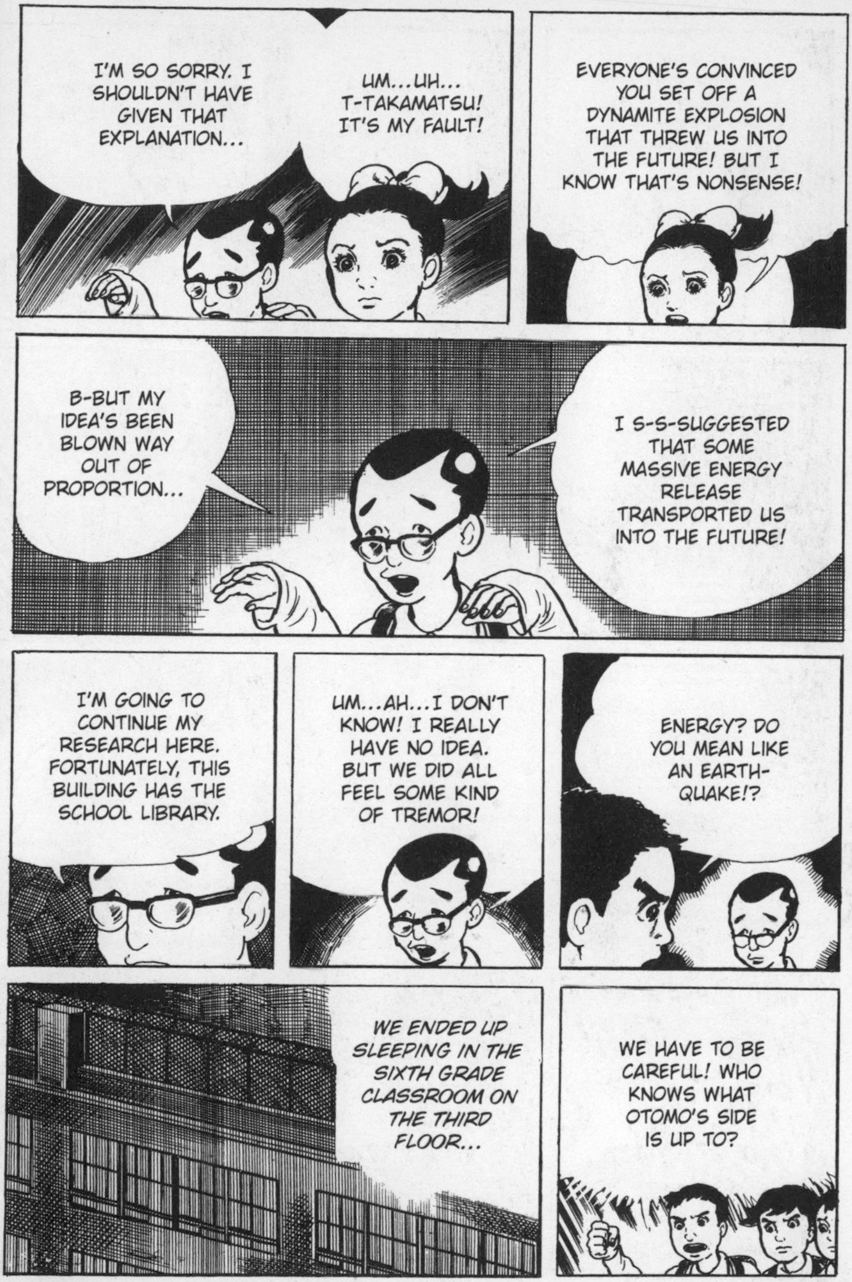
EVERYONE'S CONVINCED YOU SET OFF A DYNAMITE EXPLOSION THAT THREW US INTO THE FUTURE! BUT I KNOW THAT'S NONSENSE!
UM...UH... T-TAKAMATSU! IT'S MY FAULT!
I'M SO SORRY. I SHOULDN'T HAVE GIVEN THAT EXPLANATION...
I S-S-SUGGESTED THAT SOME MASSIVE ENERGY RELEASE TRANSPORTED US INTO THE FUTURE!
B-BUT MY IDEA'S BEEN BLOWN WAY OUT OF PROPORTION...
ENERGY? DO YOU MEAN LIKE AN EARTH-QUAKE!?
UM...AH...I DON'T KNOW! I REALLY HAVE NO IDEA. BUT WE DID ALL FEEL SOME KIND OF TREMOR!
I'M GOING TO CONTINUE MY RESEARCH HERE. FORTUNATELY, THIS BUILDING HAS THE SCHOOL LIBRARY.
WE HAVE TO BE CAREFUL! WHO KNOWS WHAT OTOMO'S SIDE IS UP TO?
WE ENDED UP SLEEPING IN THE SIXTH GRADE CLASSROOM ON THE THIRD FLOOR...

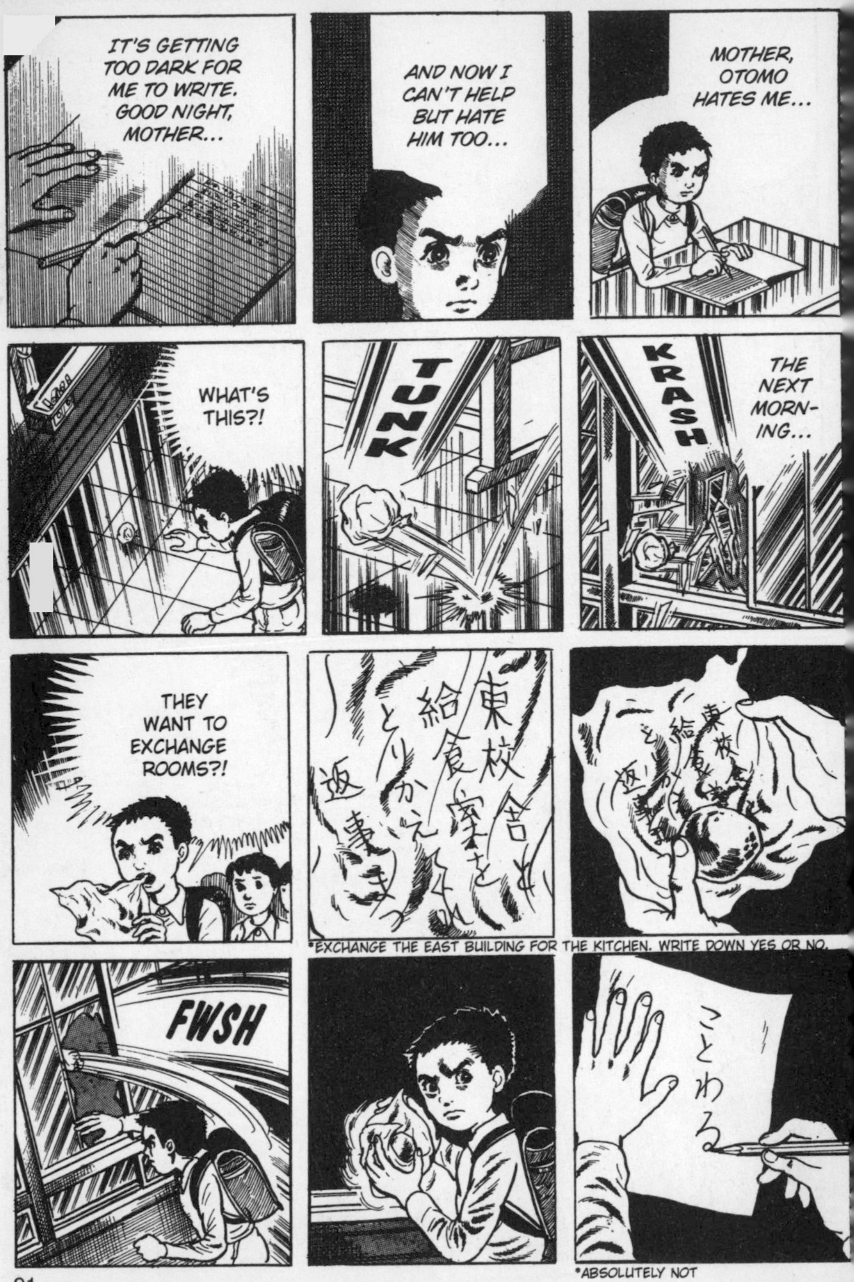
MOTHER, OTOMO HATES ME...
AND NOW I CAN'T HELP BUT HATE HIM TOO...
IT'S GETTING TOO DARK FOR ME TO WRITE. GOOD NIGHT, MOTHER...
THE NEXT MORNING...
KRASH
TUNK
WHAT'S THIS?!
東校舎と
給食室を
とりかえろ
返事まつ
THEY WANT TO EXCHANGE ROOMS?!
*EXCHANGE THE EAST BUILDING FOR THE KITCHEN. WRITE DOWN YES OR NO.
ことわる
FWSH
*ABSOLUTELY NOT

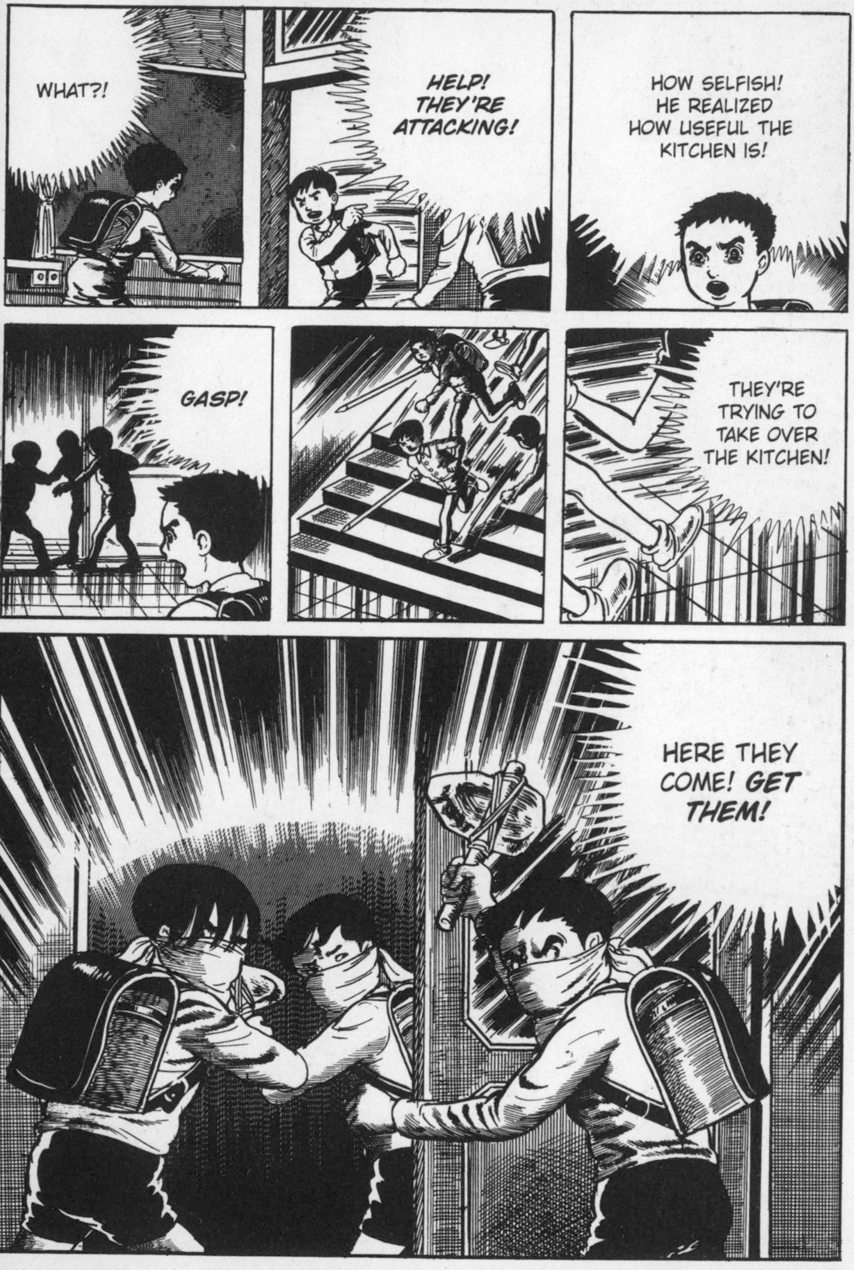
HOW SELFISH! HE REALIZED HOW USEFUL THE KITCHEN IS!
HELP! THEY'RE ATTACKING!
WHAT?!
THEY'RE TRYING TO TAKE OVER THE KITCHEN!
GASP!
HERE THEY COME! GET THEM!

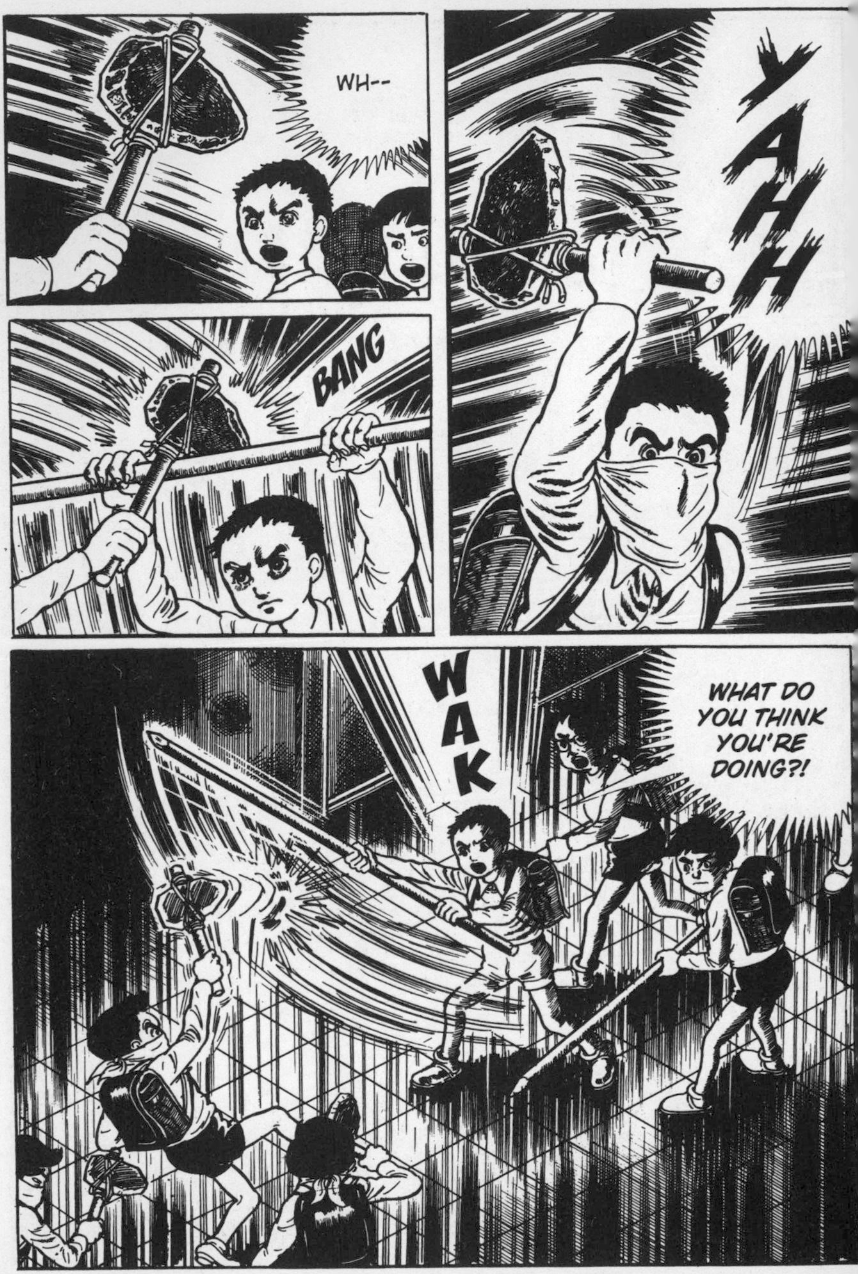
YAHH
WH--
BANG
WHAT DO YOU THINK YOU'RE DOING?!
WAK

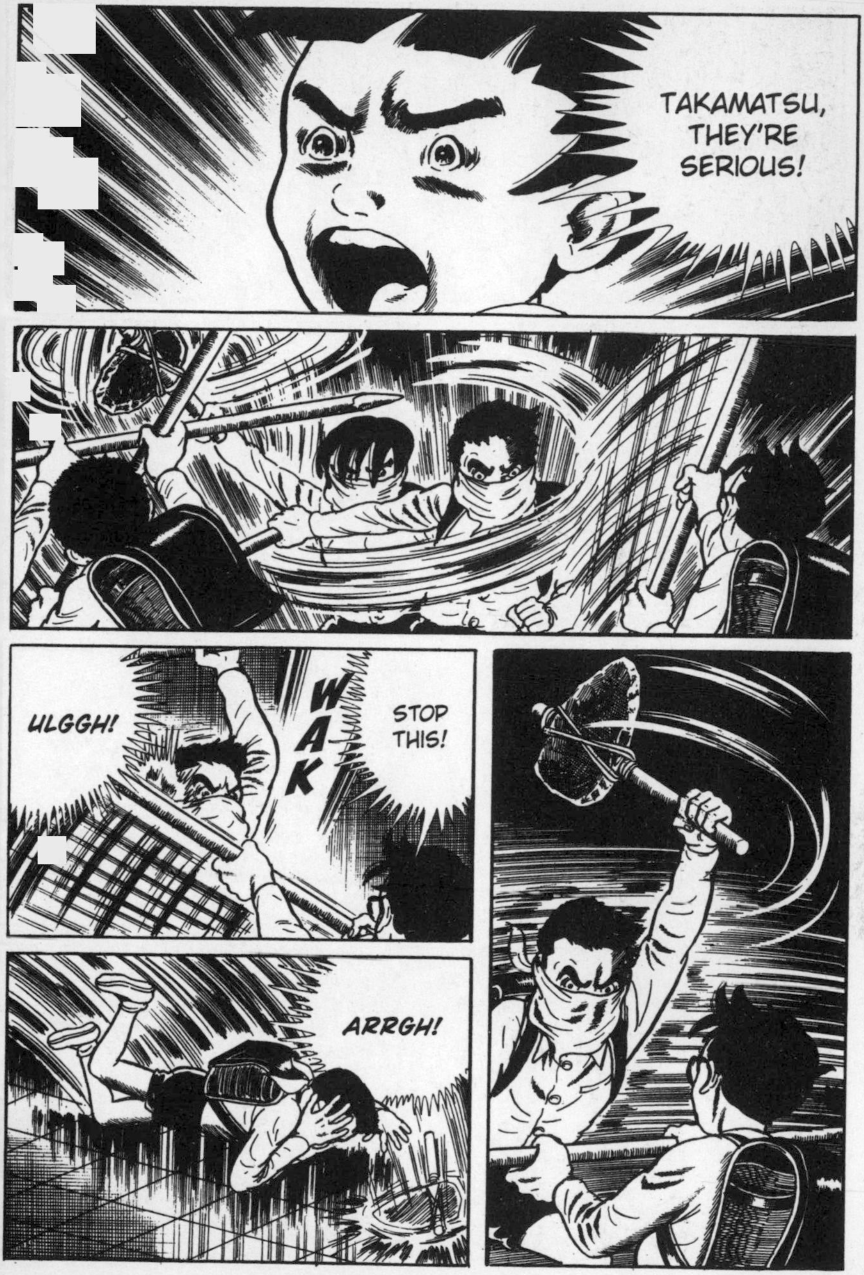
TAKAMATSU, THEY'RE SERIOUS!
STOP THIS!
WAK
ULGGH!
ARRGH!

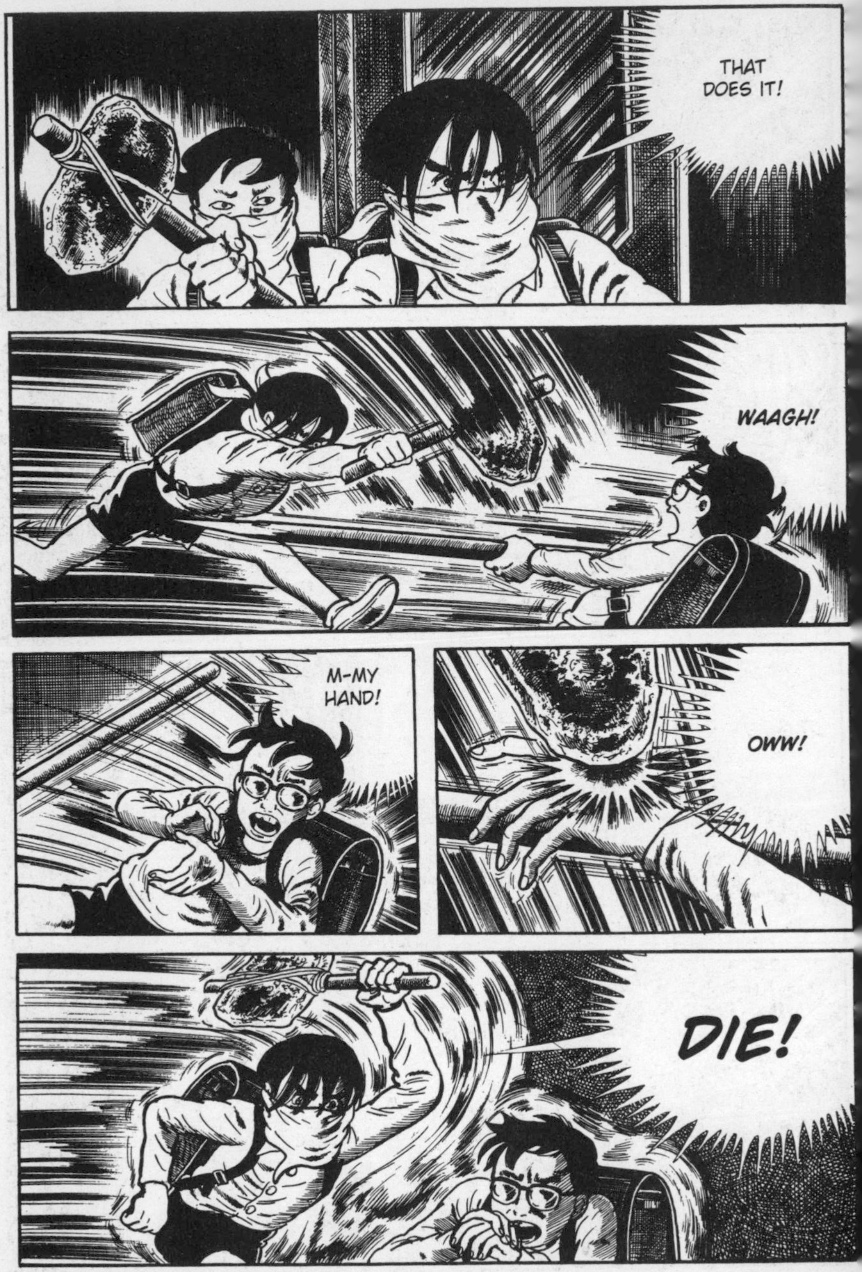
THAT DOES IT!
WAAGH!
OWW!
M-MY HAND!
DIE!

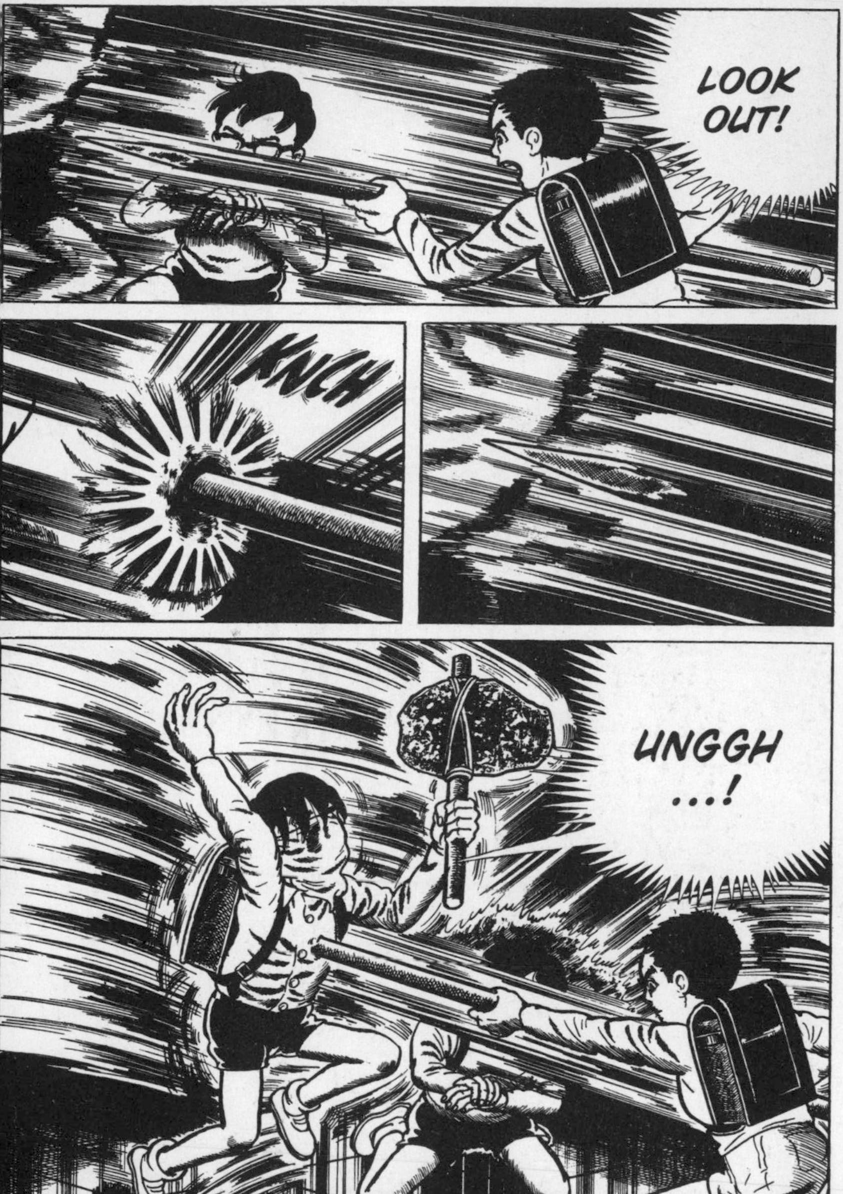
LOOK OUT!
KNCH
UNGGH ...!

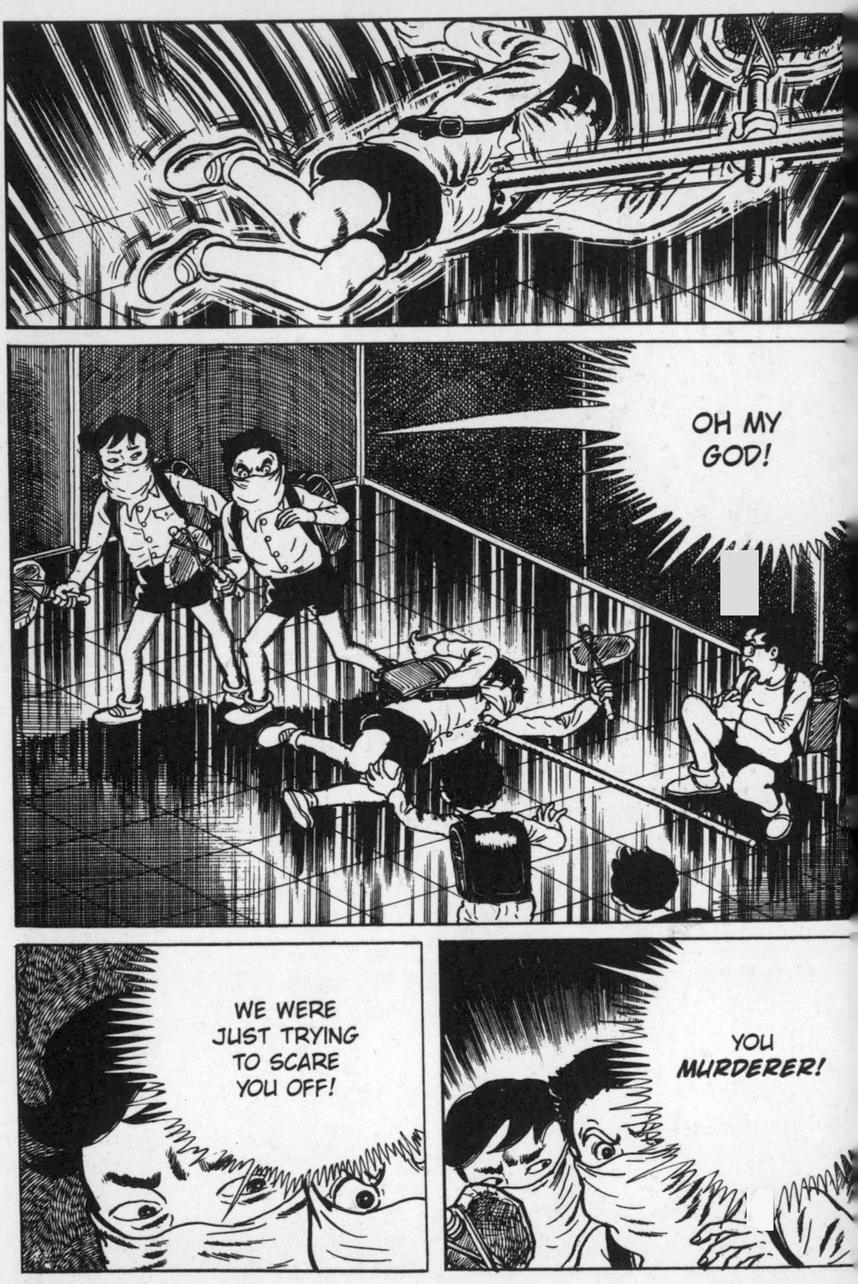
OH MY GOD!
YOU MURDERER!
WE WERE JUST TRYING TO SCARE YOU OFF!

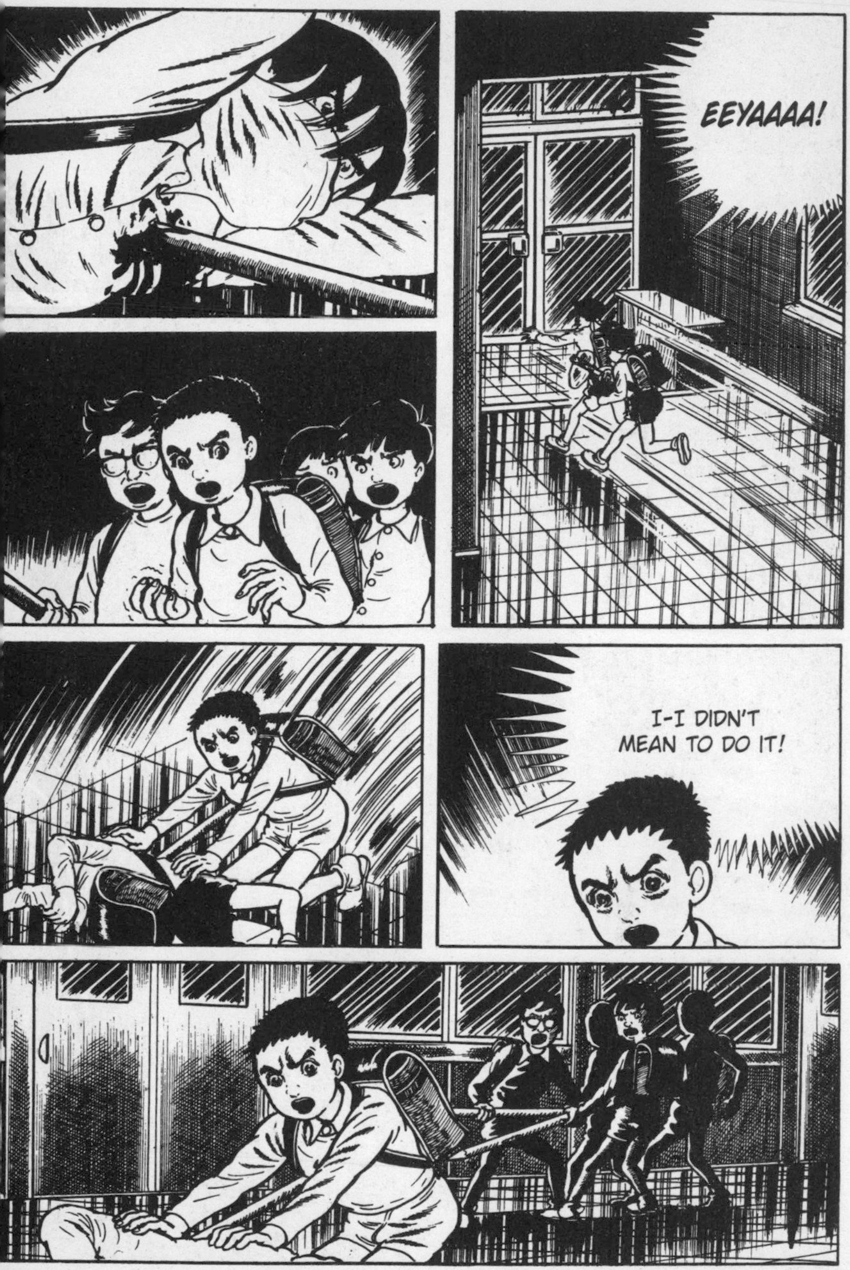
EEYAAAA!
I-I DIDN'T MEAN TO DO IT!

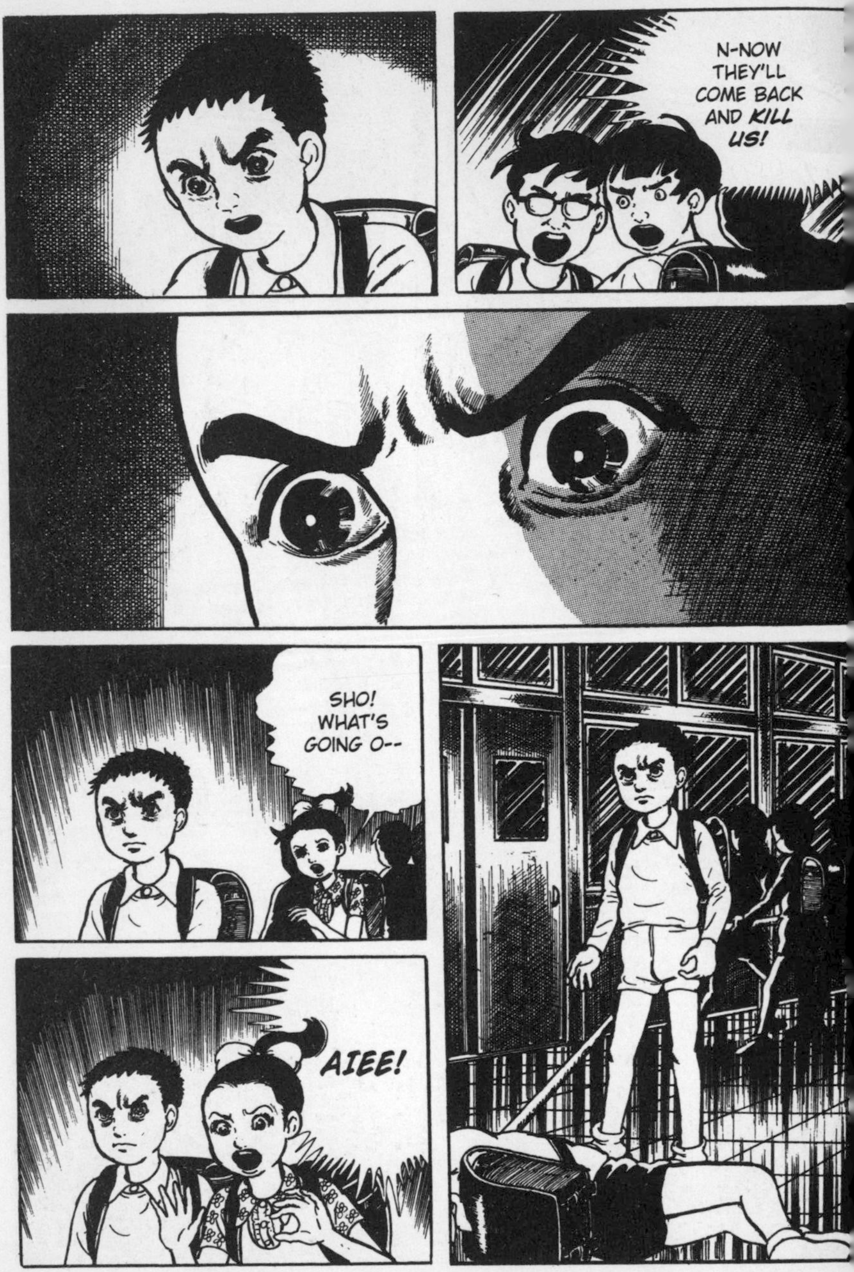
N-NOW THEY'LL COME BACK AND *KILL US!*
SHO! WHAT'S GOING O--
AIEE!

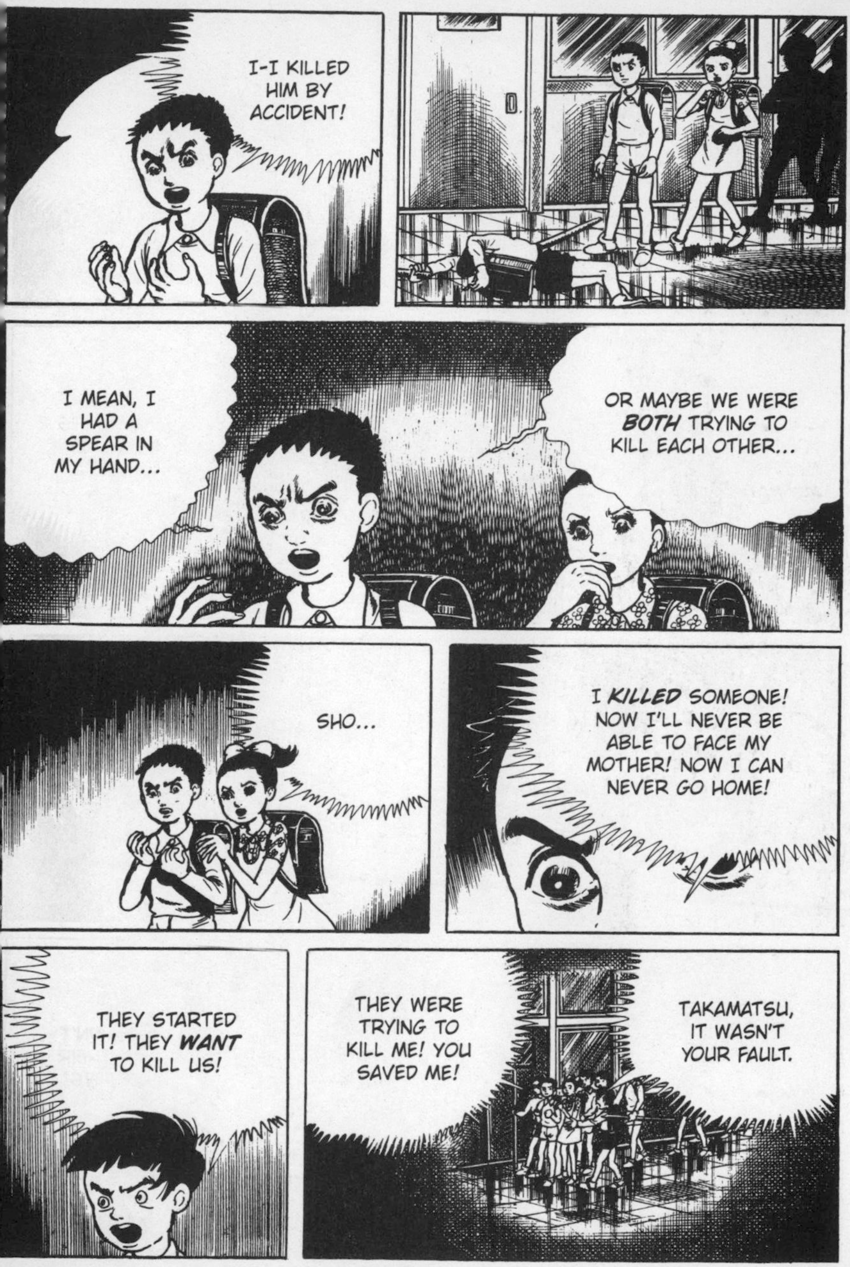
I-I KILLED HIM BY ACCIDENT!
OR MAYBE WE WERE *BOTH* TRYING TO KILL EACH OTHER...
I MEAN, I HAD A SPEAR IN MY HAND...
I *KILLED* SOMEONE! NOW I'LL NEVER BE ABLE TO FACE MY MOTHER! NOW I CAN NEVER GO HOME!
SHO...
TAKAMATSU, IT WASN'T YOUR FAULT.
THEY WERE TRYING TO KILL ME! YOU SAVED ME!
THEY STARTED IT! THEY *WANT* TO KILL US!

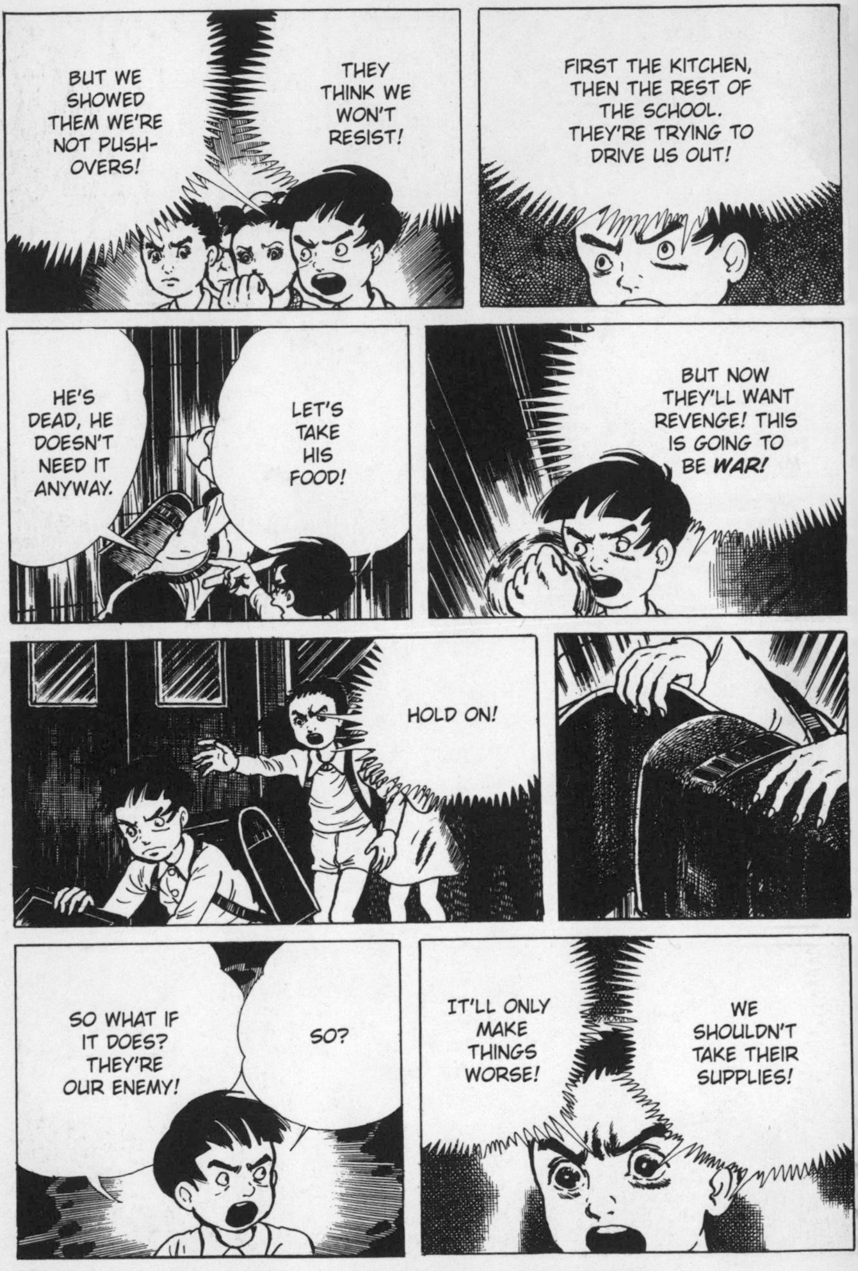
FIRST THE KITCHEN, THEN THE REST OF THE SCHOOL. THEY'RE TRYING TO DRIVE US OUT!
THEY THINK WE WON'T RESIST!
BUT WE SHOWED THEM WE'RE NOT PUSH-OVERS!
BUT NOW THEY'LL WANT REVENGE! THIS IS GOING TO BE *WAR!*
LET'S TAKE HIS FOOD!
HE'S DEAD, HE DOESN'T NEED IT ANYWAY.
HOLD ON!
WE SHOULDN'T TAKE THEIR SUPPLIES!
IT'LL ONLY MAKE THINGS WORSE!
SO?
SO WHAT IF IT DOES? THEY'RE OUR ENEMY!

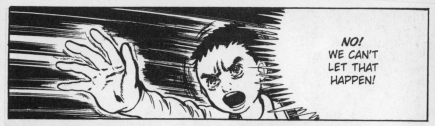

NO!
WE CAN'T
LET THAT
HAPPEN!

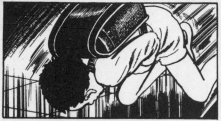

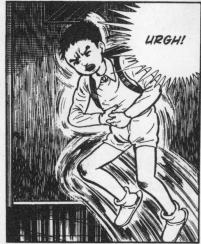

URGH!

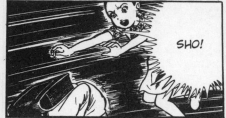

SHO!

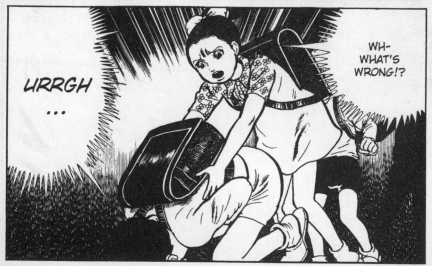

URRGH
...

WH—
WHAT'S
WRONG!?

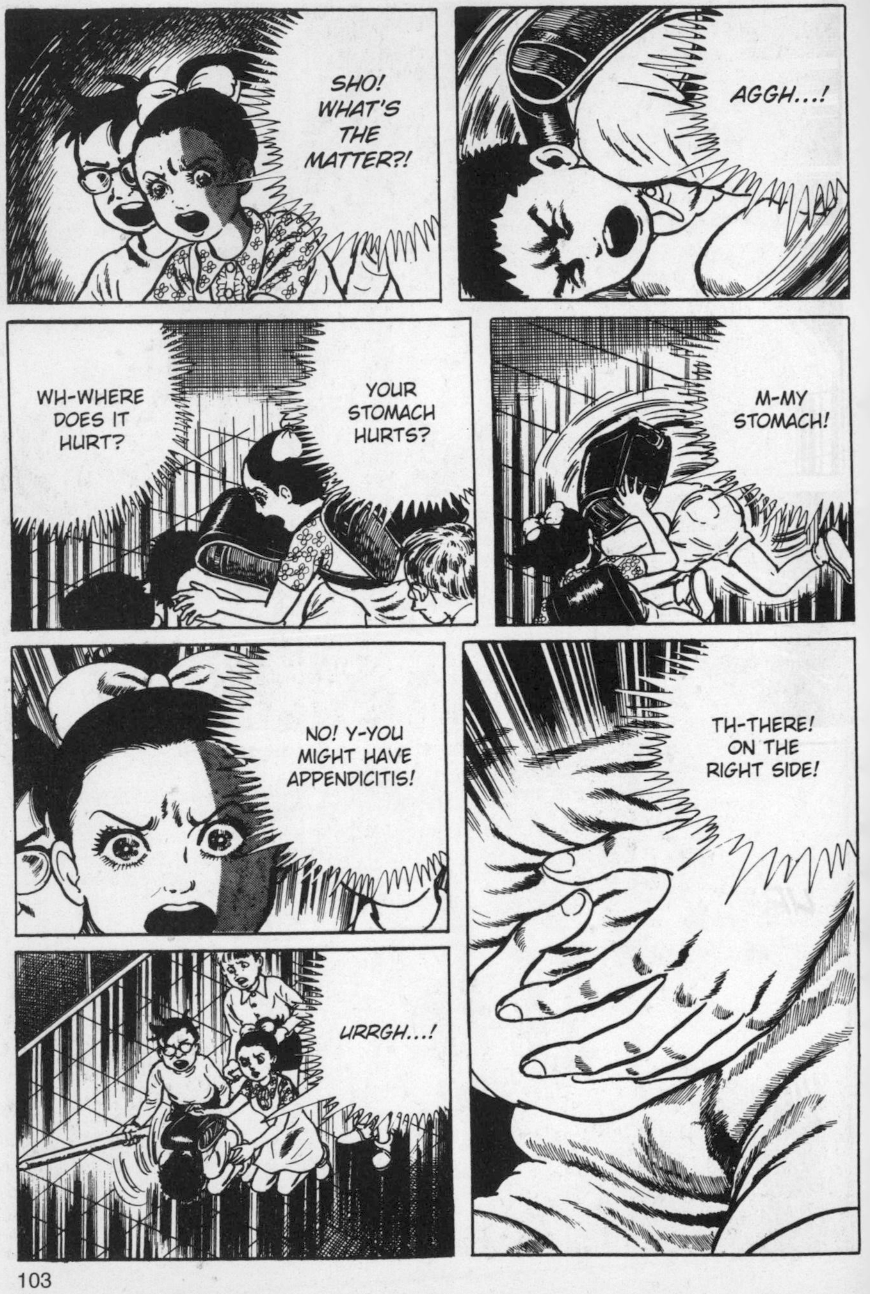
AGGH...!
SHO! WHAT'S THE MATTER?!
M-MY STOMACH!
YOUR STOMACH HURTS?
WH-WHERE DOES IT HURT?
TH-THERE! ON THE RIGHT SIDE!
NO! Y-YOU MIGHT HAVE APPENDICITIS!
URRGH...!

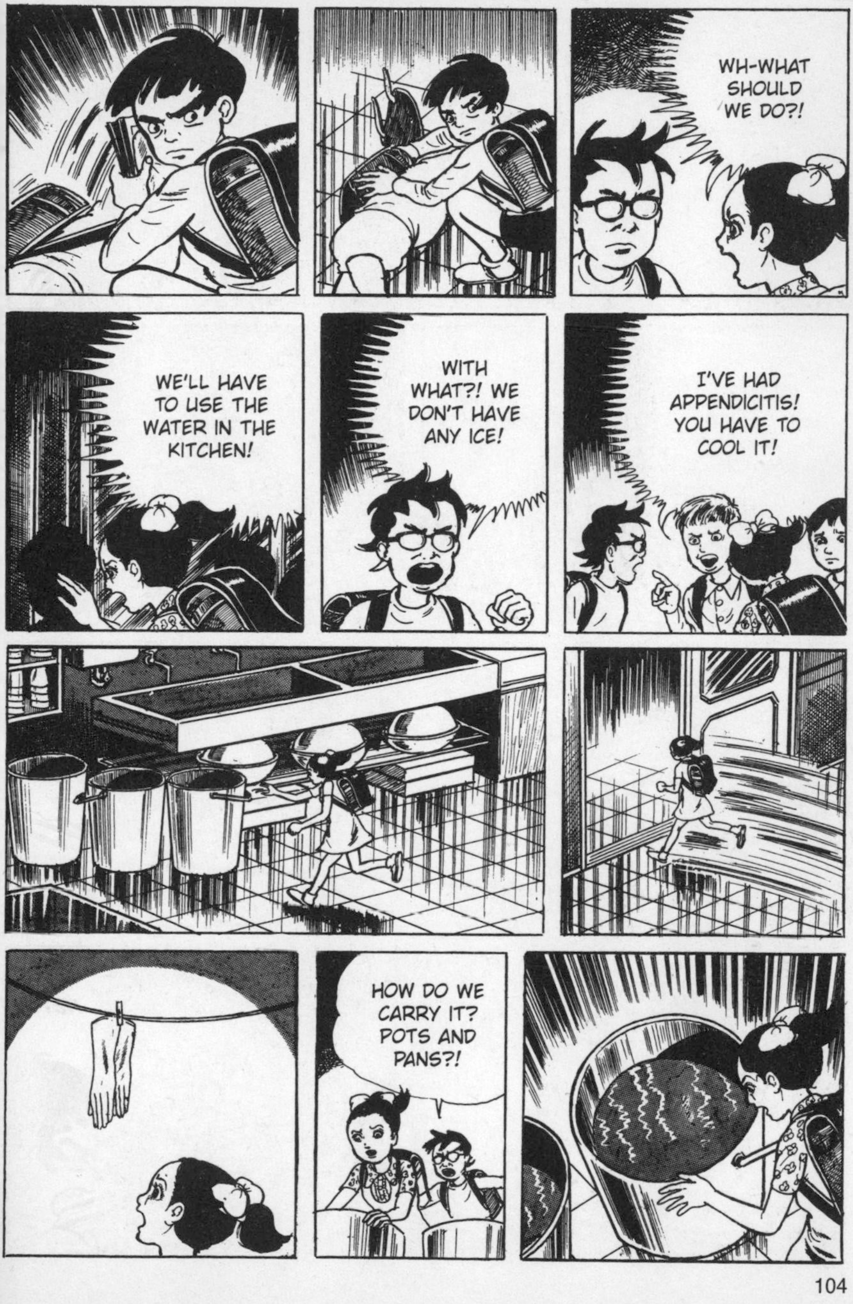
WH-WHAT SHOULD WE DO?!
I'VE HAD APPENDICITIS! YOU HAVE TO COOL IT!
WITH WHAT?! WE DON'T HAVE ANY ICE!
WE'LL HAVE TO USE THE WATER IN THE KITCHEN!
HOW DO WE CARRY IT? POTS AND PANS?!

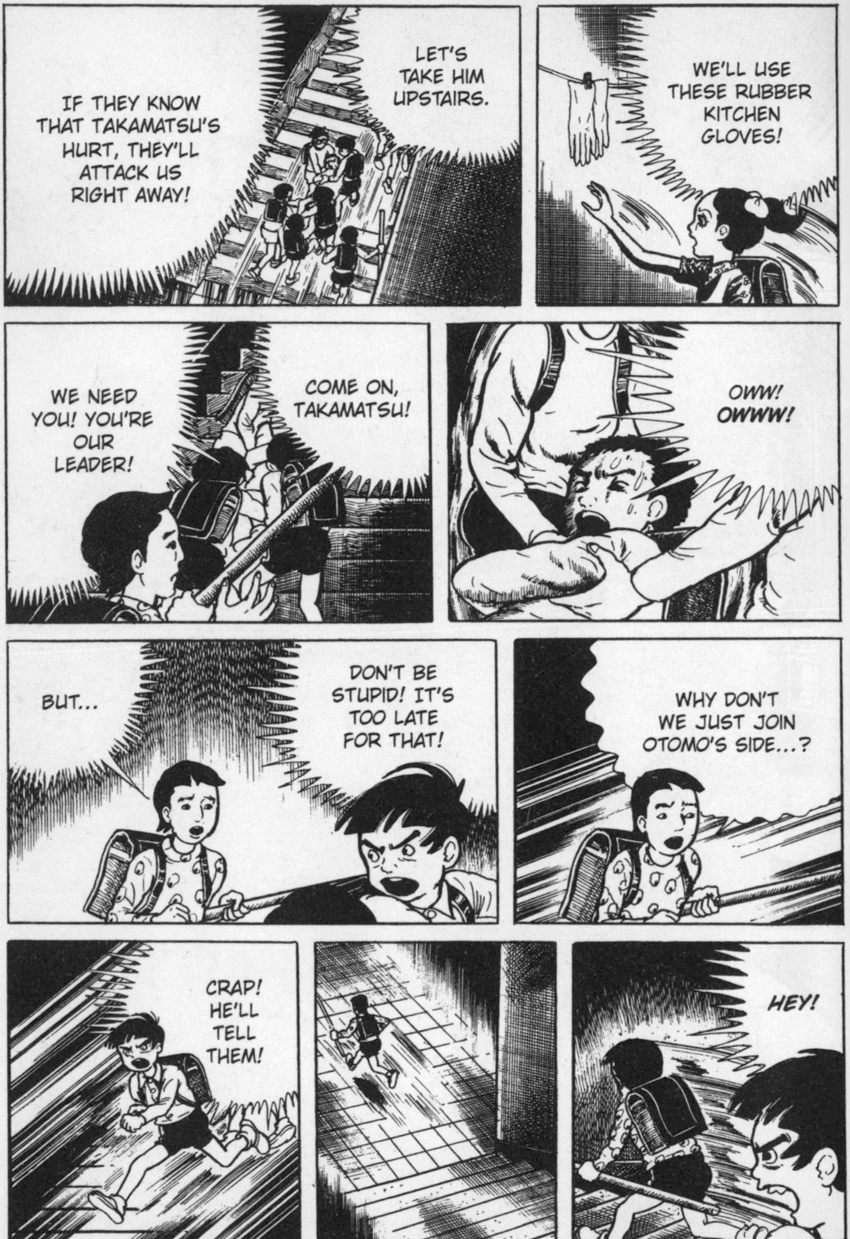
WE'LL USE THESE RUBBER KITCHEN GLOVES!
LET'S TAKE HIM UPSTAIRS.
IF THEY KNOW THAT TAKAMATSU'S HURT, THEY'LL ATTACK US RIGHT AWAY!
OWW! OWWW!
COME ON, TAKAMATSU!
WE NEED YOU! YOU'RE OUR LEADER!
WHY DON'T WE JUST JOIN OTOMO'S SIDE...?
DON'T BE STUPID! IT'S TOO LATE FOR THAT!
BUT...
HEY!
CRAP! HE'LL TELL THEM!

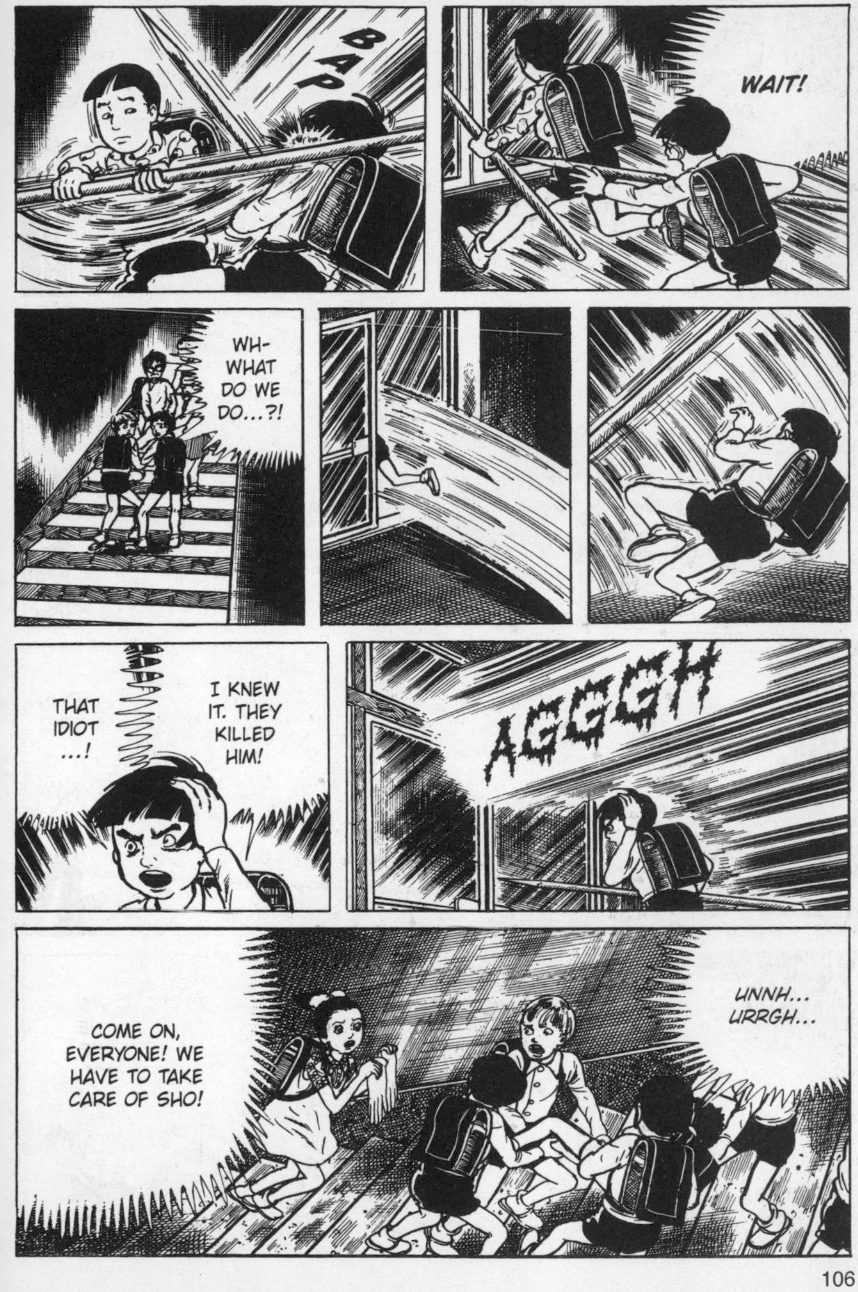
WAIT!
BAP
WH- WHAT DO WE DO...?!
AGGGH
I KNEW IT. THEY KILLED HIM!
THAT IDIOT ...!
UNNH... URRGH...
COME ON, EVERYONE! WE HAVE TO TAKE CARE OF SHO!

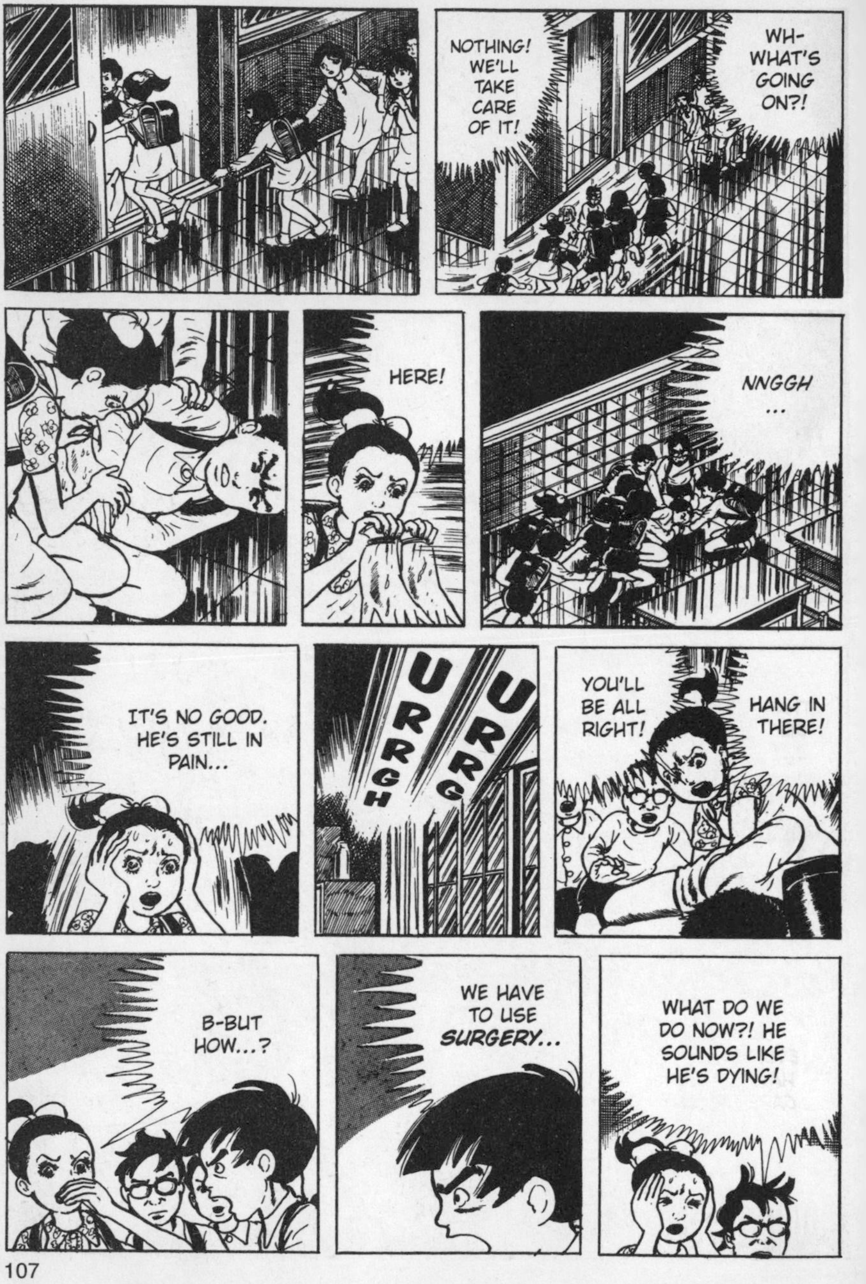
WH-WHAT'S GOING ON?!
NOTHING! WE'LL TAKE CARE OF IT!
NNGGH ...
HERE!
HANG IN THERE!
YOU'LL BE ALL RIGHT!
URRG
URRGH
IT'S NO GOOD. HE'S STILL IN PAIN...
WHAT DO WE DO NOW?! HE SOUNDS LIKE HE'S DYING!
WE HAVE TO USE *SURGERY*...
B-BUT HOW...?

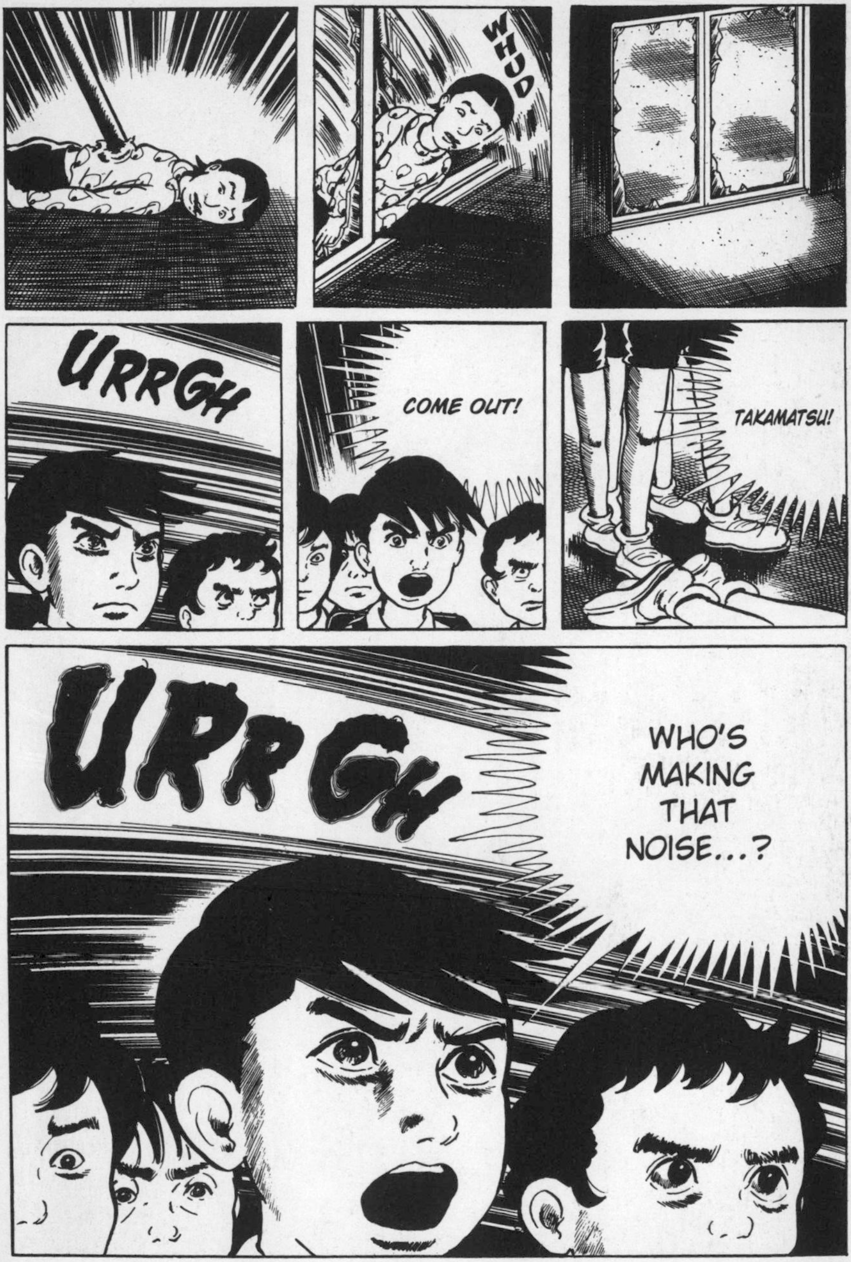
WHUD
TAKAMATSU!
COME OUT!
URRGH
URRGH
WHO'S MAKING THAT NOISE...?

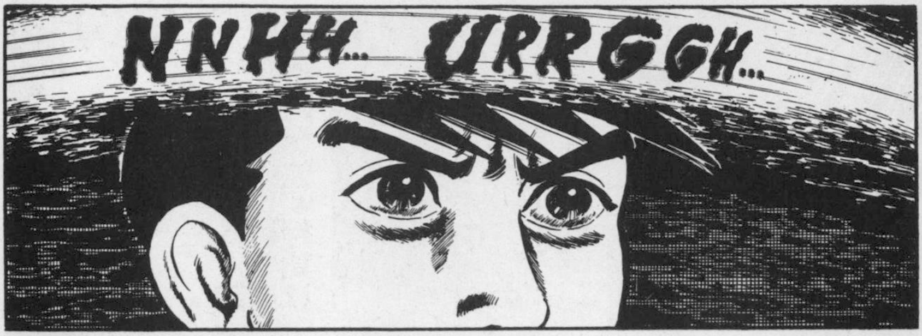
NNHH... URRGGH...
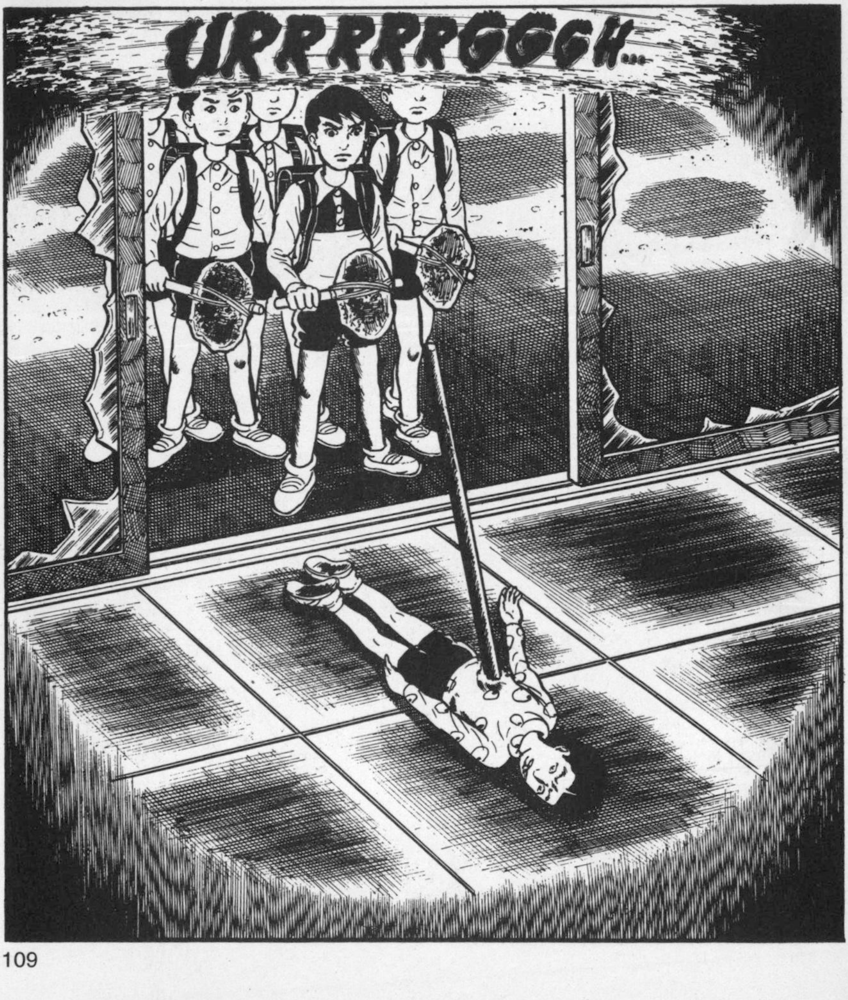
URRRRRGGGH...

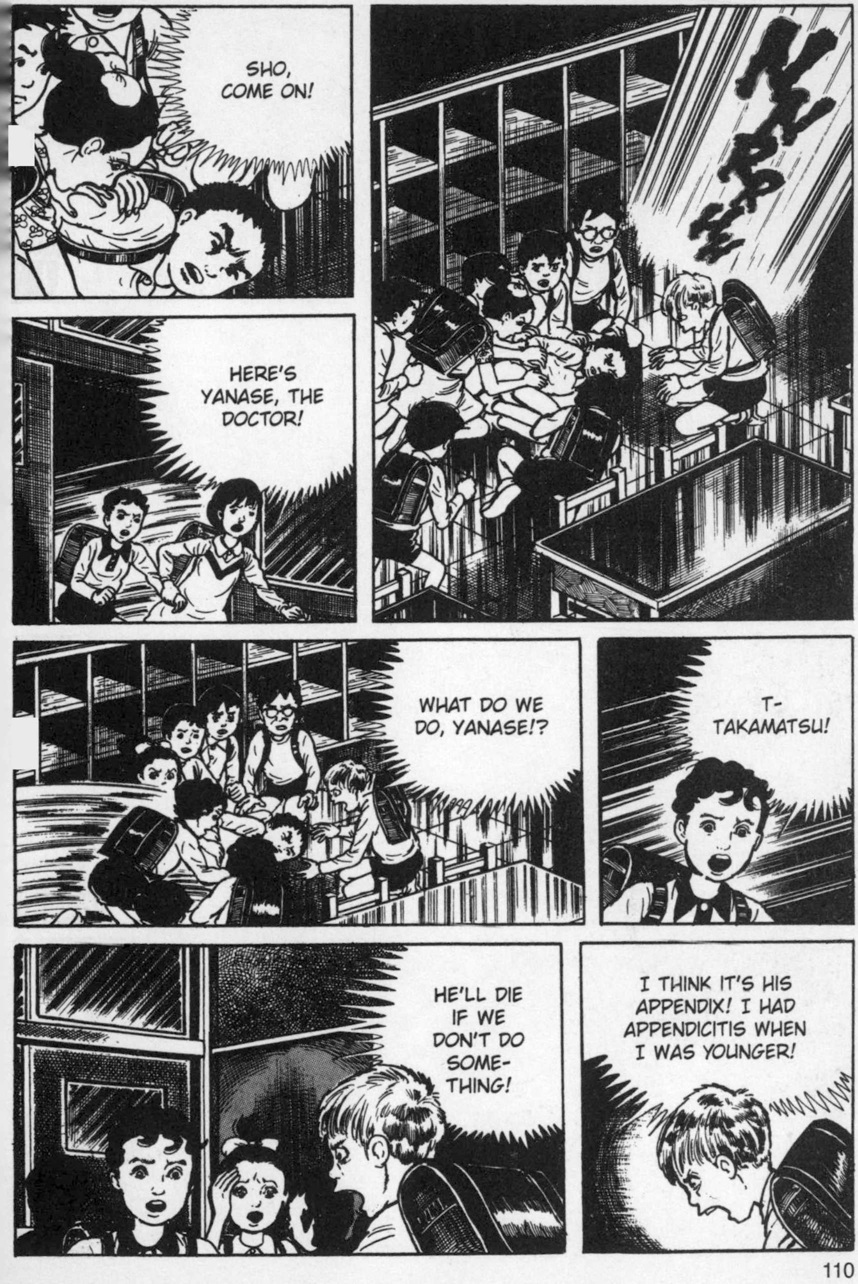
SHO, COME ON!
HERE'S YANASE, THE DOCTOR!
T- TAKAMATSU!
WHAT DO WE DO, YANASE!?
I THINK IT'S HIS APPENDIX! I HAD APPENDICITIS WHEN I WAS YOUNGER!
HE'LL DIE IF WE DON'T DO SOME-THING!

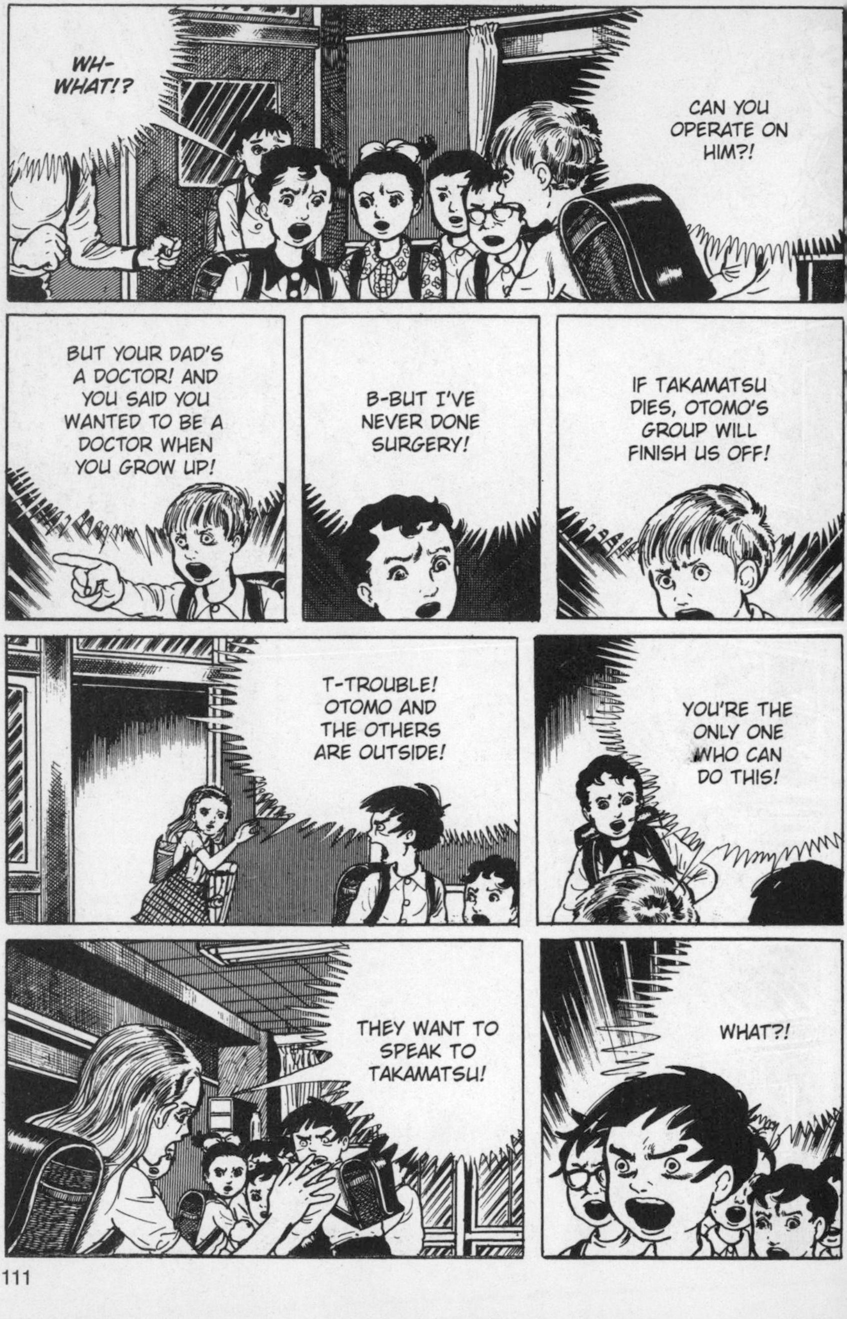
CAN YOU OPERATE ON HIM?!
WH- WHAT!?
IF TAKAMATSU DIES, OTOMO'S GROUP WILL FINISH US OFF!
B-BUT I'VE NEVER DONE SURGERY!
BUT YOUR DAD'S A DOCTOR! AND YOU SAID YOU WANTED TO BE A DOCTOR WHEN YOU GROW UP!
YOU'RE THE ONLY ONE WHO CAN DO THIS!
T-TROUBLE! OTOMO AND THE OTHERS ARE OUTSIDE!
WHAT?!
THEY WANT TO SPEAK TO TAKAMATSU!

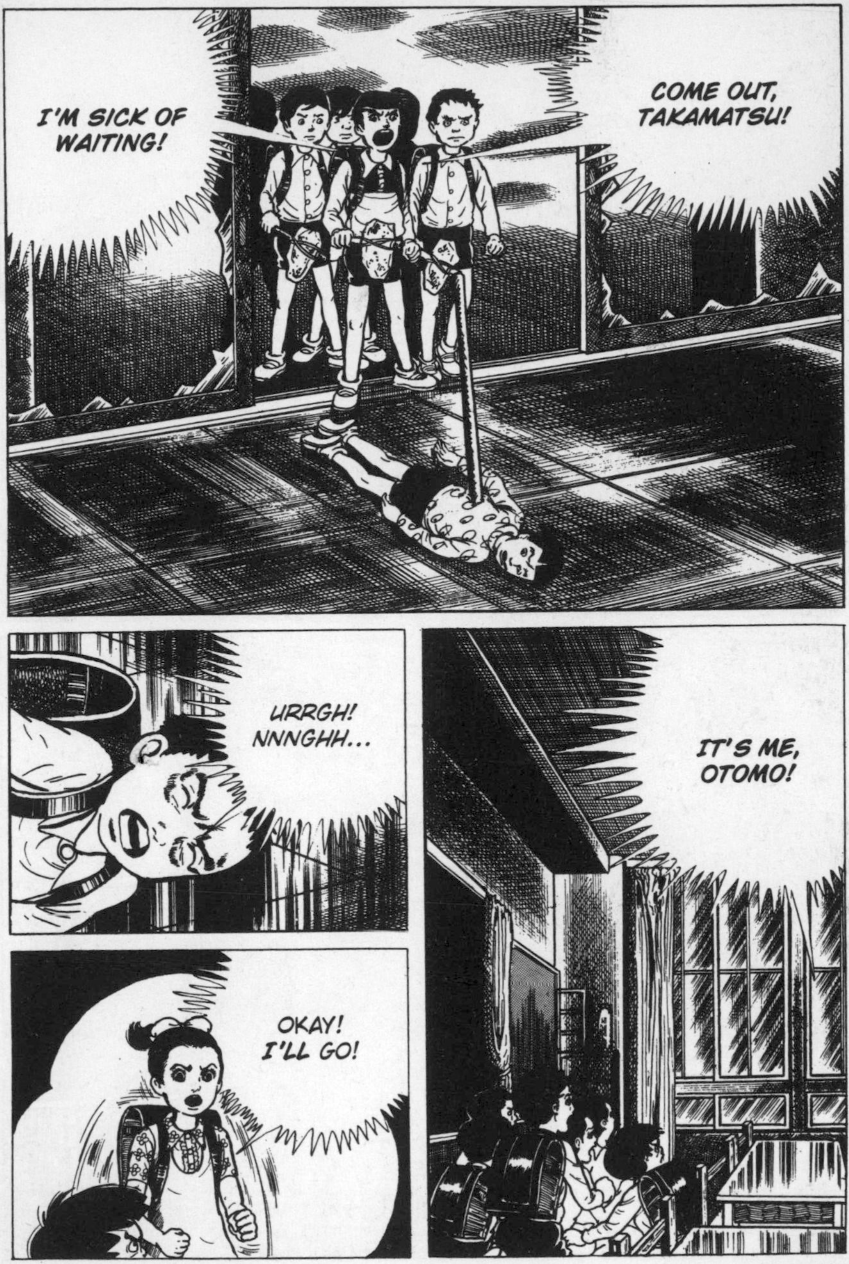
COME OUT, TAKAMATSU!
I'M SICK OF WAITING!
IT'S ME, OTOMO!
URRGH! NNNGHH...
OKAY! I'LL GO!

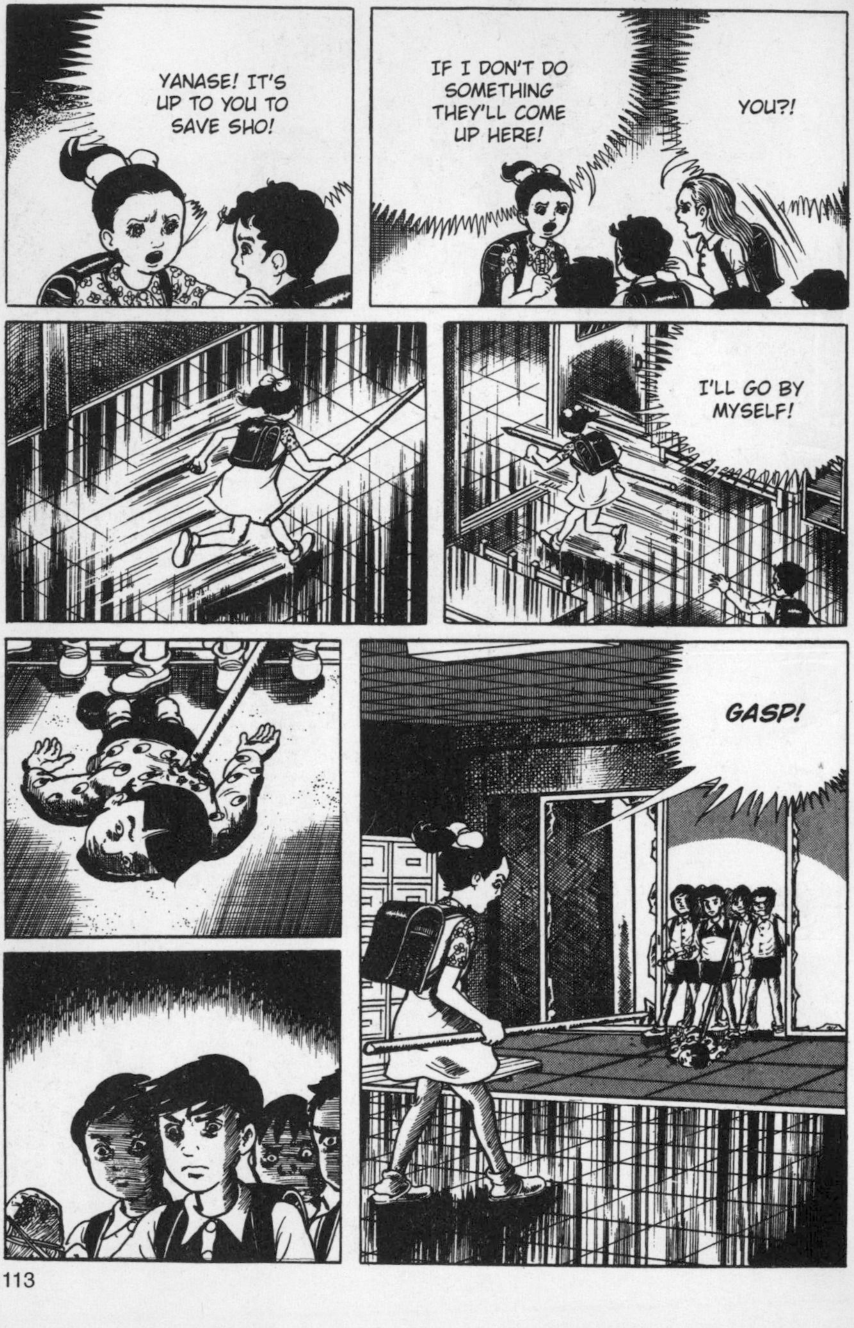
YOU?!
IF I DON'T DO SOMETHING THEY'LL COME UP HERE!
YANASE! IT'S UP TO YOU TO SAVE SHO!
I'LL GO BY MYSELF!
GASP!

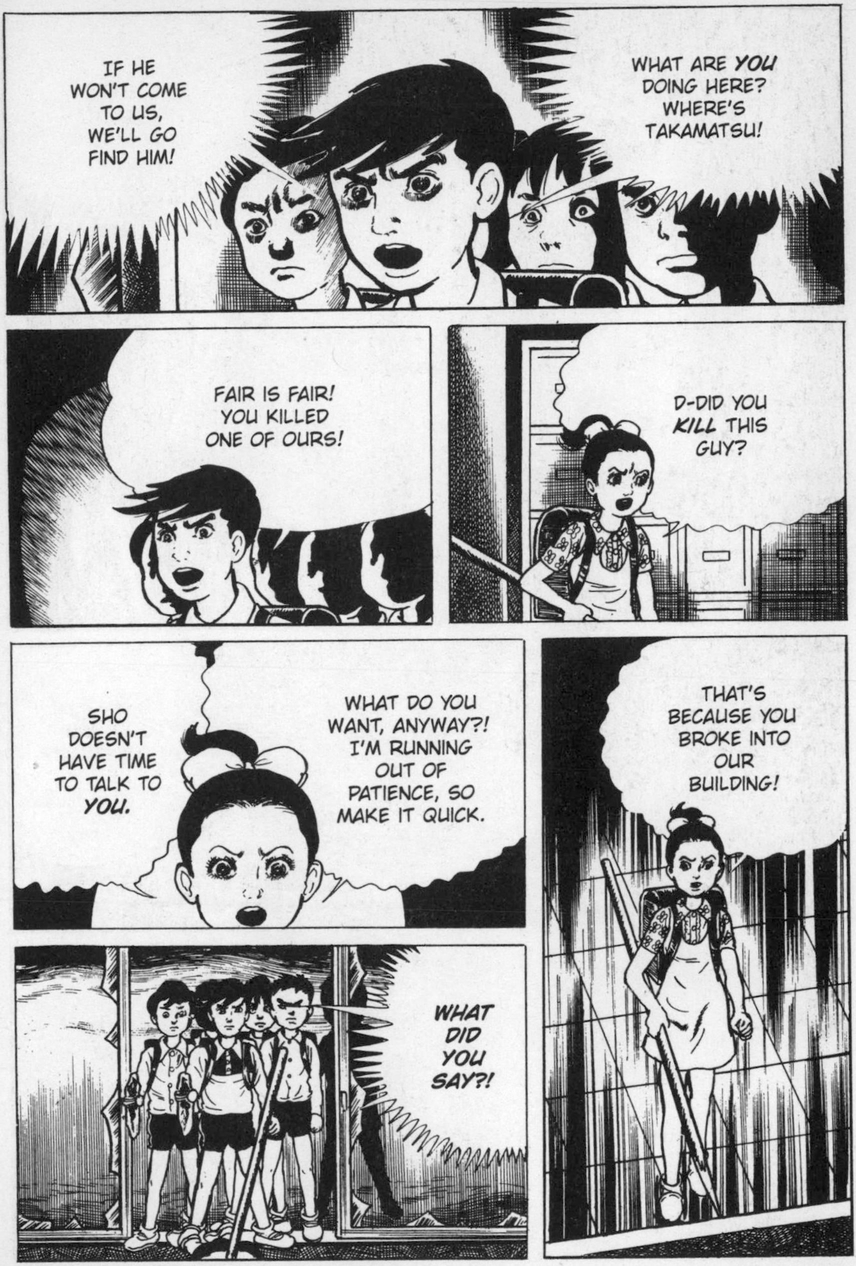
WHAT ARE YOU DOING HERE? WHERE'S TAKAMATSU!
IF HE WON'T COME TO US, WE'LL GO FIND HIM!
D-DID YOU KILL THIS GUY?
FAIR IS FAIR! YOU KILLED ONE OF OURS!
THAT'S BECAUSE YOU BROKE INTO OUR BUILDING!
WHAT DO YOU WANT, ANYWAY?! I'M RUNNING OUT OF PATIENCE, SO MAKE IT QUICK.
SHO DOESN'T HAVE TIME TO TALK TO YOU.
WHAT DID YOU SAY?!

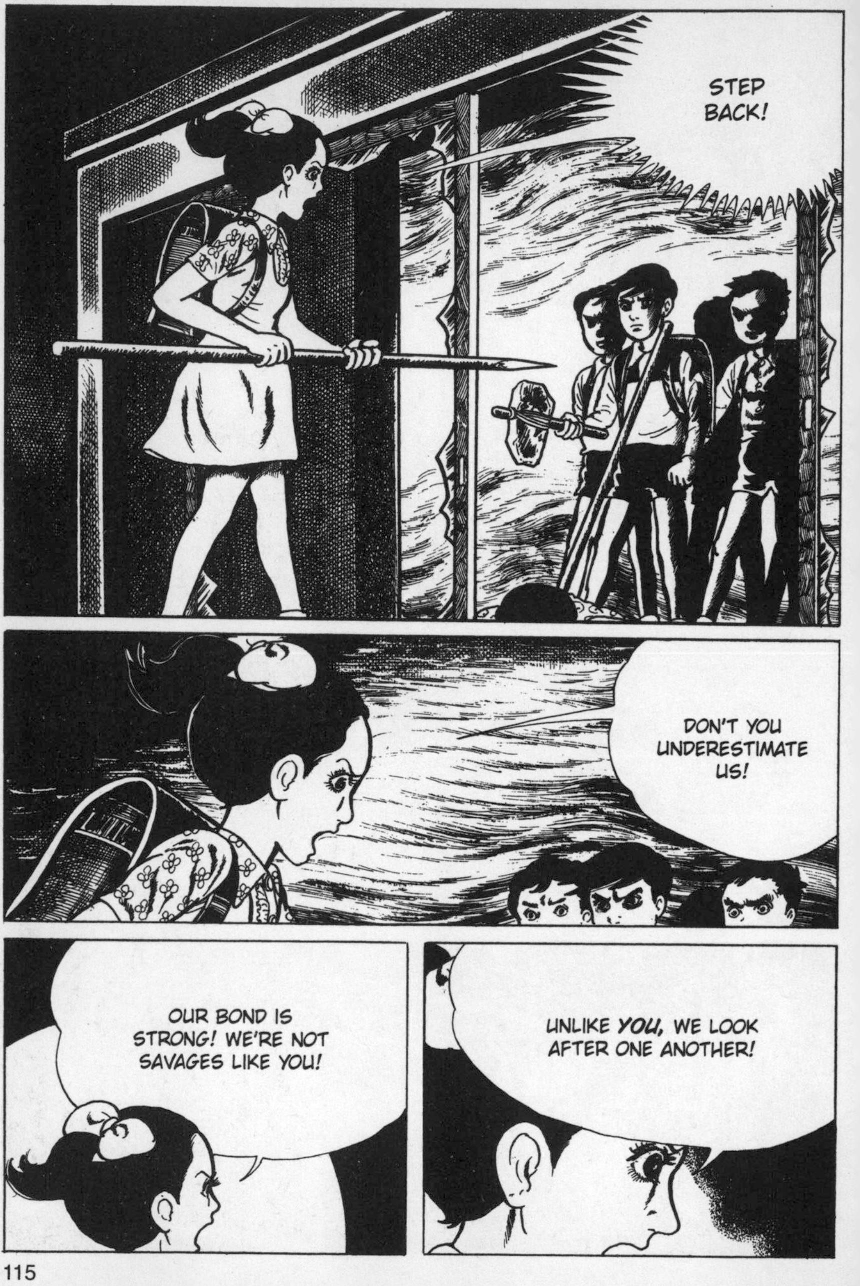
STEP BACK!
DON'T YOU UNDERESTIMATE US!
UNLIKE *YOU*, WE LOOK AFTER ONE ANOTHER!
OUR BOND IS STRONG! WE'RE NOT SAVAGES LIKE YOU!

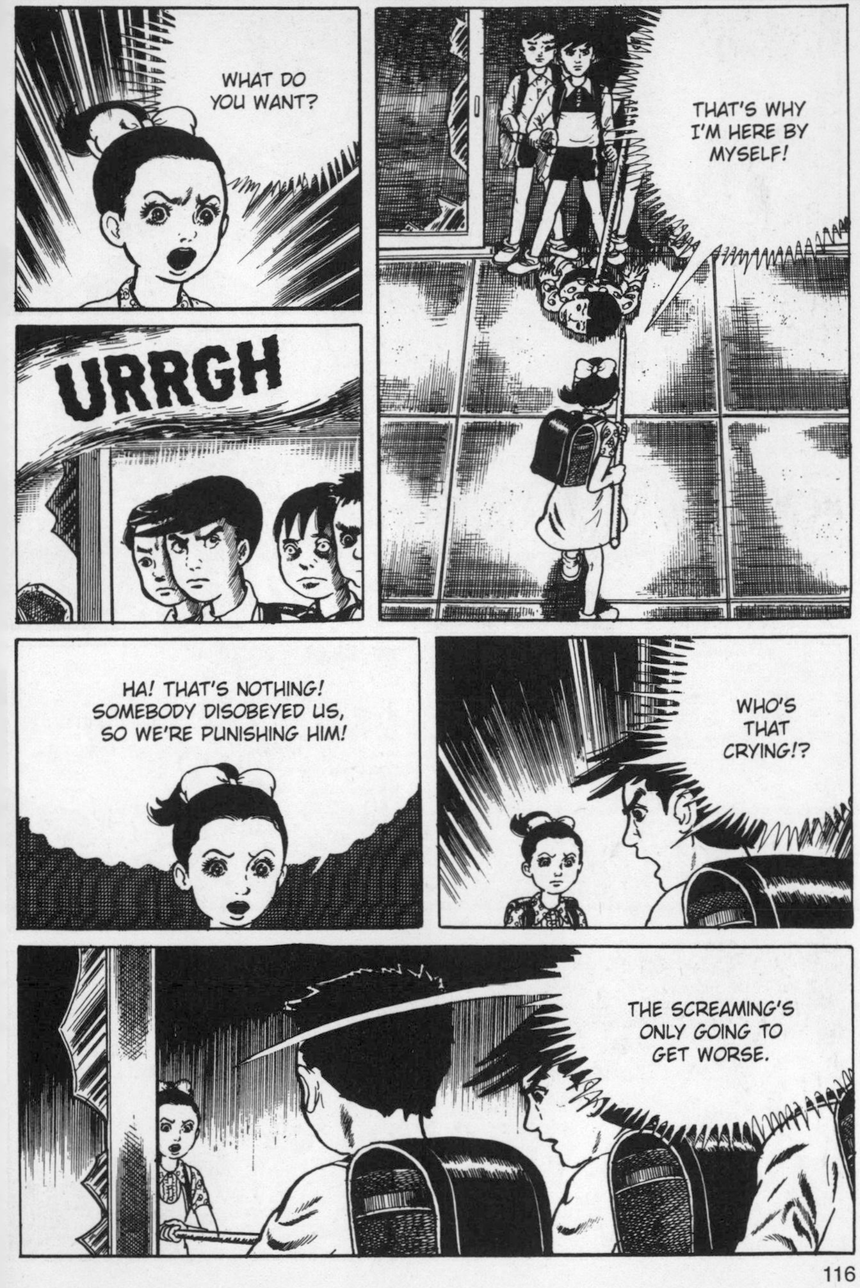
THAT'S WHY I'M HERE BY MYSELF!
WHAT DO YOU WANT?
URRGH
WHO'S THAT CRYING!?
HA! THAT'S NOTHING! SOMEBODY DISOBEYED US, SO WE'RE PUNISHING HIM!
THE SCREAMING'S ONLY GOING TO GET WORSE.

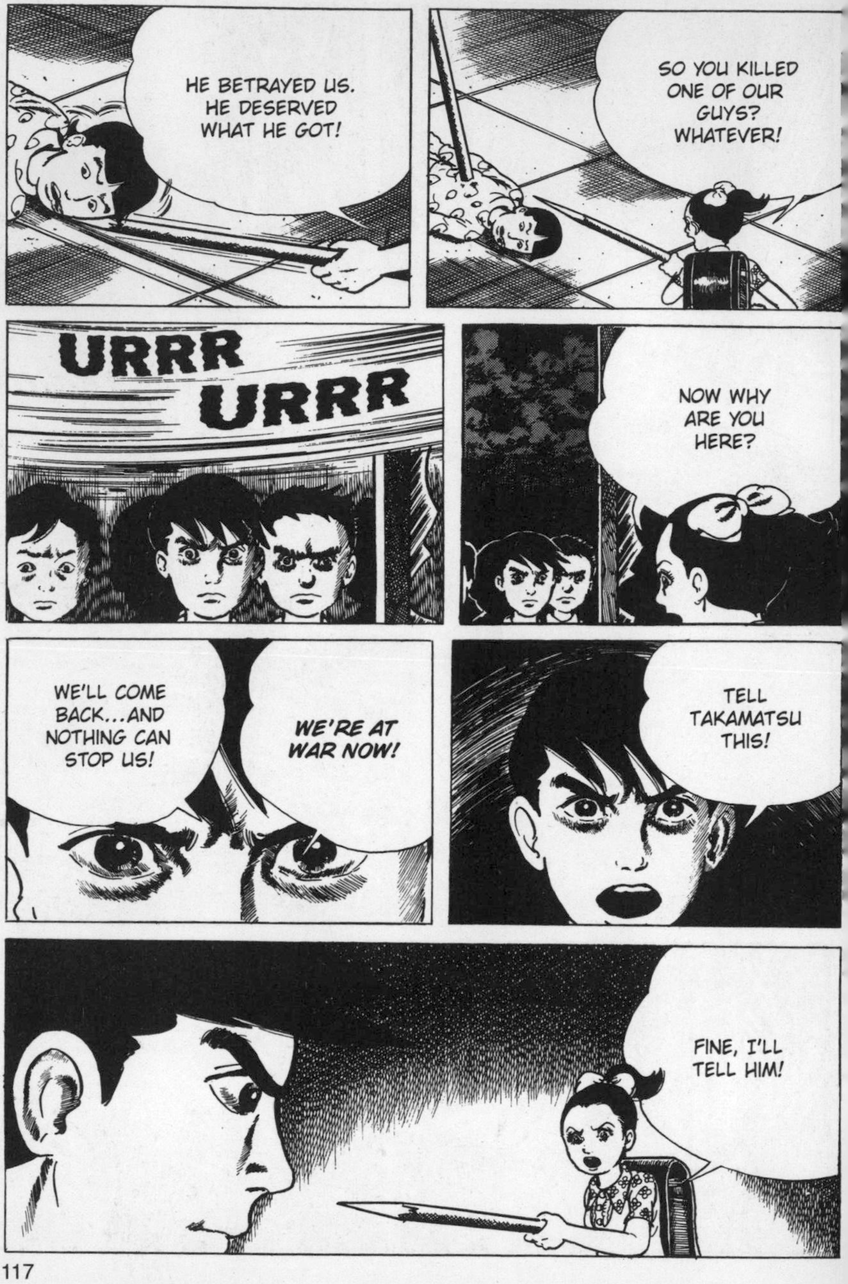
SO YOU KILLED ONE OF OUR GUYS? WHATEVER!
HE BETRAYED US. HE DESERVED WHAT HE GOT!
NOW WHY ARE YOU HERE?
URRR URRR
TELL TAKAMATSU THIS!
WE'RE AT WAR NOW!
WE'LL COME BACK...AND NOTHING CAN STOP US!
FINE, I'LL TELL HIM!

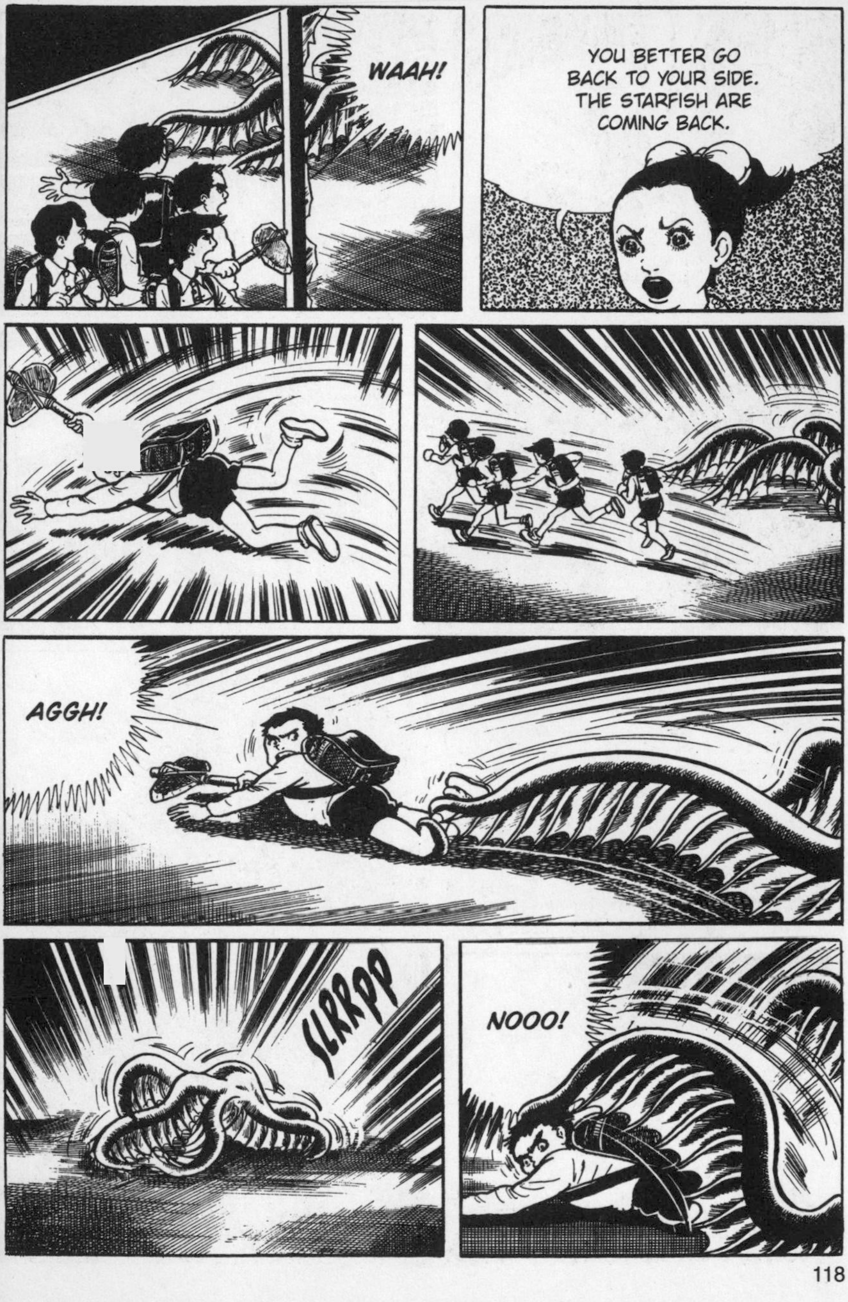
YOU BETTER GO BACK TO YOUR SIDE. THE STARFISH ARE COMING BACK.
WAAH!
AGGH!
NOOO!
SLRRPP

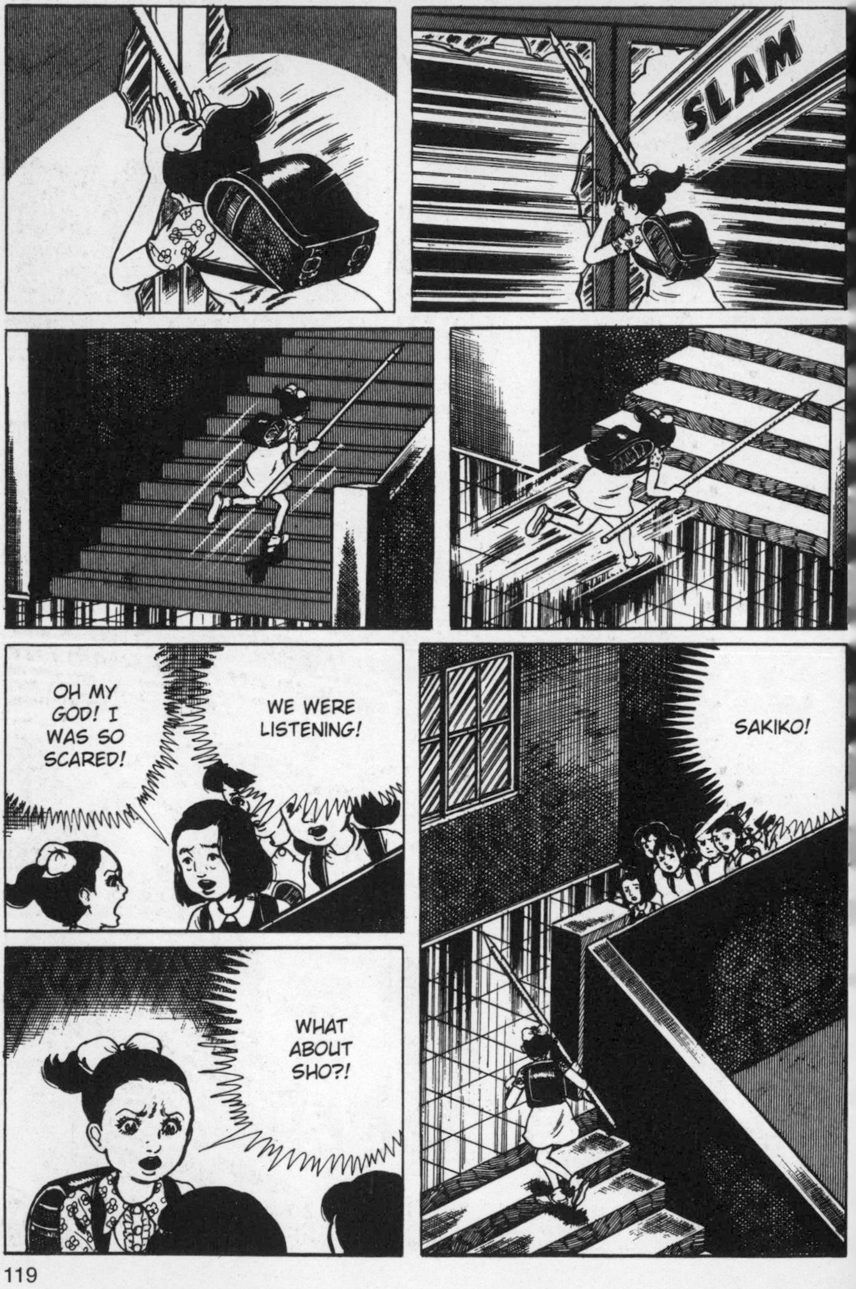
SLAM
SAKIKO!
WE WERE LISTENING!
OH MY GOD! I WAS SO SCARED!
WHAT ABOUT SHO?!

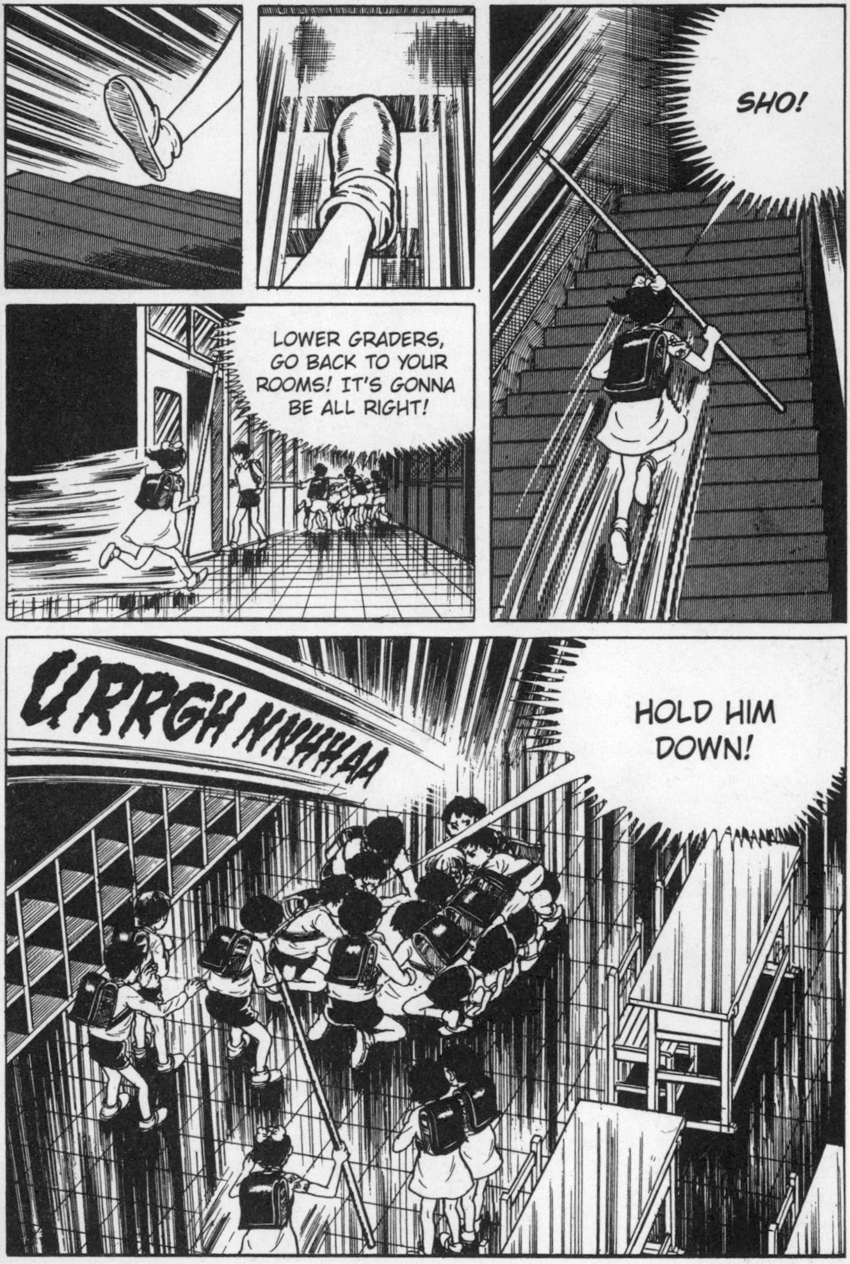
SHO!
LOWER GRADERS, GO BACK TO YOUR ROOMS! IT'S GONNA BE ALL RIGHT!
HOLD HIM DOWN!
URRGH NNHHAA

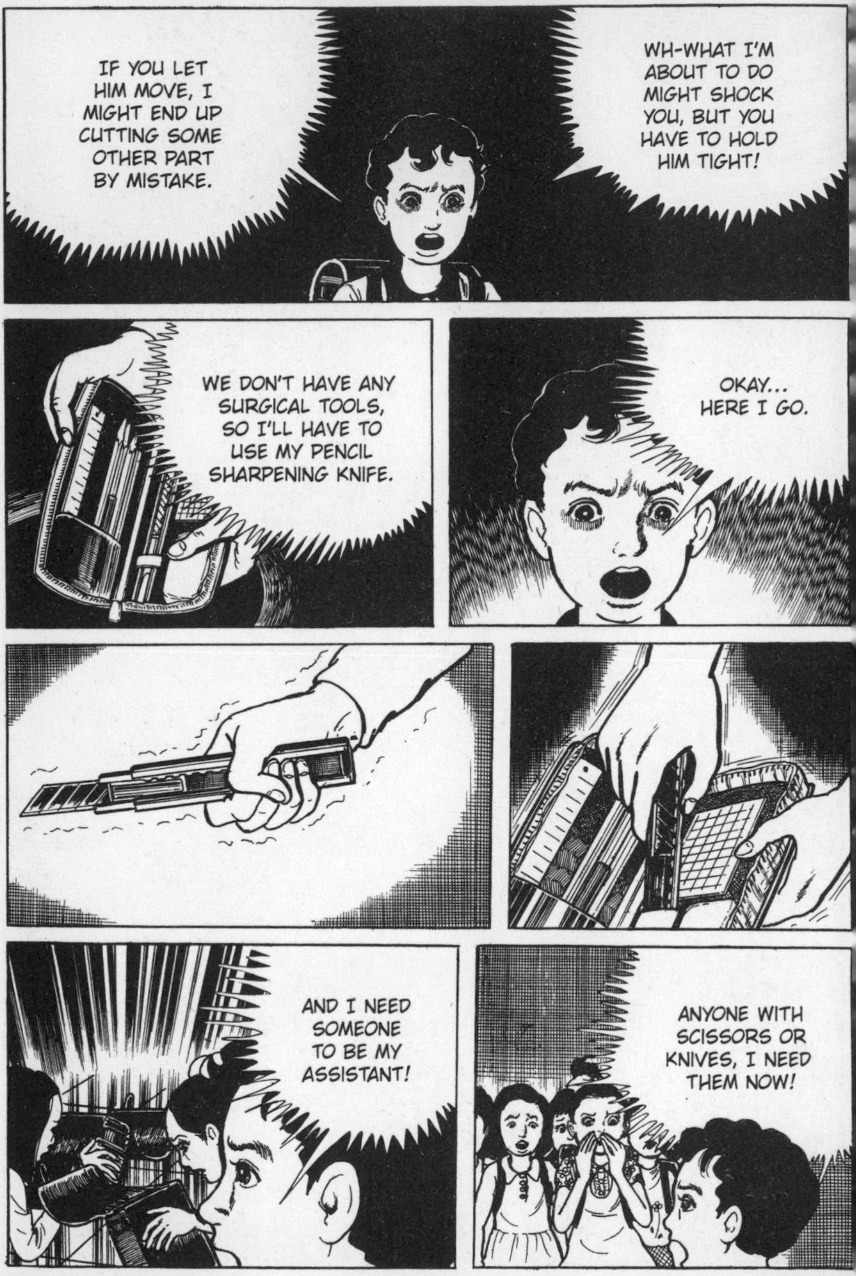
WH-WHAT I'M ABOUT TO DO MIGHT SHOCK YOU, BUT YOU HAVE TO HOLD HIM TIGHT!
IF YOU LET HIM MOVE, I MIGHT END UP CUTTING SOME OTHER PART BY MISTAKE.
OKAY... HERE I GO.
WE DON'T HAVE ANY SURGICAL TOOLS, SO I'LL HAVE TO USE MY PENCIL SHARPENING KNIFE.
ANYONE WITH SCISSORS OR KNIVES, I NEED THEM NOW!
AND I NEED SOMEONE TO BE MY ASSISTANT!

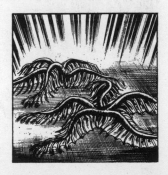

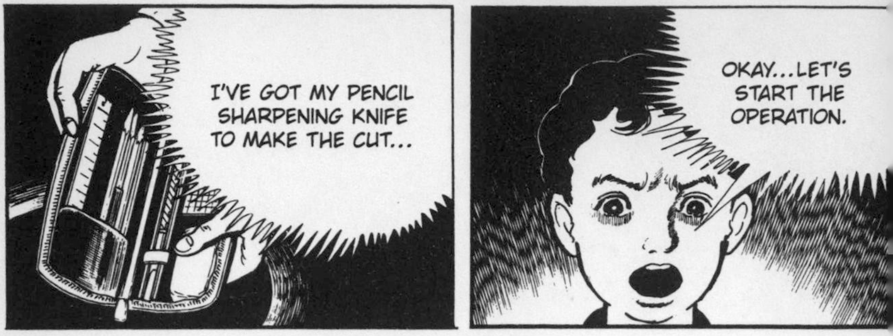
OKAY...LET'S START THE OPERATION.
I'VE GOT MY PENCIL SHARPENING KNIFE TO MAKE THE CUT...

CHAPTER 36: THE OPERATION

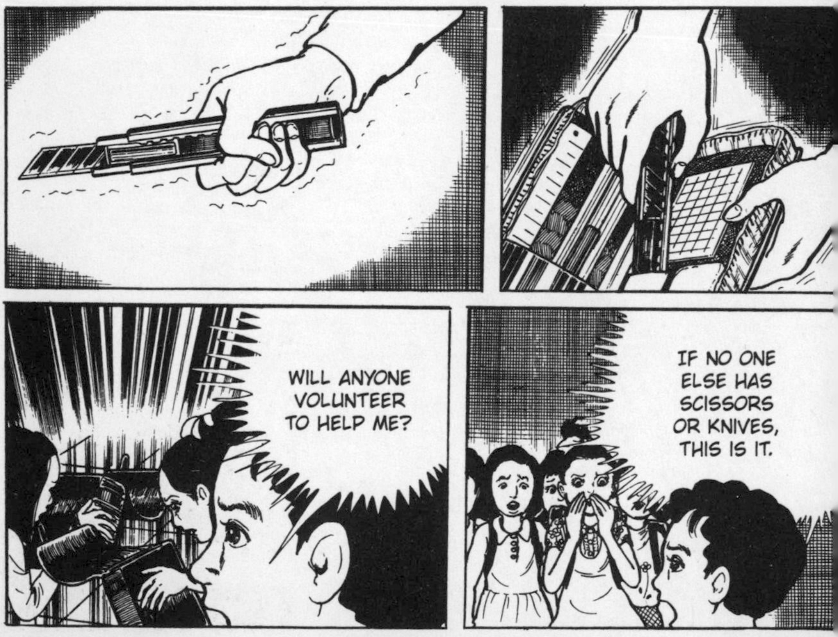
IF NO ONE ELSE HAS SCISSORS OR KNIVES, THIS IS IT.
WILL ANYONE VOLUNTEER TO HELP ME?

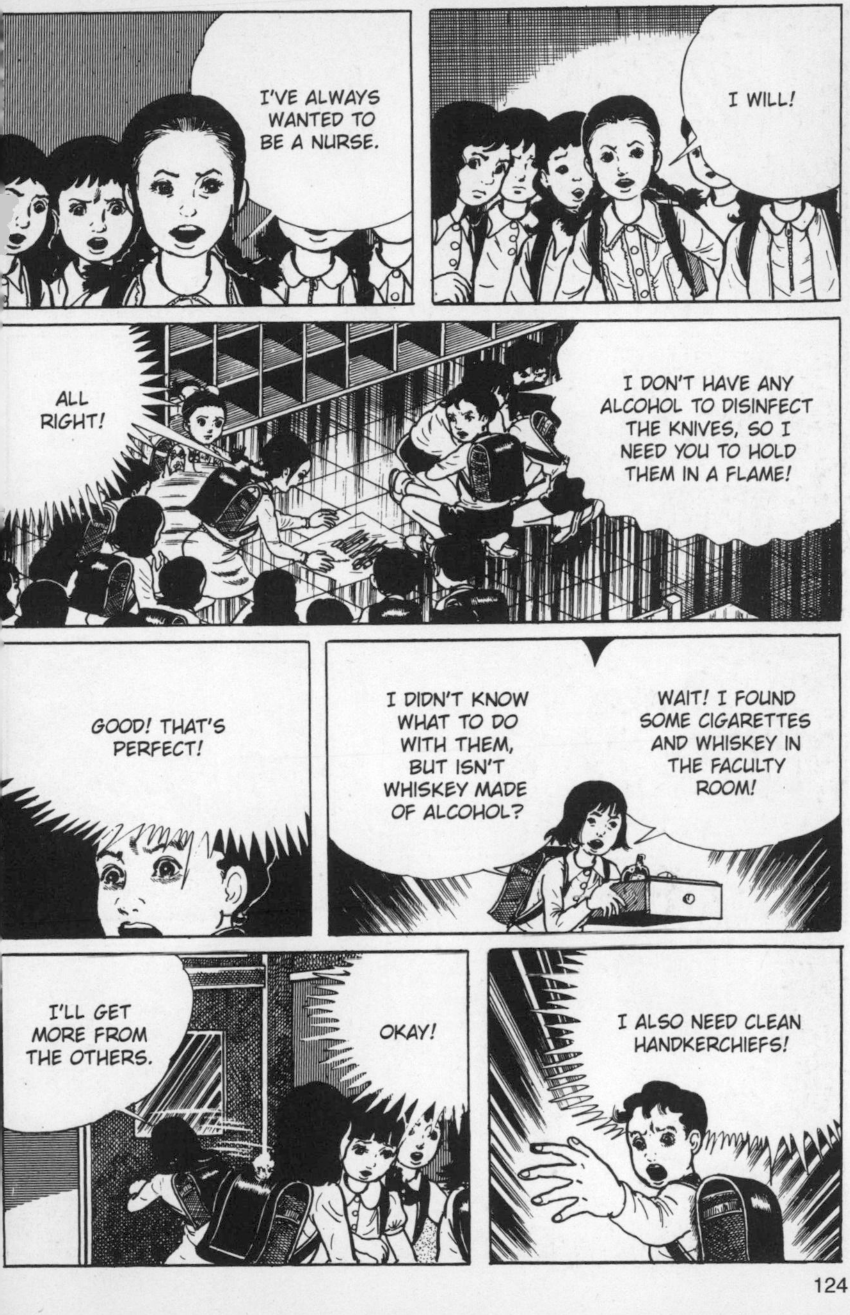
I WILL!
I'VE ALWAYS WANTED TO BE A NURSE.
I DON'T HAVE ANY ALCOHOL TO DISINFECT THE KNIVES, SO I NEED YOU TO HOLD THEM IN A FLAME!
ALL RIGHT!
WAIT! I FOUND SOME CIGARETTES AND WHISKEY IN THE FACULTY ROOM!
I DIDN'T KNOW WHAT TO DO WITH THEM, BUT ISN'T WHISKEY MADE OF ALCOHOL?
GOOD! THAT'S PERFECT!
I ALSO NEED CLEAN HANDKERCHIEFS!
OKAY!
I'LL GET MORE FROM THE OTHERS.

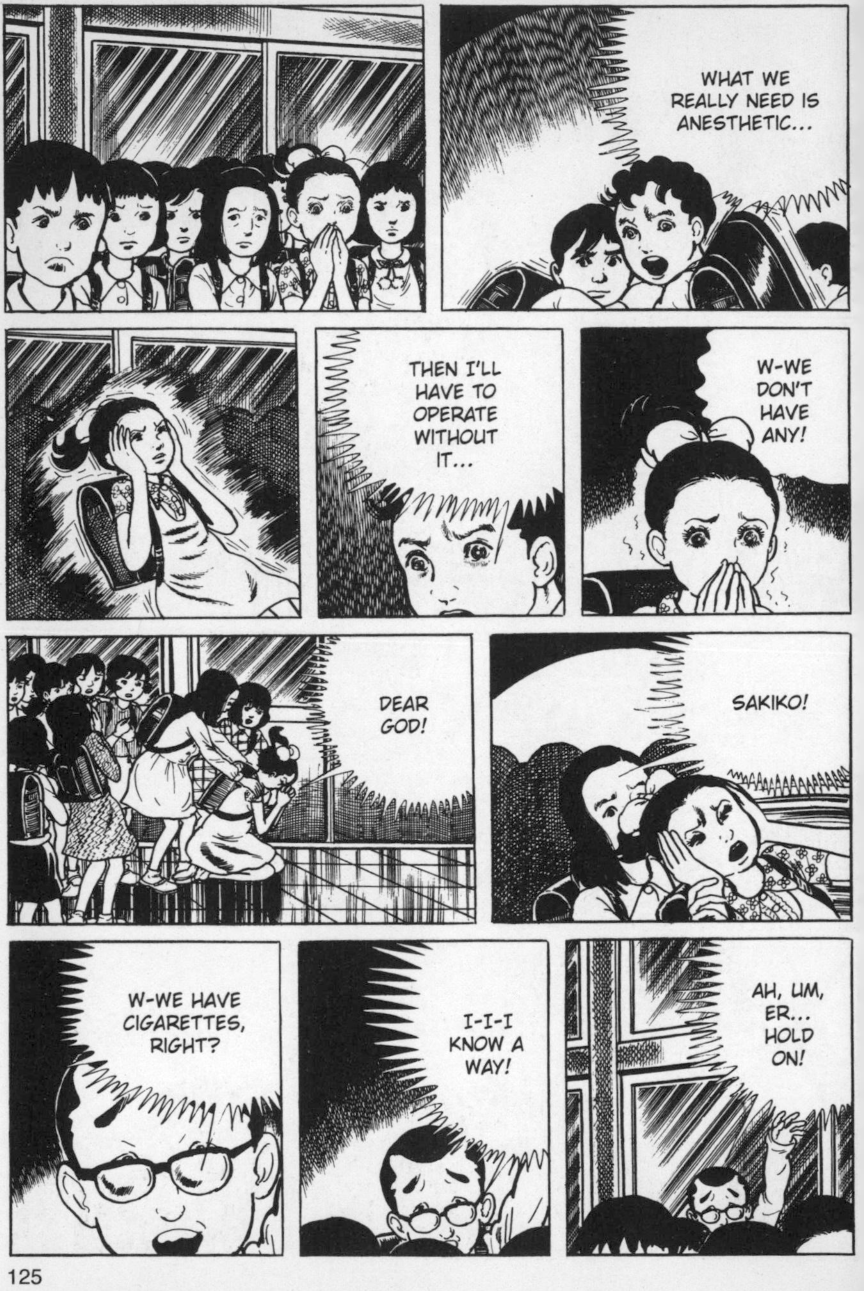
WHAT WE REALLY NEED IS ANESTHETIC...
W-WE DON'T HAVE ANY!
THEN I'LL HAVE TO OPERATE WITHOUT IT...
SAKIKO!
DEAR GOD!
AH, UM, ER... HOLD ON!
I-I-I KNOW A WAY!
W-WE HAVE CIGARETTES, RIGHT?

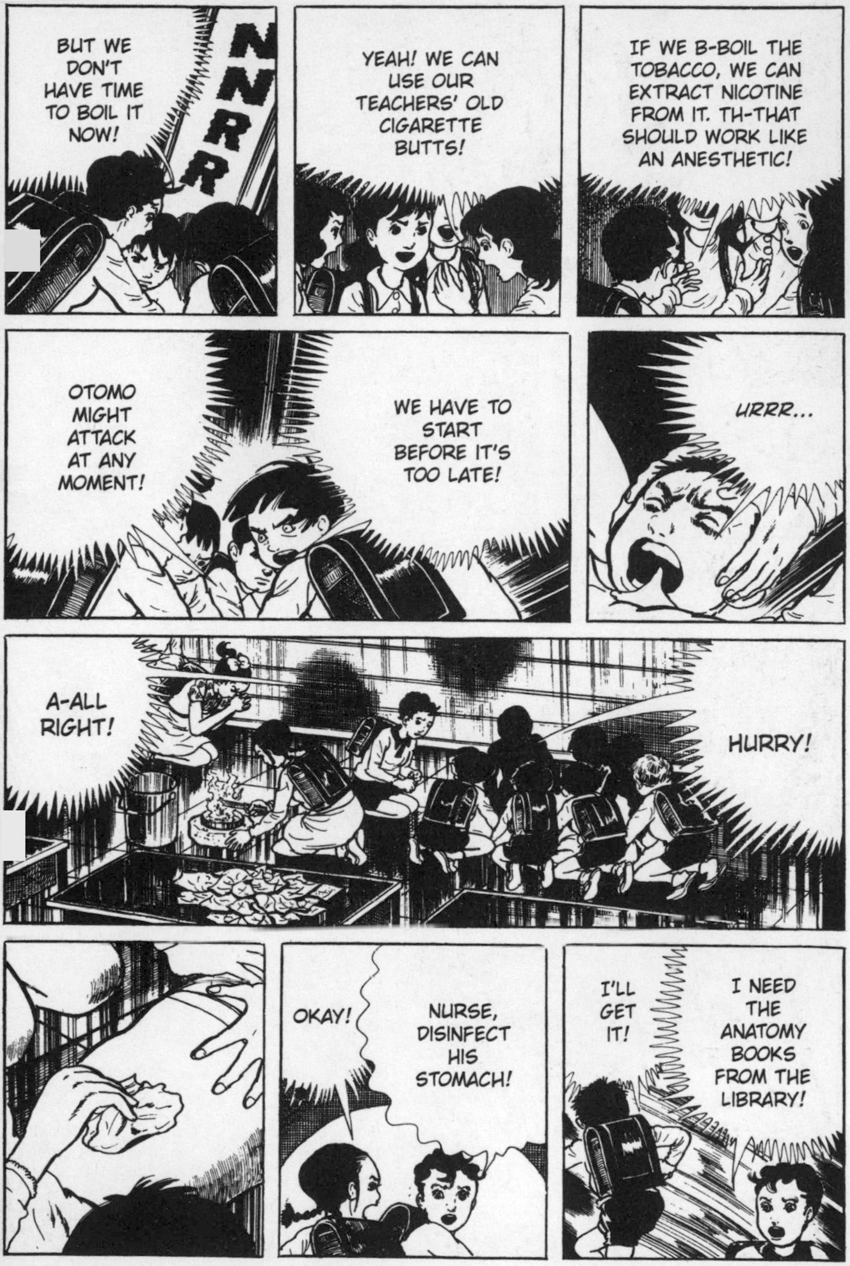
IF WE B-BOIL THE TOBACCO, WE CAN EXTRACT NICOTINE FROM IT. TH-THAT SHOULD WORK LIKE AN ANESTHETIC!
YEAH! WE CAN USE OUR TEACHERS' OLD CIGARETTE BUTTS!
NNRR
BUT WE DON'T HAVE TIME TO BOIL IT NOW!
URRR...
WE HAVE TO START BEFORE IT'S TOO LATE!
OTOMO MIGHT ATTACK AT ANY MOMENT!
HURRY!
A-ALL RIGHT!
I NEED THE ANATOMY BOOKS FROM THE LIBRARY!
I'LL GET IT!
NURSE, DISINFECT HIS STOMACH!
OKAY!

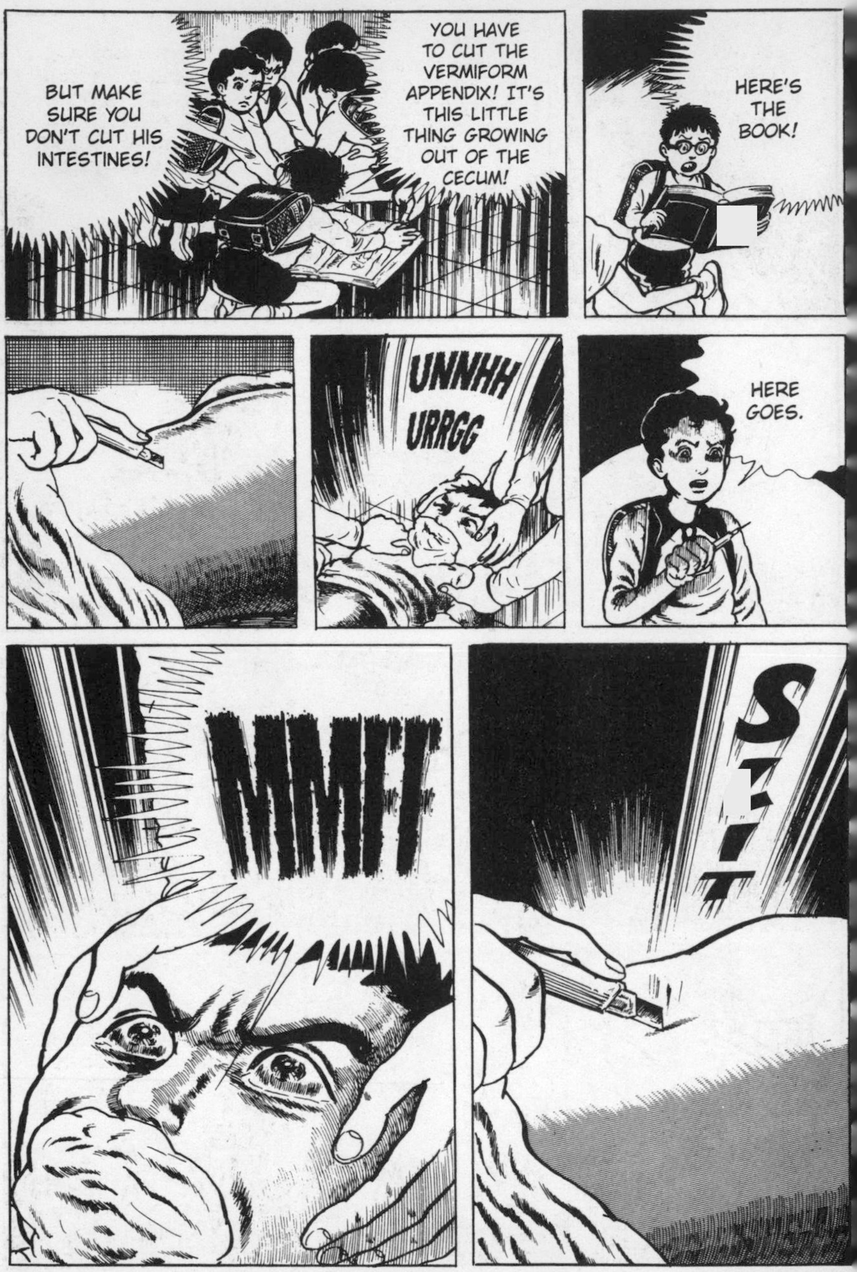
HERE'S THE BOOK!
YOU HAVE TO CUT THE VERMIFORM APPENDIX! IT'S THIS LITTLE THING GROWING OUT OF THE CECUM!
BUT MAKE SURE YOU DON'T CUT HIS INTESTINES!
HERE GOES.
UNNHH
URRGG
MMFF

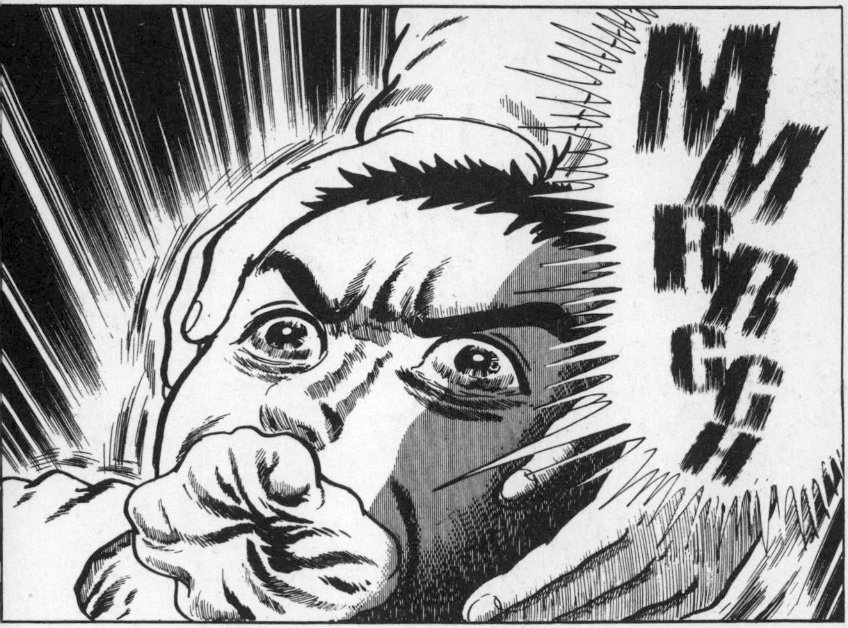
MMRGH!!
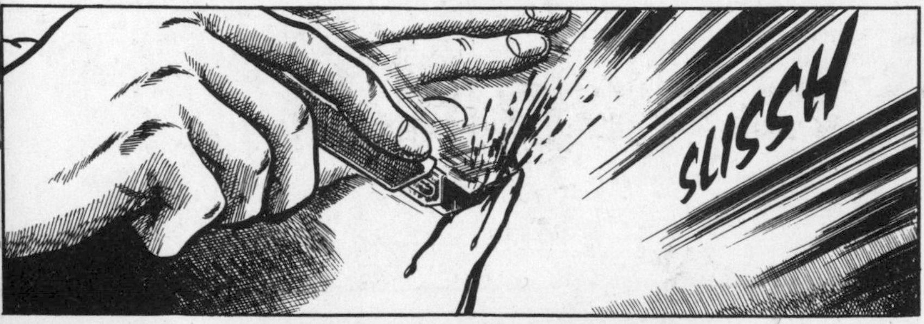
SLISSH
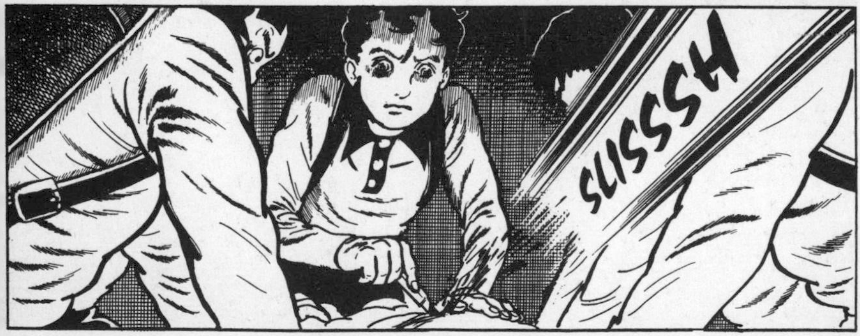
SLISSSH

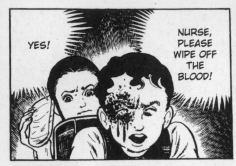

YES!

NURSE, PLEASE WIPE OFF THE BLOOD!

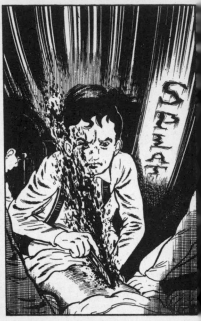

SPLAT

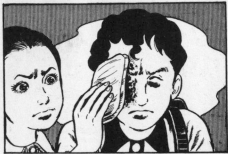

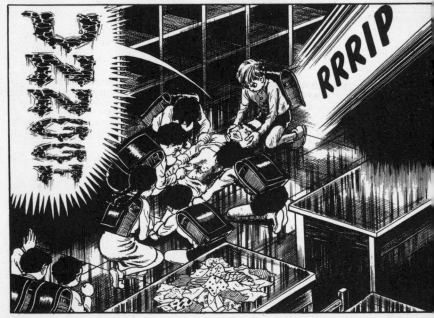

UNNGGH

RRRIP

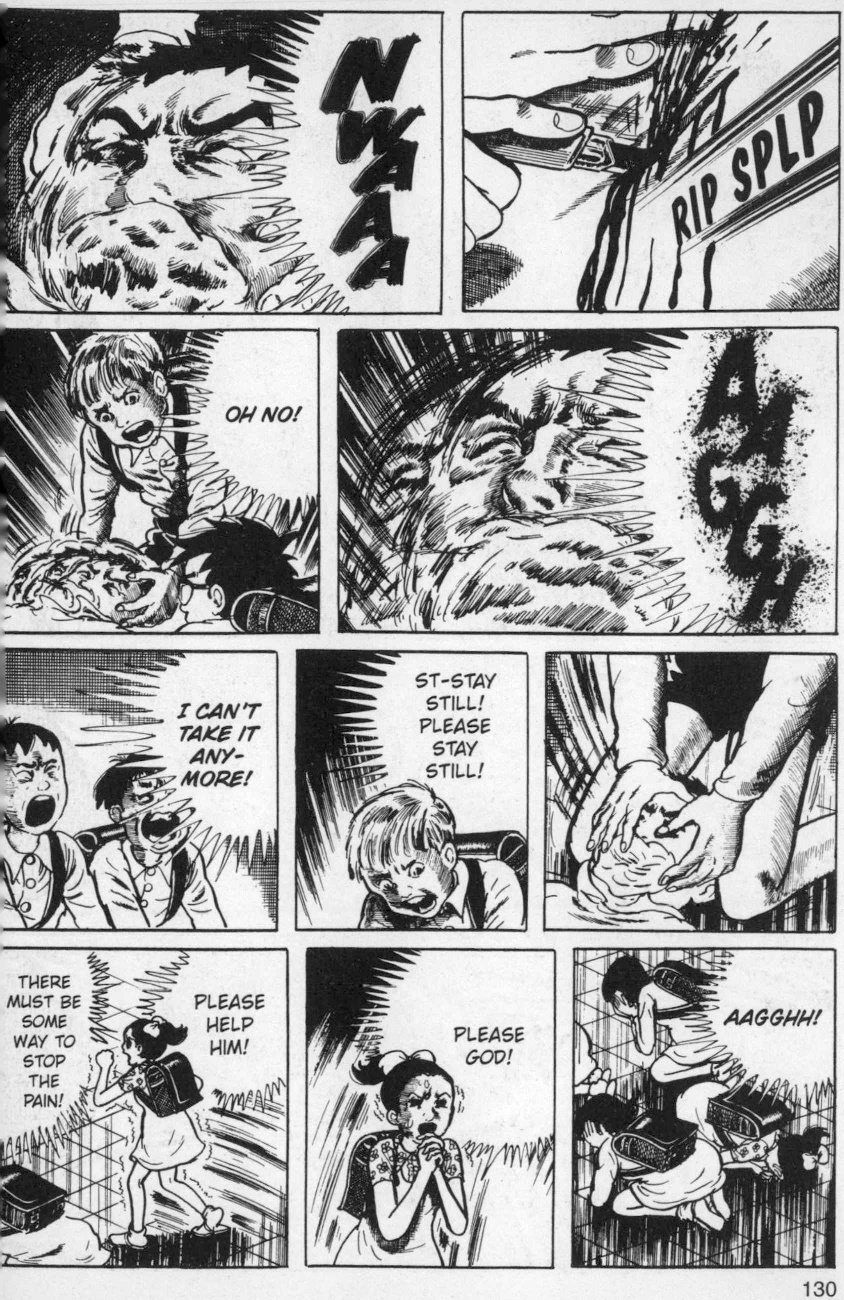
RIP SPLP
NWAAA
AAGGH
ST-STAY STILL! PLEASE STAY STILL!
I CAN'T TAKE IT ANYMORE!
AAGGHH!
PLEASE GOD!
PLEASE HELP HIM!
THERE MUST BE SOME WAY TO STOP THE PAIN!

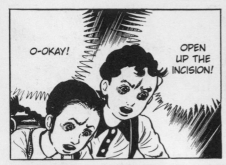

O-OKAY!

OPEN UP THE INCISION!

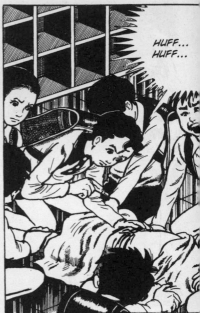

HUFF... HUFF...

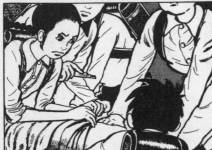

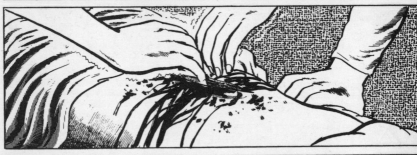

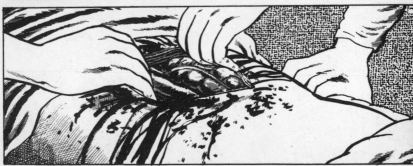

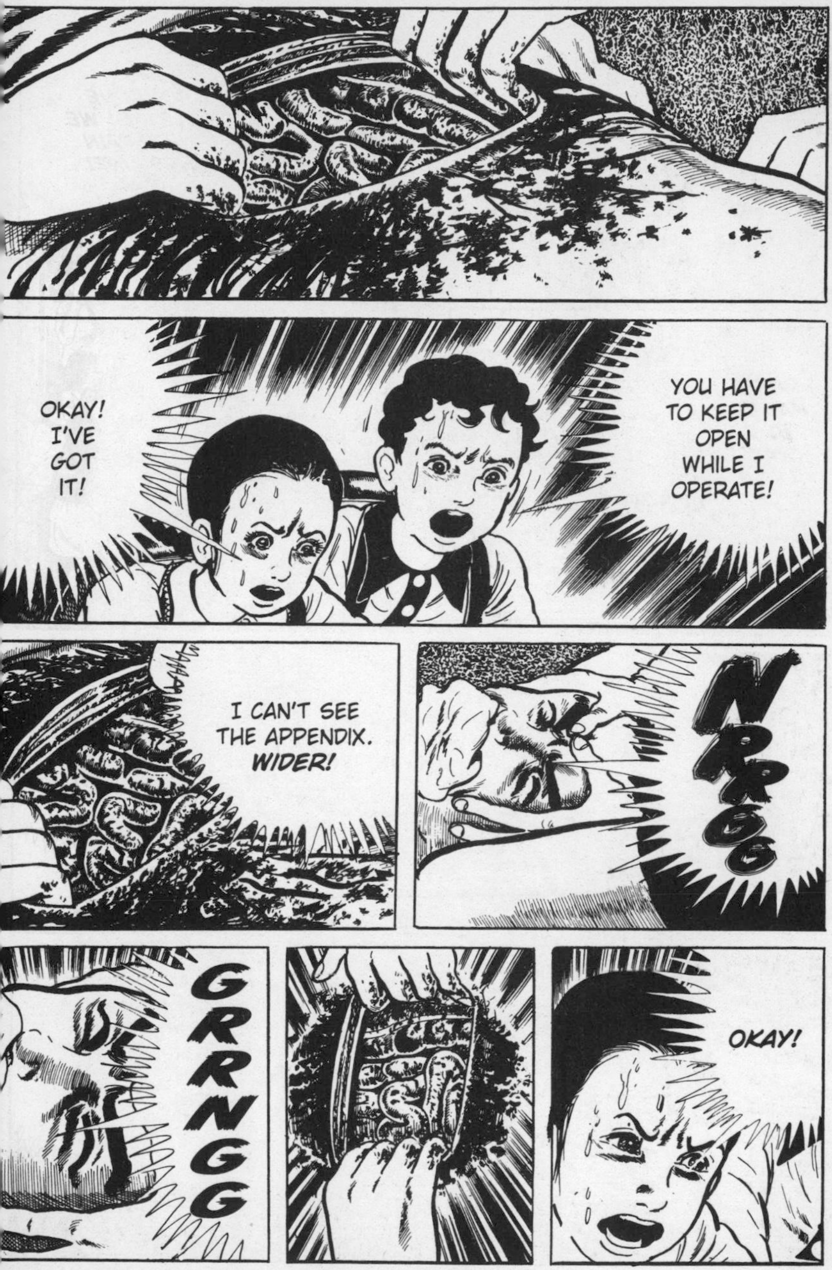
YOU HAVE TO KEEP IT OPEN WHILE I OPERATE!
OKAY! I'VE GOT IT!
NRGG
I CAN'T SEE THE APPENDIX. *WIDER!*
OKAY!
GRRNGG

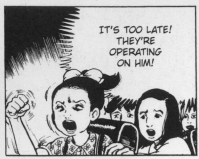

S-S- SOMEONE HELP HIM! WE NEED PAIN MEDICINE!
SAKIKO, CALM DOWN!
IT'S TOO LATE! THEY'RE OPERATING ON HIM!
NO, IT'S NOT!
THERE HAS TO BE A WAY!
UM...UH... SAKIKO, ARE THERE LILIES IN THE GARDEN?!
WE CAN USE THEM TO MAKE AN ANESTHETIC!
WHAT?!
WE CAN ALSO USE MUGWORT TO CLOT BLOOD! I'M NOT SURE HOW TO DO IT, BUT IT SAYS HERE THAT IT'S A COAGULANT!
I'LL GO GET SOME!

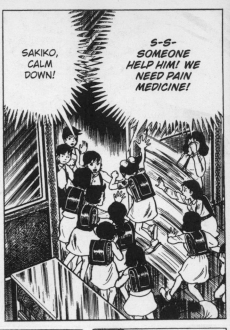

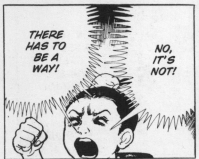

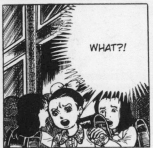

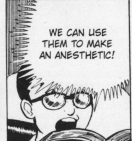

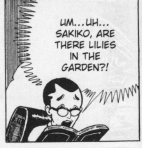

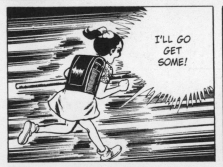

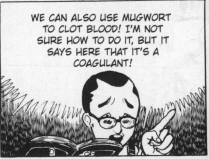

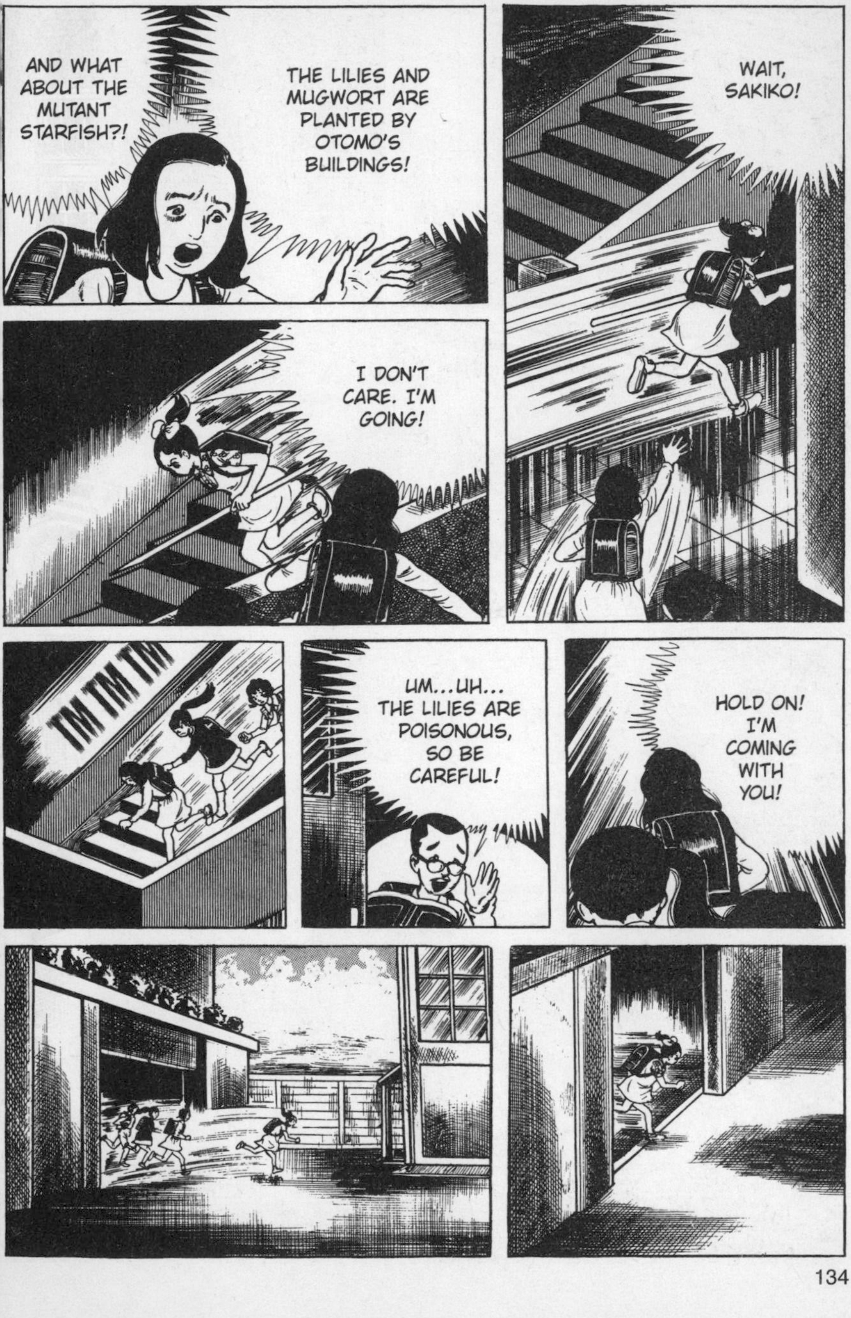
WAIT, SAKIKO!
THE LILIES AND MUGWORT ARE PLANTED BY OTOMO'S BUILDINGS!
AND WHAT ABOUT THE MUTANT STARFISH?!
I DON'T CARE. I'M GOING!
HOLD ON! I'M COMING WITH YOU!
UM...UH... THE LILIES ARE POISONOUS, SO BE CAREFUL!
TM TM TM

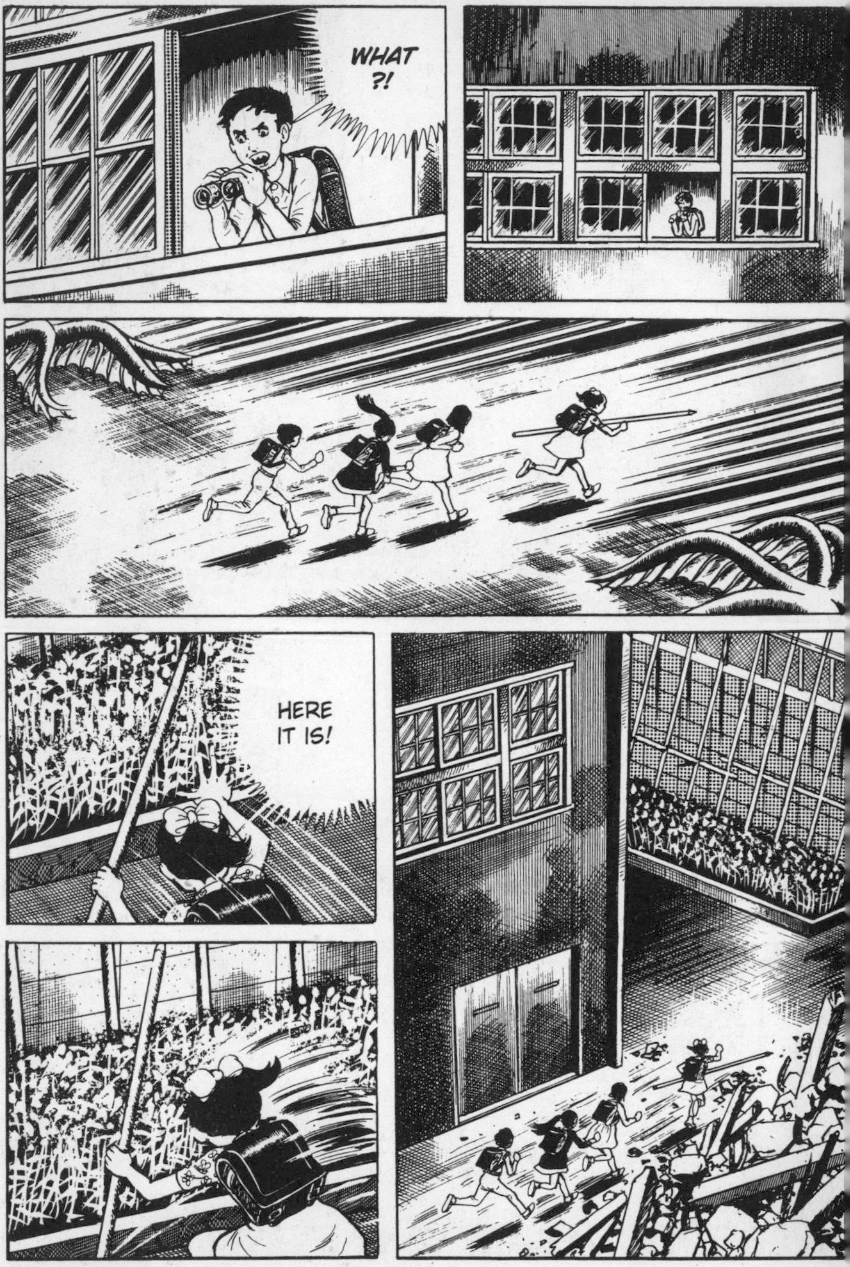
WHAT ?!
HERE IT IS!

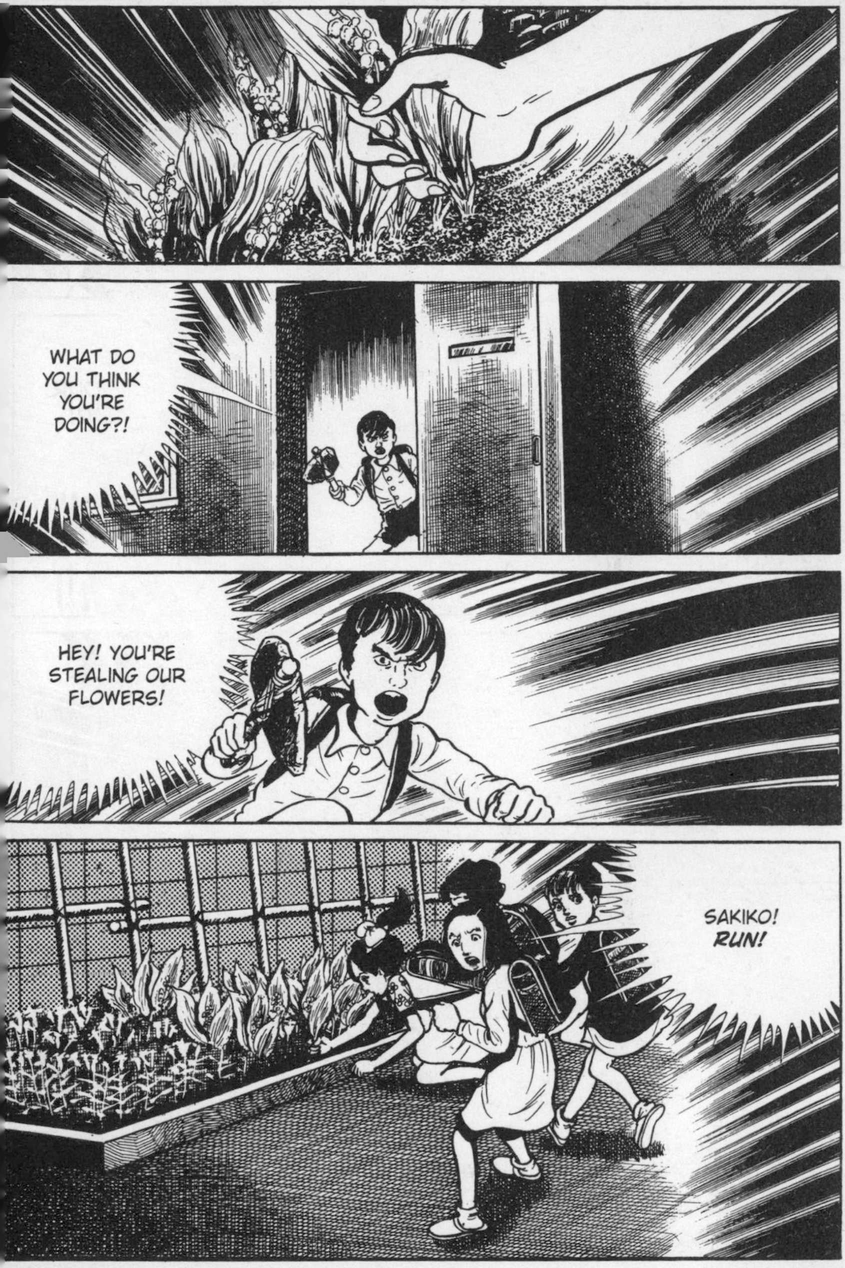
WHAT DO YOU THINK YOU'RE DOING?!
HEY! YOU'RE STEALING OUR FLOWERS!
SAKIKO! *RUN!*

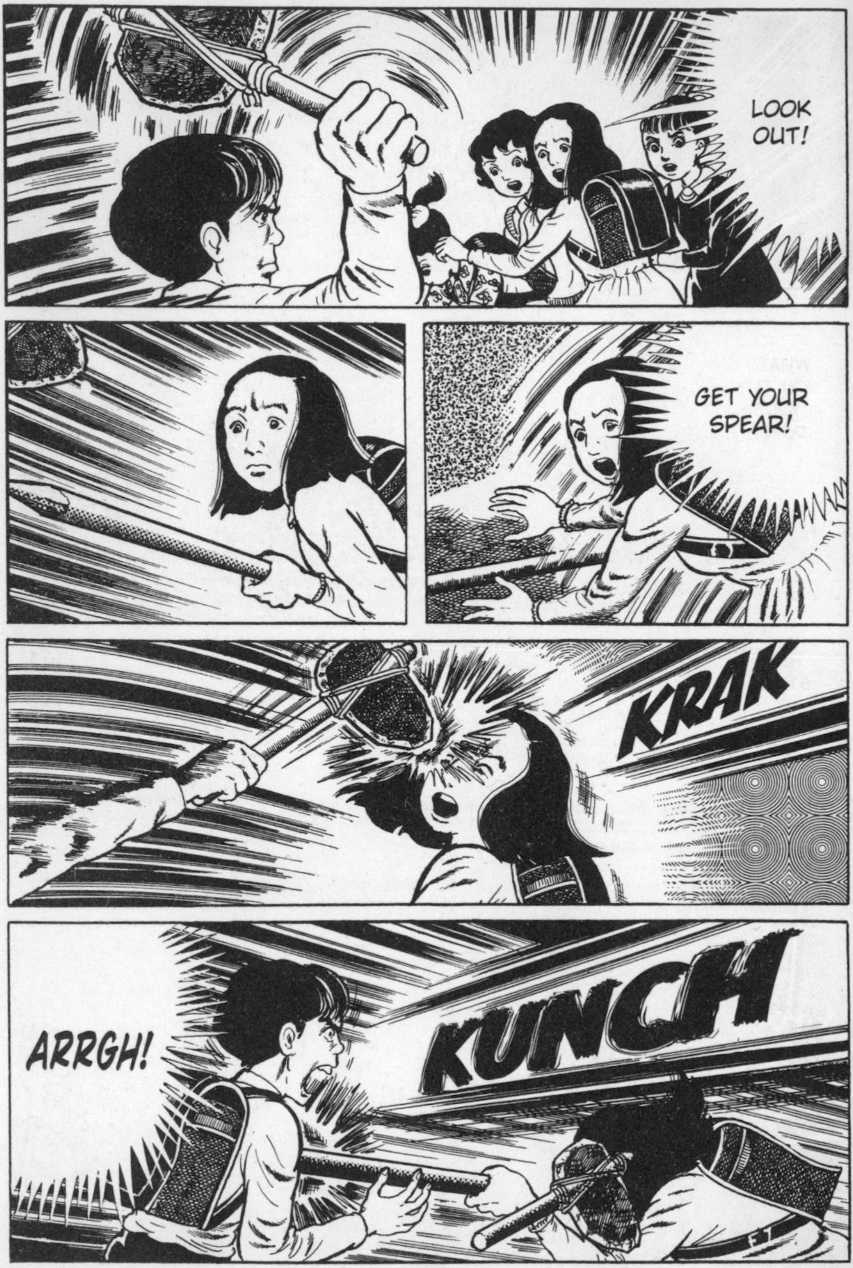
LOOK OUT!
GET YOUR SPEAR!
KRAK
KUNCH
ARRGH!

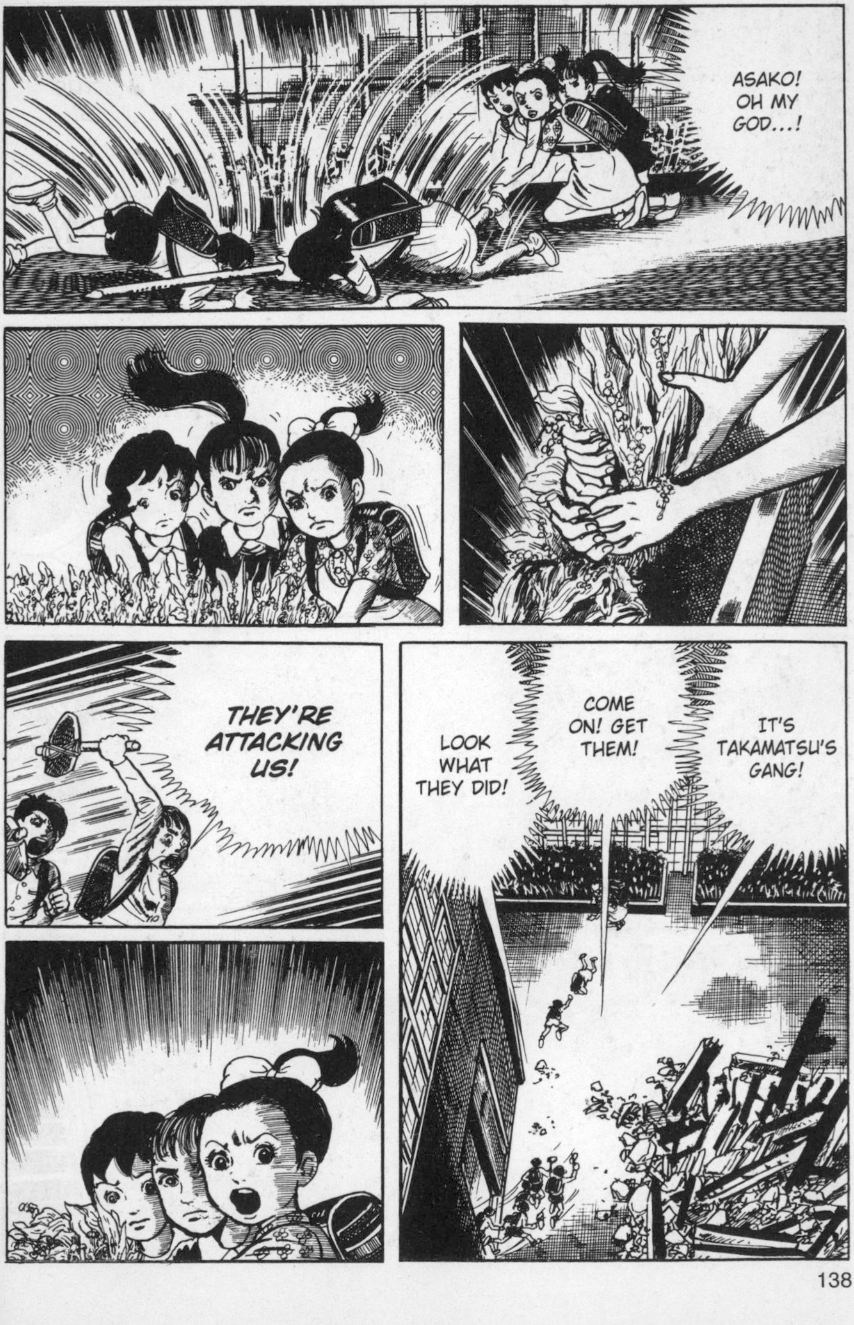
ASAKO! OH MY GOD...!
IT'S TAKAMATSU'S GANG!
COME ON! GET THEM!
LOOK WHAT THEY DID!
THEY'RE ATTACKING US!

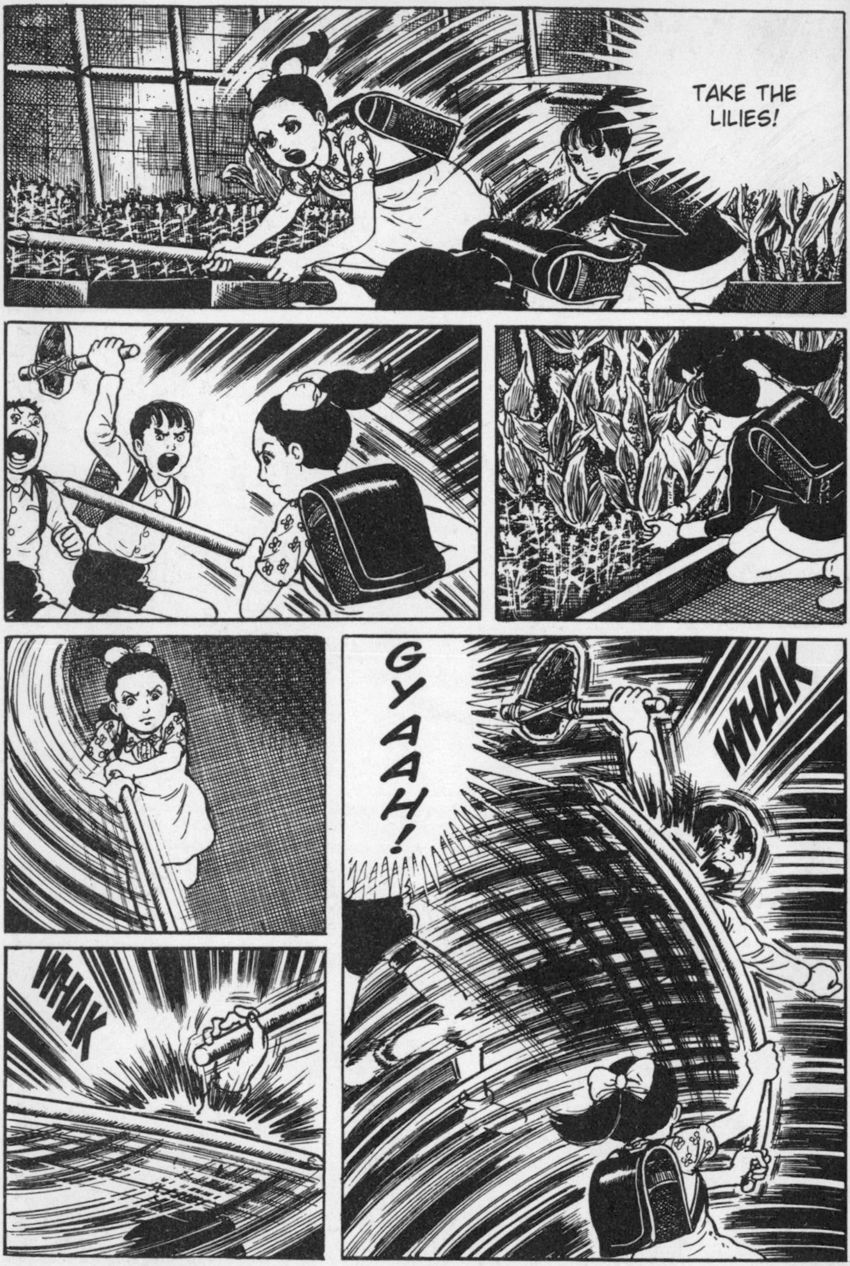
TAKE THE LILIES!
GYAAAH!
WHAK
WHAK

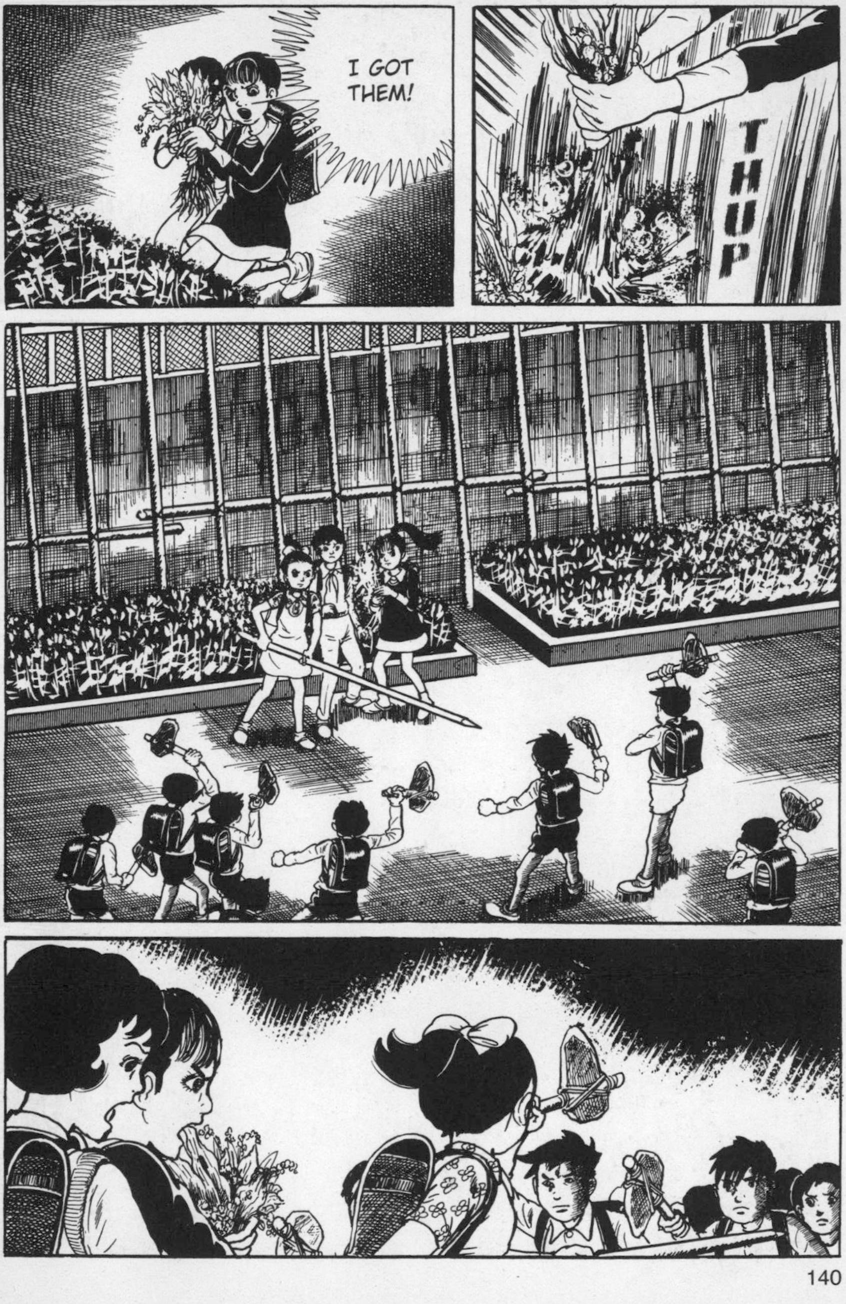
THUP
I GOT THEM!

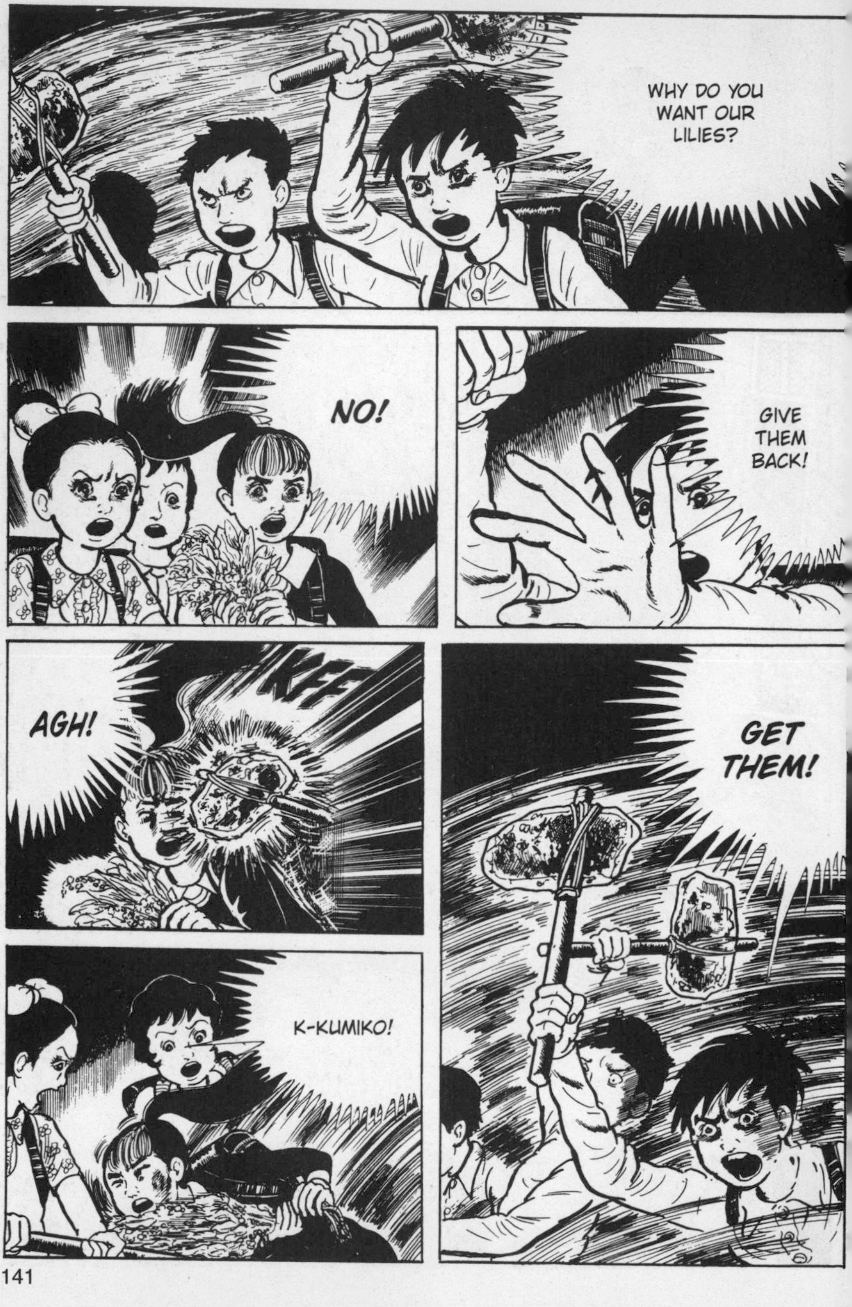
WHY DO YOU WANT OUR LILIES?
GIVE THEM BACK!
NO!
GET THEM!
AGH!
K-KUMIKO!

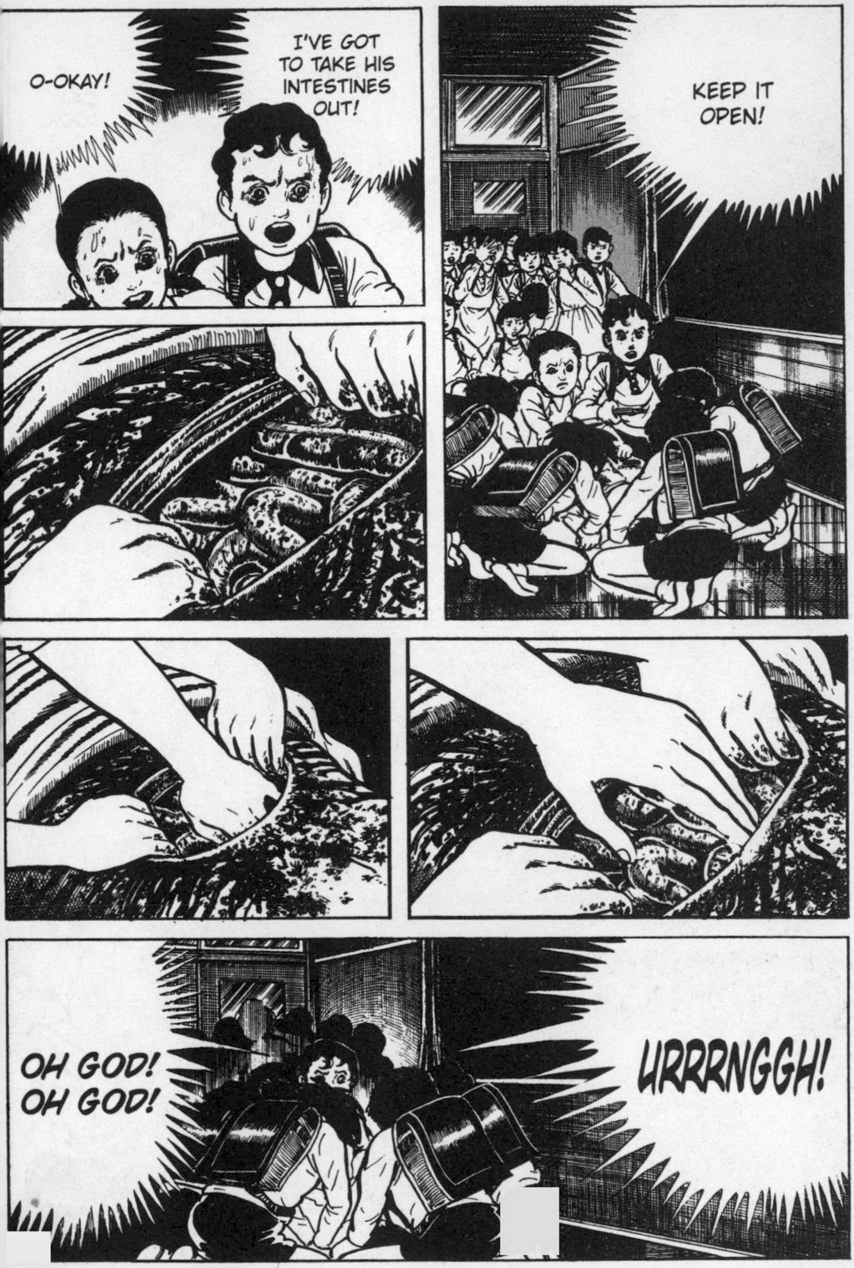
KEEP IT OPEN!
I'VE GOT TO TAKE HIS INTESTINES OUT!
O-OKAY!
URRRNGGH!
OH GOD! OH GOD!

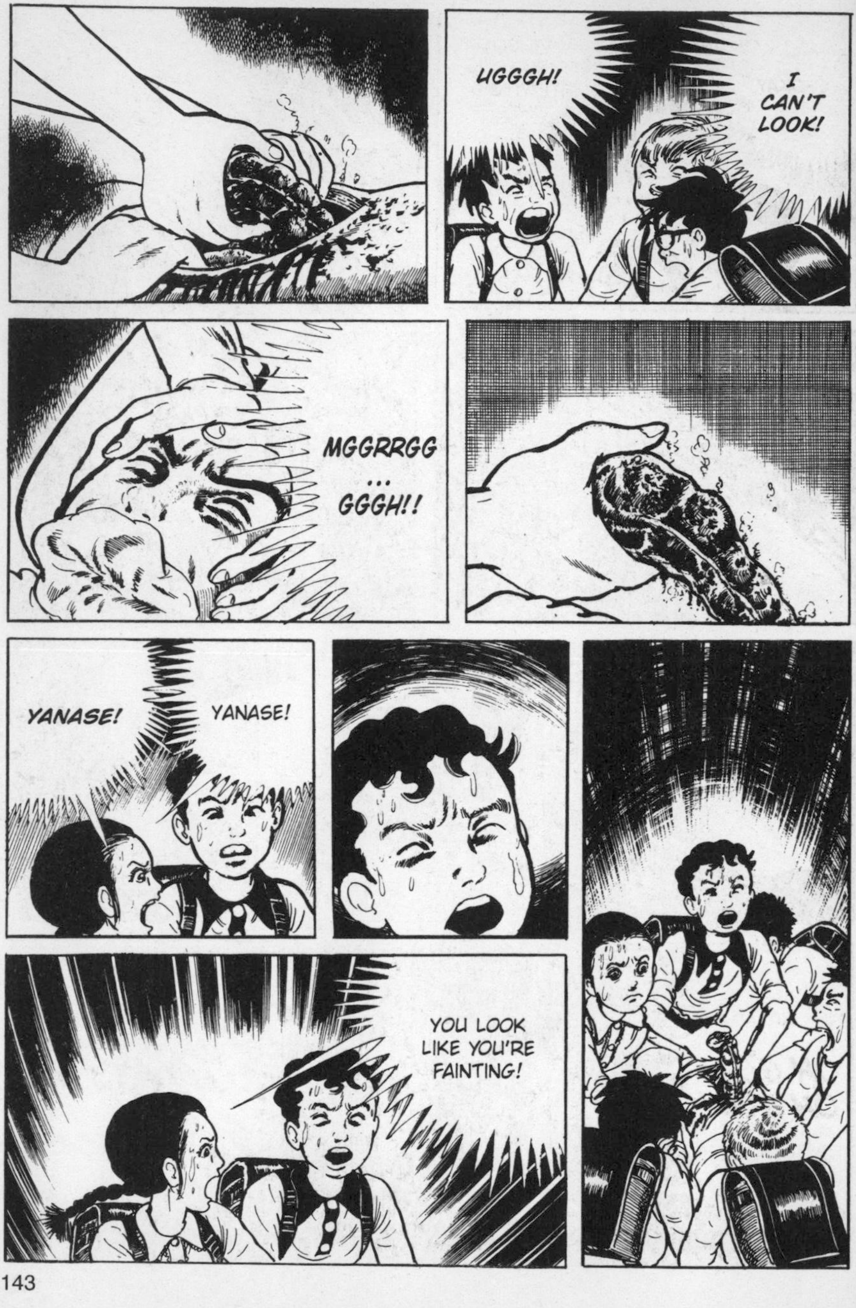
I CAN'T LOOK!
UGGGH!
MGGRRGG ... GGGH!!
YANASE!
YANASE!
YOU LOOK LIKE YOU'RE FAINTING!

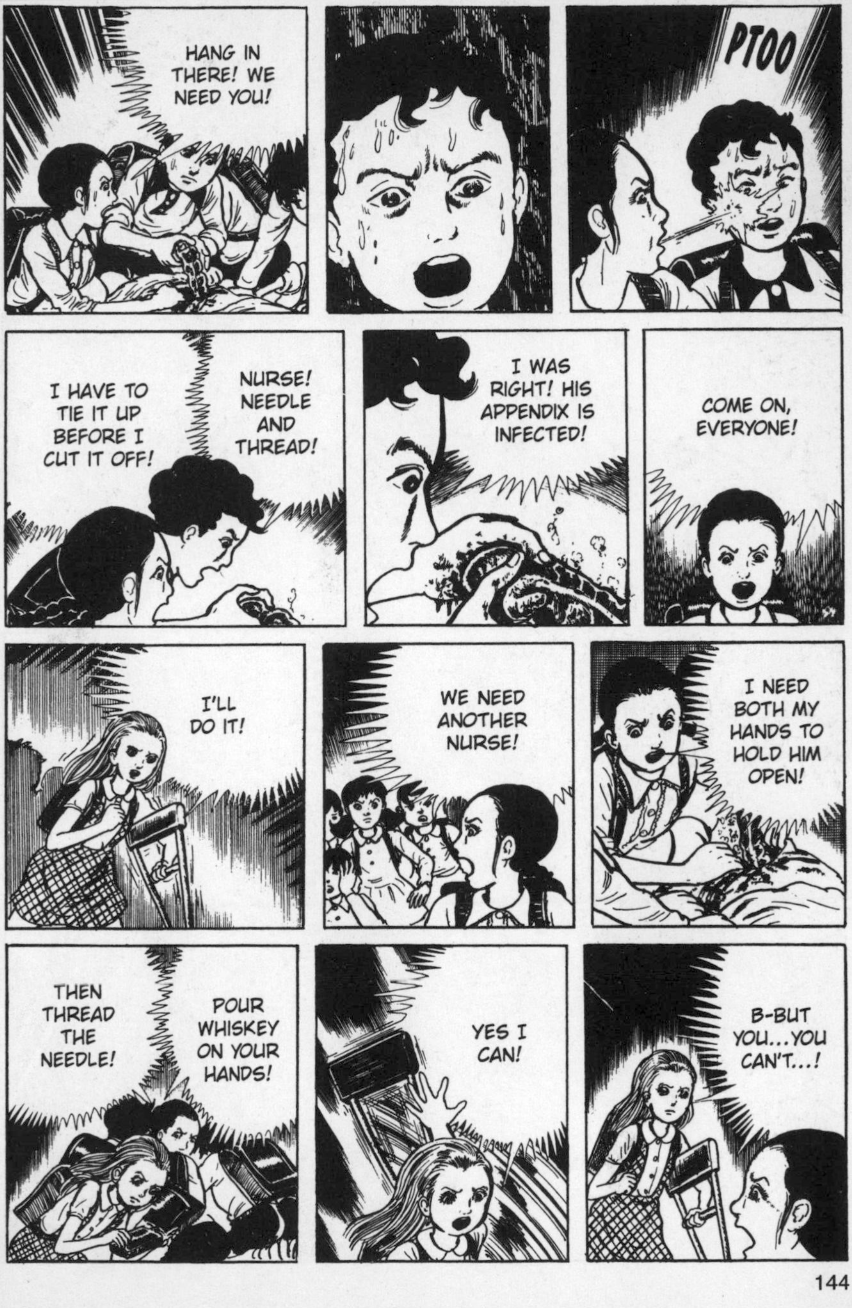
PTOO
HANG IN THERE! WE NEED YOU!
COME ON, EVERYONE!
I WAS RIGHT! HIS APPENDIX IS INFECTED!
NURSE! NEEDLE AND THREAD!
I HAVE TO TIE IT UP BEFORE I CUT IT OFF!
I NEED BOTH MY HANDS TO HOLD HIM OPEN!
WE NEED ANOTHER NURSE!
I'LL DO IT!
B-BUT YOU...YOU CAN'T...!
YES I CAN!
POUR WHISKEY ON YOUR HANDS!
THEN THREAD THE NEEDLE!

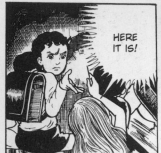

HERE IT IS!

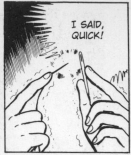

I SAID, QUICK!

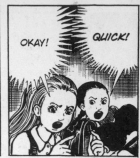

OKAY!

QUICK!

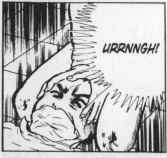

URRNNGH!

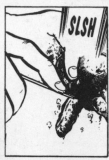

SLSH

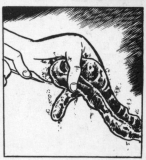

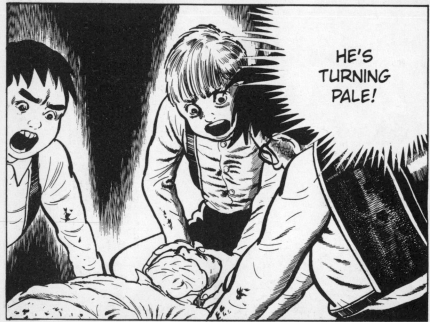

HE'S TURNING PALE!

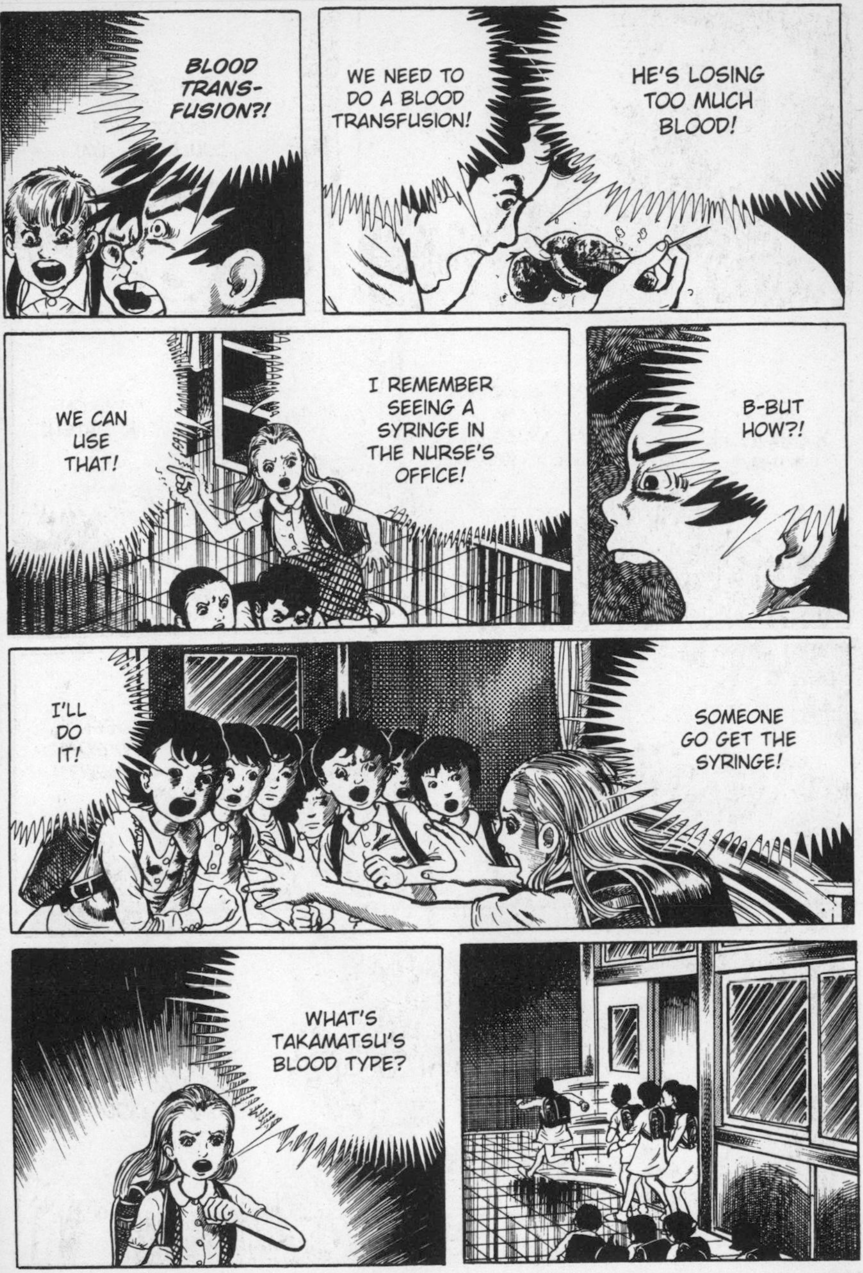
HE'S LOSING TOO MUCH BLOOD!
WE NEED TO DO A BLOOD TRANSFUSION!
BLOOD TRANS-FUSION?!
B-BUT HOW?!
I REMEMBER SEEING A SYRINGE IN THE NURSE'S OFFICE!
WE CAN USE THAT!
SOMEONE GO GET THE SYRINGE!
I'LL DO IT!
WHAT'S TAKAMATSU'S BLOOD TYPE?

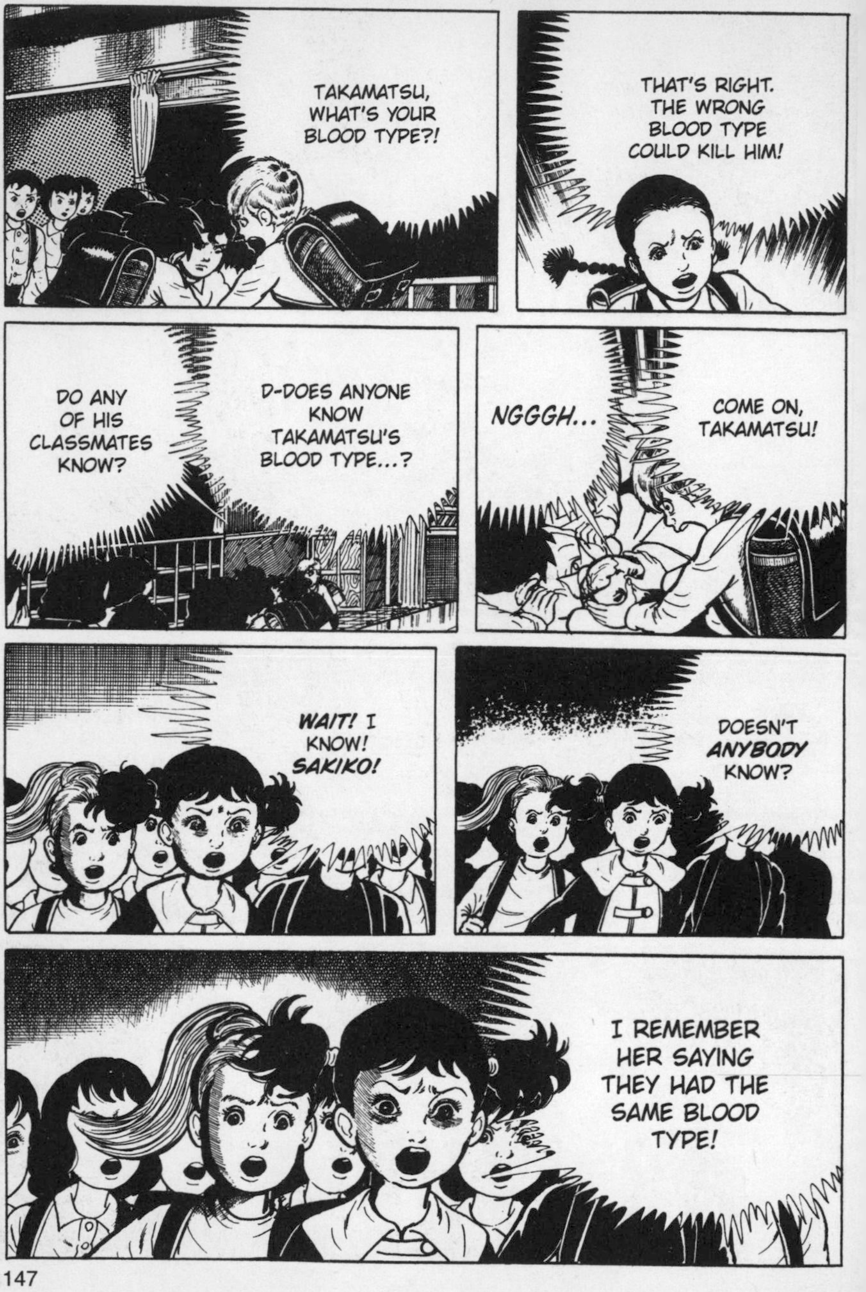
THAT'S RIGHT. THE WRONG BLOOD TYPE COULD KILL HIM!
TAKAMATSU, WHAT'S YOUR BLOOD TYPE?!
COME ON, TAKAMATSU!
NGGGH...
D-DOES ANYONE KNOW TAKAMATSU'S BLOOD TYPE...?
DO ANY OF HIS CLASSMATES KNOW?
DOESN'T *ANYBODY* KNOW?
WAIT! I KNOW! *SAKIKO!*
I REMEMBER HER SAYING THEY HAD THE SAME BLOOD TYPE!

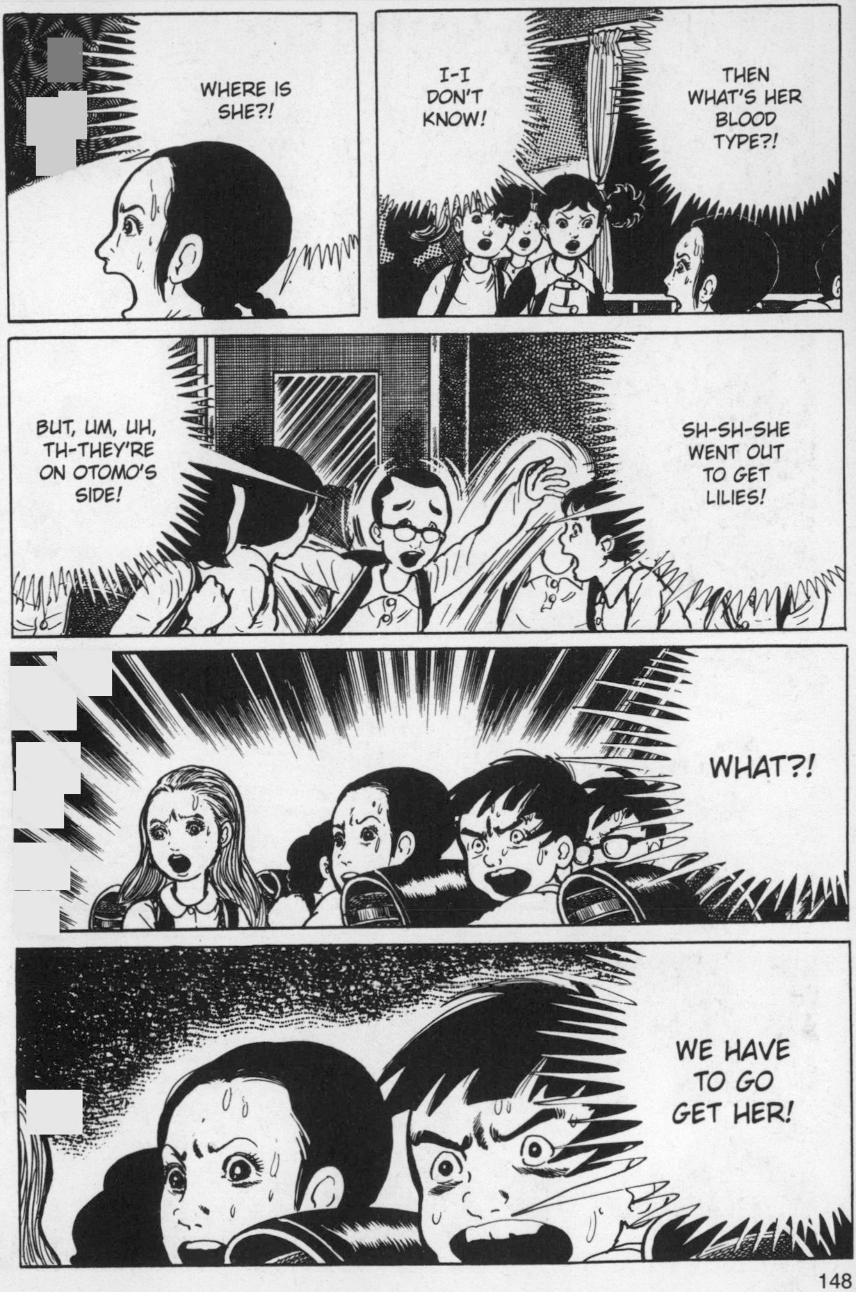
THEN WHAT'S HER BLOOD TYPE?!
I-I DON'T KNOW!
WHERE IS SHE?!
SH-SH-SHE WENT OUT TO GET LILIES!
BUT, UM, UH, TH-THEY'RE ON OTOMO'S SIDE!
WHAT?!
WE HAVE TO GO GET HER!

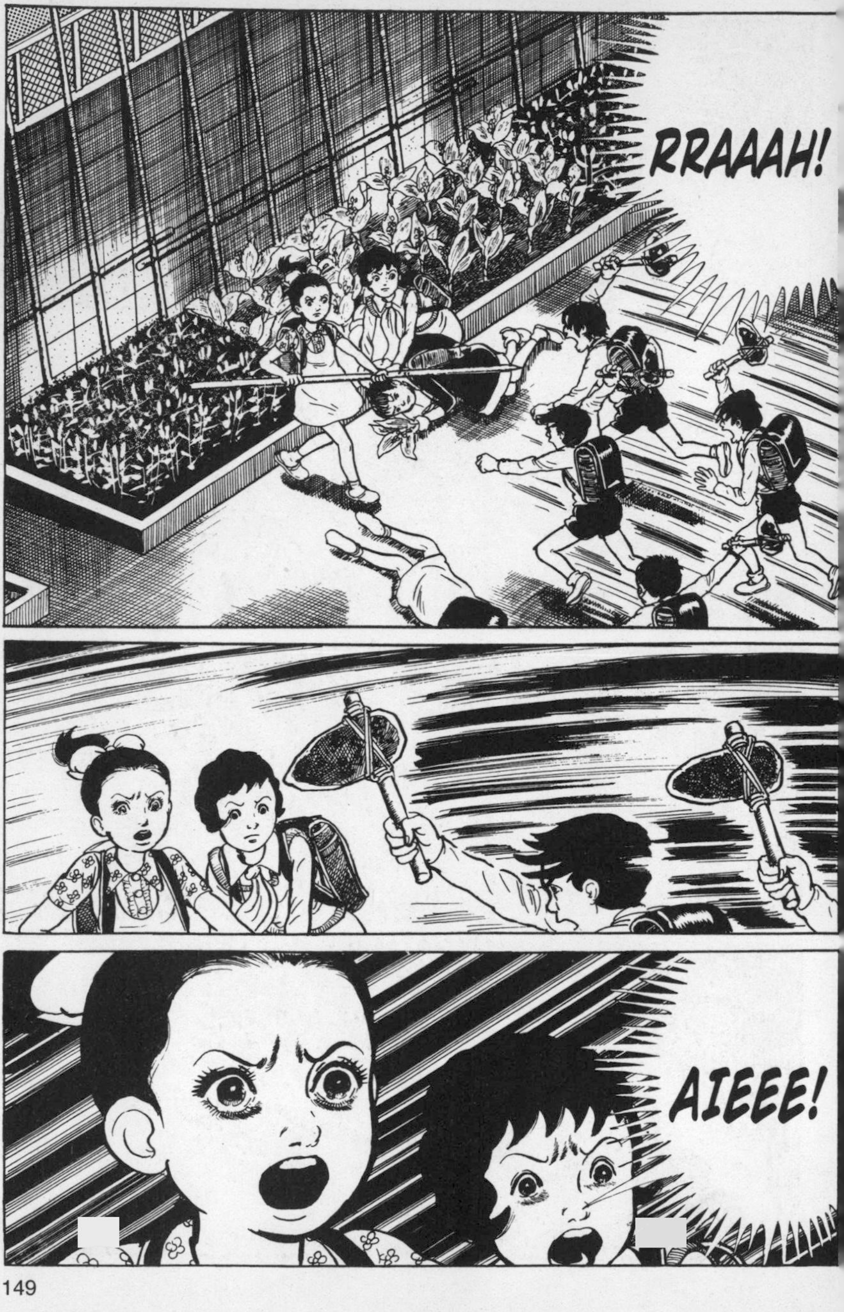
RRAAAH!
AIEEE!

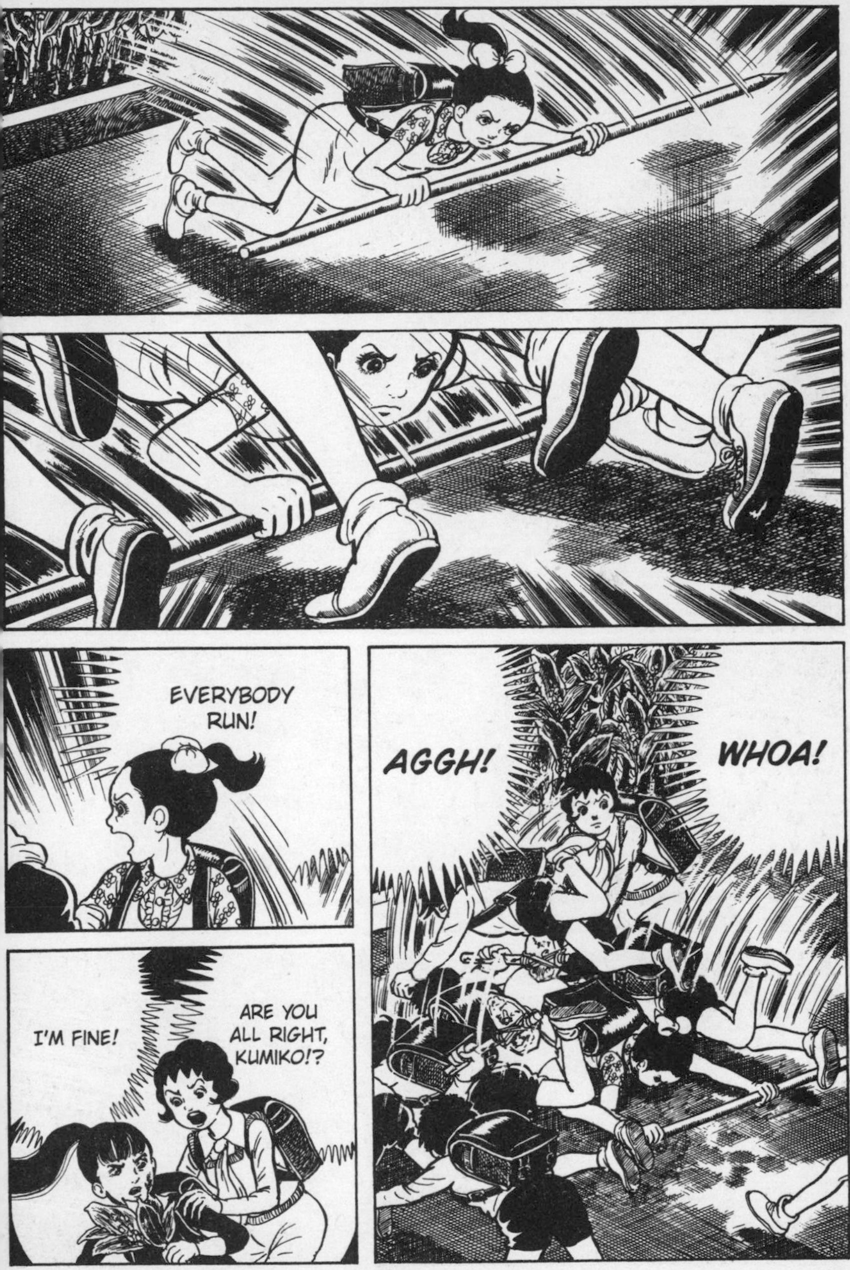
WHOA!
AGGH!
EVERYBODY RUN!
ARE YOU ALL RIGHT, KUMIKO!?
I'M FINE!

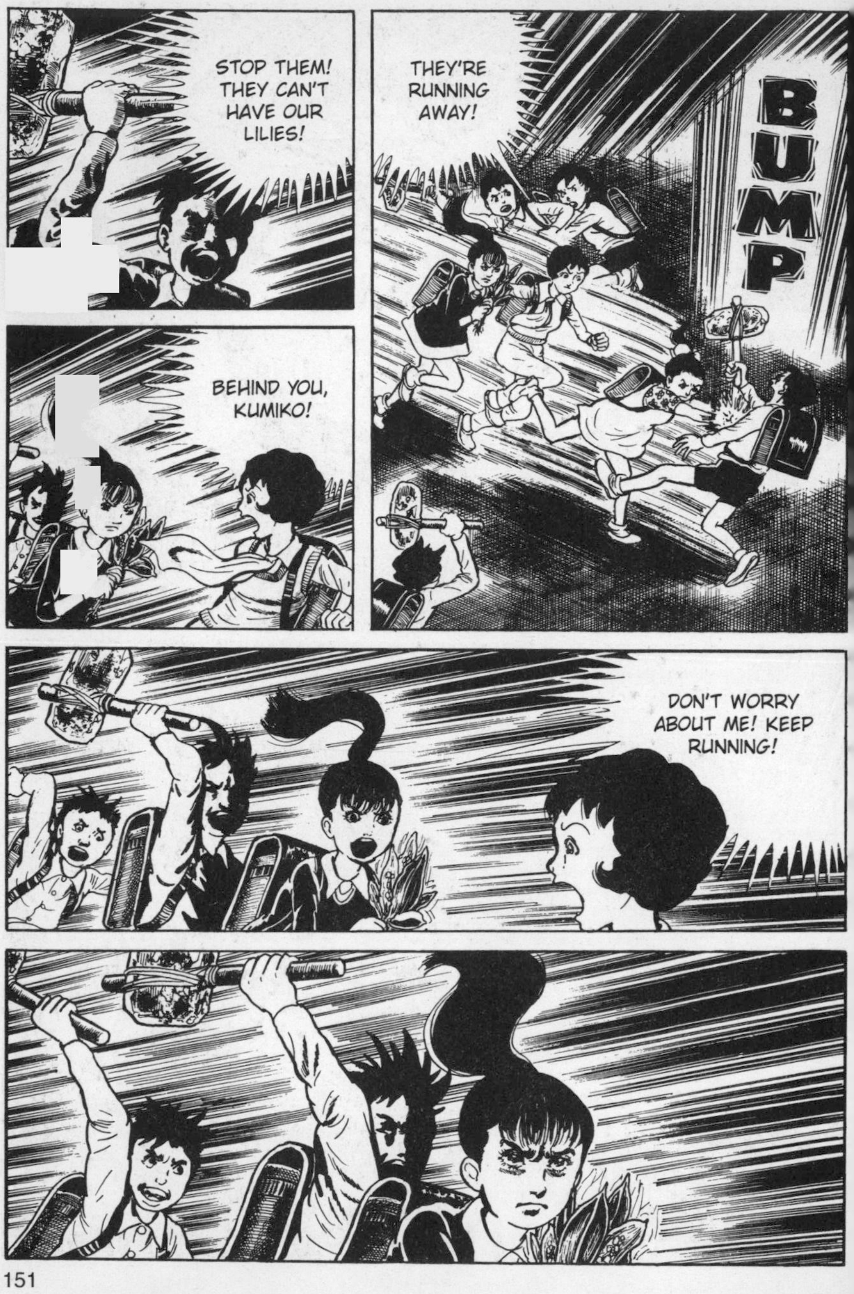
THEY'RE RUNNING AWAY!
BUMP
STOP THEM! THEY CAN'T HAVE OUR LILIES!
BEHIND YOU, KUMIKO!
DON'T WORRY ABOUT ME! KEEP RUNNING!

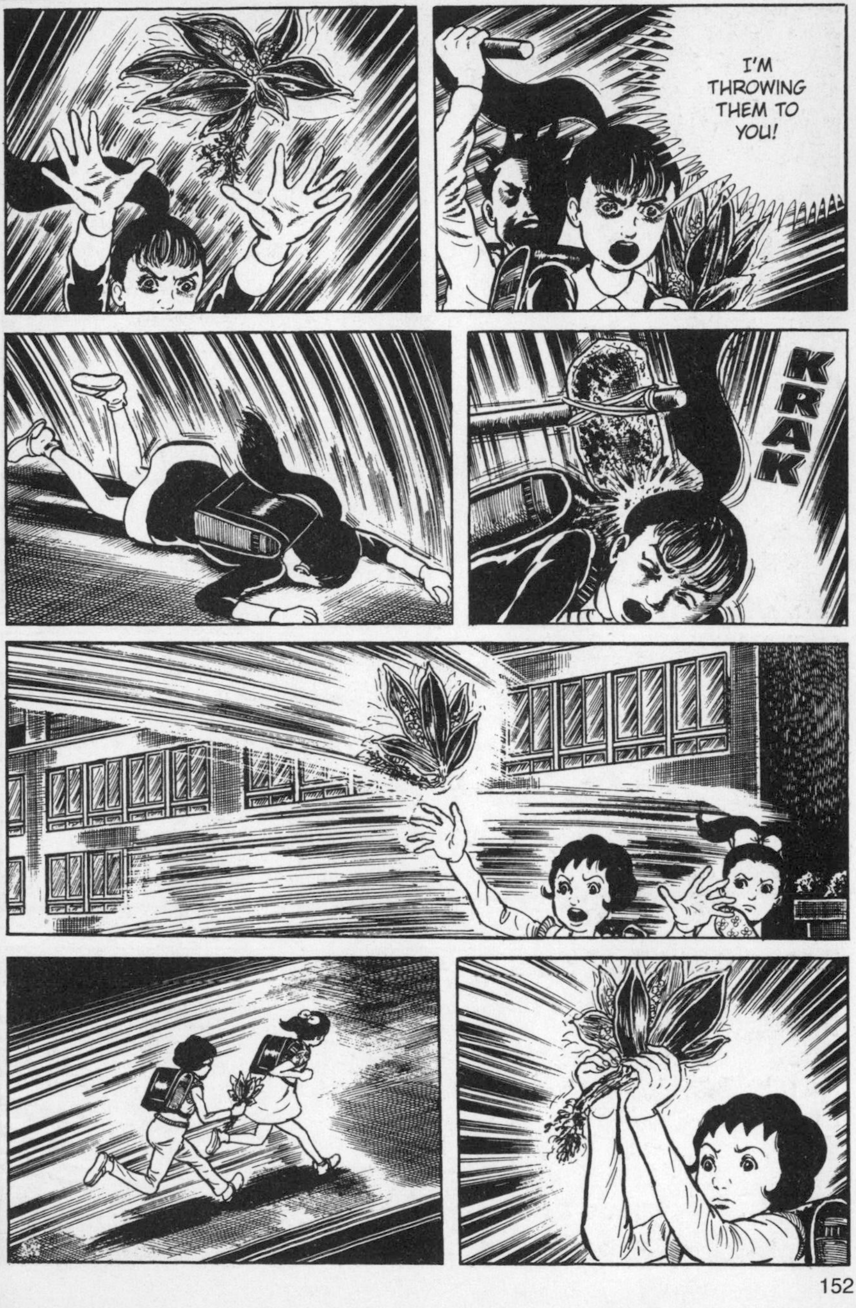
I'M THROWING THEM TO YOU!
KRAK

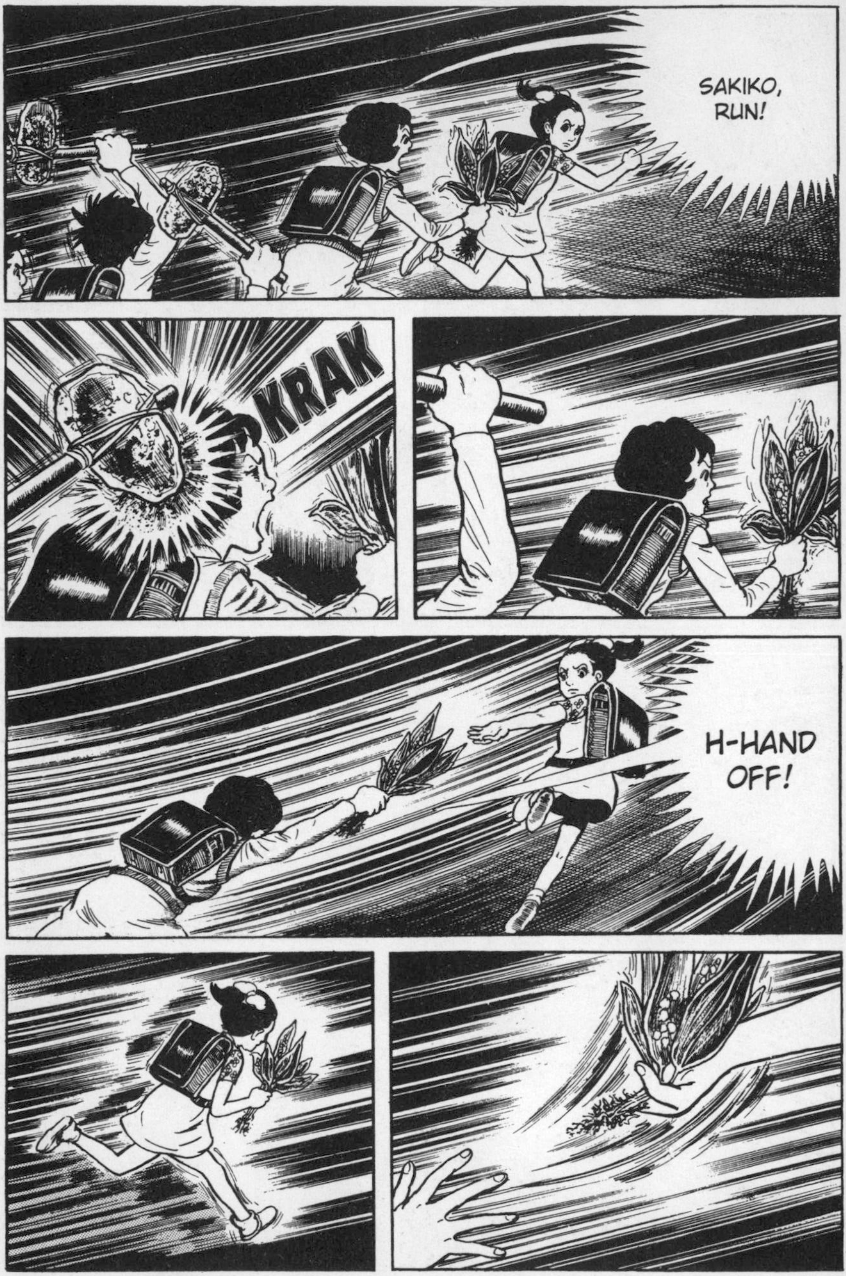
SAKIKO, RUN!
KRAK
H-HAND OFF!

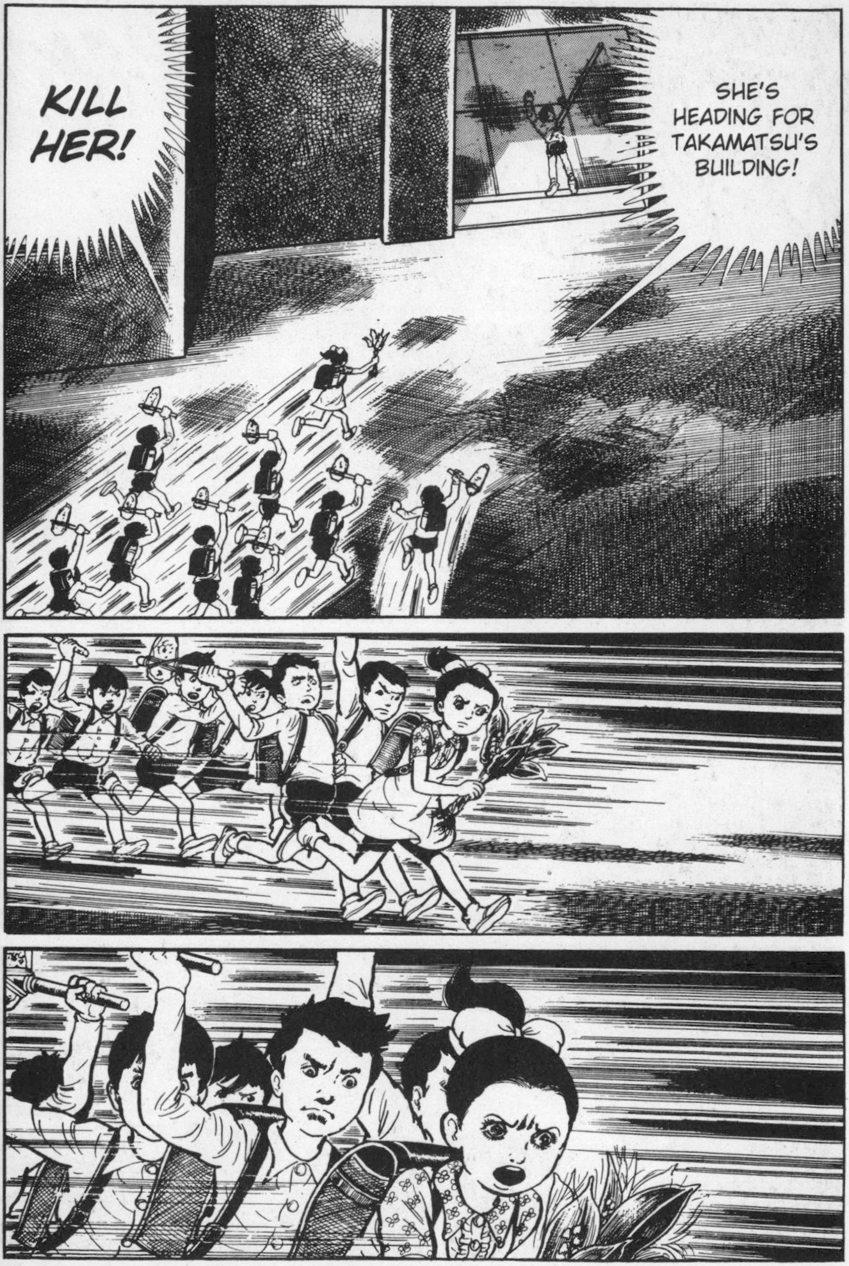
SHE'S HEADING FOR TAKAMATSU'S BUILDING!
KILL HER!

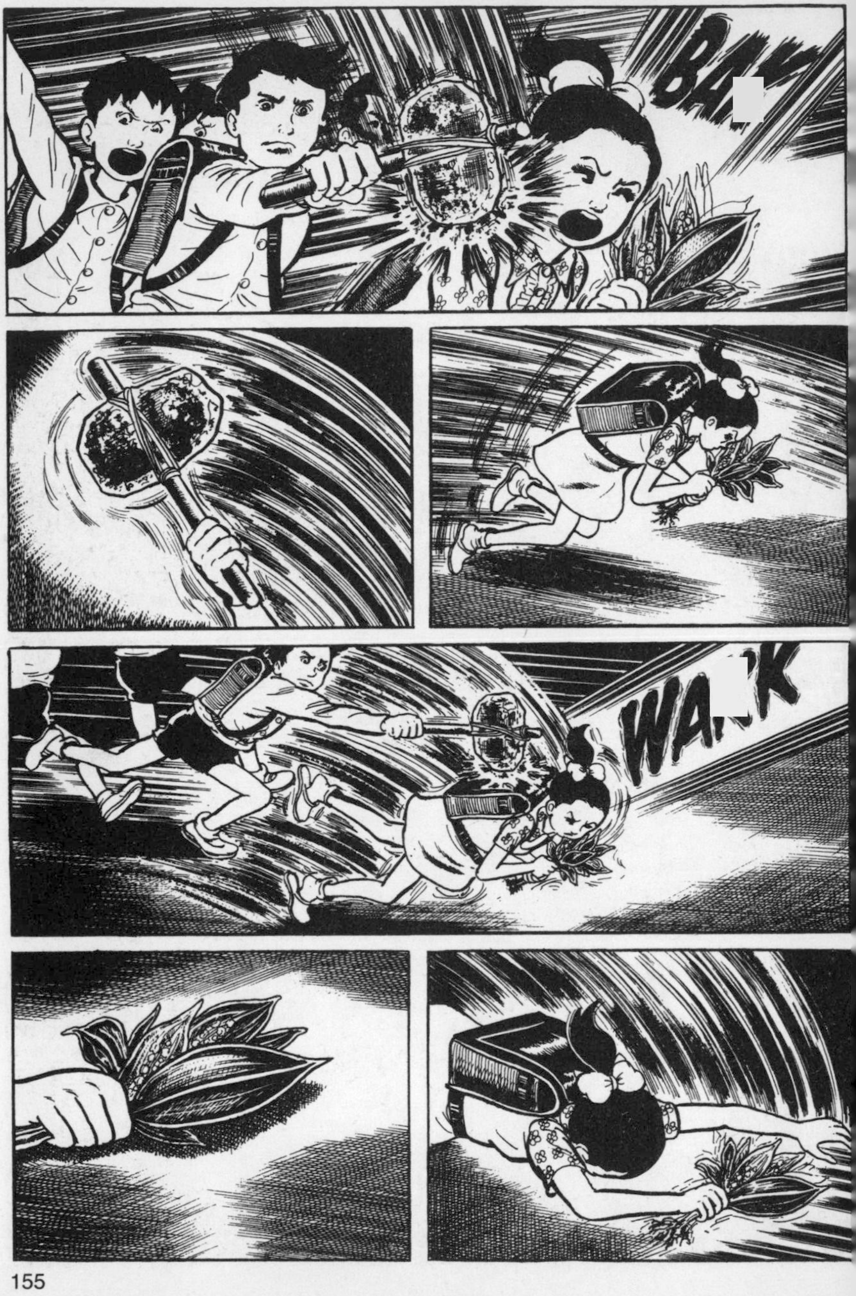
BAM
WAK

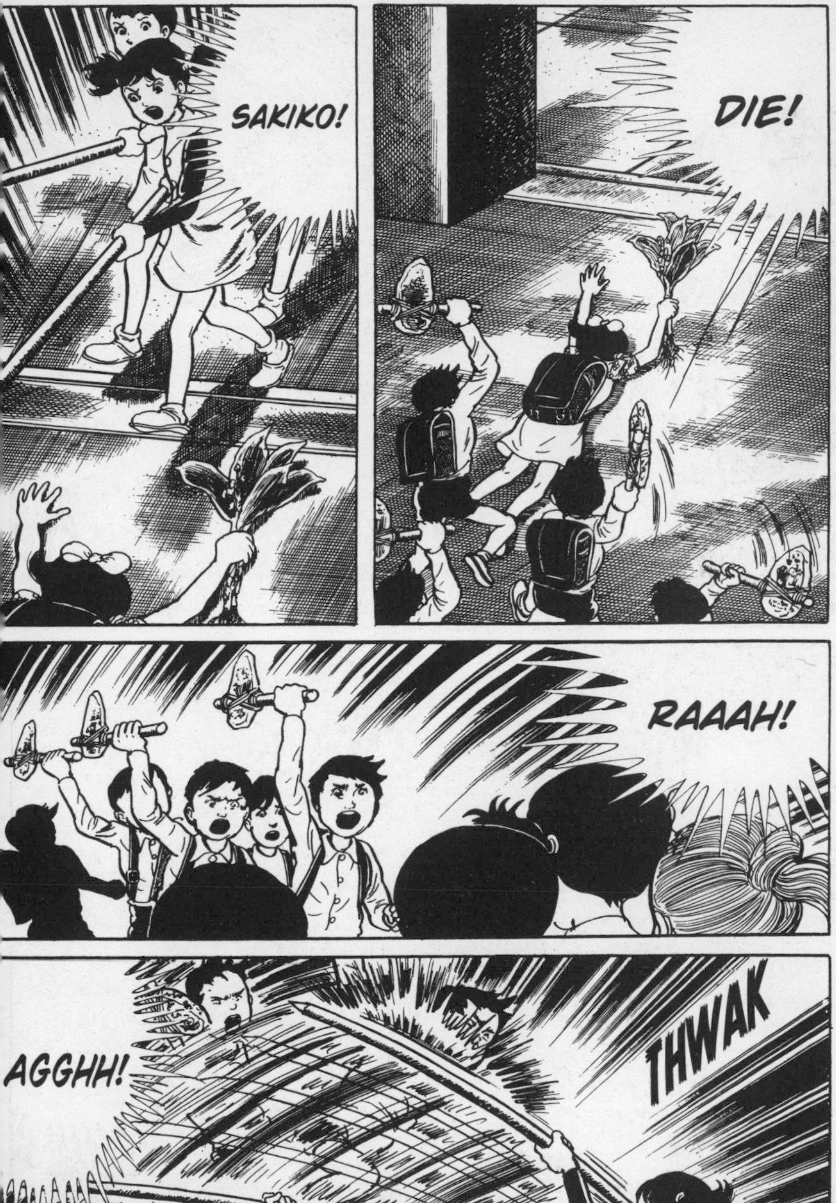
DIE!
SAKIKO!
RAAAH!
THWAK
AGGHH!

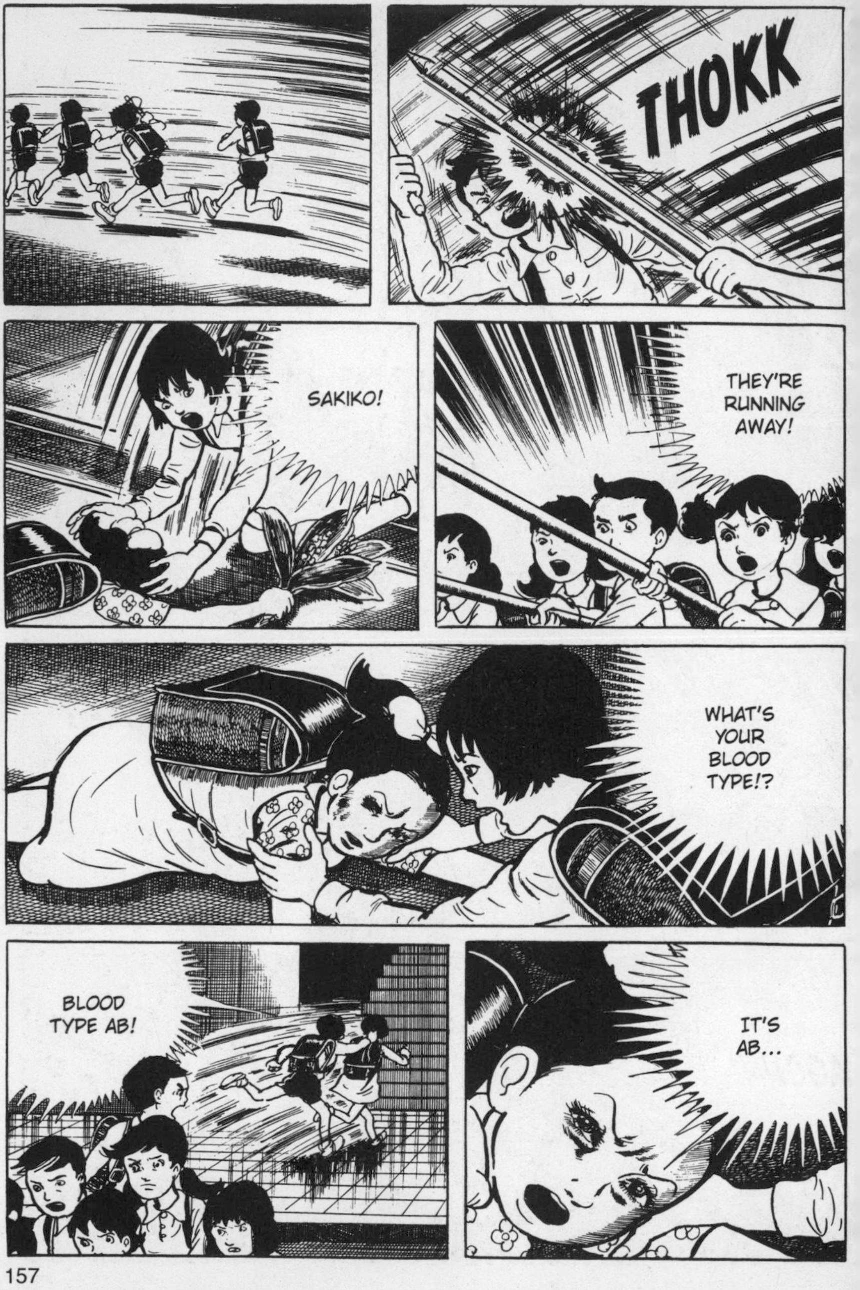
THOKK
THEY'RE RUNNING AWAY!
SAKIKO!
WHAT'S YOUR BLOOD TYPE!?
IT'S AB...
BLOOD TYPE AB!

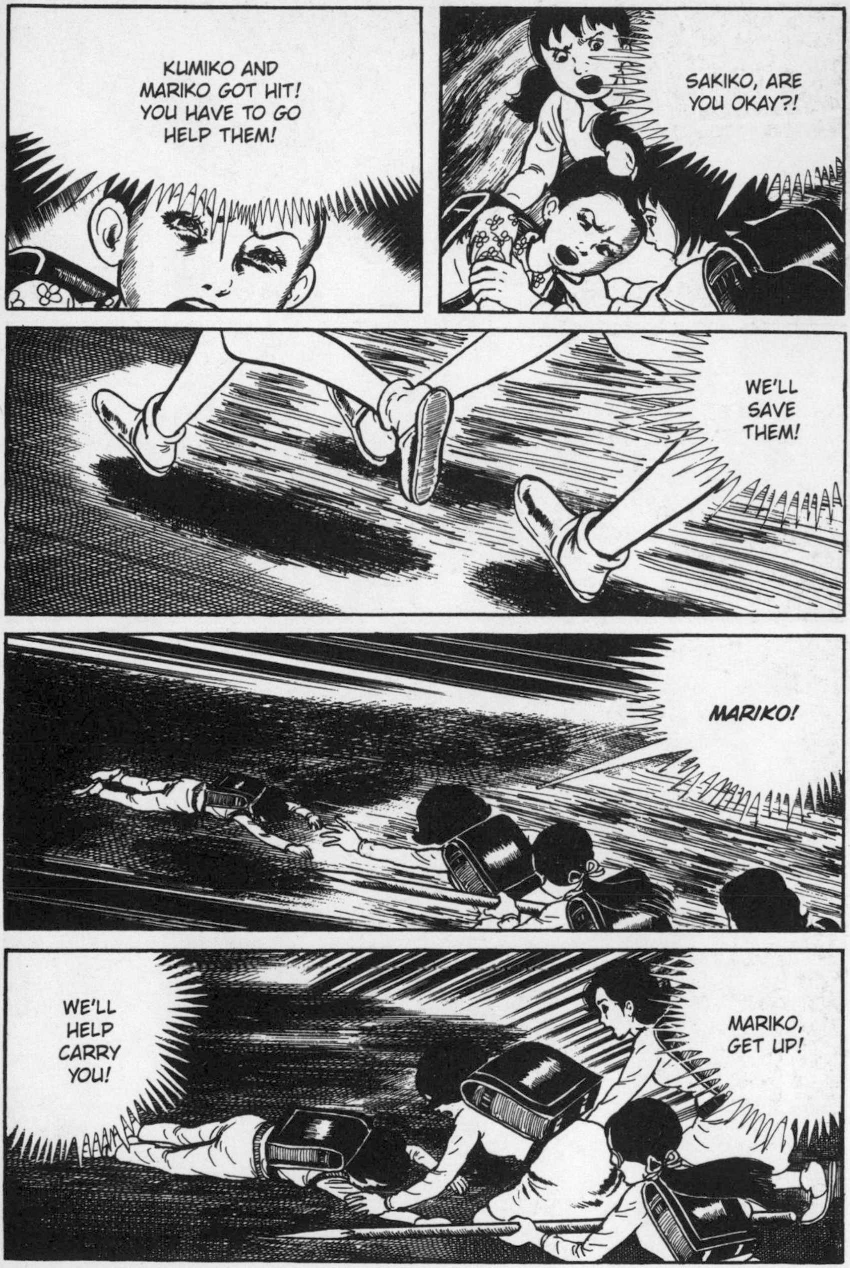
SAKIKO, ARE YOU OKAY?!
KUMIKO AND MARIKO GOT HIT! YOU HAVE TO GO HELP THEM!
WE'LL SAVE THEM!
MARIKO!
MARIKO, GET UP!
WE'LL HELP CARRY YOU!

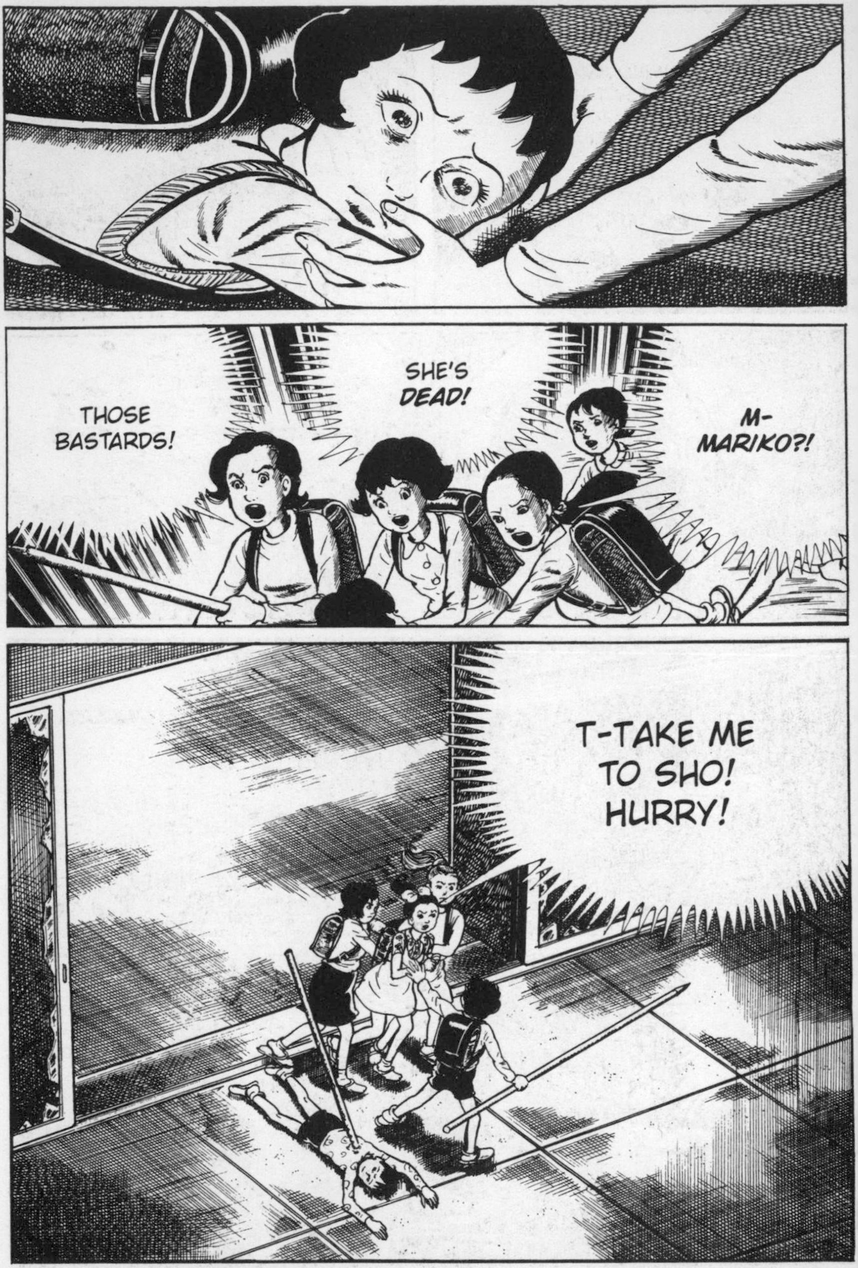
M-MARIKO?!
SHE'S DEAD!
THOSE BASTARDS!
T-TAKE ME TO SHO! HURRY!

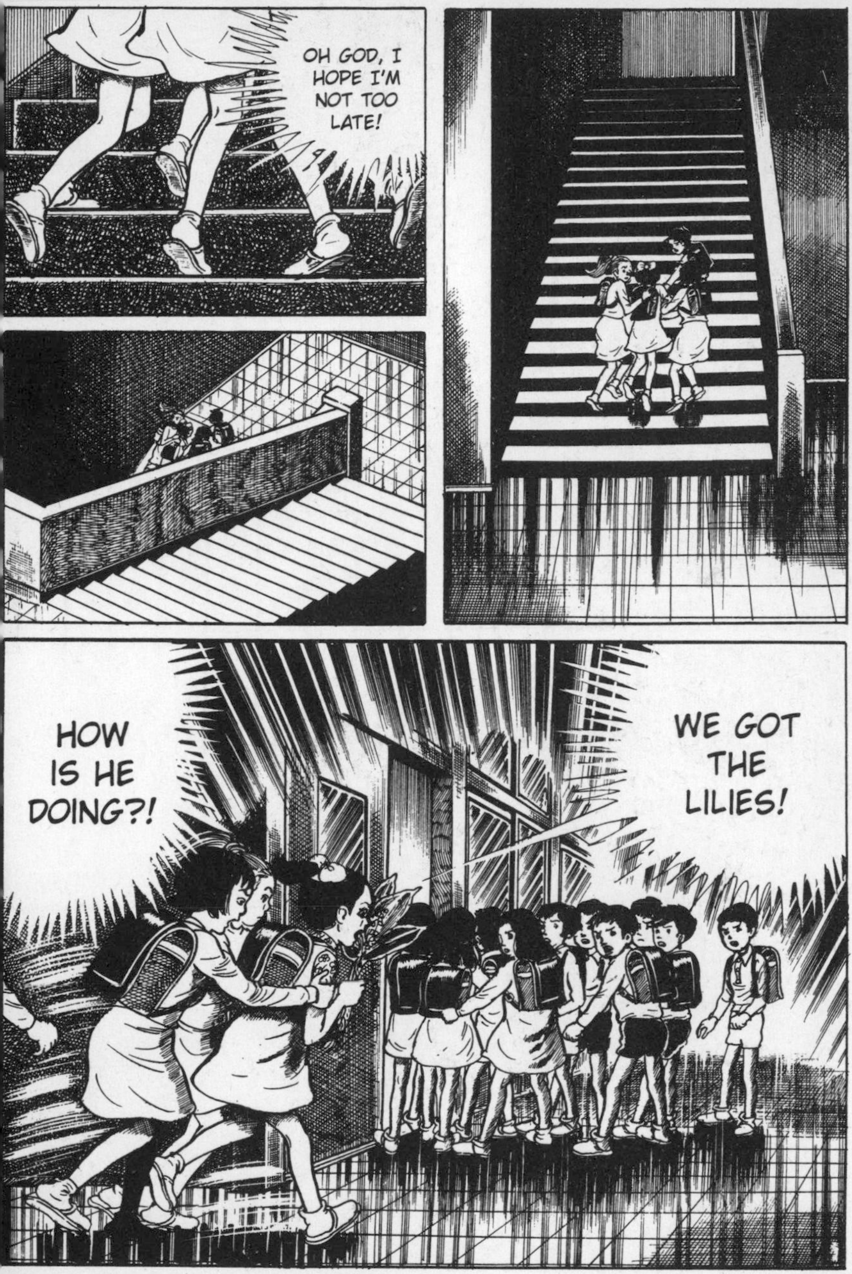
OH GOD, I HOPE I'M NOT TOO LATE!
WE GOT THE LILIES!
HOW IS HE DOING?!

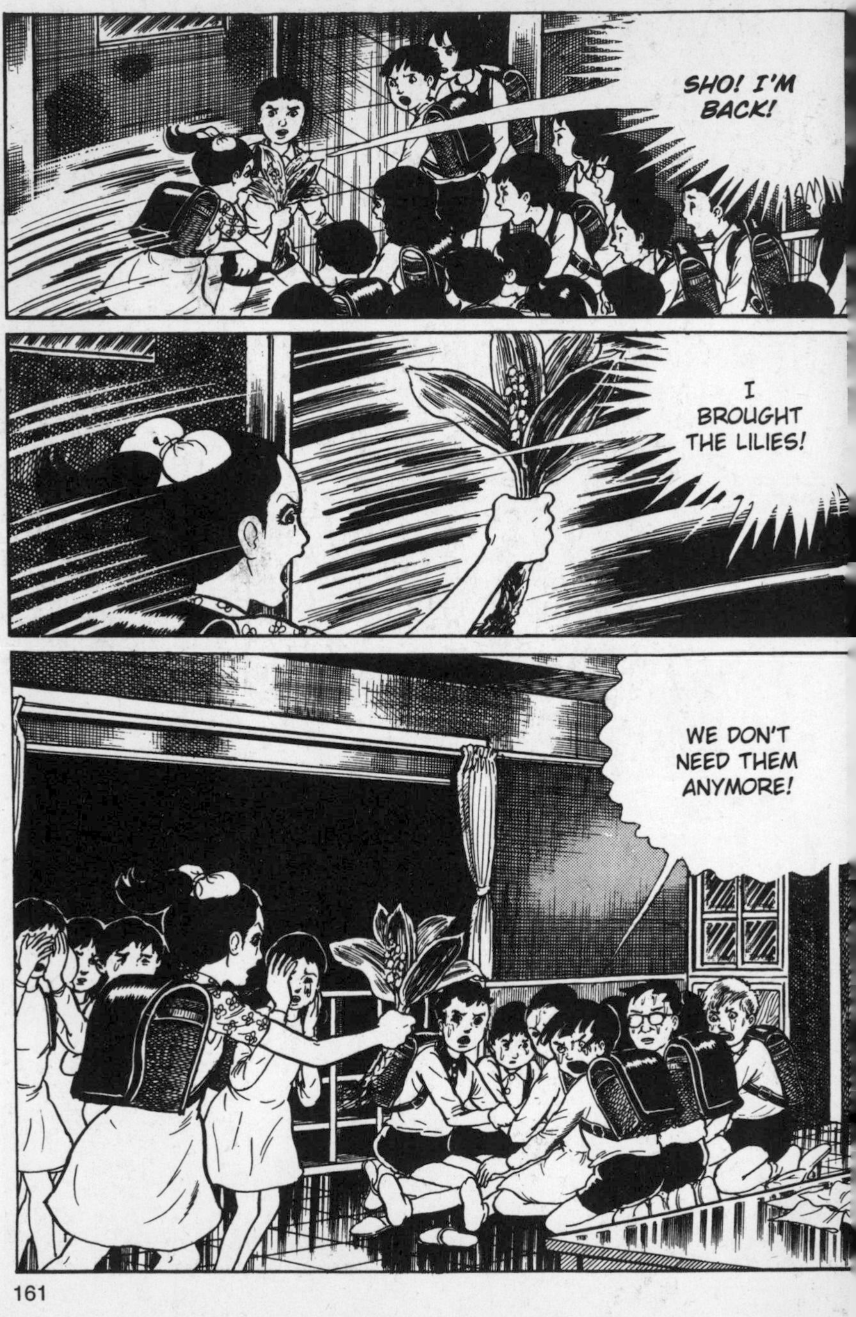
SHO! I'M BACK!
I BROUGHT THE LILIES!
WE DON'T NEED THEM ANYMORE!

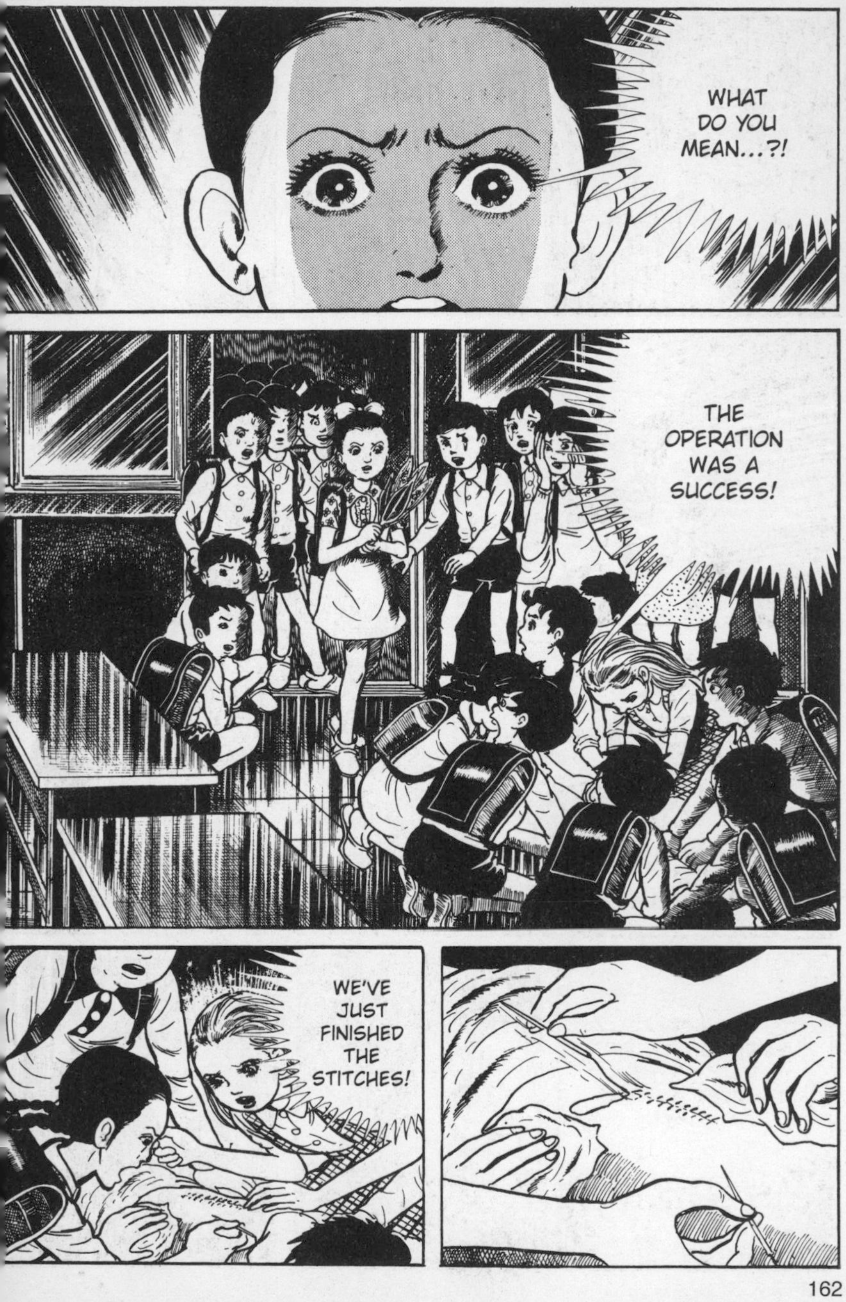
WHAT DO YOU MEAN...?!
THE OPERATION WAS A SUCCESS!
WE'VE JUST FINISHED THE STITCHES!

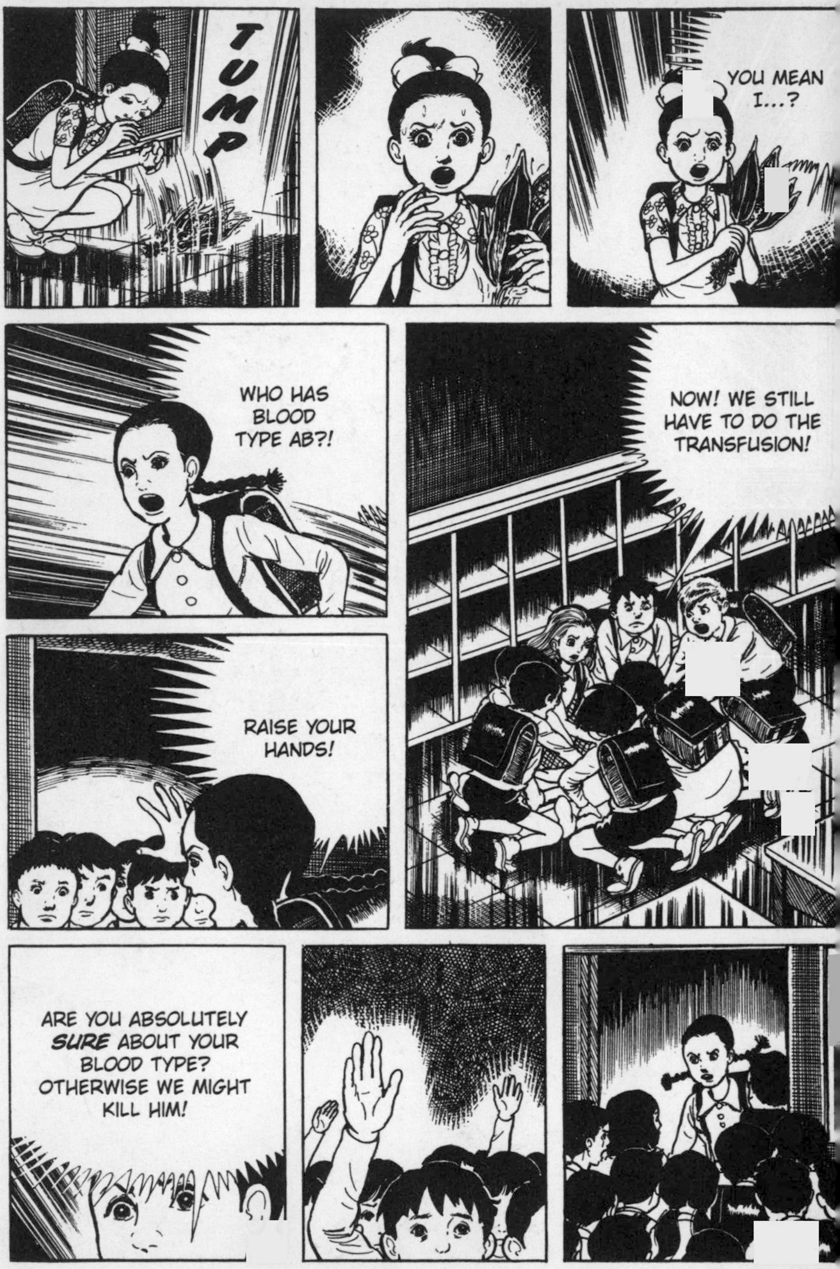
YOU MEAN I...?
TUMP
NOW! WE STILL HAVE TO DO THE TRANSFUSION!
WHO HAS BLOOD TYPE AB?!
RAISE YOUR HANDS!
ARE YOU ABSOLUTELY SURE ABOUT YOUR BLOOD TYPE? OTHERWISE WE MIGHT KILL HIM!

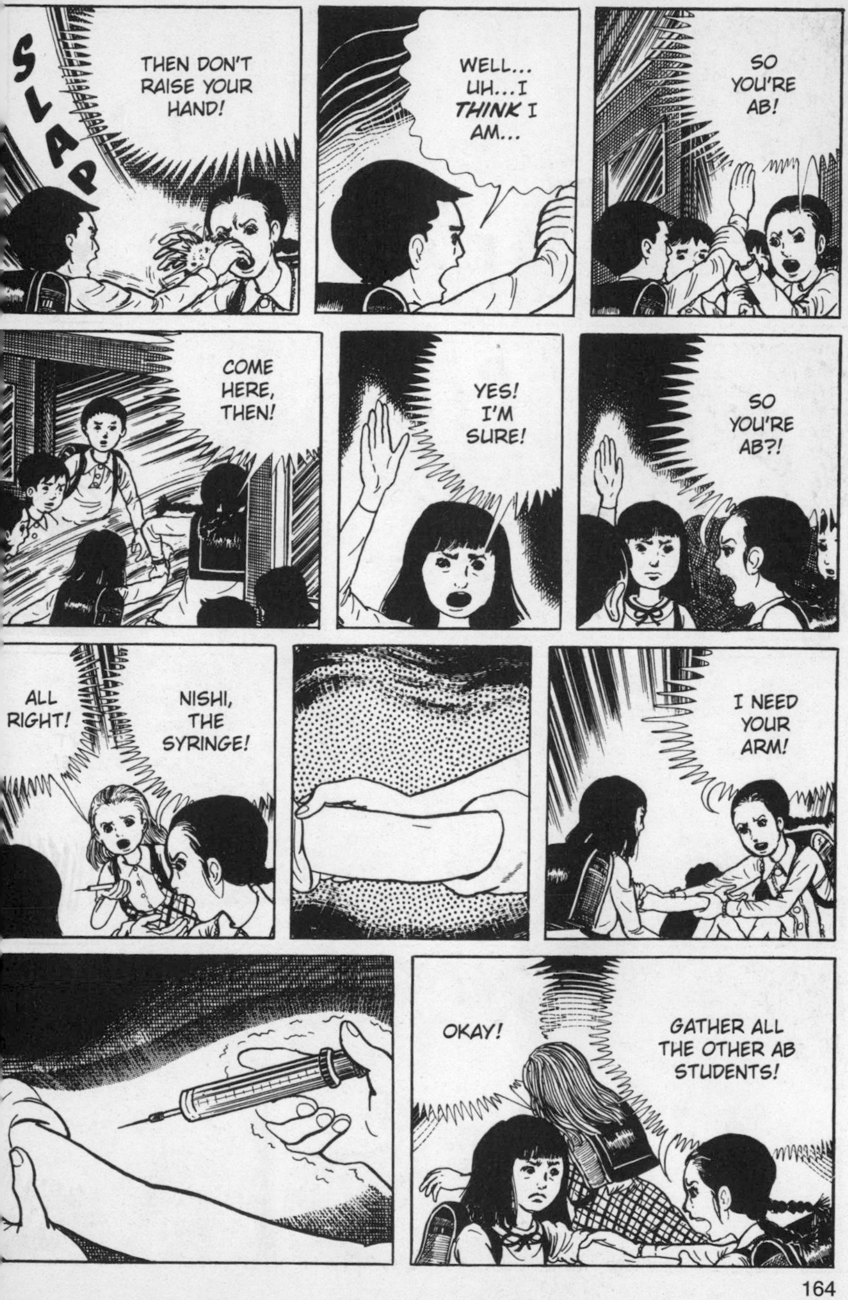
SO YOU'RE AB!
WELL... UH...I THINK I AM...
THEN DON'T RAISE YOUR HAND!
SLAP
SO YOU'RE AB?!
YES! I'M SURE!
COME HERE, THEN!
I NEED YOUR ARM!
NISHI, THE SYRINGE!
ALL RIGHT!
GATHER ALL THE OTHER AB STUDENTS!
OKAY!

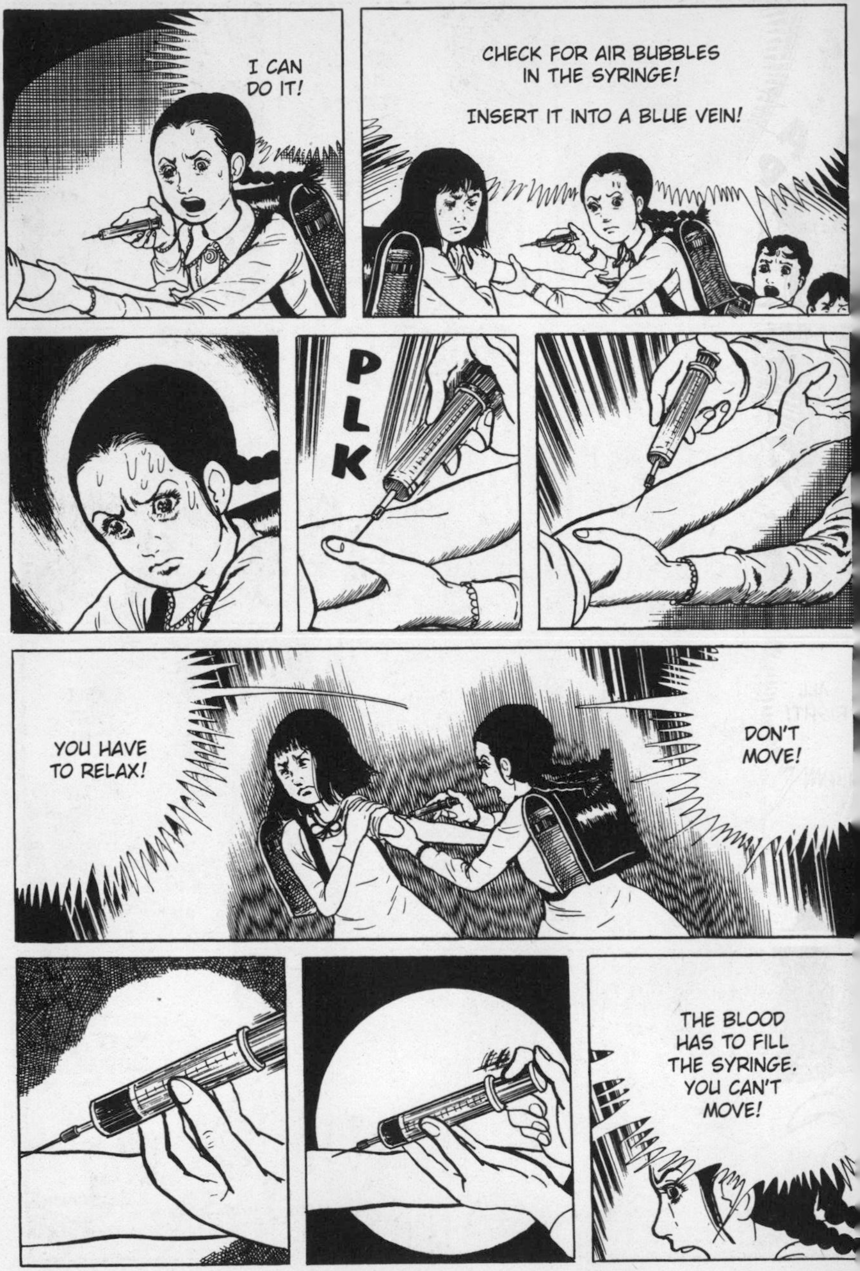
CHECK FOR AIR BUBBLES IN THE SYRINGE!
INSERT IT INTO A BLUE VEIN!
I CAN DO IT!
PLK
DON'T MOVE!
YOU HAVE TO RELAX!
THE BLOOD HAS TO FILL THE SYRINGE. YOU CAN'T MOVE!

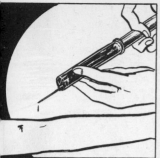

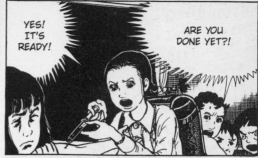
YES!
IT'S
READY!

ARE YOU
DONE YET?!

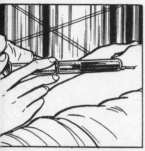

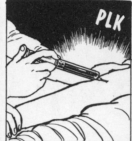
PLK

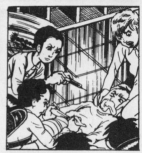

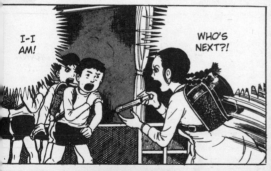
I-I
AM!

WHO'S
NEXT?!

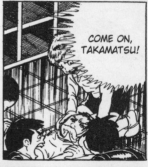
COME ON,
TAKAMATSU!

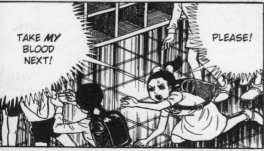
TAKE *MY*
BLOOD
NEXT!

PLEASE!

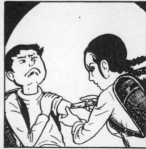

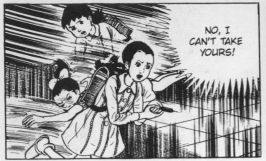

NO, I CAN'T TAKE YOURS!

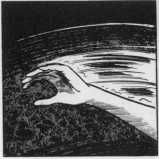

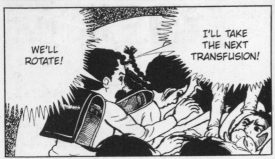

WE'LL ROTATE!

I'LL TAKE THE NEXT TRANSFUSION!

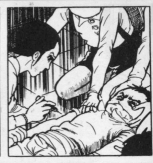

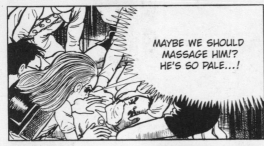

MAYBE WE SHOULD MASSAGE HIM!? HE'S SO PALE...!

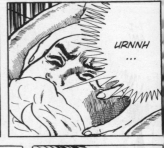

URNNH ...

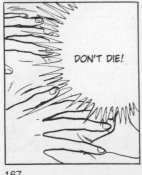

DON'T DIE!

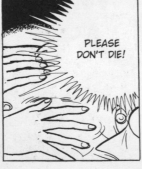

PLEASE DON'T DIE!

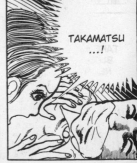

TAKAMATSU ....!

167

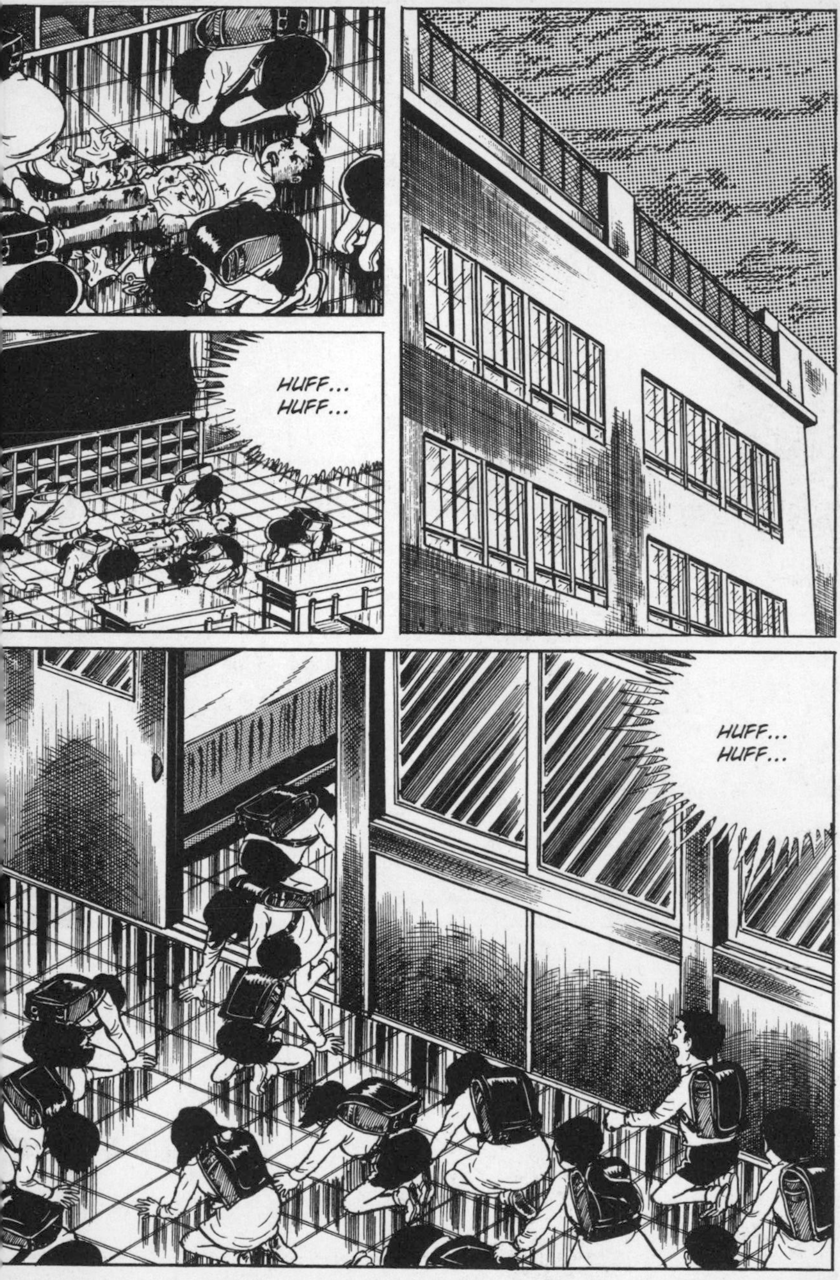
HUFF...
HUFF...
HUFF...
HUFF...

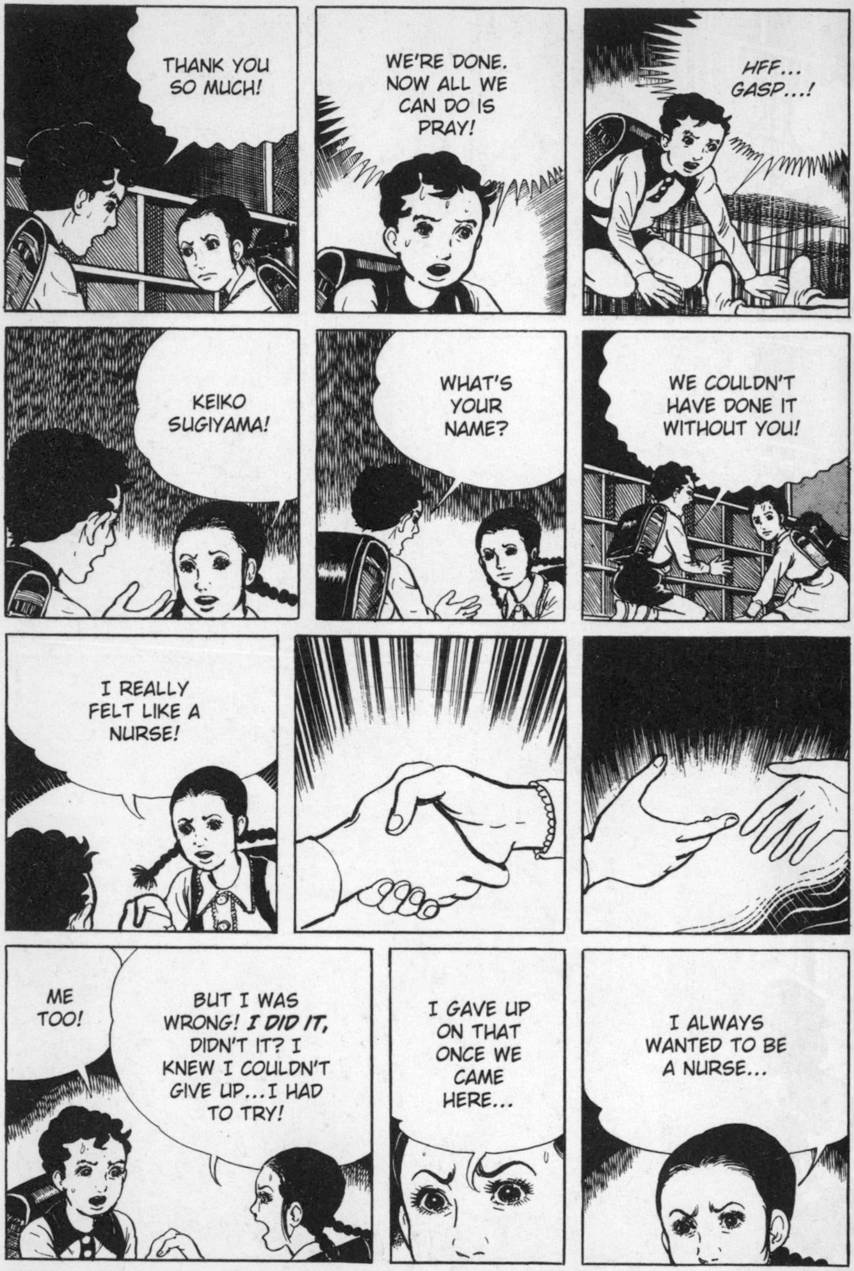
HFF... GASP...!
WE'RE DONE. NOW ALL WE CAN DO IS PRAY!
THANK YOU SO MUCH!
WE COULDN'T HAVE DONE IT WITHOUT YOU!
WHAT'S YOUR NAME?
KEIKO SUGIYAMA!
I REALLY FELT LIKE A NURSE!
I ALWAYS WANTED TO BE A NURSE...
I GAVE UP ON THAT ONCE WE CAME HERE...
BUT I WAS WRONG! ***I DID IT,*** DIDN'T IT? I KNEW I COULDN'T GIVE UP...I HAD TO TRY!
ME TOO!

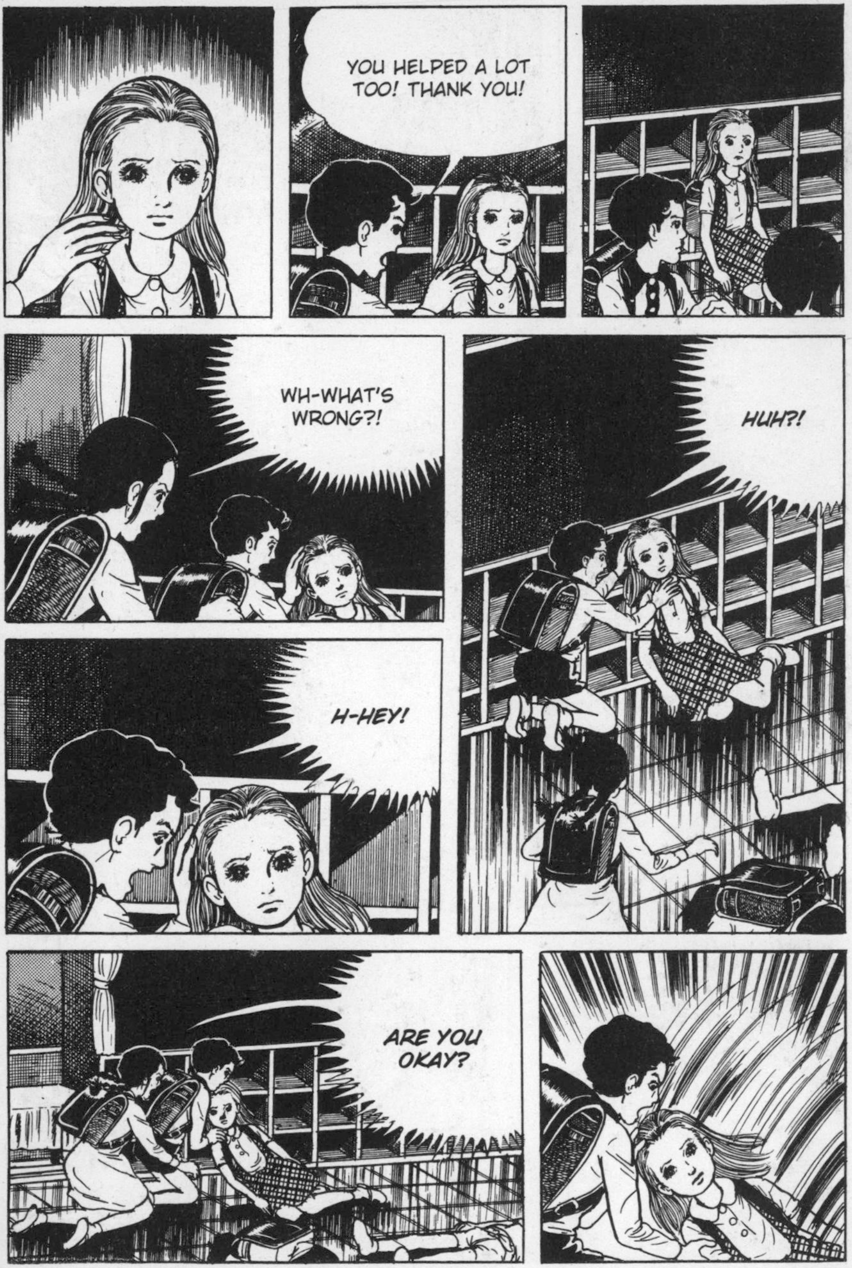
YOU HELPED A LOT TOO! THANK YOU!
HUH?!
WH-WHAT'S WRONG?!
H-HEY!
ARE YOU OKAY?

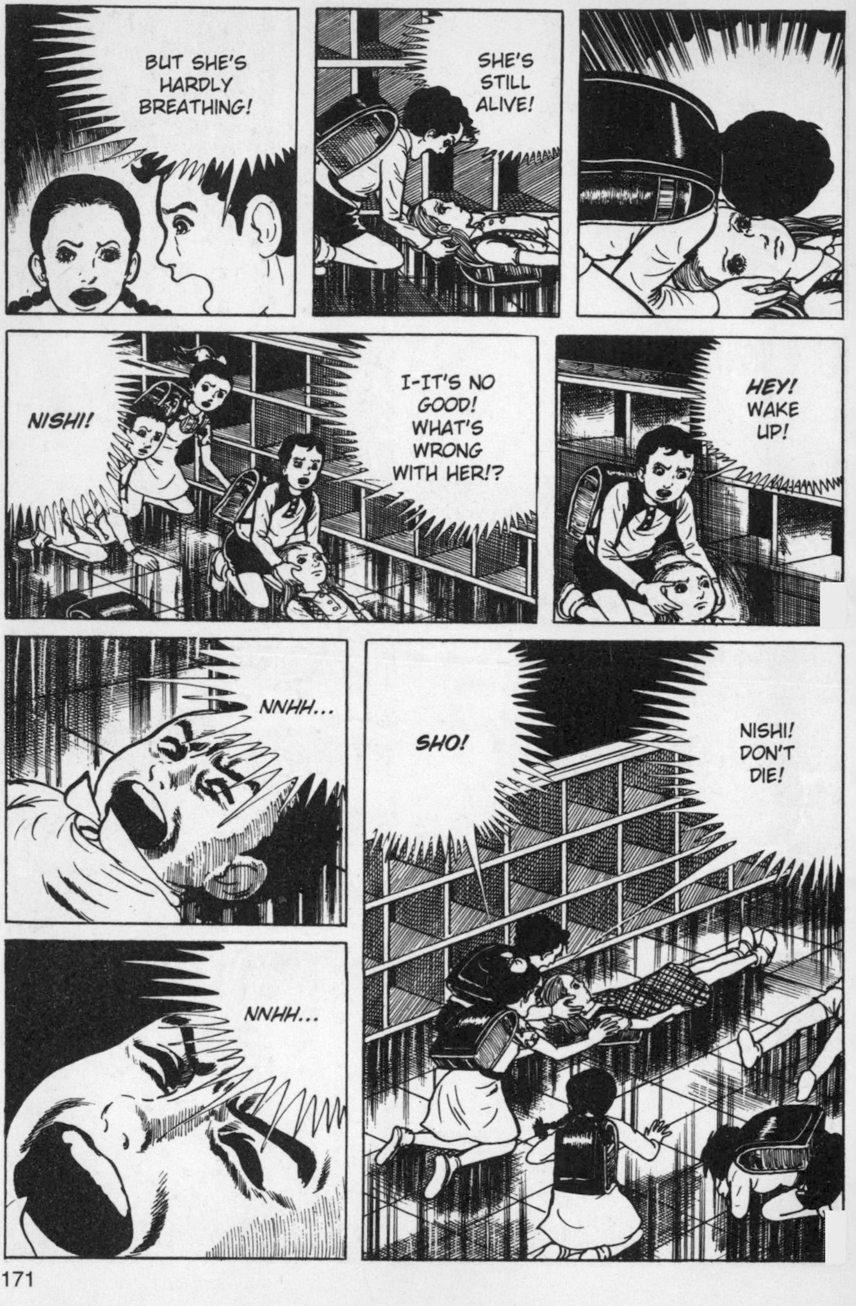
SHE'S STILL ALIVE!
BUT SHE'S HARDLY BREATHING!
HEY! WAKE UP!
I-IT'S NO GOOD! WHAT'S WRONG WITH HER!?
NISHI!
NISHI! DON'T DIE!
SHO!
NNHH...
NNHH...

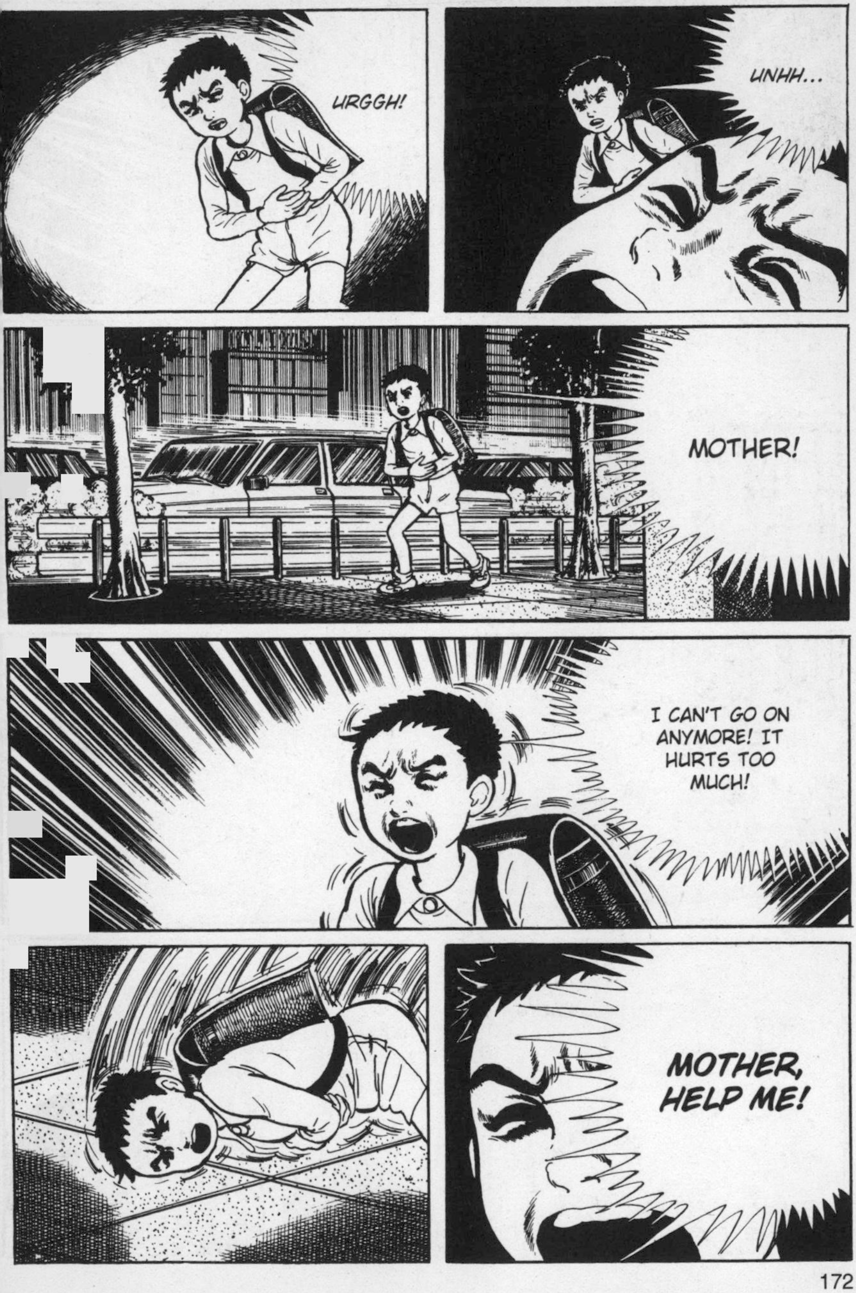
UNHH...
URGGH!
MOTHER!
I CAN'T GO ON ANYMORE! IT HURTS TOO MUCH!
MOTHER, HELP ME!

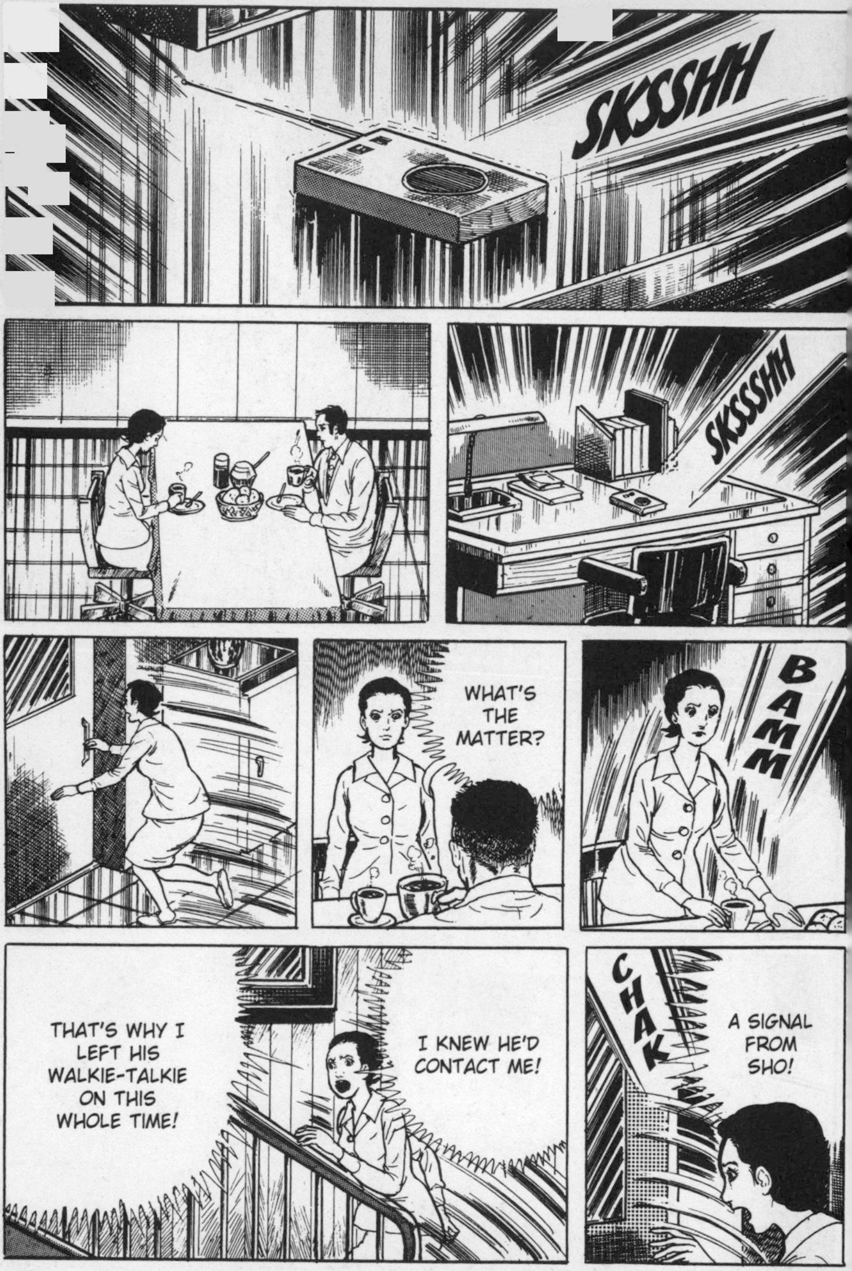
SKSSHH
SKSSSHH
BAMM
WHAT'S THE MATTER?
CHAK
A SIGNAL FROM SHO!
I KNEW HE'D CONTACT ME!
THAT'S WHY I LEFT HIS WALKIE-TALKIE ON THIS WHOLE TIME!

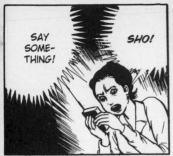

SAY SOME-THING!

SHO!

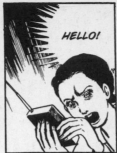

HELLO!

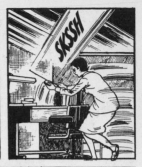

SKSSH

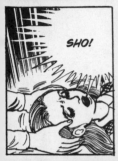

SHO!

MOTHER, MAKE IT STOP! I'M IN PAIN!

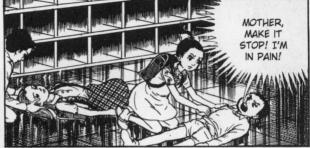

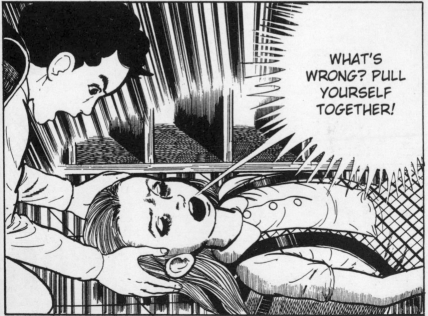

WHAT'S WRONG? PULL YOURSELF TOGETHER!

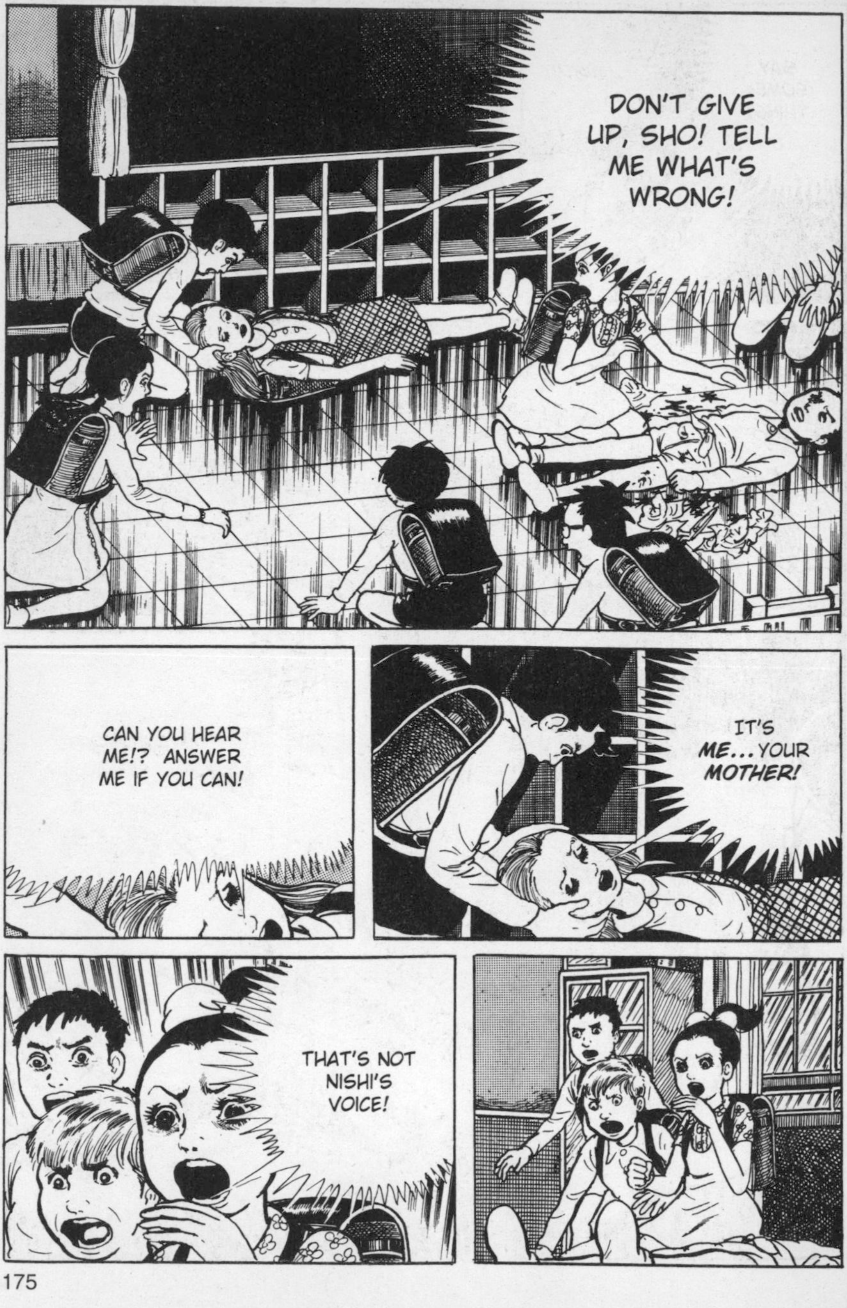
DON'T GIVE UP, SHO! TELL ME WHAT'S WRONG!
IT'S ME... YOUR MOTHER!
CAN YOU HEAR ME!? ANSWER ME IF YOU CAN!
THAT'S NOT NISHI'S VOICE!

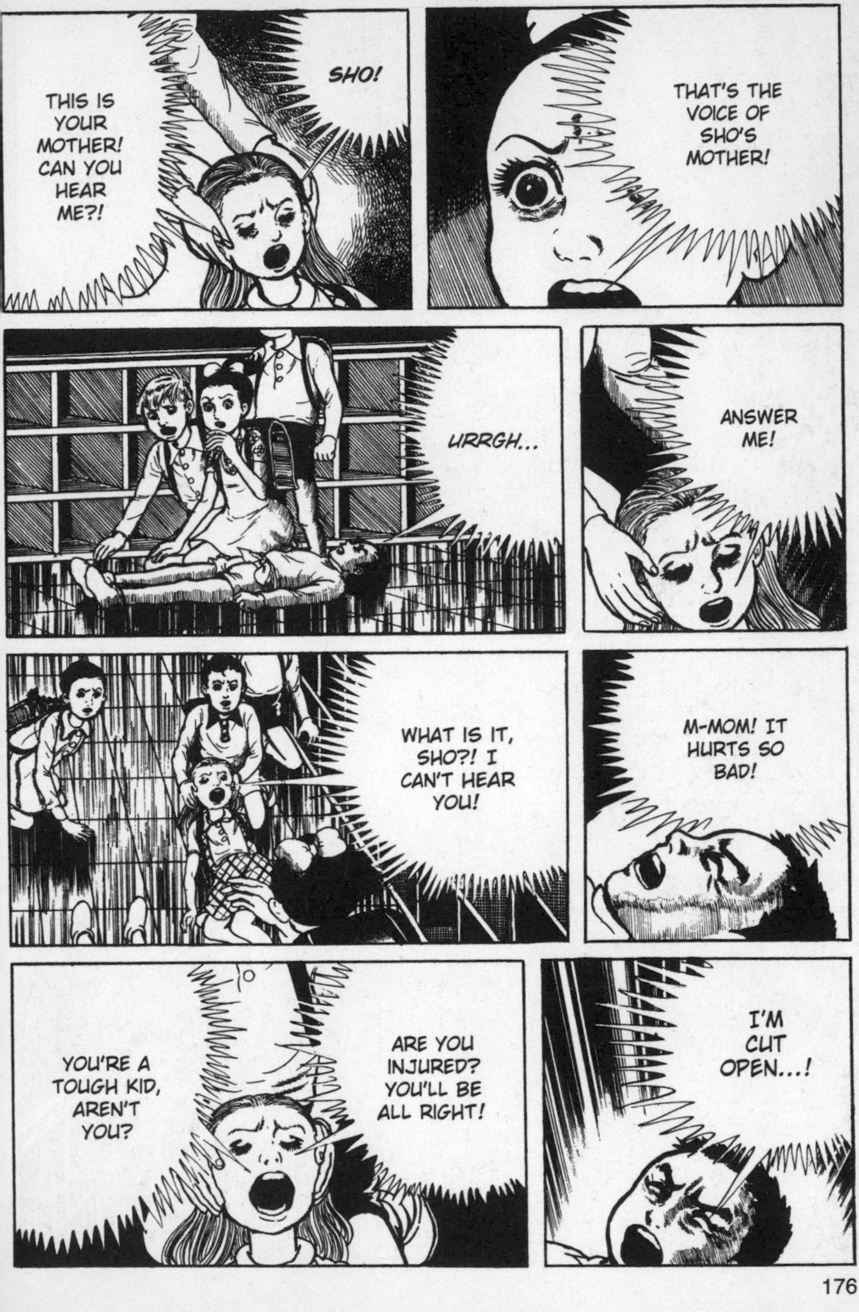
THAT'S THE VOICE OF SHO'S MOTHER!
SHO!
THIS IS YOUR MOTHER! CAN YOU HEAR ME?!
ANSWER ME!
URRGH...
M-MOM! IT HURTS SO BAD!
WHAT IS IT, SHO?! I CAN'T HEAR YOU!
I'M CUT OPEN...!
ARE YOU INJURED? YOU'LL BE ALL RIGHT!
YOU'RE A TOUGH KID, AREN'T YOU?

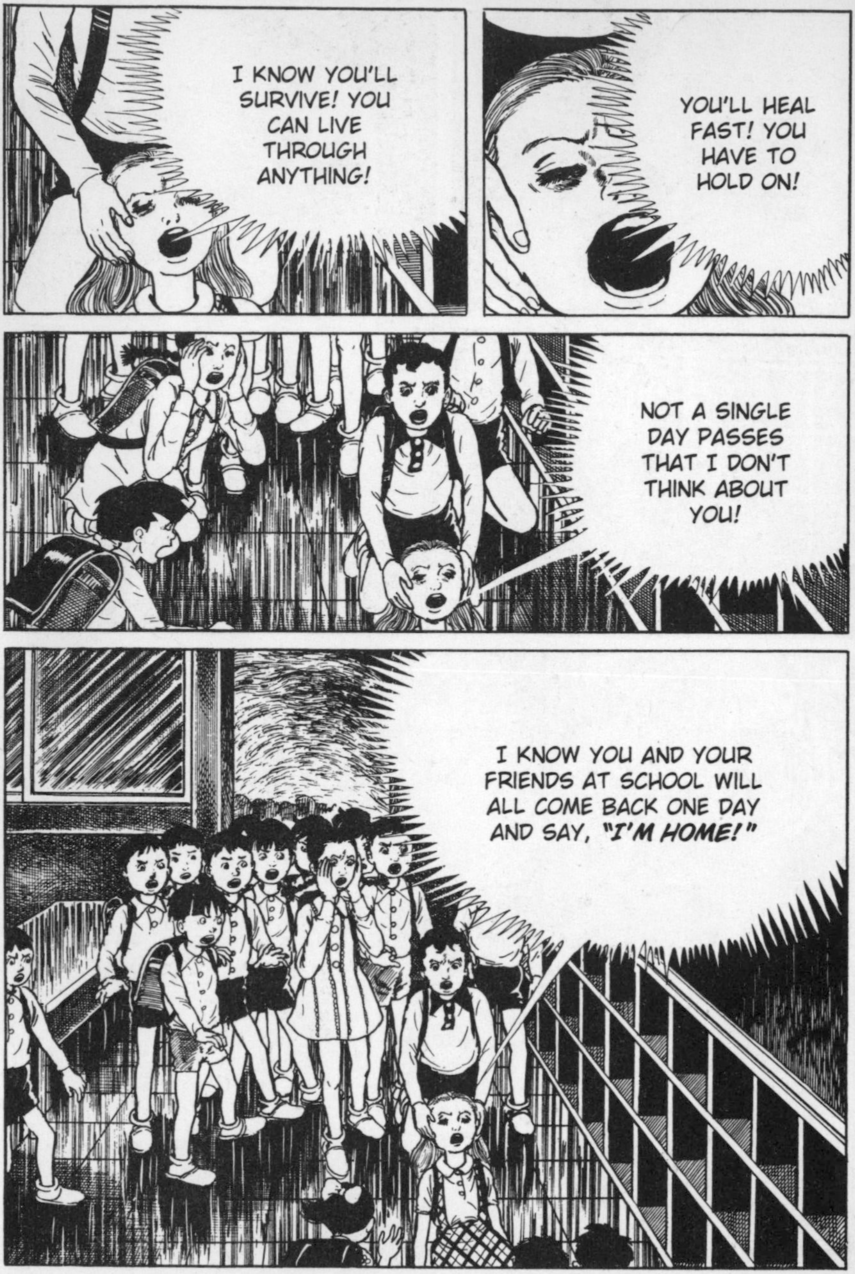
YOU'LL HEAL FAST! YOU HAVE TO HOLD ON!
I KNOW YOU'LL SURVIVE! YOU CAN LIVE THROUGH ANYTHING!
NOT A SINGLE DAY PASSES THAT I DON'T THINK ABOUT YOU!
I KNOW YOU AND YOUR FRIENDS AT SCHOOL WILL ALL COME BACK ONE DAY AND SAY, "I'M HOME!"

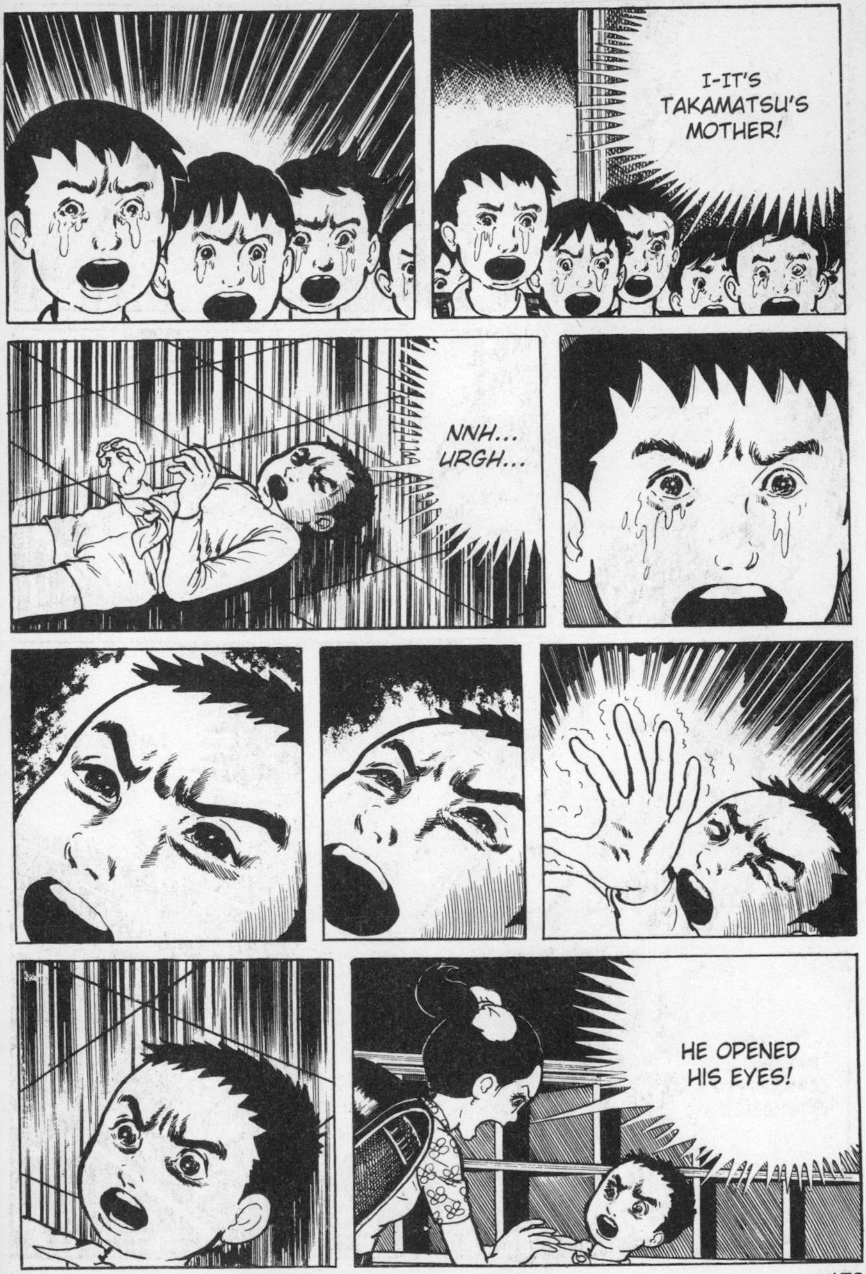
I-IT'S TAKAMATSU'S MOTHER!
NNH... URGH...
HE OPENED HIS EYES!

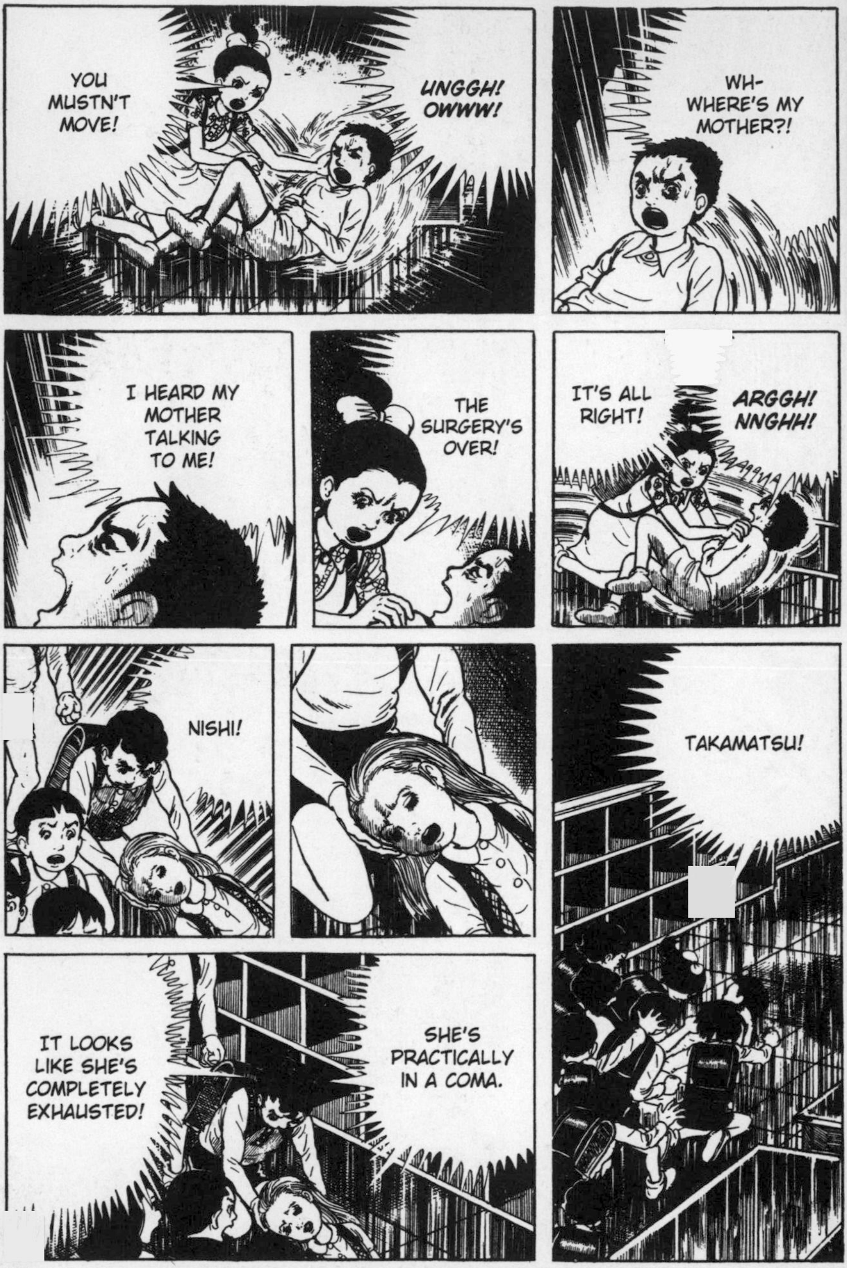
WH-WHERE'S MY MOTHER?!
UNGGH! OWWW!
YOU MUSTN'T MOVE!
ARGGH! NNGHH!
IT'S ALL RIGHT!
THE SURGERY'S OVER!
I HEARD MY MOTHER TALKING TO ME!
TAKAMATSU!
NISHI!
SHE'S PRACTICALLY IN A COMA.
IT LOOKS LIKE SHE'S COMPLETELY EXHAUSTED!

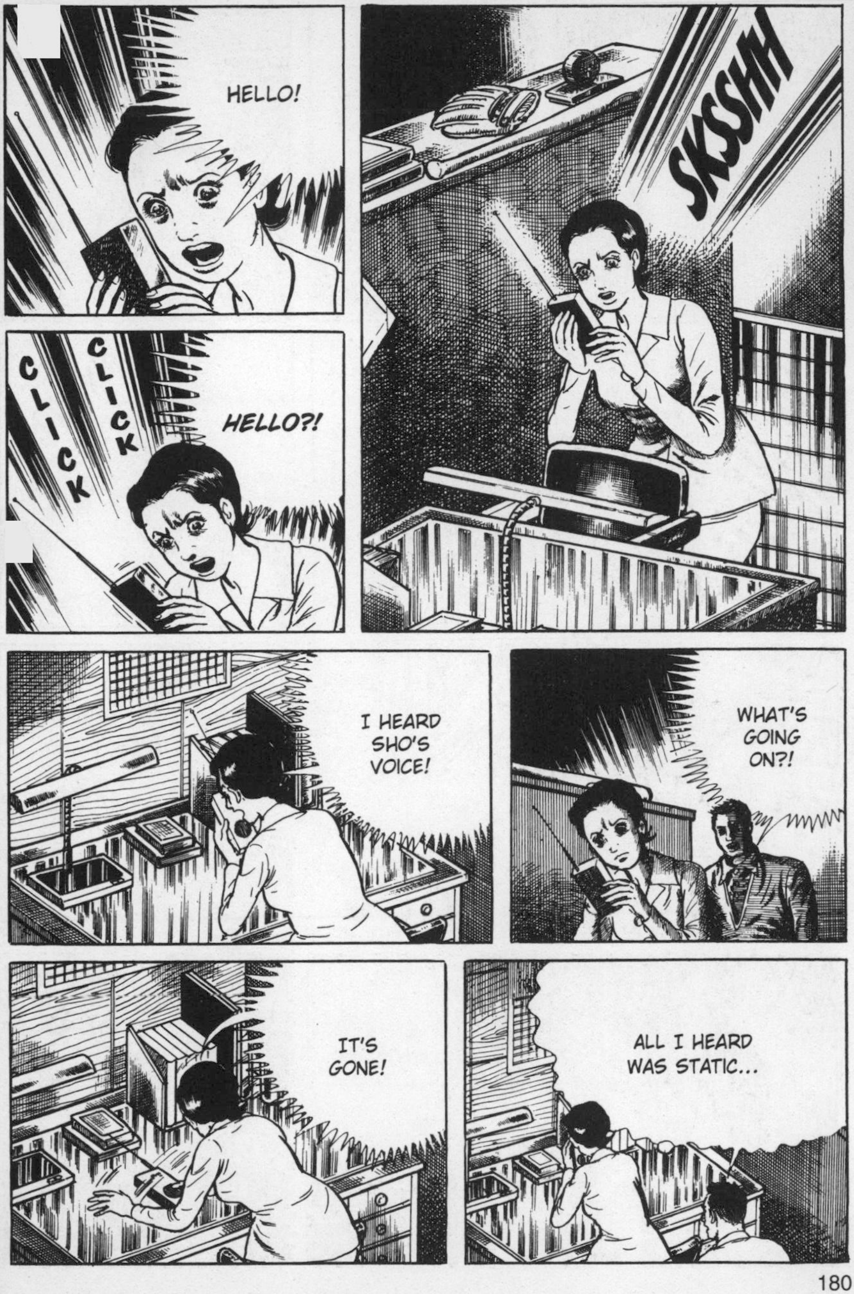
SKSSHH
HELLO!
CLICK CLICK
CLICK
HELLO?!
WHAT'S GOING ON?!
I HEARD SHO'S VOICE!
ALL I HEARD WAS STATIC...
IT'S GONE!

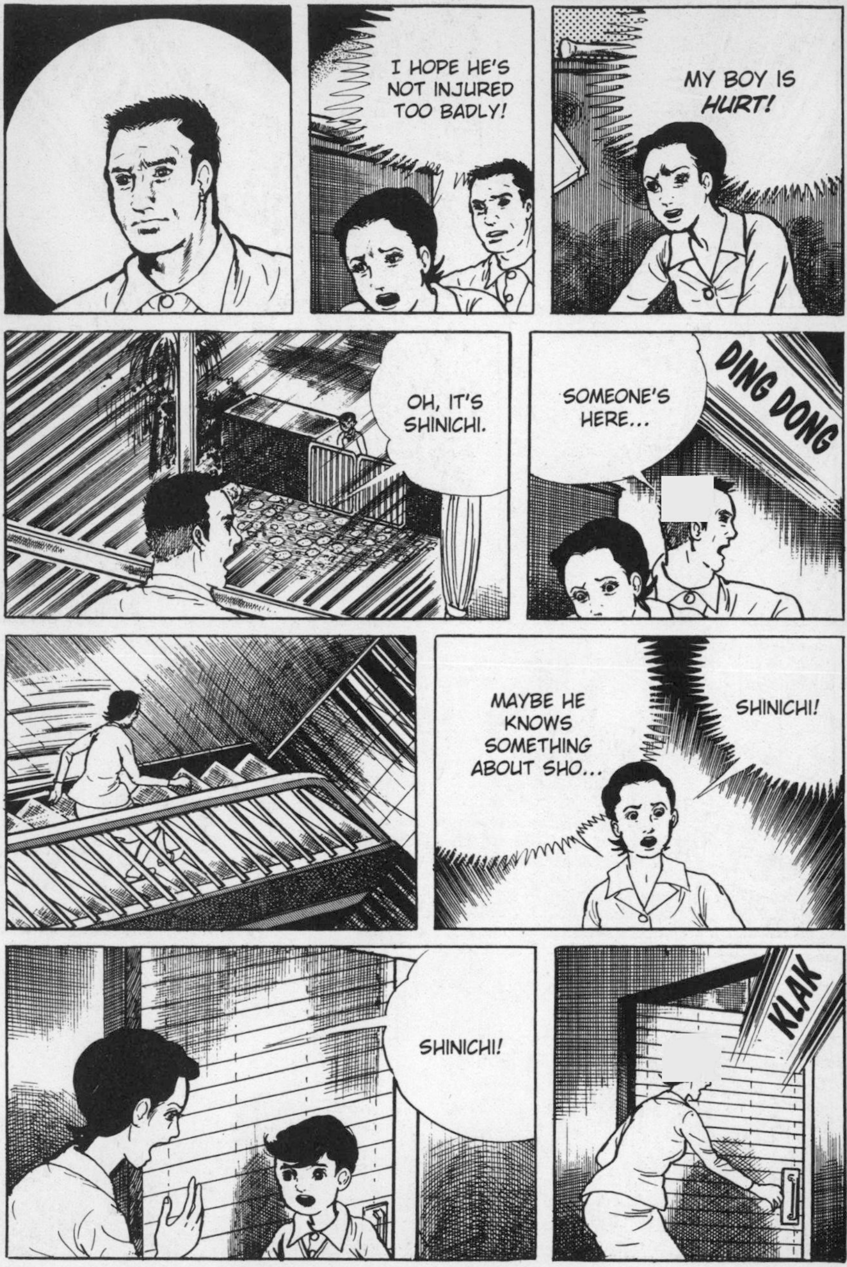
MY BOY IS *HURT!*
I HOPE HE'S NOT INJURED TOO BADLY!
DING DONG
SOMEONE'S HERE...
OH, IT'S SHINICHI.
SHINICHI!
MAYBE HE KNOWS SOMETHING ABOUT SHO...
KLAK
SHINICHI!

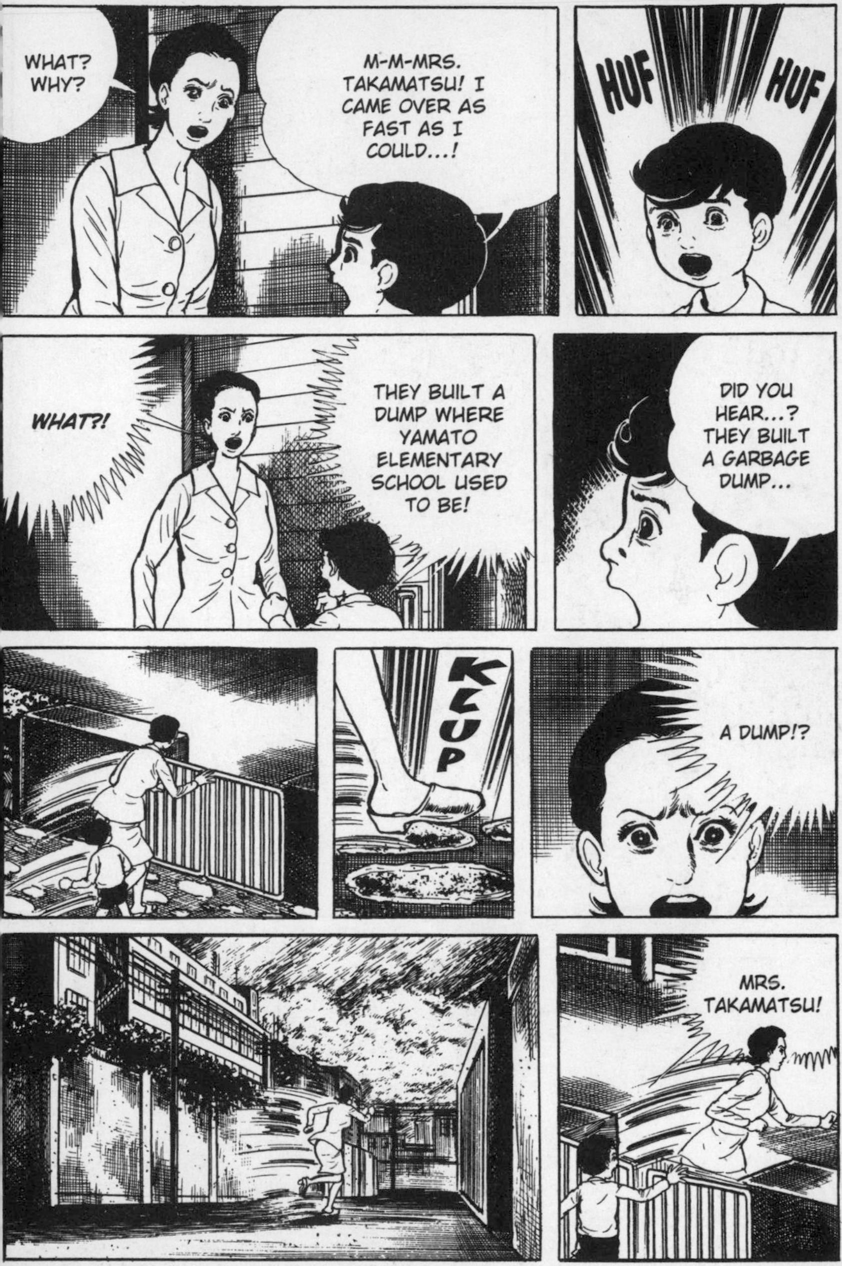
HUF HUF
M-M-MRS. TAKAMATSU! I CAME OVER AS FAST AS I COULD...!
WHAT? WHY?
DID YOU HEAR...? THEY BUILT A GARBAGE DUMP...
THEY BUILT A DUMP WHERE YAMATO ELEMENTARY SCHOOL USED TO BE!
WHAT?!
A DUMP!?
KLUP
MRS. TAKAMATSU!

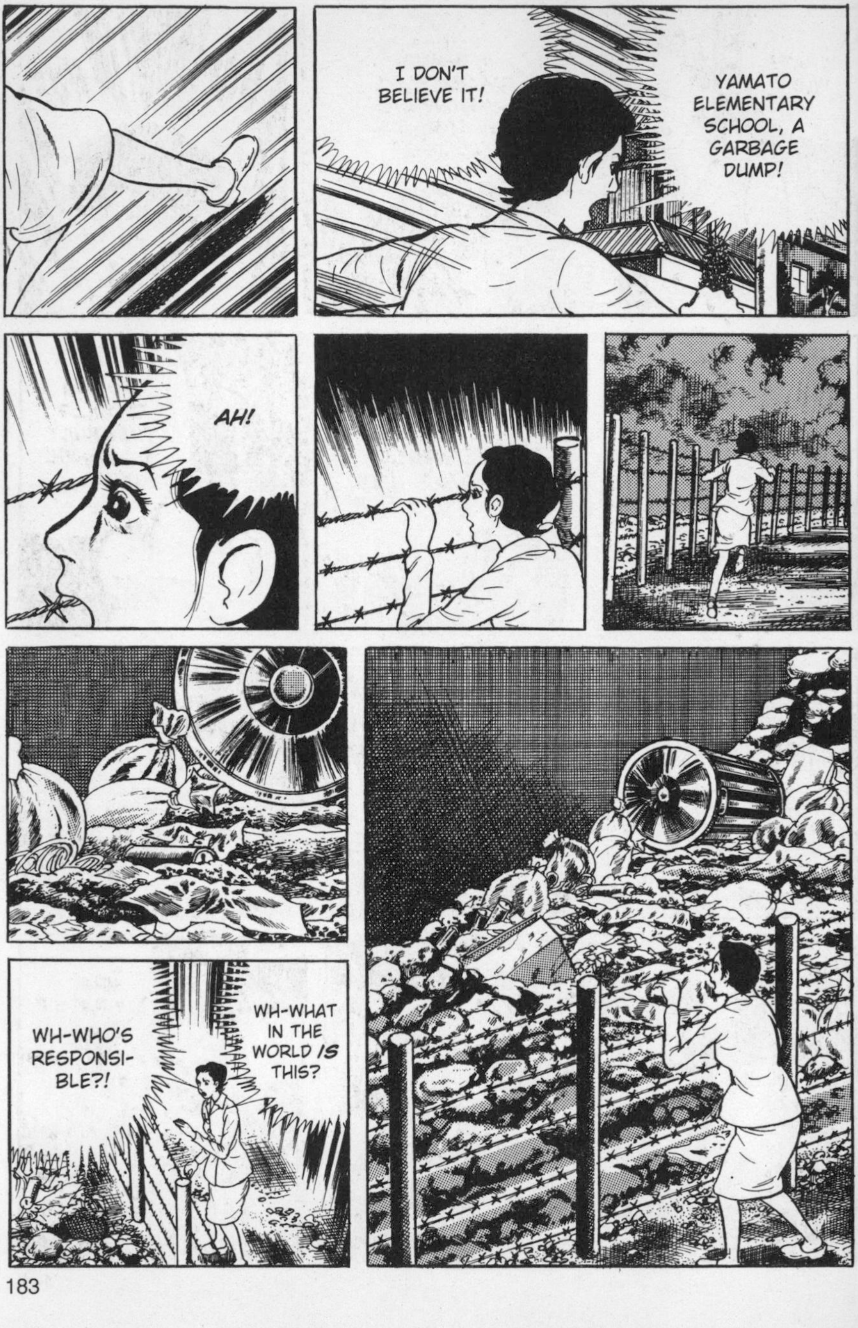
YAMATO ELEMENTARY SCHOOL, A GARBAGE DUMP!
I DON'T BELIEVE IT!
AH!
WH-WHAT IN THE WORLD *IS* THIS?
WH-WHO'S RESPONSI-BLE?!

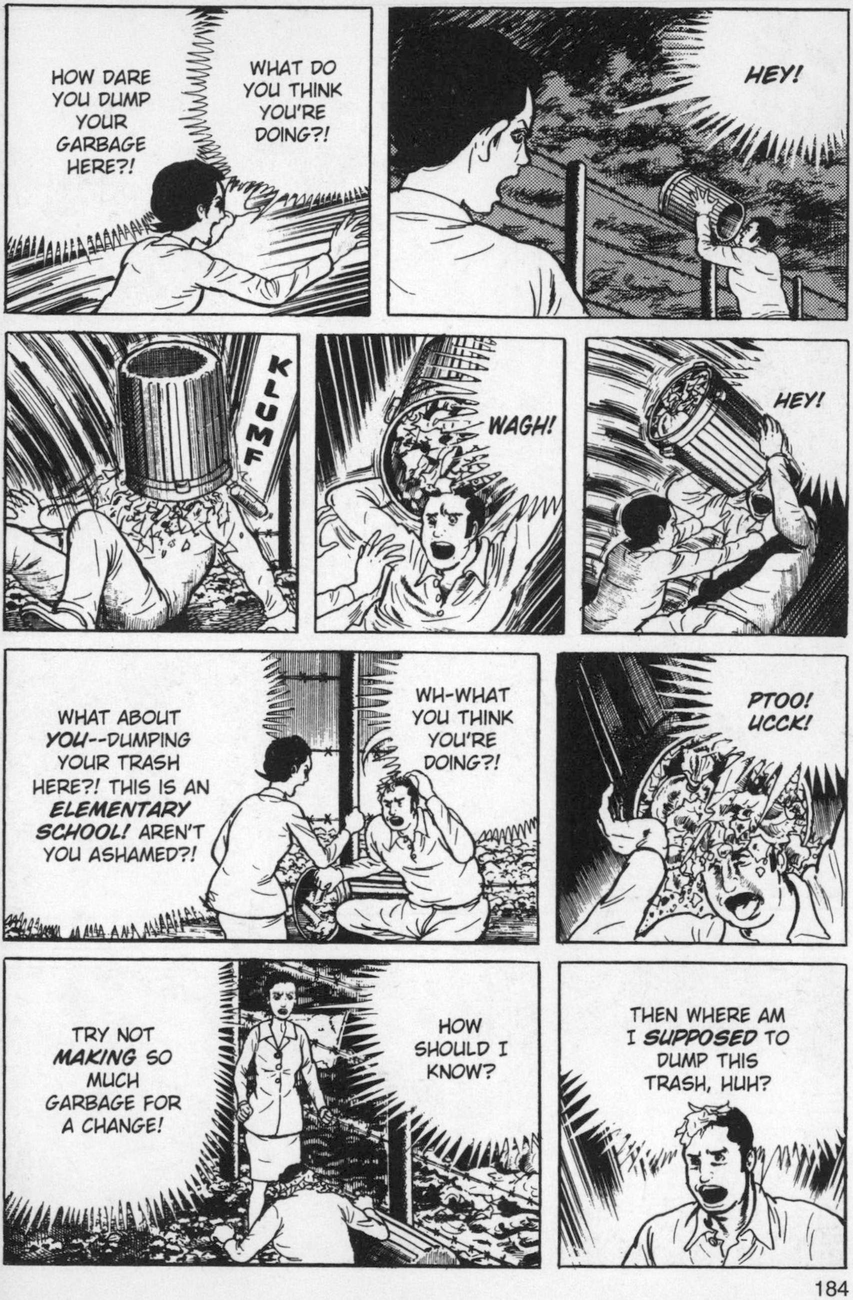
HEY!
WHAT DO YOU THINK YOU'RE DOING?!
HOW DARE YOU DUMP YOUR GARBAGE HERE?!
HEY!
WAGH!
KLUMF
PTOO! UCCK!
WH-WHAT YOU THINK YOU'RE DOING?!
WHAT ABOUT YOU--DUMPING YOUR TRASH HERE?! THIS IS AN ELEMENTARY SCHOOL! AREN'T YOU ASHAMED?!
THEN WHERE AM I SUPPOSED TO DUMP THIS TRASH, HUH?
HOW SHOULD I KNOW?
TRY NOT MAKING SO MUCH GARBAGE FOR A CHANGE!

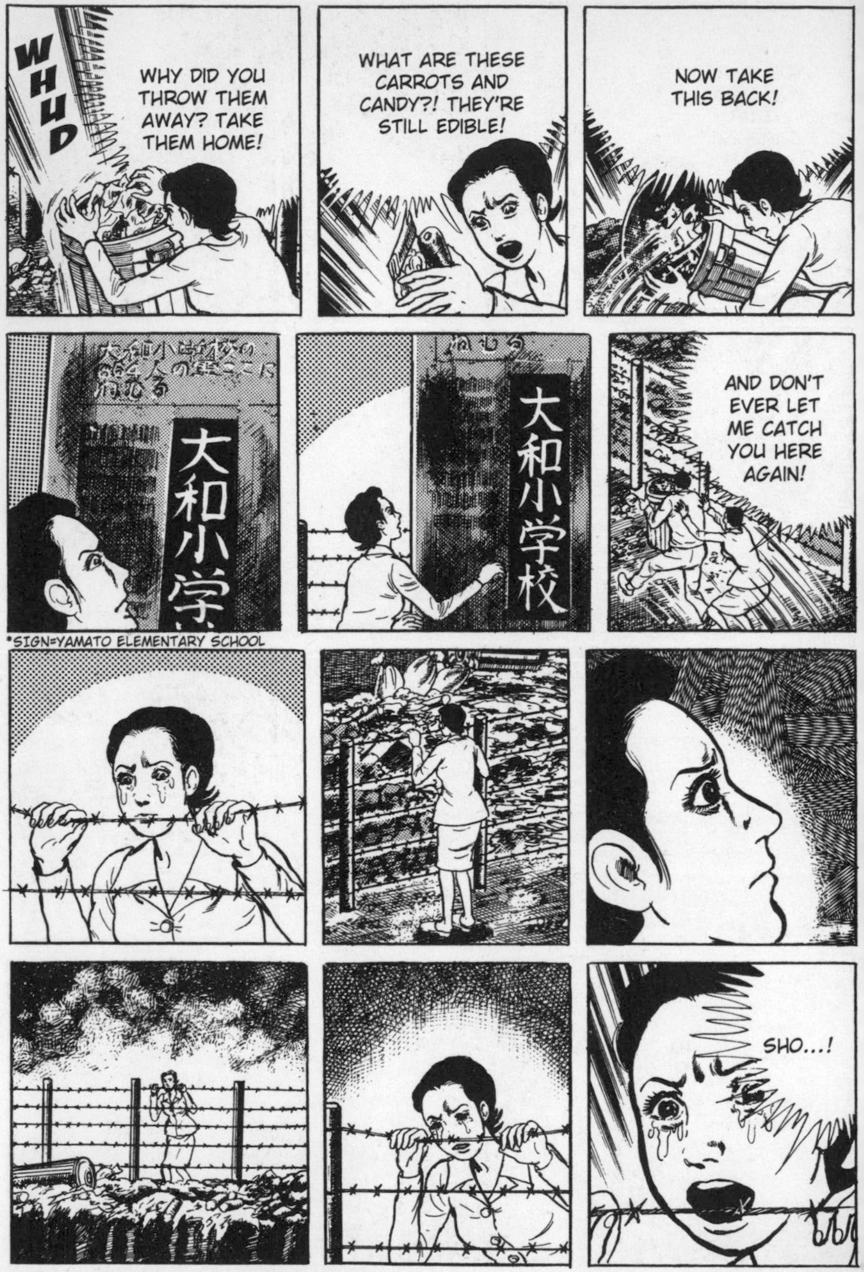
NOW TAKE THIS BACK!
WHAT ARE THESE CARROTS AND CANDY?! THEY'RE STILL EDIBLE!
WHY DID YOU THROW THEM AWAY? TAKE THEM HOME!
WHUD
AND DON'T EVER LET ME CATCH YOU HERE AGAIN!
大和小学校
大和小学
*SIGN=YAMATO ELEMENTARY SCHOOL
SHO...!

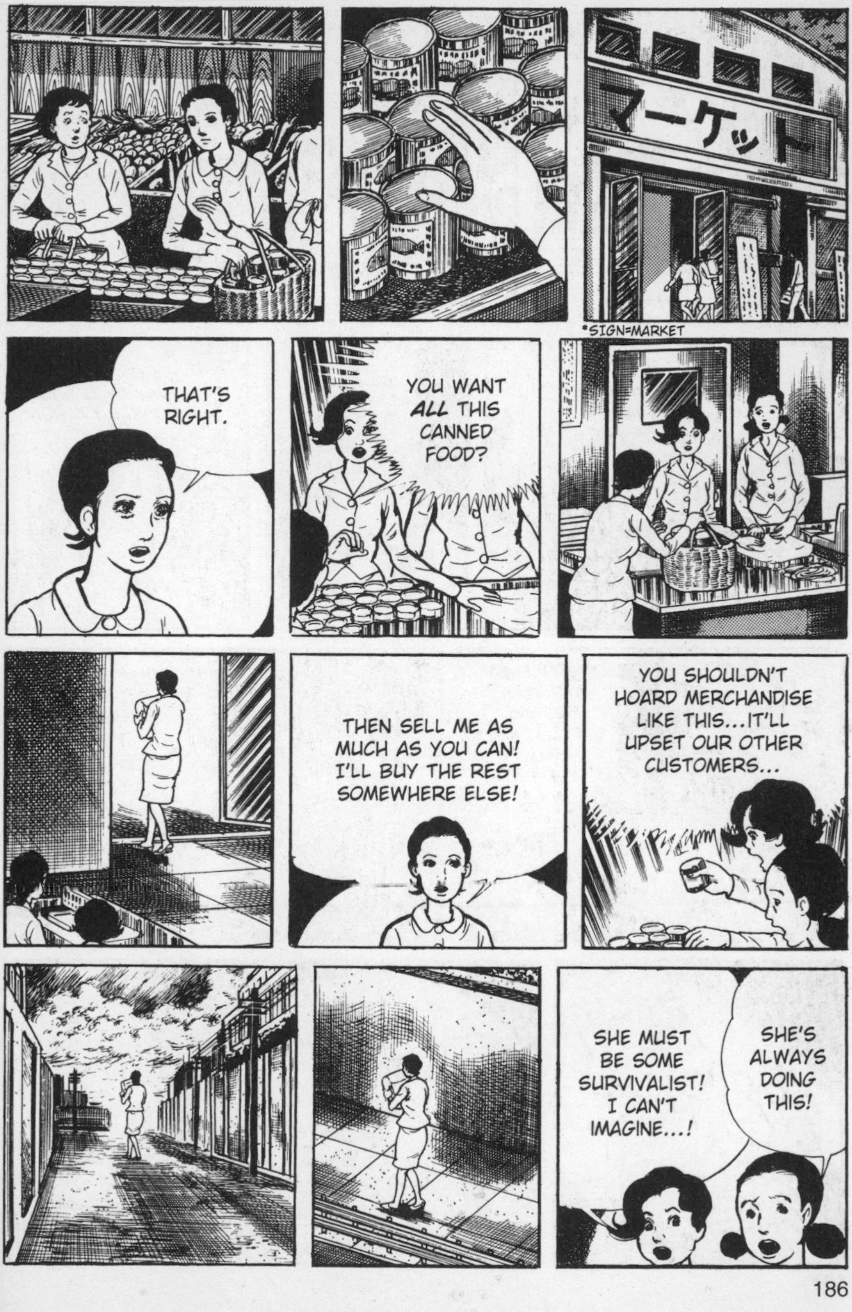
マーケット
*SIGN=MARKET
YOU WANT ALL THIS CANNED FOOD?
THAT'S RIGHT.
YOU SHOULDN'T HOARD MERCHANDISE LIKE THIS...IT'LL UPSET OUR OTHER CUSTOMERS...
THEN SELL ME AS MUCH AS YOU CAN! I'LL BUY THE REST SOMEWHERE ELSE!
SHE'S ALWAYS DOING THIS!
SHE MUST BE SOME SURVIVALIST! I CAN'T IMAGINE...!

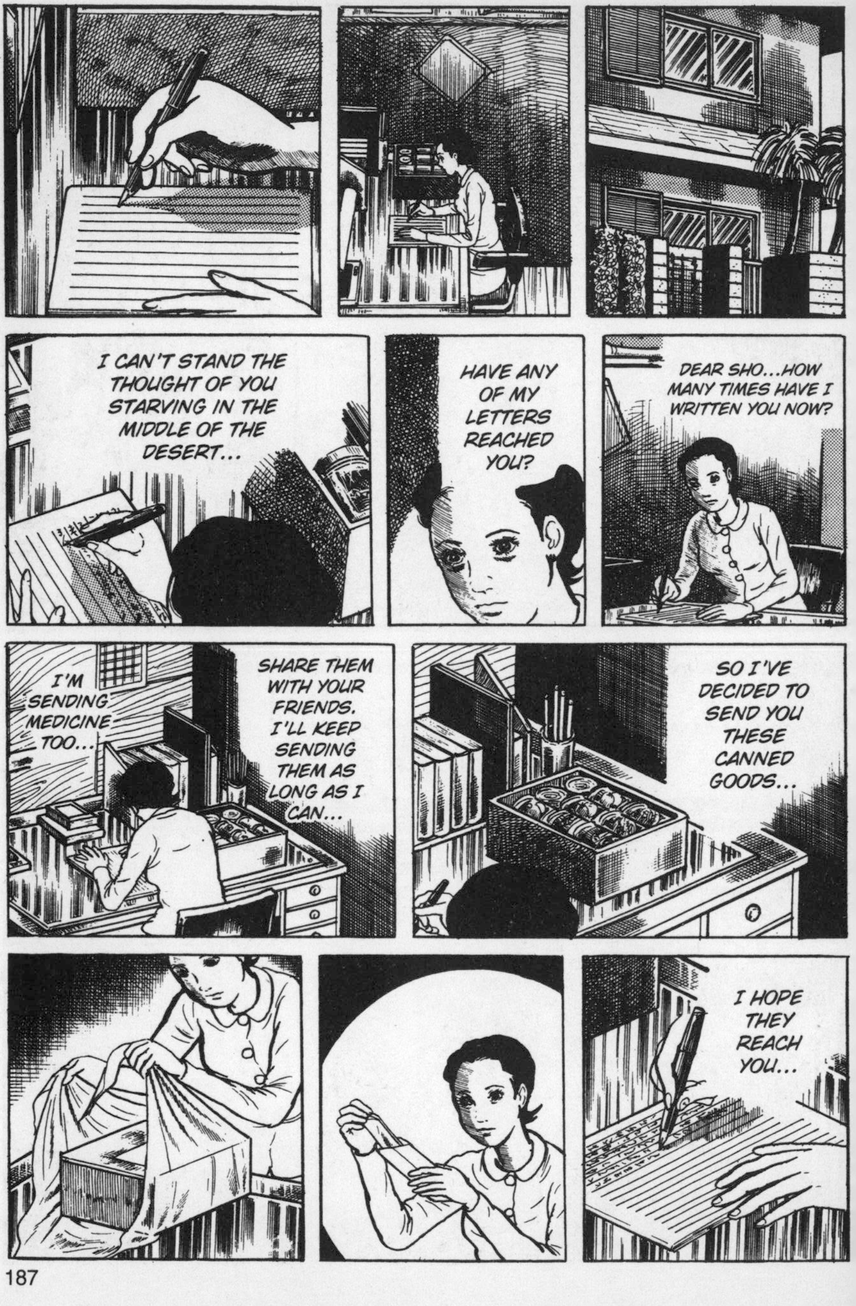
DEAR SHO...HOW MANY TIMES HAVE I WRITTEN YOU NOW?
HAVE ANY OF MY LETTERS REACHED YOU?
I CAN'T STAND THE THOUGHT OF YOU STARVING IN THE MIDDLE OF THE DESERT...
SO I'VE DECIDED TO SEND YOU THESE CANNED GOODS...
SHARE THEM WITH YOUR FRIENDS. I'LL KEEP SENDING THEM AS LONG AS I CAN...
I'M SENDING MEDICINE TOO...
I HOPE THEY REACH YOU...

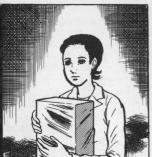
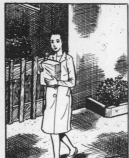
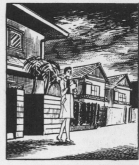
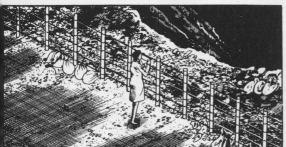
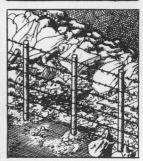
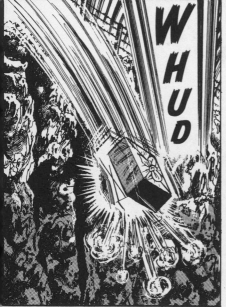
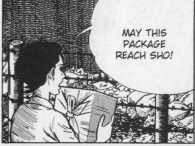

MAY THIS
PACKAGE
REACH SHO!

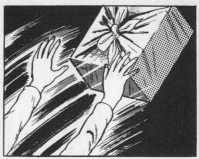

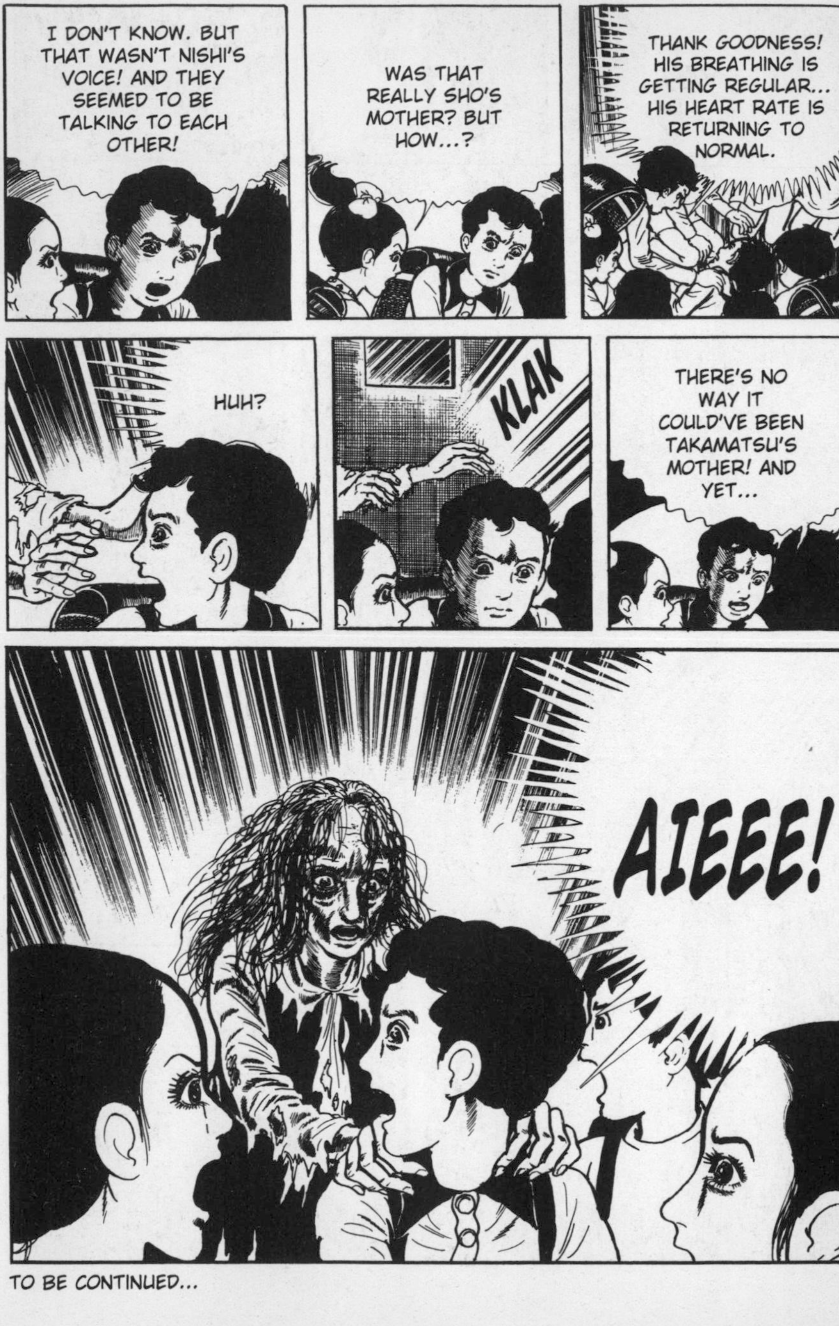
THANK GOODNESS! HIS BREATHING IS GETTING REGULAR... HIS HEART RATE IS RETURNING TO NORMAL.
WAS THAT REALLY SHO'S MOTHER? BUT HOW...?
I DON'T KNOW. BUT THAT WASN'T NISHI'S VOICE! AND THEY SEEMED TO BE TALKING TO EACH OTHER!
THERE'S NO WAY IT COULD'VE BEEN TAKAMATSU'S MOTHER! AND YET...
KLAK
HUH?
AIEEE!

TO BE CONTINUED...

IN THE NEXT VOLUME...

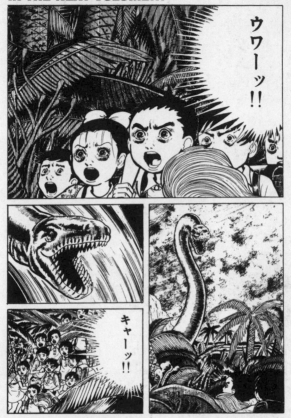

Guided by the words of their visitor, the starving children leave the school and travel across the desert in search of "paradise." But what awaits them there...and will they survive the journey through the hostile world outside?
AVAILABLE FEBRUARY 2008!